Inter-American Institute of
International Legal Studies

INSTRUMENTS RELATING TO THE

ECONOMIC INTEGRATION

OF LATIN AMERICA

1968

OCEANA PUBLICATIONS, INC. / DOBBS FERRY, NEW YORK

Manufactured in the United States of America

INSTRUMENTS RELATING TO THE

ECONOMIC INTEGRATION

OF LATIN AMERICA

Table of Contents

iii

Equalization of Import Charges

Industrial Regime

Financial Regime

APPENDIX

INTRODUCTORY NOTE

The Process of the Economic Integration of Latin America

Regional economic integration is a long-standing Latin American goal. For years it has been obvious to students of the problems of Latin American economic development that the levels of production to which the region aspires cannot be reached without the previous establishment of a common market. Integration is necessary, above all, because narrow domestic markets hinder the establishment of large-scale industries, and without them a balanced development is difficult. The broadening of the economic sphere, in addition to increasing competition, bringing to each country new ideas, products, and enterprises, would stimulate efficiency in production. The regional market—which is now comprised of 210 million persons and by 1975 will have 300 million—has sufficient amplitude for the needs of Latin American development and is its logical basis.

In recent years, with the success of the European Economic Community, the importance of the reasons of an external nature that make integration necessary have become manifest. In a world in which international trade is gradually being dominated by large economic blocs, Latin America cannot hope to solve its problems by the individual efforts of each country. Its interests in the world market will be protected and promoted adequately only when the region achieves the unity of action and of objectives which can be supplied solely by economic integration.

However, the establishment of a common market of the size and characteristics the Latin American one will have is no easy task. Obstacles of every kind hinder it—political, economic, geographic, legal, and cultural—outstanding among which are the different degrees of development in the region, the small volume of intraregional trade, as compared with the high dependency of the domestic economies on a few products exported principally to industrial countries located outside the Latin American zone.

The almost insurmountable difficulties that confront the immediate creation of a common market that would embrace all of Latin America have led the proponents of the idea of unity to divide the task, in order to gradually eliminate, through partial efforts, the obstacles to regional integration, without losing sight of the ultimate objective which is Latin American economic unity.

The first concrete initiatives of economic integration in Latin America appeared in the decade of the 50's. In contrast, the ideals and desires for political union and the efforts that were made to accomplish it, appeared practically from the time of independence. During this century and a half there also were thoughts of integrating the region in some form, and as early as the First International Conference of American States (1889-90) at the initiative of the United States, the idea of creating a customs union was discussed. But the propitious moment did not arrive until after the Second World War and it was the countries of Central America that signed the first treaties of economic integration. Seven countries of the south and Mexico created the Latin American Free Trade Association (LAFTA) in 1960. As of today one must speak of three processes: the Central American Common Market, LAFTA (comprising eleven countries today), and the Latin American common market which the Latin American Presidents agreed at Punta del Este in April 1967 to create in the period 1970-1985.

The economic integration of Latin America, considerably strengthened by its connection with the inter-American system for which it has today become a basic objective, has already reached a degree of development that demands intensified research into and study of its diverse and complex legal and institutional problems. The publication of this book, containing the up-to-date English texts of the legal instruments relative to that integration process published in Spanish three years ago, is in direct response to that demand. Its immediate usefulness for national and international officials, businessmen, practicing lawyers, and others, as well as for students and professors who are active or interested in the integration process, is also evident.

Since the publication of the Spanish text in 1964 the General Secretariat of the INSTITUTE has prepared and published several studies examining the legal and institutional problems of the economic integration of Latin America, in the light not only of the treaties and other instruments contained in that volume but also of the practice of the organs of the respective integration movements. Especially worthwhile mentioning, in this regard, is the book entitled *Problemática Jurídica e Institucional de la Integración de América Latina, Ensayo de Sistematización* [Legal and Institutional Problems of the Integration of Latin America, A Systematic Presentation], which will eventually be published in English.

The present book has been prepared with the collaboration of the Department of Legal Affairs and the Office of the Assistant Secretary for Economic and Social Affairs of the Organization of American States, as well as of the Legal Adviser of the Inter-American Development Bank. The General Secretariat also wishes to express its gratitude to the Permanent Secratariat for Central American Economic Integration (SIECA) and to the Secretariat of the Latin American Free Trade Association for their technical cooperation, as well as to the Ford Foundation which financed the publication of this English edition.

F. V. García-Amador
Secretary General
of the INSTITUTE

THE CENTRAL AMERICAN
COMMON MARKET

Free Trade

MULTILATERAL TREATY OF FREE TRADE AND CENTRAL AMERICAN ECONOMIC INTEGRATION

(Signed at Tegucigalpa, Honduras, June 10, 1958)

The Governments of the Republics of Guatemala, El Salvador, Honduras, Nicaragua, and Costa Rica, desirous of intensifying and strengthening the common bonds of origin and brotherhood uniting the five countries, and with a view to effecting the progressive integration of their economies, ensuring the expansion of their markets, promoting the production and exchange of goods and services, and raising the standards of living and employment of their respective populations, thereby contributing to the reestablishment of the economic unity of Central America, have agreed to conclude the present Multilateral Treaty of Free Trade and Central American Economic Integration, which shall be progressively achieved, and for that purpose have appointed as their respective plenipotentiaries:

[Here follow the names of the delegates]

who, after communicating their respective full powers and finding them in due and proper form, agree as follows:

Chapter I

TRADE REGIME

Article I With a view to creating a customs union between their respective territories as soon as conditions are favorable, the contracting States hereby agree to establish a free trade regime, which they shall endeavor to perfect within a period of ten years from the date on which the present Treaty enters into force. To that end, they resolve to abolish as between their territories the customs duties, charges, and conditions hereinafter mentioned, in respect of the commodities specified in the appended schedule constituting Annex A to this Treaty.

Consequently, the natural products of the contracting States and the articles manufactured in their territories, provided they are included in the aforesaid schedule, shall be exempt from import and export duties as well as all other taxes, surcharges, and charges levied on imports or exports or by reason of such importation or exportation whether they be of a national, municipal, or any other nature and whatever their purpose.

The exemptions stipulated in this article shall not include charges for lighterage, wharfage, warehousing, or handling of goods, or any other charges which may legitimately be levied for port, warehouse, or transport services; nor shall they include exchange differentials resulting from the existence of two or more rates of exchange or from other exchange regulations in any of the contracting States.

When a commodity or article included in the annexed schedule is subject to internal taxes, charges, or duties of any kind levied on production, sale, distribution, or consumption in any of the contracting States, the State concerned may levy an equivalent amount on similar goods imported from another contracting State.

Article II   Goods originating in the territory of any of the contracting States and included in the schedule appended to this Treaty shall be accorded in all the contracting States the same treatment as domestic goods and shall be exempt from any quota or other restriction except for such measures as may be legally applicable in the territories of the contracting States for reasons of public health, security or police control.

Article III   Goods originating in any of the signatory States and which are not included in the annexed schedule shall be accorded unconditional and unlimited most-favored-nation treatment in the territory of the other contracting States.

The above treatment shall not, however, be extended to concessions granted pursuant to other free trade treaties concluded between Central American States.

Article IV   The signatory States, convinced of the necessity of equalizing their customs tariffs and firmly determined to establish a customs union between their territories, undertake, subject to the opinion of the Central American Trade Commission referred to hereinbelow, to equalize the duties and other charges imposed by them individually on imports of goods listed in the schedule appended hereto, or which may be subsequently included therein, and on their principal raw materials and their containers.

For the purposes indicated in the preceding paragraph, the Commission shall prepare and submit to the signatory governments, within a period not exceeding one year, the appropriate draft contractual agreement or agreements for the equalization of import duties.

Article V   The governments of the signatory States shall endeavor to refrain from obtaining or granting customs exemptions on imports from outside Central America of articles produced in any of the contracting States and listed in the schedule appended hereto.

The signatory States shall further endeavor to equalize the advantages granted by them to industries producing any of the articles listed in the schedule, to the extent that such advantages might, in the opinion of the Central American Trade Commission, entail unfair competition in such goods.

Article VI Subject to the opinion of the Central American Trade Commission, the schedule appended to this Treaty may be extended by mutual agreement between the contracting States, by means of additional protocols and in accordance with their respective constitutional procedures.

Article VII In order that they may enjoy the advantages stipulated in this Treaty, the goods listed in the schedule appended hereto shall be entered on a customs form signed by the exporter, and containing a declaration of origin. That form shall be produced for inspection to the customs officers of the countries of origin and destination, in conformity with Annex B of this Treaty.

Article VIII The central banks of the signatory States shall cooperate closely with a view to preventing any currency speculation that might affect the rates of exchange and maintaining the convertibility of the currencies of the respective countries on a basis which, in normal conditions, shall guarantee the freedom, uniformity and stability of exchange.

Any of the signatory States which establish quota restrictions on international currency transfers shall adopt the measures necessary to ensure that such restrictions do not discriminate against the other States.

In case of serious balance of payments difficulties which affect or are apt to affect the monetary and payments relations between the signatory States, the Central American Trade Commission, acting of its own motion or at the request of one of the governments, shall immediately study the problem for the purpose of recommending to the signatory governments a satisfactory solution compatible with the multilateral free trade regime.

Chapter II

DISCRIMINATORY PRACTICES

Article IX Subject to the provisions of the bilateral Central American treaties in force and to any provisions that may be agreed upon in future treaties between Central American States, the signatory Parties agree to the following provisions with a view to ensuring a broad application of the principle of nondiscrimination in their trading relations:

a) Any goods not included in the schedule appended to this Treaty and subject to quota restrictions imposed by a contracting State shall, upon importation from the territory of another signatory State or upon exportation to such a territory, be accorded treatment no less favorable than that accorded to similar goods of any other origin or destination;

b) No signatory State shall establish or maintain any internal duty, tax, or other charge on any goods, whether or not included in the appended schedule, originating in the territory of another signatory State, nor shall it enact or impose any regulations regarding the distribution or retailing of such goods, when such charges or regulations place or tend to place the said goods in an unfavorable position by comparison with similar goods of domestic origin or imported from any other country; and

c) Should a signatory State establish or maintain a place of business or an agency or grant special privileges to a specific establishment to attend exclusively or principally, permanently or occasionally, to the production, exportation, importation, sale, or distribution of any goods, such State shall grant to the traders of the other signatory States equitable treatment with respect to purchases or sales which the said place of business, agency or establishment effects abroad. The institution concerned shall act in accordance with private business practice and shall afford the traders of the other countries reasonable opportunity to compete for participation in such purchases or sales.

Chapter III

INTERNATIONAL TRANSIT

Article X   Each of the contracting States shall ensure full freedom of transit through its territory for goods proceeding to or from another contracting State.

Such transit shall not be subject to any deduction, discrimination or quota restriction. In the event of any traffic congestion or other *force majeure,* each signatory State shall handle consignments intended for its own population and those in transit to the other States on an equitable basis.

Transit operations shall be carried out by the routes prescribed by law for that purpose and subject to the customs and transit laws and regulations applicable in the territory of transit.

Goods in transit shall be exempt from all duties, taxes, and other

fiscal charges of a municipal or other character imposed for any purpose whatsoever, except charges generally applicable for services rendered or for reasons of security, public health, or police control.

Chapter IV

EXPORT SUBSIDIES AND UNFAIR BUSINESS PRACTICES

Article XI No signatory State shall grant any direct or indirect
subsidy towards the export of any goods intended for the territory
of the other States, or establish or maintain any system resulting in
the sale of such goods for export to any other contracting State at a
price lower than the comparable price charged for similar goods on
the domestic market, due allowance being made for differences in the
conditions and terms of sale or in taxation and for any other factors
affecting price comparability.

Any measure which involves fixing of prices or price discrimination in a signatory State shall be deemed to constitute an indirect export subsidy if it involves the establishment of a sales price for specific goods in the other contracting States which is lower than that
resulting from normal competition in the market of the exporting
country.

However, tax exemptions or refunds of a general nature granted
by a signatory State with a view to encouraging the production in its
territory of specified goods, shall not be deemed to constitute an export subsidy.

Similarly, any exemption from internal taxes chargeable in the exporting State on the production, sale, or consumption of goods exported to the territory of another State shall not be deemed to constitute an export subsidy. Furthermore, the differences resulting from
the sale of foreign currency on the free market at a rate of exchange
higher than the official rate shall not normally be deemed to be an
export subsidy; in case of doubt, however, on the part of one of the
contracting States, the matter shall be submitted to the Central
American Trade Commission for its consideration and opinion.

Article XII As a means of precluding a practice which would be
inconsistent with the purposes of this Treaty, each signatory State
shall employ all the legal means at its disposal to prevent the exportation of goods from its territory to the territories of other States
at a price lower than their normal value, if such exportation would
prejudice or jeopardize the production of the other States or retard
the establishment of a domestic or a Central American industry.

Goods shall be considered to be exported at a price lower than
their normal value if their price on export is less than:

a) The comparable price, in ordinary trading conditions, of similar goods destined for domestic consumption in the exporting country; or

b) The highest comparable price of similar goods on their export to any third country in ordinary trading conditions; or

c) The cost of production of the goods in the country of origin, plus a reasonable addition for sales cost and profit.

Due allowance shall be made in each case for differences in conditions and terms of sale or in taxation and for any other factors affecting price comparability.

Article XIII   If, notwithstanding the provisions of this chapter, an unfair business practice is discovered, the State affected shall take steps with the competent authorities of the other State to ensure the elimination of that practice and, if necessary, may adopt protective measures, provided that the matter is then referred to the Central American Trade Commission for study and appropriate recommendations.

Chapter V

TRANSPORTATION AND COMMUNICATIONS

Article XIV   The signatory States shall endeavor to construct and maintain lines of communication to facilitate and increase traffic between their territories.

They shall also endeavor to standardize the transportation rates between their territories as well as the relevant laws and regulations.

Article XV   Commercial and private vessels and aircraft of any of the contracting States shall be accorded in ports and airports of the other States open to international traffic the same treatment as is extended to national vessels and aircraft. The same treatment shall be extended to passengers, crews, and freight of the other contracting States.

Land vehicles registered in one of the signatory States shall enjoy the same treatment in the territory of the other States, for the duration of their temporary stay there, as is accorded to vehicles registered in the State of visit.

Motor transport undertakings of any signatory State engaged in providing intra-Central American services for passengers and freight shall enjoy in the territory of the other States the same treatment as domestic undertakings.

Private vehicles and vehicles which are not used for the regular intra-Central American transportation of persons and goods shall be admitted to the territory of the other contracting States under a temporary duty-free importation system and shall be subject to the relevant legal provisions.

Vessels of any contracting State plying between the ports of Central America shall be subject, in the ports of the other States, to the same coastal shipping regime as domestic vessels.

The provisions of this article shall not affect the duty to comply with the formalities of registration and control prescribed in each country in respect of the entry, stay, or departure of vessels, aircraft, or vehicles for reasons of public health, security, or police control, public policy, or fiscal necessity.

Article XVI The signatory States shall endeavor to improve the telecommunications systems between their respective territories and shall direct their combined efforts towards the attainment of that objective.

Chapter VI

INVESTMENTS

Article XVII Each of the contracting States, acting within the framework of its constitution, shall grant national treatment to capital investments made by nationals of the other States, and shall recognize the right of such persons to organize or manage production, commercial, or financial undertakings, and to participate therein, on the same footing as its own nationals; each contracting State shall also extend equitable and nondiscriminatory treatment to transfers of funds accruing from capital investments made by nationals of the other States.

Chapter VII

CENTRAL AMERICAN TRADE COMMISSION

Article XVIII The signatory States agree to establish a Central American Trade Commission to which each of the contracting Parties shall appoint a representative; the Commission shall meet as frequently as its work may require or at the request of any of the contracting States.

The Commission or any of its members may travel freely in the contracting States to study matters within the Commission's competence in the field, and the authorities of the signatory States shall provide them with whatever information and facilities may be necessary for the proper discharge of their functions.

The Commission shall have a permanent secretariat, which shall be under the responsibility of the General Secretariat of the Organization of Central American States.

The Commission shall adopt its rules of procedure unanimously.

Article XIX   The functions of the Central American Trade Commission shall be as follows:

a) To propose to the contracting Parties measures conducive to the development and improvement of the Central American free trade zone referred to in the Treaty as well as measures designed to attain the objectives of Central American economic integration, and to prepare a specific plan for such purposes, including a customs union and the establishment of a Central American common market;

b) At the request of one or several governments to study questions and matters relating to the development of intra-Central American trade, in particular those connected with the application of this Treaty, and to propose measures for the solution of any problem which may arise;

c) To study production and trade in the signatory States, to recommend additions to the appended schedule, and to take appropriate measures to ensure:

   i) the standardization of customs tariffs and regulations;

   ii) the establishment of a single fiscal system for articles under state monopoly and for goods subject to production, sales, and consumption taxes;

   iii) the conclusion of agreements designed to avoid double taxation in the matter of direct taxes;

   iv) the improvement of intra-Central American transportation through the conclusion of appropriate agreements;

   v) the application of the decimal metric system of weights and measures.

d) To collect and analyze statistics and other data relating to trade between the signatory States.

In fulfilling these functions, the Commission shall avail itself of the reports and studies made by other Central American and international organizations and agencies.

The Central American Trade Commission shall give priority attention to the problem of equalizing customs tariffs and shall submit to the Economic Council of the Organization of Central American States, for consideration at its regular sessions, draft contractual agreements covering the greatest possible number of products.

Article XX   The competent authorities of the signatory States shall collect, classify, and publish the statistical data relating to import, export, and transit operations carried out under the terms of this Treaty, in accordance with the rules laid down, by mutual agreement, by the Central American Trade Commission and the statistical organizations of the signatory States.

Chapter VIII

INDUSTRIAL INTEGRATION

Article XXI With a view to promoting industrial development consistent with the purpose of this Treaty, the signatory States shall adopt, by mutual agreement, measures designed to further the establishment or expansion of regional industries directed towards a Central American common market and of particular interest to the economic integration of Central America.

Chapter IX

GENERAL PROVISIONS

Article XXII The signatory States shall adopt, as a basis for their customs tariffs and statistics, the Uniform Central American Customs Nomenclature (Nomenclatura Arancelaria Uniforme Centroamericana, NAUCA) and the Uniform Central American Nomenclature for Exports.

Article XXIII The nationals of any signatory State shall enjoy in the territory of all other signatory States national treatment in commercial and civil matters, in accordance with the internal legislation of each State.

Article XXIV Considering that this Treaty is specifically Central American in character and is designed to lay the foundations for a customs union of the contracting States and for the progressive integration of their economies, the signatory States agree that before signing or ratifying any multilateral agreements relating to commodities, trade, or customs concessions, and before joining any international organization established under those agreements or negotiating any arrangements within the framework of such an organization, they shall consult each other with a view to agreeing, if possible, on a common and united policy.

The contracting States shall also endeavor to adopt a common position at inter-American or world economic conferences or meetings.

The signatory States agree to maintain the "Central American exception clause" in any trade agreements they may conclude on the basis of most-favored-nation treatment with any countries other than the contracting States.

The contracting States declare that, in concluding this Treaty, they are prompted by the desire to establish closer mutual links as States of Central America governed by the special principles of a Central American public law.

To that end, they agree that if any of the trade agreements they may conclude with other countries or their participation in other international arrangements should constitute an obstacle to this Treaty, particularly as a result of provisions embodied in the other treaties permitting other countries to claim no less favorable treatment, they shall renegotiate or, as the case may be, denounce them at the earliest opportunity with a view to avoiding the difficulties or prejudice which might ensue for any of the contracting States as a result of claims of that nature.

The contracting Parties also undertake not to conclude any new agreements with other countries which are contrary to the spirit and purposes of this Treaty and, in particular, to the provisions of this article.

Article XXV   The signatory States agree to settle amicably, in the spirit of this Treaty, and through the Central American Trade Commission, any differences which may arise in the interpretation or application of any of its provisions. If agreement cannot be reached, they shall submit the matter to arbitration. For the purpose of constituting the arbitral tribunal, each contracting State shall propose to the Secretariat of the Organization of Central American States the names of three judges from its Supreme Court of Justice. From the complete list of candidates the Secretary General of the Organization of Central American States and the government representatives in the Organization shall select, by drawing lots, a tribunal composed of five arbitrators, no two of whom may be nationals of the same State. The award of the arbitral tribunal shall require the concurring votes of not less than three members, and shall be binding on all contracting States so far as it contains any ruling concerning the interpretation or application of the provisions of this Treaty.

Article XXVI   Any provisions of this Treaty which are broader in scope than those contained in other trade treaties between Central American countries shall prevail over the latter.

With a view to promoting the consolidation and enlargement of the multilateral free trade regime, the contracting States shall endeavor to extend free trade zones established by virtue of bilateral treaties.

Chapter X

TEMPORARY REGIMES

Article XXVII   With a view to the gradual application, whenever advisable, of the free trade regime established by virtue of the present Treaty, the contracting States may conclude special protocols for the adoption of temporary regimes introducing progressive tariff reductions, which shall be carried into effect by stages and shall be applicable to products not listed in Annex A[1], with the ultimate purpose of incorporating them in that annex.

The contracting States may also, in like manner, establish special temporary regimes for products not included in Annex A which may be subject to import or export quota restrictions.

In exceptional cases and for specified products, there may also be established, by means of additional protocols between all of the contracting Parties, a free trade regime applicable only to certain specified contracting States and providing for progressive reductions in customs tariffs with the remaining country or countries, with the ultimate aim of securing the incorporation of the products concerned in Annex A.

Chapter XI

FINAL PROVISIONS

Article XXVIII This Treaty shall enter into force, in the case of the first three States to ratify it, on the date of deposit of the third instrument of ratification; and in the case of the States which ratify it subsequently, on the date of deposit of the respective instruments of ratification.

This Treaty shall remain valid for a period of ten years from the initial date of its entry into force; it shall be tacitly renewable for successive periods of ten years.

Any contracting State may denounce this Treaty by giving notice to that effect not later than six months before the date on which the initial or any subsequent period of validity expires. Denunciation shall take effect, for the denouncing State, as from the date of expiration of the relevant period of validity of the Treaty. The Treaty shall remain in force as between the other contracting States so long as at least two States continue to be parties thereto.

This Treaty shall be submitted for ratification in each State, in conformity with its respective constitutional or legal rules.

The General Secretariat of the Organization of Central American States shall act as depository of this Treaty and shall send a certified copy thereof to the ministry of foreign affairs of each of the contracting States. It shall also notify the contracting States of the deposit of the corresponding instruments of ratification as well as of any denunciation which may occur within the prescribed time limit. When the Treaty comes into force, it shall also transmit a certified copy thereof

---

[1] Annex A not included.

to the Secretary-General of the United Nations, for registration in conformity with Article 102 of the United Nations Charter.

IN WITNESS WHEREOF, the respective plenipotentiaries sign this Treaty in the City of Tegucigalpa, D.C., Honduras, this tenth day of June 1958.

For the Government of Guatemala:

1. With reservation to Article XXV of this Treaty, in accordance with the provisions of paragraph 3, subparagraph (b) of Article 149 of the Constitution of the Republic.
2. With the reservations made by Guatemala to the schedule of articles covered by the free trade agreement (Annex A), as indicated in the notes to the said schedule.

José Guirola Leal
Minister of Economy

For the Government of El Salvador:

With the reservations made by El Salvador to the schedule of articles covered by the free trade agreement (Annex A), as indicated in the notes to the said schedule.

Alfonso Rochac
Minister of Economy

For the Government of Honduras:

With the reservations made by Honduras to the schedule of articles covered by the free trade agreement (Annex A), as indicated in the notes to the said schedule.

Fernando Villar
Minister of Economy and Finance

For the Government of Nicaragua:

With the reservations made by Nicaragua to the schedule of articles covered by the free trade agreement (Annex A), as indicated in the notes to the said schedule.

Enrique Delgado
Minister of Economy

For the Government of Costa Rica:

With the reservations made by Costa Rica to the schedule of articles covered by the free trade agreement (Annex A), as indicated in the notes to the said schedule.

Wilburg Jiménez Castro
Vice-Minister of Economy and Finance

JOINT DECLARATION OF THE PRESIDENTS OF GUATEMALA, HONDURAS, AND EL SALVADOR ON A TRIPARTITE TREATY OF ECONOMIC ASSOCIATION

(Signed January 9, 1960)

Miguel Ydígoras Fuentes, President of Guatemala, Ramón Villeda Morales, President of Honduras, and José María Lemus, President of El Salvador, having met at the common border of the three countries to make a calm review of the economic and social situation of their countries and the measures thus far put into practice to achieve integration of their economies, have agreed as follows:

ONE: The principal concern of the three governments is to promote the economic development of their respective countries in order to improve the standard of living of their peoples.

TWO: To attain this goal, the following steps, among others, are necessary:

a) To increase sources of employment;
b) To make better use of human potentialities and natural resources;
c) To promote industrial development and modernize agricultural methods;
d) To increase productivity and reduce costs for the benefit of consumers;
e) To encourage the investment of national and foreign capital in the region and facilitate access to the various sources of credit; and
f) To increase the number of consumers and their purchasing power.

THREE: For this purpose, it is essential to increase the consumption of articles produced in the region, facilitate the exchange of such goods through free trade, and accelerate the Program for the Economic Integration of Central America.

FOUR: The geographic contiguity of the three countries, the traditional existence of bilateral free trade treaties, and a relatively extensive transportation network between them have given rise to a growing exchange of persons and goods.

FIVE: These circumstances enable the three countries to adopt immediate measures of cooperation that will strengthen their existing economic relations and promote Central American economic integration.

SIX: Attainment of these purposes requires a joint effort to expand free trade, diminish the effect of any imbalance that may develop, and establish a groundwork that will make possible the balanced economic development of the three countries.

Accordingly, they declare that it is the purpose of their governments to establish in the near future an economic association among the three countries.

To that end, they authorize their respective Ministers of Economy to sign a treaty within thirty days establishing the machinery for achieving closer integration of their economies through formulas of definite and genuine Central American interdependence.

January 9, 1960

Ramón Villeda Morales

Miguel Ydígoras Fuentes   *José María Lemus*

TREATY OF ECONOMIC ASSOCIATION BETWEEN THE REPUBLICS OF HONDURAS, GUATEMALA, AND EL SALVADOR

(Signed at Guatemala City, Guatemala, February 6, 1960)

The Governments of the Republics of Honduras, Guatemala, and El Salvador,

FOR THE PURPOSE of stimulating the economic development of their respective countries in order to improve the standard of living of their peoples;

CONVINCED that it is necessary to strengthen and expand existing economic cooperation between the three countries and thus contribute to Central American integration;

CONSIDERING that the Presidents of the three republics declared that it was imperative to accelerate the integration and development of the economies of the region;

FOR THE PURPOSE of establishing in the near future a common market jointly to promote production and investment, and of establishing the necessary machinery to promote economic cooperation between them;

HAVE DECIDED to enter into this Treaty of Economic Association; and to that end have appointed the following Plenipotentiaries:

His Excellency the President of the Republic of Honduras: Jorge Bueso Arias, Minister of Economy and Finance;

His Excellency the President of the Republic of Guatemala: Eduardo Rodriguez Genis, Minister of Economy; and

His Excellency the President of the Republic of El Salvador: Dr. Alfonso Rochac, Minister of Economy;

Who having communicated to each other their full powers, found to be in good and due form, have agreed as follows:

Chapter I

BASIC PRINCIPLES

Article I The contracting Parties hereby establish an Economic Association, which will guarantee the free movement of persons, goods, and capital between their territories.

Article II The nationals of each signatory State shall enjoy the right to enter and leave the territory of the other contracting Parties with no restrictions other than those established for nationals of such contracting Parties.

Likewise, the nationals of any contracting Party shall enjoy national treatment in the territory of the others, pursuant to each State's domestic laws on civil, trade, tax, and labor matters.

Article III When the customs union referred to in Chapter III is established there shall be free movement of goods between the territories of the contracting Parties without distinction as to origin, source, or destination. In the transition period before the customs union is established, however, only natural products and manufactured articles originating in the territories of the contracting Parties shall enjoy free movement, and trade in them shall conform to the terms and conditions fixed hereinafter.

Article IV The contracting Parties shall endeavor to maintain free convertibility of their currencies, and in no case may exchange restrictions be established that discriminate against any contracting Party.

Article V Each contracting Party shall accord national treatment with respect to capital investments by natural or juristic persons of the other signatory States and the right to organize and manage companies and participate therein.

Each contracting Party shall issue regulations relating to investments by juristic persons in which nationals of third countries participate.

Article VI The contracting Parties shall see that no legislative or administrative provision unduly impedes the free movement of persons, goods, and capital between them.

Articles VII To create reasonably equitable trade conditions, the contracting Parties shall endeavor to standardize legislative or other measures that affect production activities.

Article VIII   The contracting Parties shall adopt a policy of co-operation and mutual consultation with reference to trade between them and their economic relations with countries outside Central America.

Chapter II

COMMON MARKET

Article IX   Natural products originating in the territories of the contracting Parties and those manufactured therein shall, except only for the restrictions set forth in Annex A[1] of this Treaty, enjoy immediate free trade. Accordingly, these commodities shall be exempt from all import or export charges, including consular fees.

The exemptions contemplated in this article shall not include fees for lighterage, wharfage, warehousing, handling of goods, or any others payable under law for port, custodial, or transportation services.

For the purpose of this article, products shall not be considered to be manufactured in one of the contracting Parties, when they are manufactured in a third country and are only packed, packaged, cut up, or simply diluted in the exporting country.

Article X   The products listed in Annex A shall be subject to special treatment and arrangements in accordance with the terms fixed therein.

Article XI   Goods from each contracting Party shall be subject to any national or municipal levies and taxes on production, sale, distribution, trade, and consumption that have been or may here-after be established in the importing country, and it is understood that these domestic levies and taxes shall not be different from or higher than those applied to the national goods of the said importing country.

When products subject to domestic taxes are not produced in the importing country, the latter shall also levy a duty on the importation of similar products originating in third countries.

Article XII   Products that constitute government monopolies on the date of this Treaty, pursuant to the domestic provisions of any contracting Party, shall be subject to the pertinent legal provisions of each country.

The creation of new monopolies or any change in the system of existing ones shall be preceded by consultation between the parties concerned, for the purpose of subjecting trade in the products in question to special treatment.

---

[1] Annex A not included.

Article XIII Products whose exportation or importation is governed by international agreements shall be subject to the provisions of those agreements.

Article XIV The customs authorities of the signatory States shall provide every possible facility in order that the trade established between the three countries may be conducted as expeditiously as possible. Goods for importation or exportation between the contracting Parties shall be covered by a customs form signed by the exporter, which shall contain a declaration of origin and which must be countersigned by the customs officials of the exporting and importing countries, as established in Annex B[1] of this Treaty.

Article XV When there are doubts concerning the origin of a product, the State that considers itself affected shall submit the matter to the Executive Council established by this Treaty for consideration, and if the Council deems it advisable, it shall rule that the form referred to in the preceding article must be accompanied by a declaration of origin signed by the producer of the product being exported or by a certificate issued by the Ministry of Economy of the exporting country.

Article XVI No signatory State shall grant subsidies on the exportation of goods intended for the territory of the other States, nor shall it permit goods to be exported to the territory of the other States at less than the usual price.

When there are charges of unfair trade practices, the State that considers itself affected shall submit the matter to the Executive Council for consideration, and the Council shall rule thereon.

Chapter III

CUSTOMS UNION

Article XVII The contracting Parties agree to equalize all import charges within five years of the entry into force of this Treaty. This equalization shall include all levies, taxes, and duties of any kind.

The equalization shall be carried out in accordance with the terms of the Central American Agreement on the Equalization of Import Charges, but it shall not be delayed in case the Central American levels have not been established within the five-year period provided in this article.

Article XVIII After all import charges have been equalized, the contracting Parties shall determine the bases for a Joint Customs Ad-

---

[1] Annex B not included.

ministration, revenues from which shall be equitably distributed among the signatory States.

The organization of the Joint Customs Administration and the method of distributing its revenues shall be the subject of a special protocol.

Chapter IV

DEVELOPMENT AND ASSISTANCE FUND

Article XIX The contracting Parties agree to set up a Development and Assistance Fund, which shall have juridical personality under international law and the purpose of which shall be to contribute through its activities to the economic integration and development of the associated countries, by facilitating public and private investment for production purposes.

The operation of the Fund shall be governed by its bylaws, and it shall have legal capacity to enter into and carry out active and passive financial transactions.

Accordingly, one of its functions shall be to grant loans and guaranties to the Governments of the signatory States and to private companies established in their respective territories for the following purposes:

a) Acceleration of the establishment of a balanced economic structure in the signatory countries;

b) Construction, extension, and improvement of highways connecting the territories of the contracting Parties and the execution of economic development projects of common interest;

c) Expansion or improvement of companies, especially for the purpose of diminishing the adverse effect of any imbalance that may result from the establishment of the common market; and

d) Financing of new companies that, because of their size or nature, may be established in connection with the common market.

Article XX The resources of the Fund shall be as follows:

a) The contributions or quotas paid by the governments of the contracting Parties, the understanding being that such contributions shall be in proportion to the ability of each signatory State to pay;

b) Credit resources obtained in capital markets; and

c) Any income derived from national, foreign, or international public or private organizations, on any legal basis whatsoever.

An additional protocol shall establish the method of payment, time limit, and amount of the contributions of each contracting Party. The protocol referred to in this article shall be incorporated in the bylaws of the Fund, and it shall be signed within 120 days of the signature of this Treaty.

Chapter V

ORGANS OF THE ASSOCIATION

Article XXI The organs of the Economic Association established by this Treaty shall be as follows:

a) The Committee of Directors; and
b) The Executive Council.

Article XXII The Committee of Directors shall be composed of the Ministers of Economy of the contracting Parties. It shall meet at least once every three months or at the request of any one of them, and its principal function shall be to establish the general policy to be followed in order to facilitate the economic integration of the signatory countries. Its decisions shall be implemented by the Executive Council in accordance with the terms stipulated to that effect.

The Committee of Directors shall issue the regulations necessary for facilitating the implementation of this Treaty.

Article XXIII The Executive Council shall be responsible for all activities and work whose purpose is to put into practice the economic union of the contracting Parties, and it shall submit an annual report of its work to the Committee of Directors.

The Executive Council shall be composed of one regular member and one alternate appointed by each contracting Party. It shall meet at least once a month or at the request of any signatory State, and it shall adopt its decisions by a majority vote.

The Council shall prepare its rules of procedure and submit them to the Committee of Directors for consideration. Its duties shall be those established in the said rules of procedure and those assigned to it by the Committee of Directors. It shall also have the duties and powers of the joint committees established by bilateral treaties.

Article XXIV The Executive Council shall have a permanent secretariat and shall be empowered to appoint its personnel. Administrative expenses for the maintenance and operation of the Council and the Secretariat shall be borne by the Development and Assistance Fund. The amount and distribution of the administrative expenses shall be determined by the Committee of Directors.

Article XXV The Council shall be authorized to appoint committees and working groups to function as advisory bodies.

Chapter VI

GENERAL PROVISIONS

Article XXVI   Matters relating to shipping, fishing in territorial waters, international transit, communications, customs legislation, monetary problems, and others not expressly provided for in this Treaty shall be resolved by means of additional protocols to the Treaty. These protocols shall be concluded on the recommendation of the Executive Council.

Article XXVII   The provisions of this Treaty shall not affect the provisions of bilateral or multilateral treaties on the economic integration of Central America that are not contrary to them.

However, this Treaty shall be applied in preference to any Central American bilateral or multilateral treaty, insofar as it liberalizes the provisions of such treaties.

Article XXVIII   No provision of this Treaty may be contrary to or prejudice the conclusion of agreements on Central American economic integration.

Article XXIX   Any differences that may arise concerning the interpretation or application of any clause of this Treaty shall be submitted to the Executive Council for consideration, and it shall rule on the matter.

If a contracting Party is not satisfied with the Council's decision, it may appeal to the Committee of Directors. If it does not agree with the Committee's decision, it may submit the matter to a court of arbitration made up as follows: Each contracting Party shall suggest the names of three justices of its Supreme Court to the Executive Council. From the total list of candidates, the Council shall select by lot three arbitrators to form the court, each of whom must be of a different nationality.

The judgment of the court of arbitration shall be pronounced by an affirmative vote of two members, and it shall have the force of *res judicata* for all the contracting Parties with respect to any question it resolves concerning the interpretation or application of the clauses of this Treaty.

Article XXX   In accordance with the Central American spirit that has motivated the conclusion of this Treaty, the contracting Parties shall jointly issue an invitation to the other Central American countries to participate in the Association in accordance with such bases as may be determined by common agreement.

Article XXXI   This Treaty shall be in effect for 20 years, and at the expiration of that period it may be extended indefinitely unless five years' notice of its denunciation is given. It shall continue to be in force as long as at least two countries adhere to it.

This Treaty shall enter into force on the date of the exchange of the respective instruments of ratification.

It shall enter into force with respect to the other Central American countries as soon as the pertinent instruments of ratification have been deposited in the Foreign Ministry of the country where the exchange is made.

IN WITNESS WHEREOF, the Plenipotentiaries of Guatemala, El Salvador, and Honduras sign this instrument in three original copies in Guatemala City on February 6, 1960.

GENERAL TREATY OF
CENTRAL AMERICAN ECONOMIC INTEGRATION

(Signed at Managua, Nicaragua, December 13, 1960)

Chapter I

CENTRAL AMERICAN COMMON MARKET

Article I The contracting States agree to set up among themselves a common market which should be fully established in not more than five years from the date of the entry into force of this Treaty. They also undertake to set up a customs union among their territories.

Article II For the purposes of the previous Article, the contracting Parties shall undertake to complete the establishment of a Central American free trade area within a period of five years and to adopt a uniform Central American tariff in accordance with the terms of the Central American Agreement on the Equalization of Import Charges.

Chapter II

TRADE REGIME

Article III The signatory States shall grant free trade rights for all products originating in their respective territories, with the sole limitations included in the special regimes referred to in Annex A[1] of this Treaty.

Accordingly, the natural products of the contracting countries and products manufactured in them shall be exempt from import and export duties, including consular fees, and all other taxes, surcharges and imposts levied on such imports and exports or on the occasion of their importation and exportation, whether such duties, fees, taxes,

---

[1] Annex A not included.

surcharges, and imposts are national, municipal, or of any other nature.

The exemptions provided for in this article shall not include taxes or charges for lighterage, docking, warehousing, and handling of goods or any other charges which may be legitimately levied by port, warehouse, and transport services; nor shall they include exchange differentials resulting from the existence of two or more rates of exchange or from any other exchange measures adopted in any of the contracting countries.

Goods originating in the territory of the contracting States shall be accorded national treatment in all of them and shall be exempt from any restrictions or measures of a quantitative nature, apart from control measures which are legally applicable in the territories of the contracting States for reasons of a public health, security or police character.

Article IV   The contracting Parties shall establish for given products special transitional arrangements excluding them from the direct free trade rights mentioned in Article III of this Treaty. Such products shall be automatically incorporated in the free trade regime not later than the end of the fifth year after the entry into force of this Treaty, except where specifically provided to the contrary in Annex A.

Annex A shall include products subject to special arrangements, trade in which shall comply with the conditions and requirements laid down therein. The said conditions and requirements may only be amended following multilateral negotiations in the Executive Council. Annex A shall form an integral part of this Treaty.

The signatory States shall agree that the Protocol to the Central American Agreement on the Equalization of Import Charges, concerning a Central American Preferential Tariff, shall not be applicable to trade in products subject to the special arrangements mentioned in this Article.

Article V   Goods which are accorded the advantages laid down in this Treaty must be covered by a customs form signed by the exporter which shall include a declaration of origin and shall be submitted for the visa of the customs officers of the countries of shipment and of destination, in accordance with the provisions laid down in Annex B[1] of this Treaty.

When there is doubt regarding the origin of a product and the problem has not been settled by bilateral negotiations, either of the parties affected may ask the Executive Council to intervene in order to verify the origin of the said product. The Council shall not consider as originating in one of the contracting countries, those products which have

---

[1] Annex B not included.

come from or have been manufactured in a third country and have been merely assembled, packaged, bottled, cut up, or diluted in the exporting country.

In the cases referred to in the previous paragraph, import of the goods concerned shall not be prevented, always provided that a guarantee is given to the importing country for the payment of the tariffs or other charges associated with the import. This guarantee shall become effective or shall be cancelled, as the case may be, when the problem has finally been settled.

The Executive Council shall establish, by means of regulations, the procedure to be followed in order to determine the origin of the goods.

Article VI   When the products in which trade is carried on are subject to charges, excise taxes or other internal duties of any kind, levied on production, sale, distribution, or consumption in one of the signatory countries, the latter may impose an equal duty on goods of the same nature which it imports from another contracting State, in which case it shall impose a duty of at least the same amount and under the same conditions, on imports coming from third countries.

The contracting Parties agree that internal duties on consumption shall be established in accordance with the following conditions:

a) Such duties may be established for the amount deemed necessary when the article in question is produced nationally or when the said article is not produced in any of the signatory States;

b) When an article is not produced in one of the contracting countries but is produced in another, the former may not levy duties on the consumption of the said article, except following a favorable decision by the Executive Council;

c) When one of the Parties has established an internal tax on consumption and production of the article thus taxed subsequently commences in one of the other contracting countries, although such production does not exist in the country imposing the tax, the Executive Council shall, if requested by the Party concerned, consider the case and report whether the existence of the tax is compatible with free trade. The States shall undertake to abolish, in conformity with their legal procedures, such taxes on consumption on receiving a notification calling for this from the Executive Council.

Article VII   None of the signatory States shall establish or maintain regulations on the distribution or sale of goods originating in another signatory State when such regulations tend to place or do in fact place the said goods in an unfavorable position *vis-à-vis* similar goods either of domestic origin or imported from any other country.

Article VIII   Articles which because of the internal arrangements of the contracting Parties constitute state or other monopolies on the date of entry into force of this Treaty, shall remain subject to the relevant legal provisions in each country and, where applicable, to the conditions laid down in Annex A of this Treaty.

In the event of new monopolies being created or the regime governing existing ones being modified, consultations shall take place among the Parties with the aim of providing special rules for Central American trade in the corresponding articles.

Chapter III

EXPORT SUBSIDIES AND UNFAIR BUSINESS PRACTICES

Article IX The governments of the signatory States shall not grant exemptions or reductions in customs tariffs to imports coming from outside Central America when the articles concerned are produced in the contracting States under satisfactory conditions.

When a signatory State considers it is affected by the granting of customs exemption for imports, or by government imports which are not intended for the use of the government itself or of its institutions, it may submit the problem to the Executive Council, which shall consider it and come to a decision in the matter.

Article X The central banks of the signatory States shall closely cooperate in order to prevent currency speculations which might affect the exchange rates and so as to maintain the convertibility of the currencies of the respective countries on a basis which, under normal conditions, guarantees freedom, uniformity, and stability of exchange.

In the event of one of the signatory States establishing quantitative restrictions on international monetary transfers, it shall adopt the necessary measures to ensure that such restrictions will not affect the other States in a discriminatory manner.

In the event of serious balance-of-payments difficulties which affect or might affect the monetary payment relations between the signatory States, the Executive Council either *ex officio,* or at the request of one of the Parties, shall immediately study the problem in collaboration with the central banks, for the purpose of recommending to the signatory governments a satisfactory solution compatible with the maintenance of the multilateral free trade system.

Article XI No contracting State shall grant, directly or indirectly, any subsidy in favor of the export of goods intended for the territories of the other States, or establish or maintain any system resulting in the sale of a given commodity for export to another contracting State at a price lower than the established price for the sale of the said commodity on the domestic market, making due allowance for differences in the conditions of sale and taxation, as well as for other factors affecting price comparability.

Any fixing of prices or price discrimination in one of the signatory States shall be regarded as an indirect export subsidy if it results in the establishment of a sales price for a given commodity in the other contracting States which is lower than that which would result from normal competition in the market of the exporting country.

When the import of products made in a contracting State with raw materials acquired under monopoly conditions at artificially low prices might threaten the existing production in another signatory State, the party which considers itself affected shall submit the problem for consideration by the Executive Council so that the latter can decide whether an unfair trade practice is actually involved. Within the five days following receipt of the request, the Executive Council shall issue a decision in the matter or authorize temporary suspension of free trade, while permitting trade subject to the provision of a guarantee for the amount of the customs dues. The said suspension shall be authorized for a period of 30 days, and the Council must issue a final decision before the expiry of this period. If no decision is reached within the five days laid down, the party affected may request a guarantee pending a final decision by the Executive Council. Tax exemptions of a general character granted by a contracting State with a view to encouraging production shall, however, not be deemed to constitute an export subsidy.

Likewise, exemption from internal taxes on production, sales or consumption levied in the exporting country on goods exported to the territory of another State, shall not be deemed to constitute an export subsidy. Normally, the differences resulting from the sale of foreign exchange on the free market at a rate of exchange higher than the official rate shall not be deemed to be an export subsidy; but in case of doubt on the part of one of the contracting States, the matter shall be submitted to the Executive Council for its consideration and opinion.

Article XII Since it would be a practice contrary to the aims of this Treaty, each contracting State shall, through the legal means at its disposal, prevent the exportation of goods from its territory to that of the other States at a price lower than their normal value, if this would jeopardize or threaten to jeopardize production in the other countries or retard the establishment of a domestic or Central American industry.

A commodity shall be considered to be exported at a lower price than its normal value if the price of the said commodity is less than:

a) the comparable price, under normal trade conditions, for a similar commodity when intended for consumption in the domestic market of the exporting country; or

b) the highest comparable price for a similar commodity exported to a third country under normal trade conditions; or

c) the cost of production of the commodity in the country of origin plus a reasonable addition in respect of the sales cost and profit.

In each case, due allowance shall be made for differences in conditions of sale, differences in taxation and other differences affecting price comparability.

Article XIII   If one of the contracting Parties considers that unfair business practices exist not included in Article XI, then it may not prevent trade by a unilateral decision, but shall submit the problem for consideration by the Executive Council in order that the latter may report whether such practices are in fact occurring. The Council shall render its decision within not more than 60 days from the date of receipt of the communication concerned.

When one of the Parties considers that there is evidence of unfair business practice, it shall ask the Executive Council for authorization to request a guarantee for the amount of the import duties involved.

If the Executive Council does not come to a decision within 8 days, the Party affected may request the guarantee pending a final decision by the Executive Council.

Article XIV   Once the Executive Council has come to a decision on unfair business practices, it shall inform the contracting Parties whether or not protective measures against the said practices may be applied, pursuant to this Treaty.

Chapter IV

TRANSIT AND TRANSPORT

Article XV   Each of the contracting States shall maintain full freedom of transit through its territory for goods proceeding to or from any of the other signatory States, as well as for the vehicles transporting the said goods.

Such transit shall not be subject to deductions, discrimination, or quantitative restrictions. Should there be traffic congestion or any other form of *force majeure,* each signatory State shall give equitable attention both to the forwarding of goods intended for its own population and to that of goods in transit to the other States.

Transit operations shall be carried out by the routes prescribed by law for that purpose and be subject to the customs and transit laws and regulations applicable in the transit territory.

Goods in transit shall be exempt from all duties, taxes, and other fiscal charges of a municipal or other character levied in connection with such transit, whatever the destination of the goods may be, but may remain subject to payment of the charges normally applicable for

services rendered, which may in no case exceed the cost of the latter
so that they constitute import taxes or duties.

Chapter V

CONSTRUCTION FIRMS

Article XVI The contracting States shall grant equality of treatment as compared with domestic firms to concerns of other signatory
States engaged in the construction of highways, bridges, dams, irrigation
and electrification systems, housing and other works tending to promote the development of the Central American economic infrastructure.

Chapter VI

INDUSTRIAL INTEGRATION

Article XVII The contracting Parties adopt in this Treaty all the
provisions of the Agreement on the System of Central American Integrated Industries, and so as to put the said provisions into effect as
soon as possible, they shall adopt, within not more than six months
from the date of the entry into force of this Treaty, additional protocols
in which shall be stipulated the industrial plants to be covered initially
by the said Agreement, the free trade regime applicable to their products and the other conditions provided for in Article III of the said
Agreement.

Chapter VII

CENTRAL AMERICAN BANK FOR ECONOMIC INTEGRATION

Article XVIII The signatory States agree to establish the Central
American Bank for Economic Integration which shall have the legal
status of a corporate body. The Bank shall act as an instrument for
the financing and promotion of integrated economic growth, on the
basis of balanced regional development. To this end, the contracting
States shall sign the Agreement setting up the said institution, which
Agreement shall remain open for the signature or adhesion of any
other Central American State which may wish to become a member
of the Bank.

It shall be laid down, however, that members of the Bank may not
obtain guarantees or loans from the said institution if they have
not previously deposited the instruments of ratification of the following
international agreements:

The present Treaty;

The Multilateral Treaty of Free Trade and Central American Economic Integration, signed on June 10, 1958;

The Agreement on the System of Central American Integrated Industries, signed on June 10, 1958; and

The Central American Agreement on the Equalization of Import Charges, signed on September 10, 1959, and its Protocol, signed on the same date as the present Treaty.

Chapter VIII

FISCAL INCENTIVES TO INDUSTRIAL DEVELOPMENT

Article XIX The contracting States, with the aim of providing uniform fiscal incentives to industrial development, shall agree to bring about as soon as possible a reasonable standardization of the laws and provisions in force in this connection. To this end, they shall sign within six months from the date of the entry into force of this Treaty, a special protocol in which shall be stipulated the amount and kind of exemption, the limiting dates of the latter, the conditions under which they shall be granted, the systems of industrial classification and the rules and procedures for their application. Coordination of the application of these fiscal incentives to industrial development shall be the responsibility of the Executive Council.

Chapter IX

ORGANS

Article XX To direct integration of the Central American economies and to coordinate the policy of the contracting States in economic matters there shall be set up a Central American Economic Council, consisting of the Ministers of Economy of each of the contracting Parties.

The Central American Economic Council shall meet whenever necessary or at the request of any of the contracting Parties; it shall consider the work of the Executive Council and take whatever decisions it may deem appropriate. The Central American Economic Council shall be the body responsible for expediting the implementation of the resolutions of the Economic Cooperation Committee of the Central American Isthmus relating to economic integration. It may call on Central American or international technical organizations for their advice.

Article XXI For the purpose of applying and administering the present Treaty, as well as of carrying on all negotiations and activities having as their aim the economic union of Central America, an Executive Council shall be set up consisting of one permanent member and one alternate designated by each of the contracting Parties.

The Executive Council shall meet whenever necessary, at the request of any of the contracting Parties, or when convened by the Permanent Secretariat, and its resolutions shall be adopted by a majority vote of all the members of the Council. In the event of agreement not being reached, the matter shall be referred to the Central American Economic Council so that the latter can come to a final decision concerning it.

Before coming to a decision, the Economic Council shall decide unanimously whether the matter shall be settled by the concurring votes of all its members or by a majority vote.

Article XXII The Executive Council shall lay down the measures necessary to ensure the fulfillment of the undertakings entered into pursuant to this Treaty and to solve any problems which may arise in regard to the application of its provisions. Furthermore, the Council may suggest to governments the conclusion of additional multilateral agreements required to achieve the aims of economic integration of Central America, including a customs union between their territories.

The Executive Council shall assume on behalf of the contracting Parties, the functions entrusted to the Central American Trade Commission in the Multilateral Treaty of Free Trade and Central American Economic Integration and in the Central American Agreement on the Equalization of Import Charges, as well as those entrusted to the Central American Industrial Integration Commission in the Agreement on the System of Central American Integrated Industries, and the functions and duties of the joint commissions of the bilateral treaties in force between the contracting Parties.

Article XXIII A Permanent Secretariat shall be set up, with the legal status of a corporate body, which shall be the Secretariat for both the Central American Economic Council and the Executive Council created under this Treaty.

The headquarters of the Secretariat shall be in Guatemala City, the capital of the Republic of Guatemala, and it shall be directed by a Secretary General appointed for a period of three years by the Central American Economic Council. The Secretariat shall establish whatever departments and sections may be necessary for carrying out its functions. Its expenses shall be in accordance with a general budget approved annually by the Central American Economic Council, and each of the contracting Parties shall contribute to its maintenance an annual minimum sum equivalent to fifty thousand United States dollars (US $50,000), payable in the respective currencies of the signatory countries.

The officials of the Secretariat shall enjoy diplomatic immunity. Other diplomatic privileges shall be granted solely to the Secretariat and to the Secretary General.

Article XXIV   The Secretariat shall watch over the correct application as between the contracting Parties, of this Treaty, of the Multilateral Treaty of Free Trade and Central American Economic Integration, of the Agreement on the System of Central American Integrated Industries, of the Central American Agreement on the Equalization of Import Charges, of bilateral or multilateral free trade and economic integration treaties in force between any of the contracting Parties, and of all other agreements concluded or which may be concluded with the aim of Central American economic integration and whose interpretation is not specifically entrusted to any other body.

The Secretariat shall see that the resolutions of the Central American Economic Council and of the Executive Council set up under this Treaty are implemented and shall also exercise the functions delegated to it by the Executive Council. The regulations governing its functions shall be approved by the Economic Council.

The Secretariat shall also be responsible for carrying out the activities and studies assigned to it by the Executive Council and the Central American Economic Council. In executing these functions, it shall make use of studies and work already carried out by other Central American and international bodies and shall secure their cooperation as appropriate.

Chapter X

GENERAL PROVISIONS

Article XXV   The signatory States agree not to sign unilaterally with non-Central American countries, new treaties affecting the principles of Central American economic integration. They shall also agree to maintain the "Central American exception clause" in any trade agreements they may conclude on the basis of most-favored-nation treatment with countries other than the contracting Parties.

Article XXVI   The signatory States agree to settle amicably, in conformity with the spirit of this Treaty, and through the Executive Council or the Central American Economic Council, any differences which may arise regarding the interpretation or application of any provision of this Treaty. If agreement cannot be reached, they shall submit the matter to arbitration. For the purpose of constituting the Arbitration Tribunal, each contracting Party shall nominate to the General Secretariat of the Organization of Central American States, three judges from their respective Supreme Courts of Justice. The Secretary-General of the Organization of Central American States and the government representatives attached to that body shall select, by drawing lots, one arbitrator for each of the contracting Parties, whereby all the arbitrators must be of different nationality. The award of the Arbitration Tribunal shall require the concurring votes of not less than three members and shall have the force of *res judicata* for all contracting Parties in respect of any ruling concerning the interpretation or application of the provisions of this Treaty.

Article XXVII The present Treaty shall take precedence, among the contracting Parties, over the Multilateral Treaty of Free Trade and Central American Economic Integration and over other bilateral or multilateral instruments of free trade concluded between the contracting Parties; however, notwithstanding this, the said agreement shall continue to remain in force.

Among the respective signatory States, the provisions of the trade and economic integration agreements referred to in the previous paragraph shall be applied in matters not considered in the present Treaty.

During such time as any of the contracting Parties have not ratified the present Treaty or in the event of its denunciation by any of them, the trade relations of the States concerned with the remaining signatory States shall be governed by previous commitments under the instruments in force referred to in the preamble to this Treaty.

Article XXVIII The contracting Parties agree to consult the Executive Council prior to concluding with one another new treaties which may affect free trade.

The Executive Council shall consider the matter and determine what effect the conclusion of the said agreements might have on the free trade regime established under the present Treaty. On the basis of the study made by the Executive Council, the party which considers itself affected by the conclusion of these new treaties may adopt the measures recommended by the Council with the aim of safeguarding its interests.

Article XXIX For the purposes of customs regulations connected with free trade, the transit of goods and the application of the Uniform Central American Import Tariff, the contracting Parties shall adopt within a period of not more than one year from the entry into force of this Treaty, special protocols providing for a Uniform Central American Customs Code and the necessary transport regulations.

Chapter XI

FINAL PROVISIONS

Article XXX This Treaty shall be submitted for ratification by each State, in conformity with its constitutional or legal procedures.

The instruments of ratification shall be deposited with the General Secretariat of the Organization of Central American States.

The Treaty shall come into force, in the case of the first three States to ratify it, eight days after the date of deposit of the third instrument of ratification, and for the remaining State, on the date of deposit of the corresponding instrument.

Article XXXI The duration of this Treaty shall be 20 years from the initial date of its entry into force and it may be renewed indefinitely.

On expiration of the period of 20 years mentioned in the previous paragraph, the Treaty may be denounced by any of the contracting Parties. Denunciation shall become effective, for the denouncing State, five years after notice of it has been given and the Treaty shall continue to remain in force between the remaining contracting States so long as at least two States continue to be parties to it.

Article XXXII The General Secretariat of the Organization of Central American States shall act as depository of this Treaty, of which it shall send a certified copy to the Chancellery of each of the contracting States. The said Chancelleries shall also be immediately notified of the deposit of each of the instruments of ratification, as well as as of any denunciation which may occur. Upon the entry into force of the Treaty, the General Secretariat shall also send a certified copy to the Secretary-General of the United Nations for registration, in compliance with Article 102 of the United Nations Charter.

Article XXXIII Adherence to the present Treaty shall remain open to any Central American State not among the original signatories.

Transitional Article As soon as the Government of the Republic of Costa Rica formally adheres to the provisions of this Treaty, the bodies set up by the same shall form part of the Organization of Central American States following an incorporation agreement and the remodeling of the OCAS so as to enable the bodies created under this Treaty to retain all their characteristics as regards structure and functions.

IN WITNESS WHEREOF the respective plenipotentiaries have signed this Treaty in the City of Managua, capital of the Republic of Nicaragua, this thirteenth day of December 1960.

For the Government of Guatemala:

Julio Prado García Salas
Minister of Central American Integration
Alberto Fuentes Mohr
Chief of the Office of Economic Integration

For the Government of El Salvador:
>   *Gabriel Piloña Araujo*
>   Minister of Economy
>   *Abelardo Torres*
>   Under Secretary of Economy

For the Government of Honduras:
>   *Jorge Bueso Arias*
>   Minister of Economy and Finance

For the Government of Nicaragua:
>   *Juan José Lugo Marenco*
>   Minister of Economy

The Government of Costa Rica adhered to this Treaty by means of an instrument signed on July 23, 1962, by Raúl Hess Estrada, Minister of Economy and Finance.

PROTOCOL TO THE GENERAL TREATY OF CENTRAL AMERICAN ECONOMIC INTEGRATION
LIST OF THE ARTICLES SUBJECT TO SPECIAL REGULATIONS OF EXCEPTION TO THE FREE TRADE BETWEEN COSTA RICA AND EACH OF THE OTHER MEMBER STATES

(Signed at Tegucigalpa, Honduras, November 16, 1962)

The Governments of the Republics of Guatemala, El Salvador, Honduras, Nicaragua, and Costa Rica,

CONSIDERING that the Government of the Republic of Costa Rica adhered to the General Treaty of Central American Economic Integration of July 23, 1962, by signing the corresponding instrument;

TAKING INTO ACCOUNT the provisions of Article IV of the General Treaty, and in accordance with the provisions of Articles II and III of the instrument by which Costa Rica adhered to the General Treaty of Central American Economic Integration, they have agreed among themselves on the lists of products that shall be subject to special transitory regulations for exception to the free trade between Costa Rica and each of the other member countries of the General Treaty of Central American Economic Integration; and

CONVINCED that the full participation of Costa Rica in the Common Market which they have established is of the greatest urgency to expand this market to the whole Central American territory, and thus actuate the integration of their economies,

HAVE RESOLVED to make the present Protocol, for which purpose they have appointed their respective plenipotentiaries, to wit:

[Here follow the names of the delegates]

who, after communicating their respective full powers and finding them in due and proper form, agree on the following:

Article I The signatory States agree to expand Annex A of the General Treaty of Central American Economic Integration, adding to it the lists of products that are subject to transitory regulations of exception to free trade between Costa Rica and each of the other contracting Parties.

The lists of products to which the foregoing paragraph refers, as well as the terms, conditions, and requirements to which their exchange shall be adjusted, are shown in the Annex[1] to this Protocol, which forms an integral part thereof and of the General Treaty of Central American Economic Integration.

Article II The free trade regulations provided for in the General Treaty of Central American Economic Integration for products which originate, whether natural or manufactured, in the member countries and the terms, conditions, and requirements of exchange established in the Annex to this Instrument shall become effective from the initial date of effect of this Protocol, in accordance with the stipulations of Article V thereof.

Article III Notwithstanding the provisions of the foregoing Article II, the periods of the special regulations for the products included in the Annex to this Protocol shall be counted from June 4, 1961, on which date the General Treaty of Central American Economic Integration became effective.

Article IV This Protocol shall be submitted for ratification by each signatory State, in accordance with its respective constitutional or legal rules. The instruments of ratification shall be deposited at the General Secretariat of the Organization of Central American States.

Article V This Protocol shall become effective eight days after the date on which the third instrument of ratification is deposited for the first three States ratifying it and, for the subsequent States, on the date of deposit of their respective instruments of ratification. In any case, the deposit of the ratification of Costa Rica is required for it to become effective.

Article VI The application of this Protocol, in all its terms, shall be governed by the provisions of the articles of the General Treaty of Central American Economic Integration.

---

[1] Annex not included.

Article VII The General Secretariat of the Organization of Central American States shall be the depository for the present Protocol, of which it shall send certified copies to the Ministries of Foreign Affairs of each of the contracting States, and to the Permanent Secretariat of the General Treaty of Central American Economic Integration; likewise it will immediately give notice of the deposit of each of the instruments of ratification.

When this Protocol becomes effective, a certified copy thereof shall also be sent to the General Secretariat of the United Nations for registration purposes as indicated by Article 102 of the United Nations Charter.

IN WITNESS WHEREOF, the respective Plenipotentiaries sign the present Protocol in the city of Tegucigalpa, capital of the Republic of Honduras, on the sixteenth day of the month of November, nineteen hundred sixty-two.

For the Government of Guatemala:
> *Julio Prado García Salas*
> Minister of Central American Integration

For the Government of El Salvador:
> *Salvador Jáuregui*
> Minister of Economy
> *Víctor Manuel Cuéllar Ortiz*
> Representative of El Salvador on the
> Executive Council of the General Treaty
> of Central American Economic Integration

For the Government of Honduras:
> *Jorge Bueso Arias*
> Minister of Economy and Finance

For the Government of Nicaragua:
> *Juan José Lugo Marenco*
> Minister of Economy

For the Government of Costa Rica:
> *Rodrigo Soley Carrasco*
> Special Representative of the Ministry
> of Economy and Finance

PROTOCOL TO THE GENERAL TREATY
OF CENTRAL AMERICAN ECONOMIC INTEGRATION
UNIFORM CENTRAL AMERICAN CUSTOMS CODE

(Signed at Guatemala City, Guatemala, December 13, 1963)

The Governments of the Republics of Guatemala, El Salvador, Honduras, Nicaragua, and Costa Rica,

FOR THE PURPOSE of complying with the commitment contracted under Article XXIX of the General Treaty of Central American Economic Integration;

CONSIDERING that the Central American Common Market has gone beyond the stage of signing the basic agreements which will provide its constitutional framework, and that it is evident that supplementary legislation is needed for the purpose of improving it;

CONSIDERING the desirability of creating adequate conditions for the establishment of the Central American Customs Union and thus to fulfill the intent of the General Treaty of Central American Economic Integration,

HAVE DECIDED to conclude this present Protocol, for which purpose they have designated their respective plenipotentiaries

[Here follow the names of the delegates]

who, after communicating their full powers found to be in good and proper order, agree as follows:

ARTICLE I

The contracting States by the present Protocol adopt the following Uniform Central American Customs Code.

TITLE I

General Principles

Chapter I

PURPOSES

Article 1 This Uniform Central American Customs Code establishes the basic provisions of the common customs legislation of the signatory countries for the organization of their customs services and the regulation of their administration, in accordance with the requirements of the Central American Common Market and of the Customs Union referred to in Article 1 of the General Treaty of Central American Economic Integration.

Article 2 Customs activities carried on within the territories of the contracting parties shall conform to the provisions of this Code and its regulations.

Chapter II

DEFINITIONS

Article 3   For the purpose of applying this Code, the following definitions are established:

a) Customhouse or customs office: The government office designated to conduct customs operations, pursuant to this Code and the customs tariff, and to carry out any other duties assigned to it by this Code and by other laws;

b) Storage: The fee charged for the storage of merchandise in customs warehouses;

c) Letter of correction: The document used by a shipper or exporter to amend or clarify statements contained in shipping documents that cannot be corrected by other means;

d) Certificate of origin: The written declaration issued by a competent authority of the port of origin, in which the country of origin of the merchandise subject to customs operations is indicated;

e) Bill of lading: The document containing the contract made between the shipper and the carrier for the transport of merchandise;

f) Consignee: The natural or juridical person to whom the merchandise is consigned by the shipper or sender;

g) Customs duties: Tariffs established in the schedule of import tariffs;

h) Customs exoneration or exemption: The benefit granted to merchandise carried in international trade, which, by special laws or agreements, is exempted from total or partial payment of customs duties;

i) Commercial invoice: The document issued as the result of a commercial transaction and signed by the exporter, indicating the details of the transaction, and including the value and other characteristics of the merchandise subject to customs operations;

j) Manifest: The document containing a list of the foreign cargo destined for the customhouse of arrival, or of national or nationalized cargo destined for a foreign country;

k) Merchandise: All products, articles, manufactured goods, livestock, and, in general, all tangible personal property without exception;

l) Foreign merchandise: That merchandise which proceeds from abroad and importation of which has not been legally completed, whether of national production or manufacture, or that, which having been imported conditionally, has not complied with the conditions;

m) National merchandise: That merchandise, either natural or manufactured in their territories, which, pursuant to Central American multilateral or bilateral treaties or agreements, enjoys free trade among the contracting states;

n) Nationalized merchandise: Foreign goods whose definitive importation has been legally completed;

o) Policy: The document containing data required for the respective customs operations, and which serves to indicate the destination of the goods, to declare them, to appraise them, and to withdraw them;

p) Carrier: The natural or juridical person or authorized representative who conducts a vehicle or has it conducted, and who transports merchandise or has it transported;

q) Vehicle: Any means of transportation by land (including beasts of burden or draft animals), sea, or air, with or without a motor;

r) Authorized routes: The land, sea, river, lake, or air routes authorized by law, which lead to customs offices;

s) Customs zone: The area over which the customhouse exercises jurisdiction, divided as follows:

    i) Primary zone, or customhouse premises, is that space in which are located the offices, warehouses, and premises used by the customs services, and those portions of territorial sea where such services are performed, as well as offices and installations established in the immediate vicinity, such as docks, roads, and landing strips legally authorized for such purposes;

    ii) Secondary customs zone, is that area of the customs zone not included in the primary zone or customhouse premises.

Chapter III

OTHER GENERAL PROVISIONS

Article 4   Persons crossing borders with or without merchandise, or who have it brought over a border, shall be subject to the provisions of customs legislation.

Article 5   Border crossings and arrivals of vehicles shall be effected only by authorized routes.

Anyone carrying merchandise on his person or conducting same by any means of transportation is under obligation to present and declare the goods immediately at the customhouse closest to the border crossing, without altering the state or condition of the merchandise.

Persons crossing borders who are suspected of carrying undeclared merchandise shall be subject to a search of their persons, in accordance with regulations.

Article 6   Merchandise shall be admitted for importation, exportation, or any other customs operation, with the exception of prohibitions, restrictions, or conditions prescribed by laws or regulations.

Article 7 Competent authority may, for special reasons, order that customs operations pertaining to certain types of merchandise be conducted only at specified customhouses.

Certain border zones may also be made subject to special vigilance, in which the existence and traffic of foreign merchandise shall be subject to prohibitions and restrictions established by regulations.

Article 8 Customs operations shall be conducted during normal working days and hours, within the primary zone or customhouse premises. However, in accordance with regulations and at the request of an interested party, they may be conducted outside regular hours, provided the Administrator of Customs so authorizes, or outside the customs premises if authorized by the Director General of Customs. In both cases the interested party shall defray the cost of services rendered.

Article 9 The establishment and operation of free zones and ports shall be subject to the provisions of a special Central American agreement on the subject.

Article 10 All persons arriving at authorized border ports or stations may bring their baggage into the country without payment of customs duties or taxes of any kind. Household effects shall not be considered as part of such baggage.

The regulations shall determine which merchandise is to be considered as baggage and which as household effects.

Procedures and provisions governing the introduction of household effects and baggage into the country shall be included in the uniform Central American tariff legislation.

Article 11 With regard to merchandise other than accompanied baggage, all persons shall be entitled to an exemption of up to one hundred United States dollars, or its equivalent in national currency, applicable against the total customs duties incurred.

This provision shall be applied in accordance with the regulations.

TITLE II

Customs Organization

Chapter IV

CENTRAL AMERICAN CUSTOMS SERVICE

Article 12 The customs administration in the signatory states shall be in charge of the Central American customs service.

The Central American customs service is composed of the national public agencies that in each country, in accordance with Article 13, are responsible for the application of the provisions of this Code and its regulations, of the Central American Agreement on the Equalization of Import Charges and its protocols, and of any other laws on the subject, as well as for the performance of the functions assigned to them by other legal provisions. The service shall be organized in a manner that will ensure its technical and administrative efficiency.

Article 13 In each signatory state the public agencies of the Central American customs service are the following:

a) The General Customs Aministration;
b) The customhouses or customs offices; and
c) Other agencies established by this Code and its regulations.

The customs service is subordinate to the Executive Branch through the Finance Ministry (*Hacienda*).
The organization of the General Customs Administration and of the customhouse or customs offices shall be established in the regulations of this Code.

Chapter V

GENERAL CUSTOMS ADMINISTRATION

Article 14 The General Customs Administration is the highest customs agency, on the national level, and is responsible for the technical and administrative direction of custom houses or customs offices, and other activities of the service.

Article 15 The duties of the General Customs Administration are:

a) To comply with and enforce the provisions of this Code, of uniform Central American tariff legislation, and any other applicable laws and provisions;
b) To propose to the respective Ministry the appointment of customs personnel, until such time as a civil service system is established, and perform other functions concerning the administration of personnel as assigned to it by the regulation;
c) To formulate and issue necessary instructions for a proper application of customs laws, and relations with same;
d) To propose to the respective Ministry, for decision by the pertinent branch or agency, the boundaries of the zones of customs jurisdiction, of the border zones of special vigilance, and authorized routes, as well as the establishment or elimination of customhouses;

e) To control, when necessary, the proper use and destination of merchandise imported with customs exemption, in accordance with the systems adopted by the authorities having jurisdiction under the law that established the exemption;

f) To supervise the customhouses or customs offices to ensure the enforcement of pertinent laws, regulations, and instructions, and to inspect them periodically;

g) To decide, in accordance with uniform Central American tariff legislation, as to proper classification of goods;

h) To settle claims submitted to it concerning the application of the customs tariff and of other laws and regulations on the subject, without prejudice to appropriate appeals;

i) To authorize or order inspection of goods in secondary customs zones, in accordance with applicable laws and the regulations of this Code;

j) To issue administrative instructions deemed necessary for the proper functioning of the customs service;

k) To exercise the powers assigned to it in this Code and its regulations in respect of customs brokers;

l) To reply to all inquiries relating to the field of customs;

m) To prosecute violations of this Code and its regulations and, when necessary, to impose the corresponding penalties;

n) To sell abandoned merchandise at public auction;

o) To prepare and submit to the appropriate authority, the draft budget of expenditures of the customs service;

p) To supply public agencies with basic information that may be needed in accordance with pertinent laws;

q) Any other functions assigned to it by this Code, by other laws, and by the regulations.

Chapter VI

CUSTOMHOUSES OR CUSTOMS OFFICES

Article 16 Customhouses or customs offices are agencies of the General Customs Administration, acting under its authority and supervision, and they are responsible for the control and supervision of merchandise entering or leaving the country, or in transit through same, as well as their custody and appraisal, in accordance with provisions of law.

Article 17 The customs or customhouses have the following duties:

a) To conduct customs operations and negotiations in accordance with provisions of this Code and its regulations, the Uniform Central American Import Tariff, uniform Central American tariff legislation, and all other applicable laws;

b) To receive and inspect vehicles subject to their customs jurisdiction and to authorize their departure, upon presentation of
pertinent documents when required;

c) To receive and authorize the loading, unloading, storage, and
deposit of merchandise subject to customs operations;

d) To authorize the clearance of merchandise;

e) To watch over the pertinent customs zone and propose to the
General Customs Administration the establishment of customs
surveillance posts within the zone;

f) To take any steps necessary to prevent loss and damage of merchandise in their custody;

g) To authorize and regulate access to customs premises by persons
other than their own personnel, in accordance with the regulations;

h) To authorize the berthing, mooring, or anchoring of vessels of
any kind;

i) To adopt any measures necessary to control activities carried
out in the primary zone;

j) To sell all abandoned goods at public auction, with the authorization of the General Customs Administration;

k) To prosecute violations of this Code and its regulations, and if
necessary, to impose the corresponding penalties;

l) To settle customs claims that may be submitted, when possible;
and

m) Any other functions assigned to them in this Code, in other laws,
and in the regulations.

Chapter VII

CUSTOMS PERSONNEL

Article 18 Customs personnel are required to know, comply with,
and enforce the provisions of this Code and its regulations, of the Uniform Central American Import Tariff, of uniform Central American
tariff legislation, and all other applicable laws.

Article 19 Customs officials shall be personally responsible to the
Treasury for amounts of money that they fail to collect, due to ineffi-
ciency in the performance of duties for which they are responsible,
without prejudice to the right granted them by the regulations to issue
a claim after clearance, chargeable to the persons who benefited from
the shortage. This responsibility includes cases of loss or damage of
merchandise due to negligence in their custody or handling.

Article 20 In establishing a civil service in each of the Central
American States, the customs service should be included with uniform
regulations for all.

Chapter VIII

TARIFF COMMITTEE

Article 21 A Tariff Committee is established on the national level as an agency of the Executive Branch, in the Ministry of Finance.

Article 22 The duties of the Tariff Committee are:

a) To settle, as the final administrative authority, claims concerning the proper tariff classification of merchandise in international trade. There is no right of contentious-administrative appeal against its decisions.

b) To forward to the Executive Council of the General Treaty of Central American Economic Integration, through the Permanent Secretariat, within the terms set forth in this Code and its regulations, certified copies of all decisions rendered.

Article 23 The Tariff Committee shall consist of five regular members and their alternates, one of whom shall be a representative of the Ministry of Finance, one representative of the Ministry of Economy associated with the program of Central American Economic Integration, and one representative of the General Customs Administration.

Functions of the Tariff Committee shall be governed by separate regulations in each country.

TITLE III

Customs Operations

Chapter IX

DEFINITIONS

Article 24 For purposes of the application of this Code, merchandise may be subject to any of the customs operations defined below:

a) Exportation: The departure, after completion of legal formalities, of national or nationalized merchandise for final use or consumption in a foreign country;

b) Temporary exportation: The departure, after completion of legal formalities, of national or nationalized merchandise, intended to remain outside the country for a limited time;

c) Importation: The introduction of foreign merchandise for final consumption in the country, after completion of legal formalities;

d) Noncommercial importation: The importation of merchandise which cannot be habitually and profitably marketed due to its nature, value, quantity, the status of the importer, and the frequency of such imports;

e) Temporary importation: The introduction of foreign merchandise which is to remain in the country for a limited period of time, after completing legal formalities;

f) Reexportation: The departure, after completing legal formalities, of foreign merchandise that had arrived in the country and was not nationalized;

g) Reimportation: The introduction into the country, after completing legal formalities, of previously exported goods;

h) International transit: The passage through the territory of the signatory states, after completing legal formalities, of foreign merchandise destined for another country.

Article 25   Merchandise may be subject to any of the customs procedures defined below:

a) Storage: The deposit of merchandise in warehouses under customs jurisdiction, pending a request for clearance;

b) Clearance of goods: The request of the owner, consignee, or their representative, stated according to regulations, that the appropriate customs operation be carried out;

c) Redestination: The transfer of merchandise from one customhouse to another, within the country, for subsequent customs treatment;

d) Transshipment: The transfer of merchandise from one vehicle to another for the purpose of carrying it to its destination.

Chapter X

TEMPORARY OPERATIONS

Article 26   The temporary importation and exportation of merchandise, for its exhibition, repair, scientific uses, or for any other purpose, shall be subject, in respect of its nature, proceedings, documentation, and guarantees, to pertinent provisions of the regulations, and in respect of the payment of customs duties, to uniform Central American tariff legislation.

Article 27   Temporary operations shall be authorized only when merchandise can be clearly identified, either by marks, numbers, seals, measurements, or other special characteristics.

Article 28   A period of three months is fixed during which temporarily imported merchandise may remain in the country, and the same period is fixed during which temporarily exported merchandise may remain abroad.

In computing the period, the basis to be taken is the acceptance date of the policy or document authorizing the operation. This period may be extended by the Ministry of Finance at the request of the interested party. Temporary operations contemplated in special laws or administrative contracts shall be governed by the provisions contained therein.

Temporary operations shall be guaranteed by the interested party in a form that will ensure payment of customs duties in full, with the exception of automotive vehicles, the treatment of which is governed by special provisions.

Article 29 Automotive road vehicles may be imported or exported temporarily, without payment of the usual customs duties, or guarantee for same, by fulfilling the requirements prescribed in the Regional Agreement for the Temporary Importation of Vehicles by Highway, and pursuant to the requirements governing the subject in the uniform regulations prescribed by Article XXIX of the General Treaty of Central American Economic Integration.

Chapter XI

NONCOMMERCIAL IMPORTS

Article 30 The rules governing imports of merchandise of a noncommercial nature shall be set forth in the regulations, especially with regard to procedure and documentation. The payment of customs duties shall be governed by provisions of the uniform Central American tariff legislation.

Chapter XII

INTERNATIONAL TRANSIT

Article 31 Merchandise in transit shall be exempt from any form of duties, taxes, or fiscal or municipal charges, resulting from transit operations regardless of the origin or destination of the merchandise, but it shall be subject to payment of fees normally charged for services rendered.

Article 32 Transit operations must be carried out along routes legally authorized for that purpose, subject to the provisions of this Code, its regulations, and any health, police or other laws applicable in the territory of transit.

Article 33 The Customhouse shall be permitted to request a guarantee to adequately cover the payment of taxes and other charges which might result from the importation of merchandise carried in international transit.

Article 34 The transit of merchandise among Central American countries shall be governed by the provisions of the Central American economic integration treaties.

Chapter XIII

COASTWISE TRADE

Article 35 Coastwise trade is the traffic in goods and transportation of passengers by sea between ports of the signatory states.

Article 36 Merchandise carried in coastwise trade is subject to customs control.

Where pertinent, the provisions of this Code and its regulations relating to coastwise trade are also applicable to lake and river traffic among ports of the signatory states.

Article 37 Coastwise traffic shall be subject to the requirements and other rules indicated in the regulations, and whenever applicable, to the terms of multilateral treaties or agreements on Central American economic integration.

TITLE IV

Receipt of Vehicles

Chapter XIV

ARRIVAL AND INSPECTION

Article 38 All vehicles arriving in the country shall be received by the customs authority and, when pertinent, inspected by that authority and by the health, immigration, and maritime authorities.

Aside from the authorities mentioned, only governmental authorities on a special mission and the agent or representative of the company owning the vehicle may take part in the inspection visit.

Article 39 When so required, the inspection is obligatory. No one may prevent its being immediately carried out.

Article 40 Vehicles are to be inspected in the order of their arrival, but priority shall be given to those carrying passengers, those transporting dangerous cargo or perishable merchandise, or vehicles faced with an emergency situation.

Article 41 When a vehicle has been received by the authorities indicated, passengers may be embarked or disembarked and cargo may be loaded or unloaded, in accordance with regulations.

Article 42 Gifts or sale of all merchandise on board a vehicle either to private persons, public officials, or employees, is prohibited.

Article 43 Customs administrators may order that parcels, warehouses or vehicles or sections thereof be sealed or locked with customs seals whenever there are grounds for presuming that the merchandise contained therein might be sold at the point of arrival. The breaking of locks or seals is subject to penalties established in this Code and its regulations, without prejudice to the penalties imposed by the penal laws of each country.

Article 44 Foreign vehicles transporting merchandise to the interior of the country and not departing from same within the period prescribed by regulations shall pay the respective customs charges.

Article 45 In the case of aircraft not engaged in regular international services, the posting of bond or other financial guarantee which might be required to cover customs duties on the aircraft shall be based on the provisions of the International Civil Aviation Convention.

Article 46 If by reason of *force majeure* an aircraft lands in an unauthorized zone, whether on land or water, the pilot must immediately notify the nearest authority, under whose vigilance the aircraft, the passengers, and cargo shall remain until the customs authorities appear, who shall decide as they see fit.

Article 47 In the event that a vehicle is threatened with imminent danger, the customs authorities may waive, totally or partially, the application of this Code, but only for the time necessary to safeguard lives and property.

The regulations shall establish specific rules to be applied.

Chapter XV

PRESENTATION OF MANIFEST AND OTHER DECLARATIONS

Article 48 The conductor of any vehicle coming from abroad shall present at the customhouse, immediately upon arrival or at the time of inspection, the appropriate documents duly signed, in accordance with the type of traffic concerned. The regulations of this Code shall specify the number of copies to be submitted and the requirements in connection with the necessary documents.

Article 49 For maritime traffic, the following documents shall be presented at the customhouse:

a) Manifests and checkbooks of merchandise destined for the port;

b) Manifests for merchandise discharged at the port for some other destination;

c) Passenger list;

d) Manifest of packages and other pieces brought as mail;

e) Baggage list of passengers bound for the country of arrival;

f) Voyage report; and

g) Such others as established by the regulations.

The regulations shall specify the documents required for river and lake traffic.

Article 50   The following documents shall be required for air traffic: A general declaration (departure-entry) including itineraries and cargo manifest and crew and passenger lists, as well as any other documents required by special laws and the regulations of this Code.

Article 51   For railroad traffic, the freight manifest shall be required and for highway traffic a freight manifest and passenger list.

Article 52   Mail shipments shall require postal receipts or routing slips and such documentation as considered necessary in accordance with postal conventions.

Article 53   Conductors of military vehicles authorized to circulate in national territory and of vehicles engaged in official services of foreign governments are required to submit the manifests referred to in this chapter only if transporting cargo to some point in the country, and they must also submit passenger lists as appropriate.

Article 54   The conductor of a vehicle without cargo shall present to the customhouse a written statement to that effect.

Article 55   Presentation of additional manifests shall be permitted for any merchandise destined for the port, if for unforeseen reasons it was not included in the original manifest.

Article 56   Merchandise entering the country by mail shall be delivered to the customhouse for appraisal. Parcel post packages shall receive the same treatment as parcels entering by any other means, with the exceptions and limitations established in postal conventions.

Article 57   The post office shall deliver to the customhouse, with a receipt, all parcel post packages destined for the country.

TITLE V

Discharge, Receipt, and Deposit of Merchandise

Chapter XVI

DISCHARGE

Article 58 In order to be discharged and delivered to the appropriate customhouse, merchandise shall be listed on the manifests or other documents serving in lieu thereof. Delivery may be made directly by the carrier or through a legally authorized receiving agency.

Article 59 Baggage of passengers or crew of any vehicle arriving in the country must be presented at the customhouse whether or not listed on manifests. Exception is made of baggage of crew or passengers who are continuing their voyage in the same vehicle to a foreign country.

Article 60 The carrier is responsible for the discharge of merchandise listed on the manifests.

Article 61 Carriers are charged with the transfer of merchandise from vehicles to the customhouse, or vice versa.

Fiscal and other obligations are also a responsibility of carriers as is, in general, any risk to which merchandise might be exposed in being transferred.

Carriers must furnish a general bond to cover liabilities for these operations.

Article 62 Merchandise destined for a specific customhouse may be discharged at another, if previously authorized by the General Customs Administration, provided that protection of the merchandise or of the vehicle carrying it justifies the change, if space is not available at the customhouse of destination, or if special circumstances merit such a measure.

Request for discharge at a customhouse other than that of destination may be approved and shall be for account and at the risk of the requesting party.

If customs authorities in their official capacity order the discharge of merchandise at a customhouse other than that of destination, the state shall be responsible for expenses and risks involved, provided its fault or negligence is proven.

Chapter XVII

RECEIPT OF MERCHANDISE BY CUSTOMHOUSE

Article 63 Presentation of merchandise for receipt by the customhouse shall be made at the premises of the customs zone intended to receive them.

Article 64 Receipt of merchandise is made on the basis of the manifest and in the presence of the carrier or his representative. If he is not present at the time of delivery, the notations made by the customs authority shall be considered correct and shall not be subject to appeal.

Article 65 Parcels showing evidence of damage or of having been opened shall be separated from other cargo at the time of receipt and shall be received by the customhouse only after determining the contents and weight of each parcel. Carriers or their representatives may witness this operation if they consider it necessary.

Article 66 When parcels included in the manifest are not discharged, the carrier shall have four months from the date of cancellation of the manifest to arrange for delivery of these parcels. When that period has expired, the customs administration shall impose the penalty specified by this Code and its regulations.

Article 67 Merchandise received by the customhouse cannot be changed or altered in any way, except to recondition defective packing of parcels or other preventive measures, such as repainting blurred markings that are still identifiable.

Article 68 The customhouse or customs office may require a carrier or his agents to repack goods or take other preventive measures that seem to be required, and, in emergencies, that this be done immediately. This operation is always chargeable to the consignee or his representative.

Article 69 The customhouse or customs office shall keep appropriate controls of receipt and dispatch for each type of traffic, covering all parcels delivered to its premises. Records and control systems shall be governed by rules to be set forth in the regulations.

Article 70 After being recorded in a register, merchandise shall remain in the customs office until legal importation, reexportation, or other customs clearance is effected.

Article 71 From the moment the customhouse officially receives the merchandise in its premises, as prescribed by the regulations and for a period of twelve calendar days no storage charges shall be incurred. After expiration of this period and until the date on which application for clearance of merchandise is accepted or merchandise transferred to warehouses for storage, storage charges shall be applied in accordance with the regulations of this Code.

Article 72 The period indicated in the preceding article shall be counted as from the date of receipt of merchandise by the customhouse of destination.

If redestination is requested, the storage period shall cover the time that merchandise remained at the customhouse of destination and the period it remained in the customhouse to which it was reconsigned.

If goods have been originally destined for an inland customhouse and remain in transit at a customhouse of arrival, the period shall begin as of the date of receipt by the inland customhouse.

Article 73 Storage charges shall also be applied to merchandise not withdrawn from customs within five calendar days following notification of liquidation of the respective policy. In such cases, storage charges shall be computed from that date up to and including the date of withdrawal of the parcels from customs.

Article 74 In all warehouses or other premises authorized for the storage of goods under the jurisdiction of the customhouse, inventories shall be taken as often as necessary.

Chapter XVIII

DEPARTURE OF VEHICLES

Article 75 No vehicle shall depart from the primary zone of the customhouse without a permit from the appropriate customs authority, given in accordance with the formalities specified in the regulations.

In no case may this permit be granted without previous verification that the vehicle is solvent in accordance with this Code and all other laws on the subject.

The customhouse shall prevent the departure of any vehicle not meeting the requirements referred to in the preceding paragraph, in which case it may request assistance of other governmental authorities as necessary.

TITLE VI

Customs Clearance and Withdrawal of Merchandise

Chapter XIX

CUSTOMS IMPORT POLICY

Article 76 The clearance of merchandise under the jurisdiction of the customhouse, including that which is legally exempt from payment of duties, shall be requested by means of the policy.

Notwithstanding the foregoing, the clearance of merchandise from the contracting states which are entitled to the benefits set forth in Central American free trade agreements shall be requested on uniform

customs forms established by such agreements and which shall serve
the purposes of a policy.

Article 77 The policy shall be prepared in the language of the signatory states, containing the data and other requirements specified in
this Code and the regulations. It shall be signed and presented to the
customhouse where merchandise is located, by the customs agents authorized by the consignee, or by the latter in the cases referred to in
Article 130.

Article 78 Parcel post shall require a policy, and clearance and
withdrawal of same shall be in accordance with the provisions of Articles 56 and 57.

Article 79 The interested party shall declare the merchandise in
the policy, in accordance with the Uniform Central American Tariff
Nomenclature (NAUCA), citing the item, subitem or paragraph of the
uniform tariff clause, the type and quality of merchandise, and necessary details for guaranteeing proper identification. The foregoing declaration, without prejudice to the provisions of Article 96, shall constitute
the basis for appraisal and the imposition of penalties, if any.

Article 80 The policy shall indicate as country of origin that country indicated as such on the commercial invoice or in the certificate of
origin, when required.

In cases where the declaration of country of origin is considered
doubtful, the competent authorities shall make such inquiries as necessary, in accordance with uniform Central American regulations.

The policy shall also indicate the country shipping the merchandise
and the consular registration number of the documents. In case of
doubt, the provisions of the regulations on the subject are to be followed.

Article 81 The policy shall also declare, in a common currency
unit equivalent to the United States dollar, the c.i.f. value of the goods,
determined in accordance with the uniform Central American tariff
legislation, which shall coincide with the value given on the commercial invoice.

Article 82 Notwithstanding the provisions of the preceding article,
if there is question of a difference between the value declared on the
invoice and the true value of the merchandise, the customhouse shall
determine the value in accordance with the provisions of uniform Central American tariff legislation.

Article 83 The policy shall declare the gross weight in kilograms;
but wherever the Central American Agreement on the Equalization of
Import Charges and its protocols specify some other unit of measure-

ment for applying the tax, the amount must also be declared on that basis.

Article 84 The rules set forth in the preceding articles shall be applicable to the customs forms required by Central American free trade agreements, provided these do not indicate otherwise.

Article 85 It shall be prohibited to include in the same policy merchandise shipped from different points or pertaining to different consignees.

It shall also be prohibited to include in the same policy merchandise arriving aboard different vehicles or in different voyages of the same vehicle unless merchandise is covered by a single bill of lading.

Partial contents of a parcel shall not be declared in any given policy.

Article 86 All import policies shall be presented together with the bill of lading, the commercial invoice, and any other documents required by law, all in original form, according to requisites and with the number of copies indicated in the regulations.

Chapter XX

ACCEPTANCE OF THE POLICY

Article 87 The policy shall be accepted upon presentation of all required documents, in accordance with this Code and its regulations.

However, in the cases indicated in Articles 46 and 47, when for one reason or another the interested party cannot submit the documents, the customhouse shall authorize clearance and appraisal of merchandise, provided the interested party can prove, by other means, his right to withdraw the merchandise, for which he must first guarantee, to the satisfaction and under the responsibility of the customs official, the value of the merchandise, the corresponding customs duties, and any damages that might be incurred by the Treasury and the owner or legitimate interested party should merchandise fail to be properly delivered.

Article 88 The guarantee referred to in the preceding article shall consist of a cash deposit and the interested party shall be granted a period of not more than 60 days from the date of acceptance of the policy, to submit the documents that are lacking. When that period has expired, the procedure shall be governed by the regulations.

The amount of the guarantee, after deduction of duties and other charges, shall be refunded to the interested party if the missing documents are presented to the customhouse within the period indicated above.

Article 89   The import policy shall be considered as accepted from the date of its signature by the authorized customs official. Acceptance of the policy constitutes authentic proof that appraisal of the merchandise has been requested, and the consignee thereby becomes subject to the obligations prescribed by law and regulations. After a customs policy has been accepted it cannot be canceled or changed by the applicant.

Chapter XXI

APPRAISAL AND WITHDRAWAL OF MERCHANDISE

Article 90   Appraisal of merchandise includes inspection, examination, verification, and classification of same according to the tariff, its evaluation, weight, measurement or quantity, determination of type of tariff, and liquidation of customs duties, fines, and other applicable charges.

Article 91   Prior to appraisal, and pursuant to provisions of the regulations, consignees may verify and weigh merchandise or obtain samples for proper declaration. The customhouse shall authorize this operation which shall be conducted under its supervision, all expenses incurred in this connection being for account of the consignee.

Article 92   Inspection and examination of merchandise shall include, according to the judgment of the inspector, a part of the parcels or all of them, in the manner set forth in the regulations. The right of inspection and examination is also applicable to the vehicles.

Article 93   The inspector shall review the policy and other documents, and verify the data contained therein, classify the merchandise according to the tariff, compute the customs duties, taxes, and other applicable charges, annotating on the policy any other results of his actions, and sign it.

Article 94   If, at the time of appraisal, merchandise is found to be damaged, depreciated or shrunk, this circumstance is to be noted on the policy, the extent of damage is to be determined, and the cause indicated if possible. A corresponding allowance for damage, depreciation, or shrinkage shall be made from the customs duties in the manner prescribed in the uniform Central American tariff legislation. The Administrator of Customs shall certify all annotations made by the inspector.

Article 95   Prohibited merchandise found during inspection shall be seized by the customhouse and placed at the disposal of the competent authority for pertinent legal action.

Article 96 If the inspector does not agree with the declaration of the interested party he shall act according to his own judgment in applying the tariff and rules established by uniform Central American tariff legislation. However, in case of doubt, he may refer the matter to the Administrator of Customs. The Administrator of Customs, in turn, may consult the Director General of Customs.

Article 97 Policy liquidation shall be reviewed in order to verify correct application and calculation of tariffs.

The officials who make the liquidation and review are individually or jointly liable, as the case may be.

Article 98 Notification shall be made of amounts to be paid or guaranteed for liquidation of policies in the form, time, and manner indicated in the regulations.

Article 99 The consignee or his representative shall have the right to witness inspection or examination of merchandise. If present, he may make any observations that he deems necessary for the correct tariff classification of same, presenting prospectuses, catalogs, or lists of contents.

Upon completion of appraisal, the interested party, if in disagreement with the appraisal, shall proceed in accordance with the provisions of Title XIV of this Code.

Article 100 The customs authorities, if they consider it necessary, may request that consignees appear to provide information that may be required to establish the nature of the articles being appraised.

If these do not present themselves, the customs authorities shall proceed directly with the examination of the merchandise by their own means, and all risks or expenses in this regard shall be for account of the consignee.

Article 101 The customhouse is authorized to take such samples as necessary to verify the nature of the merchandise.

Extraction of samples shall be made with the utmost care and in a minimum quantity, without damage to the merchandise.

Samples not used for analysis may be withdrawn by the consignee. The customhouse shall not be responsible for samples not withdrawn within fifteen days after date of withdrawal of the merchandise.

Article 102 Duties, taxes, fines, and other customs charges shall be those in force on the date of acceptance of the respective policy.

In the event of an auction, the duties, taxes, fines, and other applicable customs charges shall be those in force on the date of an order to auction the goods.

In cases of contraband or fraud in the customs service, the duties, taxes, fines, and other customs charges in force on the date of infraction shall be applied.

Article 103   Merchandise may be withdrawn from the customhouse only upon presentation of the canceled policy or, when pertinent, guarantee in amount of the liquidation in question.

Merchandise shall be withdrawn within the period established in this Code, under penalty of being considered abandoned.

Merchandise shall be delivered to the consignee or his representative.

Article 104   The following persons shall be compelled to pay all duties, fines, taxes, and other customs charges, as well as any other fees which may be applicable under other laws:

a) The consignee of merchandise or his customs broker, for imports;
b) The shipper of goods to a foreign country or his customs broker, for exports;
c) Persons held responsible for contraband, fiscal fraud, or other infractions indicated in this Code, its regulations, or other applicable laws.

TITLE VII

Exportation and Reexportation

Chapter XXII

EXPORTATION

Article 105   Merchandise for exportation shall be dispatched under the control of the customhouse after verification of its nature and quantity, and determination, when pertinent, of the duties, taxes, fines, and other customs charges that are due and the fulfillment of applicable provisions of law.

Article 106   The respective policy is to be submitted to the customhouse for the exportation of merchandise.

In the cases of samples of natural or manufactured products, personal effects, or used household goods, presentation of the policy shall be waived but shall be subject to requirements established in the regulations.

Article 107   The export policy shall be prepared in the official language of the signatory states, and shall be accompanied by documentation required in this Code and the regulations.

Article 108   The customs duties on merchandise for export shall be paid in full, or duly guaranteed, before the goods are loaded in the vehicle that is to transport them.

Article 109 Exportation of parcel post packages shall be governed by postal conventions and pertinent provisions of the regulations.

Article 110 The value of exported merchandise shall be indicated on the policy in FOB terms, in accordance with the provisions of uniform Central American tariff legislation.

Article 111 The country of destination shall be understood to be the one indicated on the bill of lading.

Article 112 The customhouse may inspect all or a part of the merchandise when considered advisable.

Article 113 The provisions of this Code relating to imports shall also be applicable to exports where not specifically contemplated in this chapter.

Chapter XXIII

REEXPORTATION

Article 114 Reexportation of merchandise may take place:

a) At the particular request of the interested party, provided a previous request has not been made for different customs treatment;
b) When merchandise has been discharged in error.

In either case, presentation of required documents shall be made in accordance with the regulations.

Article 115 Merchandise destined for another country and which has been discharged in error may be reexported in the original vehicle if this vehicle is still in the primary zone of the customhouse, and pertinent annotations shall be made in accordance with regulations.

If the vehicle has departed, the merchandise shall be deposited in the customhouse by order of the representative or agent of the carrier vehicle and if not withdrawn in the specified time, it shall be considered abandoned, proceeding in accordance with the provisions of Article 137 and the regulations.

TITLE VIII

Customs Lien

Chapter XXIV

Article 116 Merchandise shall be directly and preferentially liable to the Treasury, with the privilege of a legal lien in favor thereof, for customs duties, fines, and all other charges that are due. If these are not paid in full, the customhouse may retain the merchandise, and if already dispatched, the customhouse may trace and seize same if it is still in the possession of the consignee.

When this is not possible, the legal lien indicated in the preceding paragraph may be extended to other merchandise owned by the same consignee and located in the customs premises at that time or in the future.

Merchandise subject to a lien shall be sold at public auction, unless the duties, taxes, fines, and all other charges due are paid within the period indicated in the regulations.

TITLE IX

General Warehouses

Chapter XXV

Article 117   General warehouses, whether private or state-owned, offering storage facilities for foreign merchandise for a specified time, without payment of customs duties, shall operate under the supervision and control of the customhouse.

Article 118   Customs authorities shall permit the transfer of merchandise to the general warehouse provided it is properly documented in accordance with the regulations.

Merchandise, which by its nature may cause damage, shall be admitted for storage under conditions specified in the regulations.

Article 119   Transfer of merchandise to the general warehouse shall not be authorized if payment has not been made to the Treasury for services rendered in this regard.

Article 120   Transfer of merchandise to a general warehouse or from the warehouse to the customhouse must be carried out under the supervision of customs authorities.

Article 121   Merchandise may remain in deposit in the general warehouse without payment of customs duties up to a period of one year from the date of entry in the warehouse. This period may be extended by the General Customs Administration for a similar period. When these periods have elapsed without application for clearance being made, the merchandise shall be considered abandoned.

Article 122   Merchandise shall be appraised prior to its entry into the general warehouse in order to make a provisional calculation of the amount of customs duties and other applicable charges, without prejudice to a definitive appraisal to be made at the time of clearance.

Article 123   Merchandise deposited in the general warehouse may not be changed or altered in any way, except for the reconditioning of parcels, verification and extraction of samples, or the repainting of blurred markings that are still identifiable.

These operations shall be supervised by customs officials and shall be made at the risk and for account of the depositor.

Article 124   Concessionaires of general warehouses shall be responsible to the Treasury for the custody and conservation of merchandise deposited in their warehouses, as well as for customs duties and other charges incurred, without prejudice to other responsibilities indicated in this Code and other applicable laws.

Article 125   Reexportation of merchandise deposited in general warehouses shall be subject to the provisions of this Code and its regulations.

Article 126   Concessionaires of general warehouses shall be required to maintain a floater policy covering all risks to which deposited merchandise may be exposed.

The Treasury shall be the principal beneficiary of the full value of all applicable customs duties and charges.

Article 127   Customs formalities to be met by depositors of merchandise and the concessionaires of general warehouses in carrying out the respective procedures, especially in respect of transfers, deposits, guard service, terms, and withdrawal, shall be determined by the regulations.

TITLE X

Customs Brokers

Chapter XXVI

Article 128   Aside from officials of the customs service, only customs brokers may handle customs negotiations and operations set forth in this Code and its regulations, unless otherwise prescribed in Article 132.

Article 129   Natural persons authorized by the Ministry of Finance may exercise the functions of customs brokers.

Juridical persons may also engage in this activity, if authorized by the Ministry of Finance, and accredit the customs brokers to conduct the operations.

The regulations of this Code will prescribe the procedure and requirements for obtaining authorization, and in all cases the beneficiary of the authorization shall be individually bonded to cover his liabilities to the Treasury and to clients.

Article 130   Intervention of customs brokers shall not be necessary for operations and negotiations indicated below:

a) When customs operations are effected by the Government and its offices, by municipalities, or by the autonomous and semi-autonomous institutions of the state;
b) When merchandise in question comes within any of the following circumstances:
   i) When covered by a customs form authorized in any bilateral or multilateral Central American free trade agreement;
   ii) When identified as a noncommercial importation;
   iii) When received or released through the international postal system;
c) In the case of personal baggage; and
d) In the case of other merchandise specifically indicated in the regulations.

Article 131   Customs brokers shall be registered with the General Customs Administration and shall be supervised by it. Customs brokers shall be governed entirely by administrative instructions issued by that office.

The Ministry of Economy shall establish a schedule of fees applicable to the services rendered by customs brokers.

Article 132   Customs brokers, in their relations with customhouses, shall be jointly responsible, together with their clients, to the Treasury for the payment of duties, taxes, fines, or other applicable fees.

TITLE XI

Shipwrecked or Abandoned Merchandise and Sales at Public Auction

Chapter XXVII

SHIPWRECKED MERCHANDISE

Article 133   Merchandise arriving at the coasts of any of the countries as the result of shipwreck, as well as merchandise cast ashore by the sea or recovered in territorial waters, shall be delivered to the nearest customhouse by the persons or authorities recovering or receiving same.

Article 134   The Administrator of Customs shall notify the shipper or consignee of the merchandise of events, as well as the captain of the vessel in which it was transported, if possible. If not, notice shall be published as soon as possible in the official gazette, giving details by which the merchandise may be identified. This notice shall be published three times, on alternating days, summoning all persons who believe they have right thereto to appear at the customhouse to claim same within a period of sixty days after publication of the last notice, with the warning that after the expiration of the specified period, the merchandise shall be considered abandoned.

Article 135 If recovered merchandise is perishable or easily spoiled, it may be sold immediately at public auction, and the proceeds shall go to their appropriate destination.

Article 136 All persons delivering shipwrecked merchandise are entitled to reimbursement for expenses incurred in connection with its recovery and transportation to the customhouse, as well as a reward equivalent to 25% of sales price of the merchandise.

Chapter XXVIII

ABANDONED MERCHANDISE

Article 137 Except as provided in Article 121, merchandise deposited at the customs premises shall be considered as abandoned in favor of the Treasury in the following cases:

a) When request for clearance of merchandise is not made within sixty days after date of receipt by the customhouse, excepting merchandise arriving in the mails, which shall receive the treatment prescribed in postal conventions;

b) If after clearance has been requested, merchandise is not withdrawn from the custody of customs within thirty days after the notification referred to in Article 98, regardless of whether or not the amount due has been settled;

c) When, having discharged merchandise in error, the provisions of Article 115 have not been complied with;

d) When shipwrecked merchandise is not claimed within the period prescribed by Article 134;

e) If the owner or his legal representative expressly renounces the merchandise.

Merchandise involved in contraband activities or fiscal fraud shall in no instance be considered abandoned.

Chapter XXIX

SALE AT PUBLIC AUCTION

Article 138 Abandoned merchandise shall be sold at public auction.

The regulations of this Code shall include uniform procedures for determining the value of merchandise in case of auction and rules for conducting the auction sale.

Article 139   The proceeds of public auction shall be applied, except as provided in Article 140, to payment of the expenses of the auction; to duties, fines, and customs charges, and to bills pending for services of transportation, handling, and movement of goods before their delivery to the customhouse, in that order. The balance, if any, shall go to the person who proves a right to claim it within the period indicated in the regulations.

Article 140   The proceeds of public auctions of shipwrecked merchandise shall be applied to expenses incurred in salvage and transportation of same and the reward mentioned in Article 136 of this Code, as well as the expenses of the auction and customs duties, as appropriate, in that order. Any residue shall revert to the Treasury.

Excluded from this procedure are those cases in which, by special international agreements, the priorities applicable to general average and salvage are otherwise regulated.

Article 141   Until such time as an auction has taken place, the consignee or, in the case of shipwrecked merchandise, anyone who proves a right to merchandise, may recover same upon payment of amounts due for items indicated in Articles 139 and 140.

In the case of shipwrecked merchandise, if there is disagreement among the parties concerned, the payment of expenses for salvage, transportation, and reward shall be decided on the basis of an estimate made by an expert.

Article 142   Confiscated merchandise shall also be sold at public auction by competent authority in accordance with legal provisions regarding contraband and fiscal fraud.

Article 143   Judicial embargoes on abandoned merchandise shall be applicable only to the residue of income from sale at public auction after deducting the items listed in Article 139.

Consequently, the embargoes may not interrupt the process of auction nor may the sale result in claims against the Treasury or the purchasers of the merchandise.

Article 144   In auctions of merchandise whose importation is restricted or limited, only those persons legally authorized to import such merchandise may participate.

Article 145   Merchandise whose importation is prohibited shall not be sold at public auction; the regulations shall set forth the procedure to be followed in this regard.

Article 146   The regulations shall establish the procedure to be followed with regard to merchandise for which there is no bidder or whose auction is not permitted in accordance with the law.

TITLE XII

Customs Infractions and Penalties

Chapter XXX

INFRACTIONS

Article 147   Infractions which constitute contraband or fiscal fraud in the customs field are specified in the legal provisions on the subject in each signatory state and are punishable in accordance with such provisions.

Article 148   The following also constitute customs infractions:

a) Resistance to the inspection visit made by the authorities referred to in Article 38;

b) Sale or gift of merchandise as indicated in Article 42;

c) Breaking or violating seals or locks placed by the customhouse on parcels, warehouses, and vehicles or agencies thereof;

d) Failure to present manifests, declarations, and other documents required by this Code and its regulations, or delay in their presentation;

e) Presentation of the documents indicated in the foregoing clause with erroneous notations, omissions, insufficient copies, or lack of compliance with other conditions;

f) Resistance to verification or examination of merchandise in any operation in which the customhouse participates;

g) Berthing or anchoring of vessels of any type without the proper authorization from the customhouse, in those cases in which such authorization is required;

h) Moving merchandise within the customs offices in vehicles not registered in the customhouse or whose owners are not authorized to do so;

i) Unauthorized entrance into customs warehouses or vehicles subject to customs jurisdiction;

j) Contravening any measure required by the customhouse in accordance with this Code or its regulations; and

k) All others established in this Code and pertinent uniform regulations.

Article 149   Customs infractions included in the preceding article shall incur a fine in national currency equivalent to not less than five nor more than one hundred U.S. dollars.

Fines established in this article shall be applied without prejudice to civil and criminal responsibility resulting from the infraction, in accordance with respective national laws.

Article 150 Penalties for customs infractions included in the preceding article shall be applied by the administrator of the respective customs, according to their nature and the circumstances of the case, in conformity with this Code, its regulations, and any other applicable legal provisions.

Chapter XXXI

POWERS OF CUSTOMS AUTHORITIES IN PURSUING INFRACTIONS

Article 151 The Director General of Customs, the administrators of customs, and officials especially designated by the Director General, are authorized to receive declarations and to require the presentation of books, registers or other documents needed to clarify customs infractions.

Article 152 By order of competent authority, the officials referred to in the preceding article may effect searches of premises, warehouses, stores, or buildings, as well as residences and vehicles, when there is reasonable cause to assume the presence therein of merchandise of any kind which might be related to the infractions of contraband or fiscal fraud.

Article 153 Competent authorities shall issue the order referred to in the preceding article on the basis of the statement of one witness. The order shall indicate the place to be searched, the hours within which it is to take place, and the persons who shall witness same.

Article 154 Any customs authority, within the primary zone of the customhouse or within the area of a special vigilance district, may, without the need of a written order:

a) Question, examine, or detain persons suspected of contraband or fraud;

b) Examine parcels, boxes, or other containers and vehicles presumed to contain merchandise that has been brought into, or attempted to be brought into or removed from, the territory of the Republic, in violation of this Code or of other laws, and same shall be seized if necessary;

c) Detain or have detained any vehicle presumed to be transporting contraband merchandise.

In carrying out these powers an immediate report shall be made to the administrator or chief of the customs office, who shall in turn notify the competent authority, placing at his disposal the persons, vehicles, or goods that are apprehended.

Article 155 In cases of seizure of vessels, the administrator shall first notify the competent authority, and shall request his assistance in all cases, unless the urgency of the circumstances does not permit, in which case the authority shall be notified after the act is accomplished.

Article 156 Persons presumed to be responsible for infractions investigated shall be temporarily detained, and seized merchandise shall be deposited in the customhouse. Both persons and merchandise shall be immediately placed at the disposal of the competent authority.

Article 157 In carrying out the powers indicated above, the authorities shall first identify themselves by presenting, when necessary, the written order authorizing them to conduct a search.

Article 158 Any action taken by customs authorities in carrying out the powers indicated in preceding articles shall not imply the right to a claim for loss or damages resulting therefrom, if it is shown that there was justification for such action.

Article 159 Judicial or police authorities shall render immediate aid to customs officials whenever requested and they are obligated to provide the necessary personnel for carrying out the mission of the customhouse.

Article 160 Abuse of authority in enforcing the provisions of this chapter shall be punishable in accordance with penal legislation now in effect.

TITLE XIII

Responsibilities of the Customhouse

Chapter XXXII

Article 161 The Treasury shall be responsible to the consignee of the merchandise, or to its owner, as the case may be, for any loss or damage incurred while the merchandise is in the custody and control of the customhouse, except in the following cases:

a) Unforeseen causes, such as fire, earthquake, or others included in the terms "act of God" or "force majeure";
b) Decomposition, shrinkage or deterioration, or impairment due to the natural action of time, damage caused by animals, defective containers or packing, nature of the goods or defects therein; and

c) All other cases and circumstances in which the loss or damage cannot be charged to employees entrusted with the deposit.

Article 162 It shall be assumed that merchandise has been lost in a customs agency if, after being received, it does not appear when requested by an inspector or other official, for any customs operation thirty days after date of request for clearance.

Consignees or owners shall recover their right to lost merchandise, when and if located, provided they reimburse the Treasury for any amounts received as indemnity thereof.

Article 163 Customs personnel, customs brokers, or consignees or owners, as the case may be, shall be required to inform the administrator of customs, in writing, of any loss or damage of merchandise which, by any means, comes to their attention.

Article 164 Any person who through negligence or fraud, causes loss or damage to merchandise in the custody of customs shall be responsible for the damage incurred, without prejudice to any other responsibility attributable thereto.

Article 165 Whenever merchandise has been damaged or destroyed on customs premises and the corresponding customs duties have already been paid, the consignee or owner shall be entitled to a refund by the Treasury of all amounts paid, in full or in part, providing the merchandise has not been removed from customs premises. Refund shall not be in order in cases where damage or destruction is chargeable to the consignee or his representative.

When cause of damage or deterioration is due to handling or transfer by the carrier, the Treasury shall not be liable for refund of customs duties.

TITLE XIV

Customs Claims and Appeals

Chapter XXXIII

Article 166 Any person who considers himself affected by a decision of the customs authorities may file a claim in the manner and at the time indicated in this Code, its regulations, and any other laws applicable.

Article 167 Claims against acts of the customs authorities in the procedure of appraisal, including policy liquidations, or regarding fines and interpretation of this Code, shall be governed by the provisions of this title.

Article 168 Claims that are entered before liquidation of the policy shall be submitted to the appropriate administrator of customs.

The administrator shall settle the question and order liquidation of the policy.

Article 169 An appeal may be taken to the Director General of Customs against a decision rendered by an administrator of customs; it must be made in writing at the time of notification of the decision or within three working days thereafter.

The Administrator of Customs shall admit the appeal and transmit the case to the office of the Director General on the day following final notice.

The claimant shall appear in person and state his grievance within the period specified by the administrator. Both the appearance and statement of grievances shall be included in a single legal document.

Article 170 The period referred to in the preceding article shall be regulated as follows:

a) If the customhouse against which a claim is entered is located in the same place as the office of the Director General, three days shall be allowed to enter the appeal and state the grievances;

b) If the customs offices are located in a different place, one additional day shall be allowed for each twenty kilometers of distance involved.

Article 171 If a claimant fails to appear in person to state his grievances, the Director General of Customs shall declare the appeal as void and the case will be remitted to the customhouse of origin.

If the claimant appears in person and states his grievances, and there are facts to be proved, the Customs Administration shall grant a period of twenty calendar days for preparation and presentation of same. If evidence is to be obtained outside the national territory three months shall be allowed.

Upon expiration of the probatory period, the General Customs Administration shall render its decision within fifteen days and, after first notifying the claimant, shall return the case to the customhouse of origin with a certified statement of its decision.

Article 172 Without prejudice to the provisions of Article 175, decisions of the Director General of Customs may be taken to a Contentious-Administrative Tribunal in those states where such a court exists, and in the other states before whatever administrative organ is specified in their national law.

Article 173 If an administrator of customs refuses to admit an appeal for review, the claimant may appear in person and state his grievances at the office of the Director General of Customs within three working days, counted from the day following notification of the refusal plus the time for distance indicated in Article 170. The Director General shall order the administrator of customs to forward the case, by the third day, after which the proceedings shall follow the provisions of the second and third paragraphs of Article 171.

Article 174 If the claim is made by a party after the liquidation of the policy, it shall be submitted directly to the office of the Director General of Customs within thirty days following the cancellation.

Article 175 Appeal may be made to the Tariff Committee against decisions of the Director General, but only in those cases indicated in Article 22 of this Code, which must be filed in writing with the Director General within three days following the respective notification.

Article 176 Whenever a claim refers to a difference in opinion concerning the classification of merchandise, it shall be necessary to leave samples thereof in the custody of the customs, certified by the inspector who appraised them, and extracted prior to the release of merchandise from its custody.

The manner and time in which the samples shall be taken shall be set forth in the regulations. In those cases in which it is not possible to take samples, the provisions of the regulations are to be followed.

The Director General of Customs shall transmit the result to the Tariff Committee, which will act on the appeal in accordance with the procedure as indicated in Articles 169, 170, 171, 172, and 173. The Tariff Committee shall render a final decision as soon as possible.

This appeal is not admissible until after liquidation of the respective policy.

Article 177 Decisions of the Tariff Committee shall be communicated to the Executive Council of the General Treaty of Central American Economic Integration, in accordance with subparagraph (b), of Article 22.

The Executive Council shall decide as soon as possible on decisions of the Tariff Committee, and such ruling shall be binding thereafter on all the signatory states in the form and under the terms set forth in the uniform regulations.

Article 178 Claims with regard to cases not covered in Article 167 may be entered in accordance with legal provisions in force in each country, and appeals established under such laws shall be allowed against any decisions taken on such matters.

Article 179 Cases involving refund of duties, taxes, fines, or other customs charges shall be governed by the procedure established for such claims in each country.

Article 180 No claim against the Treasury shall be admitted if it derives from erroneous customs liquidations which have resulted in the payment of amounts in excess of those legally applicable for customs duties, taxes, fines, or other charges when the claims are presented more than thirty days after the date of notification of payment of account.

Article 181 The period allowed for storage referred to in Articles 71 and 73 shall not include time utilized for the process of appeals allowed under this Title.

TITLE XV

Final Provisions

Chapter XXXIV

Article 182 The Executive Power or Branch of each state shall issue regulations to this Code, as multilaterally agreed upon at a meeting of the Central American Economic Council. Changes in these regulations shall be made through the same procedure. The regulations shall not be binding until the instruments of ratification of this Protocol for the five countries have been deposited.

Article 183 These regulations shall establish administrative rules granting simplified and accelerated cutoms treatments to merchandise of Central American origin.

Article 184 The signatory countries undertake to maintain the Central American exception clause for third countries with regard to customs facilities granted among themselves.

Article 185 The signatory countries undertake not to grant to third countries customs facilities more extensive than those prescribed in this Code or its regulations.

They likewise undertake to renegotiate multilateral or bilateral agreements in force with non-Central American countries, when such agreements offer or guarantee customs facilities more extensive than those prescribed in this Code or its regulations. For this purpose they shall be released from any commitment acquired within one year from the date of entry into force of this Code.

Article 186 The five signatory countries may sign new agreements or conventions extending customs facilities to other nations only as a single unit.

Article 187   This Code revokes all provisions contained in general and special legislation which is contrary thereto.

Article 188   The contracting parties shall, until such time as the Central American Customs Union is established, make every effort to establish common facilities for customs, immigration, traffic, health, and other governmental agencies now operating or which might operate in the future at border stations in the territories of the member states of this agreement, so as to facilitate the intra-Central American transit of persons and movement of merchandise.

Chapter XXXV

TRANSITORY PROVISIONS

First Transitory Article   The agreement on free zones and ports referred to in Article 9 shall be concluded no later than one year after date of entry into force of this Code.

Free zones and ports existing on the date of entry into force of the agreement shall be governed by provisions thereof in every respect.

Second Transitory Article   Until such time as the Central American Customs Union is established, the public agencies of the national customs service shall be those indicated in Article 13 of this Code.

Third Transitory Article   Until such time as a civil service system referred to in Article 20 is promulgated in each state, the customs career may be established by these countries in accordance with national legislation.

Fourth Transitory Article   Within a period not to exceed one year from the date of entry into force of this Code, the contracting parties shall sign a uniform Central American agreement on contraband and fiscal fraud in the customs field in response to requirements of the Central American Common Market and to the constitution and operation of the Customs Union referred to in Article 1 of the General Treaty of Central American Economic Integration.

Fifth Transitory Article   In order to make this Code operative, and until such time as uniform regulations referred to in Article 182 are issued and enter into force, each signatory State may adjust its national regulations to the principles and purposes thereof.

Sixth Transitory Article   The signatory States shall standardize customs procedures, practices, and exemptions with regard to diplomatic and consular corps and official foreign missions. Aspects of a purely customs nature shall be established in the regulations to this Code.

ARTICLE II

Within a period of not more than one year from the date of signature of this Protocol, the contracting parties shall multilaterally adopt the regulations referred to in Article 183 of the Code.

ARTICLE III

This Protocol shall be submitted for ratification in each state in accordance with the respective constitutional or legal rules.

The instruments of ratification shall be deposited with the General Secretariat of the Organization of Central American States.

The Protocol shall enter into force eight days after the date of deposit of the third instrument of ratification, for the first three to ratify, and for the others on the date of deposit of their respective instruments of ratification.

ARTICLE IV

The duration of this Protocol shall be governed by that of the General Treaty of Central American Economic Integration.

ARTICLE V

The General Secretariat of the Organization of Central American States shall be the depository of this Protocol, of which it shall forward certified copies to the Foreign Office of each of the contracting states and to the Permanent Secretariat of the General Treaty of Central American Economic Integration. The Secretariat shall also immediately notify them of the deposit of each instrument of ratification. Upon entry into force of the Protocol it shall also forward a certified copy thereof to the General Secretariat of the United Nations for purposes of registration in accordance with Article 102 of the Charter of the United Nations.

IN WITNESS WHEREOF the respective plenipotentiaries sign the present Protocol in Guatemala City, capital of the Republic of Guatemala, on the thirteenth day of December, nineteen hundred and sixty-three.

For the Government of Guatemala:

Carlos Enrique Peralta Méndez
Minister of Economy

For the Government of El Salvador:

Salvador Jáuregui
Minister of Economy

For the Government of Honduras:

Tomás Cáliz Moncada
Minister of Economy and Finance

For the Government of Nicaragua:

Andrés García Pérez
Minister of Economy

For the Government of Costa Rica:

Bernal Jiménez Monge
Minister of Economy and Finance

SPECIAL PROTOCOL ON GRAINS (PROTOCOL OF LIMON)

(Signed at Limón, Costa Rica, October 28, 1965)

WHEREAS:

The General Treaty of Central American Economic Integration and its Protocol, signed in Managua on December 13, 1960 and in Tegucigalpa on November 16, 1962, respectively, provide that the regulation of regional trade in unground corn and, between some countries, the trade in rice, beans, and sorghum shall be subject to a special protocol or agreement which will also coordinate the supply policies of the States and ensure the broadest freedom for intraregional trade in such grains;

In the signatory countries there are national price stabilization programs, more or less effective, covering one or more of the above products, programs which it is necessary to coordinate and put on a regional basis in order to facilitate free trade in such articles, in conformity with the instruments cited; and

TAKING INTO ACCOUNT the recommendations made by the First Meeting of Ministers of Agriculture, as well as those agreed upon at meetings of Representatives of Price Stabilization agencies,
The Governments of Guatemala, El Salvador, Honduras, Nicaragua and Costa Rica,

HAVE DECIDED to conclude this Special Protocol (Protocol of Limón), for which they have designated their respective plenipotentiaries, to wit:

[Here follow the names of the delegates]

who, after communicating their respective full powers and finding them in due and proper form, agree on the following:

Article 1 The contracting States shall regulate the marketing and trade in basic grains of the Central American area, these being understood to include corn, rice, beans, and sorghum; they shall coordinate their national programs of production and supply, and shall ensure the broadest possible freedom of trade.

Article 2 The signatory States bind themselves to formulate and execute national programs of production and supply of basic grains and to coordinate these programs on a Central American level in accordance with the needs of integration and the balanced economic development of the contracting States, in order to adopt a uniform policy concerning these matters which will regulate and direct trade in such products.

Article 3 The Price Stabilization agencies shall be the only ones that may import basic grains from outside the region under preferential conditions, except as provided in Article 5. Based on the needs of each country, the possibilities of the internal supply of the region, and taking into account imports under international programs of assistance in kind, the Coordinating Committee on Marketing and Price Stabilization for Central America shall fix the annual volume of imports from outside the Central American area that may be permitted by the authorities of each State.

At the request of an interested country and whenever circumstances so demand, the abovementioned Committee shall make necessary readjustments in the previously established volume of imports.

Article 4 Imports of basic grains from outside the Central American area made by the Price Stabilization agencies shall be subject to payment of a customs charge that shall be equal to the difference between the guaranteed minimum price fixed by that agency and the total cost of the imported product placed in warehouse, so that it will equal the indicated guaranteed minimum price.

Article 5 Imports of basic grains coming from outside the area made by each country in the nature of a donation, shall be effected in each case, with the authorization of the government, after consultation with the appropriate Price Stabilization agency.

These imports are not subject to the provisions of Article 4 of this Protocol. In respect of other charges they shall be subject to the laws of each country.

Article 6 The Price Stabilization agencies, before negotiating exports or imports of basic grains with countries outside the Central American area, must consult with each other. In negotiating surpluses of basic grains and for meeting shortages, the signatory States shall have priority over those from outside the area.

Exports of basic grains to outside countries may be made freely whenever there is no interest in purchasing on the part of the other contracting States, manifested within a reasonable period to be fixed in the offer made by the selling country.

Whenever because of extraordinary circumstances a country must make emergency importations, it shall consult by cable with the Price Stabilization agencies, which should reply within a period of three days from the date of the cable, after which the country in question is free to import whatever is deemed necessary to solve the emergency, and it shall report to the Coordinating Committee on Marketing and Price Stabilization for Central America concerning the importation made, which shall take whatever steps it considers pertinent.

Article 7   The signatory States bind themselves to strengthen and maintain adequate programs of price stabilization for basic grains, to coordinate such programs, and to give them a Central American scope to the extent that circumstances permit.

Article 8   The signatory States also bind themselves to provide their Price Stabilization agencies with the economic resources with which they can fully carry out their functions, principally to establish an adequate system of centers for conservation and storage.

Article 9   The Coordinating Committee on Marketing and Price Stabilization for Central America shall be composed of one proprietary delegate and one alternate, proposed by the board of directors of each Price Stabilization agency of the member states and appointed by their respective governments. The delegates must have sufficient authority to decide on the matters to be dealt with, provided the powers granted to such delegates are not limited by the laws and regulations of their country.

Article 10   The Coordinating Committee on Marketing and Price Stabilization for Central America shall have the following powers and duties:

a) To coordinate the national price stabilization policies and programs on a Central American level.

b) To establish, modify, and watch over the proper application of the standards of quality for grains and other agricultural products that it considers advisable.

c) To maintain an exchange of information on the production, marketing, and prices of basic grains and any other agricultural or livestock product that it considers advisable.

d) To coordinate and procure uniformity in the working procedures of the Price Stabilization agencies.

e) To seek to establish measures by which selling prices in the domestic market for imports of basic grains from outside Central America shall be equivalent to the selling prices for basic grains purchased under stabilization programs in the importing country.

f) To establish the machinery for consultations to determine the needs for importation or exportation from or to outside countries.
g) To see that resolutions of the Committee are complied with on a national level, for which it may take action, when appropriate, to obtain the approval and support of competent authorities.
h) To coordinate its activities with those of the Executive Council of the General Treaty of Central American Economic Integration.
i) Any others assigned to it by the Central American Economic Council.

Article 11 On the Coordinating Committee on Marketing and Price Stabilization for Central America, each country shall have the right to one vote, and its decisions shall be taken by a majority of its members.

Whenever a country considers itself affected by a decision, it may take its case before the Executive Council of the General Treaty of Central American Economic Integration for settlement. In accordance with the General Treaty, these decisions may be appealed to the Economic Council.

Article 12 Differences that may arise over compliance with obligations acquired under this Protocol, or over rules and regulations legally issued by the Coordinating Committee on Marketing and Price Stabilization for Central America, may be submitted, by the country that believes it is affected, for consideration by that body, and the Committee, within a period no longer than eight days, shall recommend the measures deemed suitable, in order to neutralize the adverse effects originating from the nonobservance of such obligations or rules; such measures may be adopted by the country affected.

If within the indicated time limit the Committee has not ruled on the matter, the affected country may adopt any measures that it believes suitable for the purpose indicated.

In the event that the question is not solved within a period of thirty days or that any party is dissatisfied with the decision of the Committee, the procedure to be followed is that prescribed by the last paragraph of the preceding article.

Article 13 The Coordinating Committee on Marketing and Price Stabilization for Central America shall meet regularly twice a year and extraordinarily at the request of one of its members. The date and place of meetings shall be established by the Committee itself. The Committee must adopt its own internal regulations.

The functions of the Secretariat of the Committee shall be performed by the Permanent Secretariat of the General Treaty of Central American Economic Integration (SIECA).

Article 14 This Protocol shall be submitted for ratification in each

State, in accordance with its respective constitutional or legal procedures.

The Protocol shall come into force eight days after the date of deposit of the third instrument of ratification for the first three depositing States and for the others, on the date of deposit of their respective instruments.

Article 15   The duration of the present Protocol shall be subject to that of the General Treaty of Central American Economic Integration.

Article 16   The General Secretariat of the Organization of Central American States (ODECA) shall be the depository of the present Protocol, of which it shall transmit certified copies to the Chancellery of each contracting State and to the Permanent Secretariat of the General Treaty of Central American Economic Integration (SIECA), and shall immediately notify them of the deposit of each instrument of ratification. When the Protocol comes into force, it shall also transmit a certified copy thereof to the General Secretariat of the United Nations for purposes of registration as prescribed by Article 102 of the Charter of that Organization.

IN WITNESS WHEREOF, the several plenipotentiaries sign this Protocol in the city of Limón, Costa Rica, on October 28, 1965.

For Guatemala:

Carlos Enrique Peralta M.
Minister of Economy
Carlos Humberto de León
Minister of Agriculture

For El Salvador:

Víctor Manuel Cuéllar Ortiz
Under Secretary for Economic Integration and
International Trade
René David Escalante Orozco
Minister of Agriculture

For Honduras:

Manuel Acosta Bonilla
Minister of Economy and Finance

For Nicaragua:

Silvio Argüello Cardenal
Minister of Economy
Rodrigo A. Salmerón Argüello
Vice Minister of Agriculture

For Costa Rica:

Bernal Jiménez Monge
Minister of Economy and Finance
Abundio Gutiérrez Matarrita
Minister of Agriculture

Equalization of Import Charges

CENTRAL AMERICAN AGREEMENT ON THE EQUALIZATION OF IMPORT CHARGES

(Signed at San José, Costa Rica, September 1, 1959)

The Governments of the Republics of Guatemala, El Salvador, Honduras, Nicaragua, and Costa Rica,

BEARING IN MIND the commitments contracted under the terms of the Multilateral Treaty of Free Trade and Central American Economic Integration, signed at Tegucigalpa on June 10, 1958, and being convinced that, if the Central American free trade area is to be established in its final form within ten years, pursuant to the provisions of the said Treaty, their respective customs tariffs must be equalized,

HAVE DECIDED to conclude the present Agreement, and for that purpose have appointed as their respective plenipotentiaries:

[Here follow the names of the delegates]

who, after communicating their respective full powers and finding them in due and proper form, agree as follows:

Chapter I

SYSTEM OF EQUALIZATION OF IMPORT CHARGES

Article I The contracting States agree to establish a common tariff policy and decide to set up a Central American import tariff consistent with the integration and economic development requirements of Central America. To this end, they agree to equalize import duties and charges within not more than five years from the date on which the present Agreement enters into force.

The signatory States shall maintain the Standard Central American Tariff Nomenclature as the basis of the customs tariff for imports.

Article II For the purpose of Article I hereof and of Article IV of the Multilateral Treaty of Free Trade and Central American Economic Integration, the contracting States agree to adopt forthwith the tariffs

79

and tariff denominations specified in Schedule A.[1] They likewise agree to establish an interim system of exemptions, with a view to progressive equalization, in respect of the items included in Schedule B.[1] The two schedules form an integral part of the present Agreement.

Article III The contracting Parties, besides aiming at tariff equalization in conformity with Article IV of the Multilateral Treaty of Free Trade and Central American Economic Integration and with a view to expediting the establishment of the Central American import tariff, pledge themselves, with respect to additions to Schedules A and B, to observe, by preference, the following order of priorities:

a) Commodities in respect of which the immediate or progressive liberalization of trade is provided for under the terms of bilateral free trade treaties concluded between the contracting Parties to the Agreement;

b) Goods manufactured in Central America;

c) Imported goods for which goods produced in Central America may be substituted over the short term;

d) Raw materials, intermediate products, and containers, priority being given to those required for the production and sale of the items included in the foregoing subparagraphs; and

e) Other goods.

Article IV Once tariff equalization has been achieved in respect of the items comprised in the groups of products referred to in the foregoing article, the contracting States pledge themselves to apply to these same items multilateral free trade treatment within not more than five years, without exceeding the ten-year time limit stipulated in Article I of the Multilateral Treaty for the establishment of the free trade area in its final form.

Article V The Parties engage not to impose or levy any tax other than those provided for in this Agreement on imports of goods included in Schedules A and B. The bases for valuation adopted are the c.i.f. import value in the case of the *ad valorem* part, and, for the specific component, the standard physical units set forth in Schedules A and B.

If any of the signatory States is not in a position to abolish consular fees immediately in respect of the goods included in Schedules A and B, it shall be entitled to maintain the fees as such, discounting the value they represent from the *ad valorem* part of the duty and/or charge agreed upon. The term "duty and/or charge agreed upon" shall be understood to mean the duty and/or charge immediately applicable by all Parties to the goods included in Schedule A; that which all Parties pledge themselves to reach by the end of the interim period,

------

[1] Schedules A & B not included.

in the case of goods included in Schedule B; and the tariffs established by any of the Parties with a view to progressive equalization in respect of the goods included in Schedule B and to attainment of the stipulated standard duty by the end of the interim period.

In the case of items which are equalized at levels below the consular fee—either immediately (Schedule A) or by the end of the interim period (Schedule B)—the signatory States shall not charge consular fees.

Article VI The contracting States agree to the establishment of fixed equivalences, solely for equalization purposes, between the currency units in which each country's tariff duties are expressed and a common currency unit equivalent to the United States dollar. These equivalences, which are those existing at the date of signature of the present Agreement, are established as follows: Guatemala, 1 quetzal; El Salvador, a currency unit equivalent to the United States dollar; Honduras, 2 lempiras; Nicaragua, a currency unit equivalent to the United States dollar; and Costa Rica, 5.67 or 6.65 colons, according to the exchange provisions applicable to the item in question. If a country makes any change in the equivalence of its currency unit *vis-à-vis* the United States dollar in respect of goods included in Schedules A and B, it shall be under the obligation to alter its tariffs immediately in the proportion necessary to maintain equalization.

Article VII In order to make the equalization of import duties and charges effective, the contracting Parties shall renegotiate any multilateral or bilateral pacts that remain in force with nonsignatories of the present Agreement whereby tariffs lower than those established herein are consolidated, and shall release themselves from the consolidation commitment assumed within not more than one year from the date of deposit of the corresponding instrument of ratification of this Agreement. Likewise, the contracting Parties undertake to refrain from signing new agreements or tariff concessions with other countries which are contrary to the spirit and objectives of the present Agreement and, in particular, to the provisions of this article.

Article VIII When the duty agreed upon for a specific product is higher than the tariff in force in one or more of the contracting Parties, the countries concerned shall apply, in intra-Central American trade not covered by the free trade regime, the lower tariff in force, unless the Central American Trade Commission decides otherwise.

The preferential tariffs which the Parties pledge themselves to establish are set forth in Schedule A and in Annex 6 of Schedule B (this annex forms an integral part of the schedule in question).

"Tariff in force" shall be understood to mean the sum of the tariff duties, consular fees and other duties, charges and surcharges levied on imports of the goods listed in Schedules A and B at the time the present Agreement is signed. Legal rates and charges for services rendered are not included.

As this Agreement is specifically Central American in character and constitutes one of the bases for the customs union of the contracting Parties, the signatory States agree to maintain the "Central American exemption clause" with respect to third countries, to the extent that the application of the preferential tariff system established by the present article is concerned.

Article IX The Schedules appended to this Agreement shall be expanded, by agreement among the contracting States, through the signing of successive protocols and in accordance with respective constitutional procedures.

Chapter II

CENTRAL AMERICAN TRADE COMMISSION

Article X The signatory States agree to set up a Central American Trade Commission, made up of representatives of each of the contracting Parties, which shall meet as often as its work requires or when any of the contracting States so requests.

The Commission (or any of its members) shall be entitled to travel freely in the territory of the contracting Parties in order that matters within its purview may be studied on the spot, and the authorities of the signatory States shall provide such information and facilities as it/ they may need for the discharge of its/their functions.

The Commission shall have a permanent Secretariat which shall be responsible to the Secretariat of the Organization of Central American States.

The Commission shall adopt its own rules of procedure unanimously.

Article XI The following shall be the terms of reference of the Central American Trade Commission:

a) To recommend to the contracting Parties measures conducive to the establishment of the Central American customs tariff referred to in this Agreement;

b) To study, at the request of one or more governments, topics or matters relating to the development of tariff equalization and in particular to the implementation of the present Agreement, and to propose the measures that should be adopted in order to solve such problems as may arise;

c) To study production and trade activities in the signatory States and recommend additions to Schedules A and B;

d) To act as the agency responsible for coordinating tariff equalization, taking into special consideration the progress made in this field by virtue of bilateral treaties signed between Central American countries, with a view to submitting early proposals for standard duties and charges and endeavoring to promote their adoption by all the contracting Parties. In this connection, the Parties undertake to notify the Commission of bilateral tariff equalization agreements as soon as these are negotiated;

e) To study the various aspects of the maintenance of uniformity in the application of the Standard Central American Tariff Nomenclature and to recommend to the contracting Parties such amendments as may seem advisable in the light of experience and from the standpoint of increased diversification of production in Central America;

f) To take steps calculated to establish and maintain uniformity in customs regulations.

In the discharge of its functions, the Commission shall utilize the studies carried out by other Central American international bodies.

Chapter III

GENERAL PROVISIONS

Article XII   The contracting Parties agree to renegotiate at the request of any one of their number, and through the Central American Trade Commission, the standard duties and charges agreed upon and the standardized tariff classification. The renegotiation shall affect only those goods in respect of which it is applied for.

Decisions in this connection shall be adopted by the unanimous vote of the States for which the Agreement is in force. In any event, every change shall be introduced at uniform levels.

Article XIII   The signatory States agree that differences arising in connection with the interpretation or application of any of the provisions of this Agreement shall be settled amicably, in accordance with the spirit of the Agreement, through the Central American Trade Commission. In the event of failure to reach agreement, controversies shall be decided by arbitration. To form the tribunal of arbiters, each of the contracting Parties shall submit to the Secretariat of the Organization of Central American States the names of three magistrates from its respective Supreme Court of Justice. From the complete list of candidates, the Secretary General of the Organization of Central American States and government representatives to this Organization shall choose by lot five arbiters to form the tribunal, each of whom must be of a different nationality.

The ruling of the tribunal of arbiters shall be awarded on the affirmative vote of at least three of the members present and shall have the effect of *res judicata* for all the contracting Parties in respect of any point settled in connection with the interpretation or application of the provisions of the Agreement.

Chapter IV

INTERIM SYSTEM

Article XIV To facilitate the equalization of import duties and charges in the case of products with respect to which, for economic, fiscal, or other motives, it is impossible to establish a standard tariff to be applied immediately by all Parties, the contracting States establish an interim system of progressive equalization.

The contracting States agree to adopt progressively, for the goods included in Schedule B, the standard duties given in column I of the said Schedule, each Party conforming to the time limit (column II), to the initial tariffs (column III) and to the tariff denomination established therein.

The first change in the initial tariffs shall be introduced twelve months after the date on which the present Agreement enters into force, and succeeding modifications shall be effected for periods of twelve months exactly, until the duty agreed upon is reached.

In annexes 1 to 5 of Schedule B, the tariffs applicable by the contracting Parties during each year of the interim period are set forth. These annexes form an integral part of Schedule B.

While progressive equalization is being put into effect, the annual decrease or increase in tariffs which must be introduced by each contracting Party shall not be less than the quotient resulting from division of the total amount of the decrease or increase to be effected by the number of years in the interim period. This commitment shall be binding on the contracting States except insofar as, during the interim period, they may have introduced annual changes exceeding those agreed upon.

This interim system does not preclude the immediate adoption of the standard duty by a group of countries smaller than the total number of the contracting Parties, or release the remaining country or countries from the commitment to attain the said standard duty by means of progressive equalization.

When the interim period ends for each of the goods or articles included in Schedule B, these shall be automatically transferred to Schedule A.

Chapter V

FINAL PROVISIONS

Article XV This Agreement shall be submitted by each State for ratification in conformity with the pertinent constitutional and legal procedure and shall enter into force, for the first three States to deposit the instrument of ratification, on the date of deposit of the third such instrument, and, for States acceding thereafter, on the date of deposit of their respective instruments of ratification. Its duration shall be twenty years from the date of its entry into force, and it shall be tacitly renewed for successive ten-year periods.

The contracting States agree that the tariff equalization of goods included in Schedule B shall be completed by the end of the interim period which shall begin upon the entry into force of the Agreement. Consequently, they agree to effect progressive tariff equalization within the time limit established for the end of the interim period, without changing the year-by-year tariffs established in the relevant annex of Schedule B, each State taking as a base the level which it would have reached if it had deposited its instrument of ratification upon the entry into force of the Agreement.

The present Agreement may be denounced by any of the signatory States at least two years before the date of expiration of the initial period or of the succeeding periods during which it is in force. Denunciation shall become effective for the denouncing State at the date on which the corresponding period of validity of the Agreement ends, and the Agreement shall remain in force for the other Parties so long as at least two of them continue to uphold it.

Article XVI The present Agreement shall be deposited with the Secretariat of the Organization of Central American States, which shall send certified copies to the foreign ministries of the contracting States and shall also notify them of the deposit of the pertinent instruments of ratification, as well as of any denunciation which may take place within the time limits established in that connection. Upon the entry into force of the Agreement, it shall also transmit a certified copy to the Secretariat of the United Nations for registration in conformity with Article 102 of the United Nations Charter.

Provisional Article With respect to the implementation of Article VIII of this Agreement the contracting Parties agree that preferential duties shall not be applicable to the items or subitems of the Standard Central American Tariff Nomenclature which are included both in Annex A of the Multilateral Treaty and in Schedules A and B of the present Agreement.

Provisional Article The signatory States agree that representatives of the Parties for which the Agreement has not entered into force shall be entitled to attend meetings of the Central American Trade Commission as observers with the right to speak but not to vote.

IN WITNESS WHEREOF, the respective plenipotentiaries sign the present Agreement at the city of San José, capital of the Republic of Costa Rica, the first day of September, one thousand nine hundred fifty-nine.

For the Government of Guatemala:

Eduardo Rodríguez Genis
Minister of Economy

For the Government of El Salvador:

Alfonso Rochac
Minister of Economy

For the Government of Honduras:

Jorge Bueso Arias
Minister of Economy and Finance

For the Government of Nicaragua:

Enrique Delgado
Minister of Economy

For the Government of Costa Rica:

Alfredo Hernández Volio
Minister of Economy and Finance

NOTES ON THE
PROTOCOLS AND SPECIAL AGREEMENT ON
EQUALIZATION OF IMPORT CHARGES

Protocol on Central American Tariff Preference   By virtue of this Protocol, signed in San José on September 1, 1959, the Governments of Guatemala, El Salvador, Honduras, Nicaragua, and Costa Rica agreed to a tariff preference of 20% on imports of natural products and manufactured articles of those countries. This reduction applies to the total amount of import charges, including customs duties, consular fees, and other charges and surcharges.

The signatory countries also agree to maintain the "Central American Exception Clause" in relation to the application of this tariff preference.

Ratification of this Protocol is independent of the ratification of the Central American Agreement on Equalization of Import Charges, signed on the same date, and its denunciation is also independent of that instrument. This Protocol was in force for the five Central American countries. It is no longer in effect as a result of Article IV of the General Treaty of Central American Economic Integration.

Protocol of Managua   By virtue of this Protocol, signed in Managua on December 13, 1960, the Governments of Guatemala, El Salvador, Honduras, and Nicaragua agree to expand schedules A and B of the Central American Agreement on the Equalization of Import Charges which refer, respectively, to the immediate equalization and to the progressive equalization of import charges.

The Protocol of Managua contains two lists of products: list A, for which the tariff designations and rates are to be applied immediately, and list B, for which the tariff designations and rates are to be applied progressively.

In the same manner it provides that, in respect of the contracting parties that had adopted free trade as a general system for commerce, as well as specific preferential treatment in exceptional cases, the provisions of paragraphs one and two of Article VIII of the Central American Agreement on the Equalization of Import Charges, relating to preferential duties, are no longer in effect.

The duration of this Protocol is dependent on that of the aforementioned Central American Agreement.

The tariff rates established in this Protocol and in the Agreement may not be applied to products originating in Costa Rica. They are not applicable to natural products originating in the territory of British Honduras, to which Guatemala extends special treatment.

Costa Rica adhered to the Protocol of Managua by a Protocol signed on July 31, 1962, and it is in force between all five Central American countries.

Protocol of San José By virtue of this Protocol, signed in San José on July 31, 1962, the Governments of Guatemala, El Salvador, Honduras, Nicaragua, and Costa Rica agreed to expand schedules A and B of the Central American Agreement on the Equalization of Import Charges, which refer, respectively, to the immediate equalization and to the progressive equalization of import charges.

The Protocol of San José, in turn, contains two lists of products: list A, the tariff rates and designations of which are to be applied immediately, and list B, on which the tariff rates and designations are to be applied progressively. Lists A and B of the Protocol of Managua are also amended by the Protocol.

This Protocol also contains special provisions concerning milk products and unfair trade practices. It is in force between all five Central American countries and its duration is dependent on the time the Central American Agreement cited above remains in force.

Protocol of San Salvador By virtue of this Protocol, signed in San Salvador on January 29, 1963, the Governments of Guatemala, El Salvador, Honduras, Nicaragua, and Costa Rica agree to amend the uniform charges and tariff classification agreed upon in the Central American Agreement on the Equalization of Import Charges and its Protocols, for the items and in the manner indicated in lists A and B, which form an integral part of this Protocol.

This Protocol is in force between all five Central American countries and its duration is dependent on the time that the Central American Agreement on the Equalization of Import Charges remains in force.

Protocol of Guatemala By virtue of this Protocol, signed in Guatemala City on August 1, 1964, the Governments of Guatemala, El Salvador, Honduras, Nicaragua, and Costa Rica agree to expand Schedules A and B of the Central American Agreement on the Equalization of Import Charges, which refer, respectively, to immediate equalization and to progressive equalization of import charges.

This Protocol, like others, contains two lists of products: list A, whose tariff rates and designations are to be applied immediately, and list B, for which the rates and designations are to be applied progressively.

The Protocol of Guatemala also amends Schedule B and appendixes of the Central American Agreement and lists A and B and annexes of the Protocols of Managua and San José, as indicated in appendixes 1 and 2 of the Protocol of Guatemala.

Appendix 3 of this Protocol contains the import charges and tariff designations that the parties agree to adopt, within maximum and minimum levels; and they agree to attain uniformity within a period of four years.

The duration of this Protocol will depend on the time that the Central American Agreement is in force.

Special Central American Agreement on Equalization of Import Charges on Rayon Textiles and other Artificial or Synthetic Fibers By this Special Agreement, signed in San Salvador on February 7, 1965, the Governments of Guatemala, El Salvador, Honduras, Nicaragua, and Costa Rica agree to apply a progressive tariff rate on the products indicated and which must be reached within a maximum period of five years counting from April 29, 1964. To accomplish this, list B of the Protocol of San José was amended.

The duration of this Agreement will depend on that of the Central American Agreement on the Equalization of Import Charges.

Second Protocol of San Salvador By virtue of this second Protocol of San Salvador, signed in that city on November 5, 1965, the Governments of Guatemala, El Salvador, Honduras, Nicaragua, and Costa Rica agree to expand Schedule A of the Central American Agreement on the Equalization of Import Charges, which refers to the immediate equalization of charges.

This Protocol contains a list A, as an appendix, the tariff rates and designation of which are to be adopted immediately.

The contracting States also agree to amend the uniform charges and tariff classification agreed to in the abovementioned Central American Agreement and its Protocols, for the items and in the manner indicated in the appendix to this Protocol, which forms an integral part thereof.

The duration of this Protocol will depend on that of the Agreement.

Industrial Regime

AGREEMENT ON THE SYSTEM OF CENTRAL AMERICAN INTEGRATED INDUSTRIES

(Signed at Tegucigalpa, Honduras, June 10, 1958)

The Governments of the Republics of Guatemala, El Salvador, Honduras, Nicaragua, and Costa Rica,

HAVING REGARD TO the objectives of the Central American Economic Integration Program which was undertaken through the Central American Economic Cooperation Committee and, in particular, to Article XXI of the Multilateral Treaty of Free Trade and Central American Economic Integration,

DESIROUS OF strengthening the natural and traditional bonds of brotherhood which unite their countries, and of cooperating towards the solution of their common economic problems,

HAVING AS THEIR BASIC AIM the improvement of the living standards of the Central American people and the rational use, for that purpose, of their natural resources, and being convinced that, within the economic development programs of the Central American Isthmus, the integration of their economies offers favorable prospects for the expansion of trade between their countries and for a more rapid industrialization process on the basis of mutual interest,

HAVE DECIDED to conclude the present Agreement, which prescribes a system of Central American Integrated Industries, and for that purpose have appointed as their respective plenipotentiaries:

[Here follow the names of the delegates]

who, after communicating their respective full powers and finding them in due and proper form, agree on the following:

Article I The contracting States undertake to encourage and promote the establishment of new industries and the specialization and expansion of existing industries within the framework of Central American economic integration, and agree that the development of the various activities which are or may be included in such a program shall be effected on a reciprocal and equitable basis in order that each and every Central American State may progressively derive economic advantages.

Article II The contracting States declare their interest in the development of industries with access to a common Central American market. These shall be designated Central American integrated industries and shall be so declared jointly by the contracting States, through the agency of the Central American Industrial Integration Commission established in conformity with Article VIII of this Agreement.

The contracting States shall regard as Central American integrated industries those industries which, in the judgment of the Central American Industrial Integration Commission, comprise one or more plants which require access to the Central American market in order to operate under reasonably economic and competitive conditions even at minimum capacity.

Article III The application of the present System of Central American Integrated Industries is subject to signature by the contracting States, in respect of each of the said industries, of an additional protocol stipulating:

a) The country or countries in which the industrial plants covered by this System are to be initially situated, the minimum capacity of the said plants and the conditions under which additional plants are to be subsequently admitted into the same or other countries;

b) The quality standards for the products of the said industries and any other requirements that may be deemed convenient for the protection of the consumer;

c) The regulations that may be advisable as regards the participation of Central American capital in the enterprises owning the plants;

d) The common Central American tariffs which shall be applied to the products of Central American integrated industries; and

e) Any other provisions designed to ensure the attainment of the objectives of this Agreement.

Article IV The products of plants which form part of a Central American integrated industry and which are covered by the present System, shall enjoy the benefits of free trade between the territories of the contracting States.

The products of plants which form part of the same industry but which are not covered by the System, shall enjoy in the contracting States successive annual reductions of ten percent in the applicable uniform Central American tariff, from the date specified in the relevant additional protocol. As from the tenth year, such products shall enjoy the full benefits of free trade.

Except as provided in the preceding paragraph and in any other provisions of this Agreement or of the additional protocols, all trade in commodities produced by the Central American integrated industries shall be governed by the provisions of the Multilateral Treaty of Free Trade and Central American Economic Integration.

Article V   In conformity with the provisions of Article IV of the Multilateral Treaty of Free Trade and Central American Economic Integration, the Central American Trade Commission shall give priority consideration to the equalization of the customs duties and other charges levied upon imports of commodities that are similar to or substitutes for the commodities produced by the Central American integrated industries covered by the additional protocols to this Agreement, as well as upon imports of raw materials and of the containers necessary for their production and distribution.

Article VI   Since the contracting States intend to grant to the Central American integrated industries ample fiscal incentives, the enterprises owning industrial plants covered by the present System shall enjoy, in the territory of the countries where such plants are or may be established, the benefits and exemptions prescribed by the national legislation of the country concerned.

Article VII   Except in cases of emergency, the governments of the contracting States shall not grant customs duty exemptions or reductions below the Central American common tariff on any imports from countries outside Central America of goods which are equal or similar to or substitutes for goods manufactured in any of the Central American countries by plants of industrial integrated industries, nor shall they apply to such imports preferential exchange rates equivalent to such exemptions or reductions.

The governments and other state bodies shall also give preference in their official imports to the products of the Central American integrated industries.

Article VIII   In order to ensure due application of this Agreement and of the additional protocols, the signatory States agree to establish a Central American Industrial Integration Commission, to which each of the contracting States shall appoint a special representative; the Commission shall meet as frequently as its work may require or at the request of any of the participating States.

The Commission or any of its members may travel freely in the contracting States in order to study matters within the Commission's competence in the field, and the authorities of the contracting States shall provide them with whatever information and facilities may be necessary for the proper discharge of their functions.

The Commission shall have a permanent secretariat which shall be under the responsibility of the General Secretariat of the Organization of Central American States.

The Commission shall adopt its rules of procedure unanimously and shall prescribe the regulations relating to the conduct of matters within its competence, in particular the regulations relating to the conditions and form in which, in each specific case, the views of private enterprise shall be heard.

Article IX   Individuals or legal entities desiring the incorporation of a given plant into the present System shall present an application to that effect to the Secretariat of the Central American Industrial Integration Commission and accompany it with the required information.

When the Secretariat has sufficient information available, it shall advise the Commission of the application. If the Commission finds that the project meets the aims of this Agreement, the application shall be referred for an opinion to the Central American Institute for Industrial Research and Technology or to any other person or body that the Commission considers competent. Such opinion shall take into account the technological and economic aspects of the project and, in particular, the market prospects, and the costs incurred shall be borne by the interested parties.

The Commission shall decide on the project on the basis of the said opinion, and if it finds the project capable of being realized, shall make whatever recommendations it considers pertinent to the governments of the contracting States on the conclusion of the protocol covering the industry concerned and on the conditions to be stipulated.

When the project refers to a plant which forms part of an industry already covered by a protocol, the Commission may, in conformity with the terms of the relevant protocol and of this article, declare that the plant shall be admitted to the benefits of the present System and advise the governments of the contracting States to that effect.

Article X   The Central American Industrial Integration Commission shall submit an annual report on its activities to the contracting States.

The Commission shall periodically carry out studies with a view to enabling the governments to evaluate the results of the application of the present System.

The Commission may propose to the contracting States measures favorable to the development of the Central American integrated industries and to the efficient functioning of their plants. The Commission may also propose to the governments any measures necessary to resolve any problems arising from the application of this Agreement.

Article XI The contracting States agree to settle amicably, in the spirit of this Agreement, any differences which may arise in the interpretation or application of any of its provisions or of the additional protocols. If agreement cannot be reached, they shall submit the matter to arbitration. For the purpose of constituting the arbitral tribunal, each contracting State shall propose to the General Secretariat of the Organization of Central American States the names of three judges from its Supreme Court of Justice. From the complete list of candidates, the Secretary General of the Organization of Central American States and the government representatives in the Organization shall select, by drawing lots, a tribunal composed of five arbitrators, no two of whom may be nationals of the same State. The award of the arbitral tribunal shall require the concurring votes of not less than three members and shall be binding on all the contracting States so far as it contains any ruling concerning the interpretation or application of the provisions of this Agreement and of the additional protocols.

Article XII This Agreement shall be submitted for ratification in each contracting State in conformity with its constitutional or legal norms.

This Agreement shall come into force on the date of deposit of the last instrument of ratification. It shall remain in force for twenty years and shall be tacitly renewable for successive periods of ten years.

Any contracting State may withdraw from this Agreement provided notice of withdrawal is given not later than two years before the date on which the initial or any other subsequent period of validity expires.

If a contracting State gives notice of withdrawal after the prescribed time limit but before a new period of validity has commenced, such notification shall be valid, but the Agreement shall remain in force for two years after the beginning of the new period.

In the event of denunciation of this Agreement, the same shall remain in force as regards its additional protocols until the expiration of the latter.

Should a contracting State denounce this Agreement, the other contracting States shall determine whether the Agreement shall cease to have effect between all the contracting States or whether it shall be maintained between such contracting States as have not denounced it.

The additional protocols to this Agreement shall be approved in conformity with the constitutional or legal norms of each country.

Article XIII The General Secretariat of the Organization of Central American States shall act as depository of this Agreement and shall send a certified copy thereof to the ministry of foreign affairs of each of the contracting States. It shall also notify the contracting States of the deposit of the relevant instruments of ratification as well as of any denunciation which may occur within the prescribed time limit. When the Agreement comes into force it shall also transmit a certified copy thereof to the Secretary-General of the United Nations for registration in conformity with Article 102 of the United Nations Charter.

Transitional Article In order to promote an equitable distribution of the Central American industrial integrated plants, the contracting States shall not award a second plant to any one country until all of the Central American countries have each been assigned a plant in conformity with the protocols specified in Article III.

IN WITNESS WHEREOF, the respective plenipotentiaries have signed this Agreement in the city of Tegucigalpa, D.C., capital of the Republic of Honduras, on June 10, 1958.

For the Government of Guatemala:

With reservation regarding Article XI of this Treaty, in accordance with the provisions of paragraph 3, sub-paragraph (b) of Article 149 of the Constitution of the Republic.

José Guirola Leal
Minister of Economy

For the Government of El Salvador:

Alfonso Rochac
Minister of Economy

For the Government of Honduras:

Fernando Villar
Minister of Economy and Finance

For the Government of Nicaragua:

Enrique Delgado
Minister of Economy

For the Government of Costa Rica:

Wilburg Jiménez Castro
Vice-Minister of Economy and Finance

PROTOCOL TO THE AGREEMENT ON THE SYSTEM OF CENTRAL AMERICAN INTEGRATED INDUSTRIES

(Signed at San Salvador, El Salvador, January 29, 1963)

HAVING AS A FUNDAMENTAL OBJECTIVE the raising of standards of living and living conditions of the peoples of Central America through the integration of their respective economies;

CONVINCED of the importance of the establishment of integrated Central American industries in their territories in order to promote economic development, a rational use of resources, and a balanced growth among countries;

RECOGNIZING that it is necessary to apply the Agreement on the System of Central American Integrated Industries, and to carry out the provisions of Article XVII of the General Treaty of Central American Economic Integration;

CONSIDERING THAT the granting of the benefits prescribed herein or in other additional Protocols to the Agreement on the System should not restrict or limit the trade that has been carried on under free trade before those protocols were signed; and in the case of the plants to which this instrument refers, the granting of free trade to their products, under the terms of Article IV of the Agreement, does not restrict any previously existing trade; and

THAT the desirability of creating complementary systems of stimulation for the establishment of industrial activities of particular interest to the economic development of the region,

The Governments of the Republics of Guatemala, El Salvador, Honduras, Nicaragua, and Costa Rica

HAVE DECIDED to conclude the present Protocol, for which purpose they have designated their respective plenipotentiaries, to wit:

[Here follow the names of the delegates]

who, having communicated their respective full powers and found them to be in due and proper form, agree to the following:

Chapter I

GENERAL PROVISIONS

Article 1 The benefits of the Agreement on the System of Central American Integrated Industries may not restrict or limit trade that is being carried out under the provision of the General Treaty of Central American Economic Integration.

Article 2 The signatory States declare that integrated industries are those covered by this Protocol and they bring within the terms of the Agreement on the System of Central American Integrated Industries the plants pertaining to those industries which are indicated in this instrument.

Article 3 The products of the integrated plants shall enjoy free trade within the territories of the contracting Parties, as soon as the present protocol comes into force.

The products of plants that may be established within the same branch of industry subsequent to the date this Protocol is signed, but which are not covered by the Agreement on the System of Central American Integrated Industries, shall be entitled to successive tariff reductions of ten percent a year from the uniform Central American rates established in this Protocol. These reductions shall begin as of the date the corresponding instrument takes effect, in the case of plants that are declared to be integrated and that are already established, and as of the date that they are required to begin production, in the case of proposed plants or those in process of installation.

Article 4   The products of integrated plants must meet the standards of quality formulated by ICAITI [Central American Institute of Industrial Research and Technology] and approved by the Executive Council.

ICAITI is charged with periodically verifying the enforcement of those specifications, and reporting the results to the Permanent Secretariat. The Executive Council, by a majority vote, shall determine what measures to adopt in case of noncompliance, including among them the authorization of imports subject to payment of the rates indicated in Articles 15 and 23 below.

Article 5   The customs tariff system prescribed by this Protocol shall take effect thirty days from the date that the Permanent Secretariat gives written notice to the member States that the initial capacity of the integrated industries is of the volume indicated in the corresponding protocol and that their products meet the quality requirements referred to in the preceding article.

Article 6   Integrated plants shall be entitled, for a period of ten years, to exemption from charges on imports of raw materials or intermediate products utilized by such plants; they shall also be exempt from taxes levied on the production or consumption of such raw materials or intermediate products, or when pertinent, the amount paid will be refunded. All other tax benefits shall be governed by the Central American Agreement on Fiscal Incentives to Industrial Development.

Article 7   Enterprises that are owners of integrated plants may not become distributors of products specifically covered by this System nor sell them through exclusive distributors; likewise, they shall not refuse to fill orders submitted by distributors, without justifiable reasons.

Article 8   Whenever at the request of any contracting Party the Executive Council has proof of the existence of imports made at a price lower than their normal value, or below regular quotations of the international market, or under unfair trade practices that cause or threaten to cause harm to integrated plants, the governments shall order the suspension of imports coming from exporters who have engaged in such practices, without prejudice to other measures that may be taken by the Executive Council in accordance with the provisions of Chapter III of the Protocol of San José of July 31, 1962, concerning tariff equalization. The suspension shall continue for such time as is deemed necessary.

Article 9   An article of foreign merchandise will be regarded as having been imported at a price below its normal value whenever the factory price for the article in the exporting country is less than:

a. The comparable price, under normal trading conditions, for a similar article intended for consumption in the domestic market of the exporting country; or
b. The highest comparable price, under normal trading conditions, of a similar article, intended for export to a third country; or
c. The cost of production of this article in the country of origin plus a reasonable increase for sales expenses and a profit.

Article 10   The Executive Council, through the Permanent Secretariat, shall watch over compliance with the provisions of this Protocol in reference to the rights and obligations relating to the integrated plants; to this end these plants must submit to the Secretariat a monthly report on production and stocks of their products and any additional information that may be requested.

Chapter II

CAUSTIC SODA AND CHLORINATED INSECTICIDES

I. *Field of application*

Article 11   The contracting States declare as integrated the caustic soda and chlorinated insecticides industry and place under the Agreement on the System of Central American Integrated Industries the plants producing caustic soda and chlorinated camphene insecticide which are to be established in the Republic of Nicaragua. Enterprises owning the integrated plants must become organized within a period of twelve months counting from the date this Protocol comes into force. Not later than eighteen months after that date construction of the installations must be started, and production shall begin within three and a half years, again counting from the date this instrument takes effect.

Article 12   The rights and obligations that are stipulated in this Protocol shall be applicable to the plants covered by Resolution 7 of the Executive Council, referring to caustic soda and chlorinated camphene insecticide.

II. *Investment and composition of capital*

Article 13   The company or companies owning the integrated plants shall invest the approximate equivalent of four and a half million dollars United States currency. At least forty percent of the capital shall be offered for sale to capital of Central American origin, during a period of not less than one hundred and eighty days prior to the date of organization of the company or companies.

III. *Capacity*

Article 14   The integrated plants shall have an initial minimum capacity of 4,700 metric tons annual production of caustic soda and 2,700 metric tons of chlorinated camphene insecticide, to supply the market of the signatory countries in the manner prescribed in this Protocol.

The incorporation of additional plants that may be required to meet the demand of the Central American market shall be effected by decision of the Executive Council adopted by a majority vote in accordance with the procedure prescribed in Article IX of the Agreement on the System of Central American Integrated Industries, and they shall be subject to the same obligations with respect to offer of capital, prices, quality, and guaranty of supply, required by this Protocol for the original plants, and they shall have equal general rights.

IV. *Guaranty of market supply*

Article 15   The enterprises owning the plants are obligated to guarantee an adequate and constant supply of chlorinated camphene insecticide.

The Permanent Secretariat shall determine, at the request of any contracting Party, whether there are cases of nonfulfillment of this guaranty. In doing so it shall take into account the volume of stocks on hand and other criteria considered pertinent. In such cases, the governments may authorize the importation of shortages substantiated by the Permanent Secretariat, subject to a duty equivalent to $0.05 US currency per kilogram gross weight, of chlorinated camphene insecticide.

Article 16   If production or supply of chlorinated camphene insecticide becomes interrupted the enterprise shall immediately notify the Permanent Secretariat of the Executive Council. In case of an interruption the Council shall adopt any measures deemed necessary to ensure an adequate supply for the market of the member countries. On the basis of the resolution adopted by the Council, the governments may issue licenses for the importation of this product, subject to payment of the charge indicated in the final paragraph of Article 15 above. Resolutions are to be adopted by a majority vote.

V. *Price Guaranty*

Article 17 The enterprises are obligated to supply the market of the signatory countries under reasonable and competitive price conditions, which may in no case exceed one hundred twenty dollars ($120) per metric ton of caustic soda or six hundred fifteen dollars ($615) per metric ton of chlorinated camphene one hundred percent technical grade.

They are also obligated to sell the caustic soda at the same factory prices and the insecticide at the same prices at the distribution points in each of the signatory countries.

The Executive Council, through its Secretariat, shall be the agency entrusted with supervision of the proper application of the foregoing provisions and shall authorize, if necessary, price changes that it may be desirable to make, by reason of variations in production costs.

VI. *Tariff schedule*

Article 18 The contracting States hereby adopt the uniform classification and charges on imports as indicated below:

NAUCA item or subdivision or uniform tariff item	Description	Unit	Uniform charges on imports	
			Specific (dollars per unit)	Ad valorem (percent C.I.F.)
511–03–00	Sodium hydroxide (caustic soda)	G.K. (gross kg.)	0.04	10%
512–09–01	Camphor (natural or artificial) and derivatives n.s.p.	G.K.		
512–09–01–01	Chlorinated camphene for insecticides	G.K.	0.10	14
512–09–01–09	All others	G.K.	0.15	15
512–09–03	Halogen derivatives of hydrocarbons, n.s.p.	G.K.		
512–09–03–01	Chloroform	G.K.	0.05	10

NAUCA item or subdivision or uniform tariff item	Description	Unit	Uniform charges on imports	
			Specific (dollars per unit)	Ad valorem (percent C.I.F.)
512–09–03–02	Refrigerant gases liquefied or not (freon gas, etc.)	G.K.	Free	10
512–09–03–03	Dichlorodiphnyl-trichloroethane (DDT) and other chlorinated chemical products for making insecticides	G.K.	Free	10
512–09–03–04	Nonchlorinated chemical products for making insecticides	G.K.	Free	5
512–09–03–09	All others	G.K.	0.05	15
512–09–12	Amidophenol n.s.p.	G.K.		
512–09–12–01	For making insecticides	G.K.	Free	6
512–09–12–09	All others	G.K.	0.05	15
599–02–00	Insecticides, fungicides, disinfectants (including those prepared for animals) and similar products, not used as medicinals, fumigants, soaps or deodorants			
599–02–00–01	Chlorinated camphene derived from turpentine, prepared as insecticides	G.K.	0.10	10

NAUCA item or subdivision or uniform tariff item	Description	Unit	Uniform charges on imports	
			Specific (dollars per unit)	Ad valorem (percent C.I.F.)
599–02–00–02	Chlorinated insecticides prepared for immediate consumption; mixtures and solutions, concentrated or not, containing any of the products indicated in 512–09–01–01 512–09–03–03 599–02–00–01	G.K.	Free	15
599–02–00–03	Other insecticides, n.s.p.	G.K.	Free	10
599–02–00–09	All others (Note item 599–02–00 of the Uniform Central American Tariff: Any preparation not ready for immediate use as an insecticide is considered a technical grade)			

(Tariff item 599–02–00–09 is given solely to ensure a uniform application of the Uniform Central American Tariff Nomenclature)

Chapter III

TIRE AND TUBE INDUSTRY

I. *Field of application*

Article 19 The contracting States declare as integrated the tire and tube industry and place under the Agreement on the System of Central American Integrated Industries the plant producing those articles established in the Republic of Guatemala as of the date of this Protocol.

Article 20   The rights and obligations stipulated in this Protocol shall be applicable to the plant in respect of the tires and tubes produced by it for automobiles and trucks.

The Executive Council shall determine the list of types and sizes to be covered by this Protocol as of the date it takes effect. This list may be expanded by the Executive Council upon proof that the factory can produce additional types of tires and tubes under adequate conditions to supply the Central American market. Additions to the list may be made every six months, and shall be published by the Executive Council for purposes of appropriate customs classification. The initial list of tires and tubes for automobiles and trucks referred to in this article will be published for the same purpose.

II. *Investment and composition of capital*

Article 21   The enterprise owning the integrated plant has invested therein the approximate equivalent of $5,000,000. Capital in the enterprise equivalent to $2,500,000 comprises a majority share of capital of Central American origin. An equal proportion of any future expansion of capital shall be offered for sale, by public advertisement, to capital of Central American origin for a period of not less than 180 days.

III. *Capacity*

Article 22   The integrated plant shall maintain an initial capacity of 145,000 tires and 116,000 tubes, which must be expanded to 225,000 tires and 180,000 tubes annually within a period of not more than one year, counted from the date this Protocol takes effect.

IV. *Guaranty of market supply*

Article 23   The plant is obligated to guarantee an adequate and constant supply of the types of tires and tubes specified in the list to which Article 20 refers, and it shall maintain on the market of the five member countries stocks equal to the average monthly consumption of those articles during the preceding year.

The Executive Council, by a majority vote and at the request of any contracting Party, shall determine cases of nonfulfillment of this guaranty. In doing so it shall take into account the volume of existing stocks in the signatory countries and any other criteria deemed pertinent. In case of nonfulfillment, the governments, on the basis of a resolution of the Executive Council, also by majority vote, may authorize an import license for the products covered by this Protocol, which shall be subject to payment of the uniform duty on tires and tubes included in tariff item 629–01–02–01. The authorization will be granted for the quantity necessary to ensure an adequate market supply.

Article 24 If production or the supply of tires and tubes becomes interrupted, the enterprise shall immediately notify the Permanent Secretariat. The Council shall adopt any measures deemed necessary to ensure an adequate market supply for the member countries. On the basis of a resolution adopted by the Council, the governments may issue import licenses for tires and tubes from third countries which will be subject to payment of the uniform duty indicated in tariff item 629–01–02–01. Resolutions pursuant to this article are to be adopted by a majority vote.

V. *Price guaranty*

Article 25 The enterprise agrees to sell the products covered by this Protocol at the same price, under equal conditions, to all distributors of the region; and it also agrees to ensure that the selling price to the ultimate consumer shall in no case exceed the lowest list price quoted on December 1, 1962, in any of the contracting countries, under conditions of quality comparable to the products manufactured by the plant.

The Executive Council shall in due course fix the selling prices for tires and tubes produced in the plant, on the basis of a report prepared by the Permanent Secretariat concerning the actual prices quoted in the Central American countries for similar products on the aforementioned date.

The Executive Council, through its Secretariat, shall be the agency entrusted with overseeing the proper enforcement of the foregoing provisions and with authorizing, when pertinent, any changes that it may be desirable to make in prices by reason of variations in costs of production.

Article 26 The contracting States hereby adopt the classification and uniform duties on tires and tubes as indicated below:

NAUCA item or subdivision or uniform tariff item	Description	Unit	Uniform charges on imports	
			Specific (dollars per unit)	Ad valorem (percent C.I.F.)
629–01–02	Tires, n.s.p., and tubes, for vehicles of all kinds	G.K.		

NAUCA item or subdivision or uniform tariff item	Description	Unit	Uniform charges on imports	
			Specific (dollars per unit)	Ad valorem (percent C.I.F.)
629–01–02–01	Tires and tubes, n.s.p., in types and sizes not produced by integrated industry		0.10	10%
629–01–02–02	Tires, n.s.p., for any use, weighing up to 20 kilograms per unit, of sizes produced by the integrated industry and which appear in the list referred to in Art. 20 of the Protocol to the Agreement on the System of Central American Integrated Industries, and tubes for such tires	G.K.	0.90	10
629–01–02–09	Tires, n.s.p., for any use, weighing over 20 kilograms per unit, of sizes produced by the integrated industry and which appear in the list referred to in Art. 20 of the Protocol to the Agreement on the System of Central American Integrated Industries, and tubes for such tires	G.K.	0.75	10

Article 27 The incorporation of additional plants shall be effected by decision of the Executive Council adopted by majority vote in accordance with the procedure outlined in Article IX of the Agreement on the System of Central American Integrated Industries, and they shall be subject to the same obligations with respect to prices, quality, and guaranty of supply as required by this Protocol for the original plant, and they shall have equal general rights. At least sixty percent of the capital for new plants shall be offered by public advertisement to capital of Central American origin, and at least thirty percent must be subscribed by Central American investors.

Chapter IV

SPECIAL PROVISIONS

Article 28 The contracting States agree to establish a special system for the promotion of productive activities, aimed at stimulating the establishment of new industries in Central America that will be of particular significance to the economic development of the region.

Article 29 Commercial intercourse in the products covered by Article 31 of this Protocol shall be subject to the provisions of the General Treaty of Central American Economic Integration.

Article 30 Without prejudice to the uniform levels already agreed upon or that may be agreed upon pursuant to the Central American Agreement on Equalization of Import Charges and its protocols, a system of tariffs is hereby established the application of which shall follow the conditions stipulated in this chapter.

Article 31 Under the system to which the preceding article refers, the following uniform rates are agreed upon:

NAUCA item or subdivision or uniform tariff item	Description	Unit	Uniform charges on imports	
			Specific (dollars per unit)	Ad valorem (percent C.I.F.)
664–03–00	Plate glass (commonly used for windows), undecorated, with or without color	G.K.	0.10	10%

NAUCA item or subdivision or uniform tariff item	Description	Unit	Uniform charges on imports	
			Specific (dollars per unit)	Ad valorem (percent C.I.F.)
665–01–00	Glass containers (with or without caps of any materials), not ornamental (carboys, bottles, demijohns, flasks, jugs, tubular receptacles and similar containers of glass), including caps and stoppers of ordinary glass, and glass interiors for thermos bottles and similar vessels.			
665–01–00–02	Containers of any capacity for beer, carbonated waters, wines and liquors (including soft drinks)	G.K.	0.06	10
699–12–01	Hand tools for artisans			
699–12–01–01	Machetes	G.K.	Free	20
721–03–01	Bulbs and incandescent tubes for electric lighting of all kinds and voltage, including sealed beams for vehicles			
721–03–01–01	Light bulbs, of all kinds and voltage (except incandescent tubes and sealed beams)	G.K.	1.00	10

Article 32   The tariff rates listed in the preceding article shall take effect whenever Central American production of the items listed exists, and provided that the effective installed capacity will cover at least fifty percent of the regional demand.

Article 33   The Permanent Secretariat, at the request of an interested country or countries, shall verify, in collaboration with ICAITI, the requirements of the preceding article and notify the member governments of the result of its investigations. The customs charge will be applicable thirty days after the date of written notice thereof.

Article 34   If the system established in accordance with the foregoing rules might give rise to the speculative importation of foreign products, the Executive Council, at the request of any contracting Party, may decide whether the countries should subject those products to import restrictions or quotas at any time before the date on which Central American production shall have commenced.

The governments shall take action in accordance with the resolutions adopted by the Council.

Article 35   The addition of new items to the list of products contained in Article 31 shall be subject to the signing of additional protocols to be negotiated by the Executive Council.

Article 36   The industrial activities that are covered by the special system for the promotion of productive activities established by this chapter may not receive the benefits of the Agreement on the System of Central American Integrated Industries; likewise, the industrial activities covered by the latter Agreement shall not be entitled to the benefits of this special system.

Article 37   The Executive Council shall maintain a strict vigilance over the prices of articles covered by this special system. Whenever it is found that such prices are unduly high in comparison with the normal market prices for similar articles, the Executive Council, on the basis of a study made for this purpose by the Permanent Secretariat in collaboration with the Central American Institute of Industrial Research and Technology (ICAITI), may authorize that imports shall be subject to payment of the uniform customs duties agreed upon in the Central American Agreement on the Equalization of Import Charges and its protocols or, if these are lacking, to the national duties in force on the date of signing the present Protocol.

The Council may authorize imports in the quantity necessary to cover any shortage determined from its findings based on a study to be made by the Permanent Secretariat, which imports shall be subject to payment of the duties to which the preceding paragraph refers.

Chapter V

FINAL PROVISIONS

Article 38   This Protocol shall be submitted for ratification in each State in accordance with its constitutional or legal rules.

The instruments of ratification are to be deposited in the Secretariat of the Organization of Central American States. The Protocol will come into force eight days from the date of deposit of the third instrument, for the first three States to ratify, and for the others, on the date of deposit of their respective instruments.

Article 39   The duration of this Protocol shall be subject to that of the General Treaty of Central American Economic Integration.

Article 40   The Organization of Central American States shall be the depository of the present Protocol, certified copies of which shall be transmitted to the Foreign Ministry of each of the contracting States and to the Permanent Secretariat of the General Treaty of Central American Economic Integration; it shall also give notice immediately of the deposit of each instrument of ratification. When the Protocol comes into force, a certified copy shall also be transmitted to the General Secretariat of the United Nations for registration as required by Article 102 of the Charter of that Organization.

IN WITNESS WHEREOF, the respective plenipotentiaries sign the present Protocol in the city of San Salvador, Republic of El Salvador, on January 29, 1963.

For the Government of Guatemala:

Julio Prado García Salas
Minister of Central American Integration

For the Government of El Salvador:

Salvador Jáuregui
Minister of Economy

For the Government of Honduras:

Jorge Bueso Arias
Minister of Economy and Finance

For the Government of Nicaragua:

Gustavo A. Guerrero
Minister of Economy

For the Government of Costa Rica:

Rodolfo Trejos Donaldson
Director of Economy

SECOND PROTOCOL TO THE AGREEMENT ON THE SYSTEM OF CENTRAL AMERICAN INTEGRATED INDUSTRIES

(Signed at San Salvador, El Salvador, November 5, 1965)

CONSIDERING the importance of establishing within their territories Central American integrated industries to encourage economic development, the rational use of resources, and a balanced growth among the countries;

CONSIDERING the desirability of creating complementary systems for stimulating the establishment of industrial activities of particular significance to the economic development of the region; and

BASED ON the provisions of Article IX of the Agreement on the System of Central American Integrated Industries and Article 35 of its Protocol,

The Governments of the Republics of Guatemala, El Salvador, Honduras, Nicaragua, and Costa Rica

HAVE DECIDED to conclude this Second Protocol to the Agreement, for which purpose they have designated their respective Plenipotentiaries,

[Here follow the names of the ministers]

whose powers are found to be in due and proper form, and who agree as follows:

Chapter I

WINDOW OR PLATE GLASS INDUSTRY

I. *Field of Application*

Article 1 The contracting States declare the window glass industry to be an integrated industry and place the window or plate glass plant to be established in Honduras under the Agreement on the System of Central American Integrated Industries.

The company owning the integrated plant must be organized within six months from the date this Protocol comes into force, and must begin construction of the installations not later than twelve months from that date.

Production must be started within twenty-four months, again counting from the date this instrument takes effect.

Article 2 The Executive Council, through an agreement and on the basis of the production program of the plant and a report to be prepared by ICAITI (Central American Institute of Industrial Research and Technology) shall determine the classes and thicknesses of window or plate glass to be covered by this Protocol at the time it takes effect. In addition, it may include new classes and thicknesses, also by agreement, if it is first shown that the factory can produce them in such a way so as to adequately supply the Central American market. These agreements shall be published in the official gazette of each country, for appropriate legal effects, within the period of 30 days to which Article 16 refers.

II. *Investment and Composition of Capital*

Article 3 The company owning the integrated plant shall invest the approximate equivalent of two million dollars. The initial capital of the company, of approximately one million dollars, shall consist of not less than sixty percent capital of Central American origin.

This proportion of Central American capital must be maintained at all times, even in case of an increase in the capital, and shall be applicable to any other natural or juridical person who may acquire ownership of the plant or the right to its operation.

The certificates representing the capital of Central American origin shall always be registered.

III. *Capacity*

Article 4 The integrated plant shall have a minimum initial installed capacity for an annual production of 6,100 metric tons of window or plate glass, in the furnace section. It must also have a minimum installed lamination capacity of 8,500 metric tons to satisfy the demand of the signatory countries in the manner prescribed in this Protocol.

IV. *Guaranty of Market Supply*

Article 5 The company owning the integrated plant may not become a distributor of the products specifically covered by this System, nor may it sell through exclusive distributors; moreover, without justifiable reasons it may not refuse to fill orders made by distributors.

Article 6 The company owning the plant must guarantee an adequate and constant supply of window or plate glass, of the classes and thicknesses covered by the Tariff Schedule set forth in this Protocol, and within the capacity referred to in Article 4.

At the request of any of the contracting Parties, the Permanent Secretariat shall determine whether this guaranty has not been complied with. In doing so, it shall take into account the volume of existing stocks and other criteria deemed pertinent. In such cases and in the event that the total capacity of the plant may become insufficient to satisfy Central American demand, the governments, on the basis of resolutions of the Executive Council adopted by majority vote, may authorize licenses for the importation of the products covered by this Protocol, subject to the payment of a duty of US $0.05 per kilogram, gross weight, and 15 percent ad valorem cif. The authorization shall be for the volume necessary to ensure an adequate market supply.

Article 7 If the production or supply of window or plate glass, of any class or thickness to which the preceding article refers, is interrupted, the company shall immediately notify the Permanent Secretariat, which in turn shall notify the Executive Council.

In case of an interruption, the Council shall adopt all measures deemed necessary to ensure an adequate supply for the market of the member countries. On the basis of a resolution adopted by the Council, the governments may issue licenses for the importation of this product from outside countries, subject to payment of the duty indicated in the final paragraph of Article 6. Such resolutions shall be adopted by majority vote.

V. *Price Guaranty*

Article 8 The company must supply the market of the signatory countries at reasonable and competitive prices.

The Executive Council, by agreement, shall get the prices per square meter to the distributor and consumer, based on a study by the Permanent Secretariat taking into account prices and normal conditions of the trade in window or plate glass, over a period prior but close to the date of this Protocol. The prices shall be those for the product placed in the distributor's warehouse, including insurance. In setting prices for the consumer, account should also be taken of the different factors involved in the marketing of glass, such as additional services provided by the distributor and the loss and waste resulting from handling the product.

In every case, maximum prices per square meter for distributors shall be set by the Executive Council, on the basis of an exhaustive study to be made by the Permanent Secretariat within three months after the signing of this Protocol. These maximum prices shall be set in such a way that the consumer will be adequately protected, but at the same time ensuring the economic feasibility of the integrated plant.

The Executive Council shall be the organ entrusted with overseeing, through the Permanent Secretariat, the proper application of these provisions, and of authorizing, if necessary, and always by agreement, any changes that it may be advisable to make in prices because of variations in the costs of production. The agreements referred to shall be published in the official gazette of each country, for legal effects, within the 30 days indicated in Article 16.

VI. *Standards of Quality*

Article 9 The products of the integrated plant must meet the standards of quality that are to be specified by ICAITI and approved by the Executive Council.

ICAITI is charged with periodically verifying compliance with those specifications and communicating the result of its check to the Permanent Secretariat. The Executive Council, by a majority vote, shall determine what measures should be applied in the event of noncompliance, including among them authorization of imports and payment of the duties indicated in Article 6.

VII. *Tariff Schedule*

Article 10 The contracting States hereby adopt the classification and duties on imports as indicated below:

Item in NAUCA	Description	Unit	Uniform import charges	
			Specific (dollars per unit)	Ad valorem (Percent CIF)
664–03–00	Plate glass (commonly used for windows), plain, with or without color	G.K. (gross kilograms)	0.10	10%
664–04–00	Plate glass, clear, flat, burnished and polished on both sides (commonly used for mirrors, showcases, counters, etc.), no other processing	G.K.	0.10	10%
664–05–00	Cast or rolled glass, ribbed, imprinted, waved, frosted, ground, embossed, pressed, or reinforced with wire, with or without color, but no other processing	G.K.	0.10	10%

VIII. *General Provisions*

Article 11   The products of the integrated plant shall be entitled to free trade between the territories of the contracting Parties.

The products of plants that may be established in the same branch of industry subsequent to the date this Protocol is signed, but which are not covered by the Agreement on the System of Central American Integrated Industries, shall be entitled to successive tariff reductions of 10 percent annually from the uniform Central American duties established in Article 10 of this Protocol.

These reductions shall begin to be counted as of the date that the plant covered by this Protocol is required to begin production.

Article 12   The benefits of the Agreement on the System of Central American Integrated Industries may not restrict or limit the commercial intercourse that is being carried out under the General Treaty of Central American Economic Integration.

Article 13   For a period of ten years the integrated plant will be entitled to exemption from charges on imports of raw materials or intermediate products utilized by the plant; it shall also be exempt from taxes levied on the production or consumption of such raw materials or intermediate products, or if levied, the amount will be reimbursed. All other tax benefits shall be governed by legislation in force relating to industrial promotion.

However, a government may not grant exemptions or reductions in customs duties on imports coming from outside Central America, for articles produced in the contracting States in adequate quantities.

Article 14   The incorporation of additional plants that may be required to meet the demand of the Central American market, shall be effected without the necessity of a new Protocol, by decision of the Executive Council adopted by majority vote and in accordance with the procedure prescribed in Article IX of the Agreement on the System of Central American Integrated Industries, and they shall be subject to the same conditions as to composition of capital, prices, quality, and guaranty of supply, as are required by this Protocol for the original plants, and the same privileges will be granted.

Article 15   If the company is not organized within the period stipulated in Article 1 or construction of the installations and production are not begun within the indicated time limits, the provision under which the plant will be covered by the terms of the Agreement on the System of Central American Integrated Industries will be void, and any other plant in another Central American country may obtain the benefits, in accordance with the procedure stipulated in the foregoing Article 14.

Notwithstanding the provisions of the preceding paragraph, the Executive Council must extend the periods mentioned for duly justifiable reasons.

Article 16   Agreements by the Council referred to in Articles 2 and 8 above must be entered into not later than 15 days after the Permanent Secretariat has notified the governments that the initial capacity of the plant is the volume indicated in Article 4 and that its products meet the requirements as to quality indicated in Article 9, both of this Protocol.

The Tariff Schedule indicated in Article 10 shall take effect 30 days after SIECA notifies the governments of the agreements referred to in the foregoing paragraph. The Permanent Secretariat must publish this notification and the agreements in question on the same date and in the same form in a newspaper of wide circulation in each country.

Article 17   The company owning the plant referred to in Article 1 must submit to its government a duly legalized statement binding it to comply with all the conditions established in this Protocol, as a requirement for enjoying the benefits of the System of Central American Integrated Industries. This statement shall be transmitted to the Permanent Secretariat, for legal purposes, pursuant to Article XXIV of the General Treaty on Central American Economic Integration. The Permanent Secretariat shall in turn communicate this to the Executive Council.

Article 18   In order to prevent speculative importation of foreign products, the Executive Council, at the request of any of the contracting Parties, may decide whether it is necessary for the countries to submit the importation of window or plate glass to restrictions or quotas, at any time before the date on which Central American production is begun. The governments shall act according to the decisions adopted by the Council.

Article 19   Whenever at the request of any of the contracting Parties the Executive Council proves the existence of imports made at a price lower than their normal value, or lower than regular quotations of the international market, or by unfair trade practices which cause or threaten to cause injury to the integrated plant, the governments shall order the suspension of imports from exporters who have been guilty of the practices indicated, without prejudice to any other measures agreed upon by the Executive Council pursuant to the provisions of Chapter III of the Protocol of San José on tariff equalization, of July 31, 1962. The suspension shall be maintained for as long as necessary.

Article 20   Foreign goods will be regarded as imported at a price lower than their normal value, whenever the factory price charged for the goods in the exporting country is less than:

a) The comparable price, under normal trade conditions, for similar goods intended for consumption in the domestic market of the exporting country;

b) The highest comparable price, under normal trade conditions, for a similar article, intended for exportation to a third country; or

c) The cost of production of the article in the country of origin, plus a reasonable increase for sales expenses and profit.

Article 21 The Executive Council, through the Permanent Secretariat, shall see to the enforcement of the provisions of this Protocol in regard to the rights and obligations of the integrated plant; for which purpose the plant must submit to the Secretariat a monthly report on production and stocks of its products and any additional information that may be requested.

Chapter II

SPECIAL PROVISIONS

Article 22 The contracting States agree, in the present Protocol, to add to the list of products contained in Article 31 of the Protocol to the Agreement on the System of Central American Integrated Industries, signed in the city of San Salvador, Republic of El Salvador, on January 29, 1963, the following items, to which the pertinent provisions of Chapter IV of that Protocol shall be applicable:

Subitem of NAUCA or uniform tariff	Description	Unit	Uniform import duties	
			Specific (dollars per unit)	Ad valorem (Percent CIF)
511–01–02	Sulfuric acid	G.K.	0.04	13%
641–19–08	Paper, n.s.p., in rolls or sheets			
641–19–08–01	Absorbent paper, uncut, in large rolls or spools for sanitary uses	G.K.	0.10	12
642–09–06	Toilet paper in sheets or rolls	G.K.	0.20	10

Subitem of NAUCA or uniform tariff	Description	Unit	Uniform import duties	
			Specific (dollars per unit)	Ad valorem (Percent CIF)
684–02–01	Thin aluminum sheets or foil, with or without paper lining, with or without printing	G.K.	0.20	25
699–21–04	Metal cylinders for compressed gases and similar containers that resist pressure, unwelded or with welded bottoms	G.K.	0.10	10

Chapter III

FINAL PROVISIONS

Article 23   This Protocol shall be submitted for ratification in each State, in accordance with its constitutional or legal rules.

The instruments of ratification are to be deposited with the General Secretariat of the Organization of Central American States. The Protocol shall come into force eight days from the date that the third instrument of ratification is deposited, for the first three depositors, and for the remaining ones, on the date of deposit of the respective instrument.

Article 24   The General Secretariat of the Organization of Central American States shall be the depository of this Protocol and shall transmit certified copies thereof to the Foreign Ministry of each contracting State and to the Permanent Secretariat of the General Treaty, all of whom shall be immediately notified of the deposit of each instrument of ratification. When the Protocol comes into force, the General Secretariat shall also transmit a certified copy thereof to the General Secretariat of the United Nations, for purposes of registration as prescribed by Article 102 of the Charter of the United Nations.

Article 25   The duration of this Protocol shall be subject to that of the General Treaty of Central American Economic Integration.

IN WITNESS WHEREOF, the Plenipotentiaries hereby sign this

Protocol in the city of San Salvador, Republic of El Salvador, on November 5, 1965.

For Guatemala:

Carlos Enrique Peralta Méndez
Minister of Economy

For El Salvador:

Abelardo Torres
Minister of Economy

For Honduras:

Manuel Acosta Bonilla
Minister of Economy and Finance

For Nicaragua:

Silvio Argüello Cardenal
Minister of Economy

For Costa Rica:

Bernal Jiménez Monge
Minister of Economy and Finance

CENTRAL AMERICAN AGREEMENT ON FISCAL INCENTIVES TO INDUSTRIAL DEVELOPMENT

(Signed at San José, Costa Rica, July 31, 1962)

The Governments of the Republics of Guatemala, El Salvador, Honduras, Nicaragua, and Costa Rica,

WITH THE OBJECTIVE of stimulating jointly the industrial development of Central America, in order to improve the living conditions and the well-being of their peoples;

CONSIDERING that industrialization contributes substantially to the accomplishing of this objective and assures a more efficient utilization of the human and material resources of their countries;

CONVINCED that it is necessary to unify the provisions on fiscal incentives to industrial development and to coordinate their application among the member countries; and

IN FULFILMENT of Article XIX of the General Treaty of Central American Economic Integration, signed in Managua, Nicaragua, on December 13, 1960,

HAVE DECIDED to conclude the present Agreement, for which purpose they have designated their respective plenipotentiaries as follows:

[Here follow the names of the delegates]

who, after communicating their respective full powers and finding them in due and proper form, agree as follows:

Chapter I

OBJECTIVES OF THE AGREEMENT

Article 1 The contracting States agree to establish a uniform Central American regime of fiscal incentives to industrial development, in accordance with the needs of the integration and the balanced economic development of Central America, and in accordance with the following provisions.

Chapter II

FIELD OF APPLICATION

Article 2 The regime referred to in the preceding article will be applied to the establishment or the amplification of manufacturing industries which contribute effectively to the economic development of Central America.

Article 3 The contracting States will not grant to manufacturing industries fiscal privileges of a kind, amount, or duration different from those provided in this Agreement. Excepted from this provision are exemptions granted with respect to municipal or local taxes.

The contracting States will not grant fiscal exemptions to productive activities not included in Article 2 above, except to the following, which may be regulated by laws or provisions of a national character:

a) Mineral-extracting industries;
b) Industries extracting petroleum and natural gas;
c) Forestry and the extraction of lumber;
d) Pisciculture and fishing;
e) Service industries and activities;
f) Agricultural activities; and
g) The construction of low-cost housing. In this case it will be possible to grant exemptions from customs on imports of construction materials only when Central American substitutes adequate in quality, quantity, and price are not available.

The exceptions referred to in the foregoing subheadings shall not include typically manufacturing processing of the products obtained, which will be controlled by the provisions of this Agreement.

Chapter III

QUALIFICATION OF ENTERPRISES

Article 4 Eligible for benefits of the regime of fiscal incentives established in this Agreement are those enterprises whose industrial plants, utilizing modern and efficient processes of fabrication in the transformation of raw materials and semimanufactured products, produce articles which are necessary for the development of other productive activities, or to satisfy basic needs of the population, or to replace articles that are being imported in considerable quantities, or to increase the volume of exports.

In evaluating the contribution of these plants to economic development, account will also be taken of whether the value added in the industrial process is important in absolute or relative terms; whether they contribute to a greater utilization of national or regional raw materials or semimanufactured products; and whether, in general, they increase the use of the natural human and capital resources of Central America.

Chapter IV

CLASSIFICATION OF ENTERPRISES

Article 5 Enterprises which fulfill the conditions enumerated in Chapter III will be classified as belonging to one of the following groups: A, B, and C.

Classified in Group A will be those enterprises which:

a) Produce industrial raw materials or capital goods; or
b) Produce articles of consumption, containers, or semimanufactured products, provided that at least fifty percent of the total value of the raw materials, containers, or semimanufactured products used are of Central American origin.

Classified in Group B will be those enterprises which combine the three following requirements:

a) Produce articles of consumption, containers, or semimanufactured products;
b) Give rise to important net benefits in the balance of payments and to a high value added in the industrial process;
c) Utilize entirely, or in a high proportion, in terms of value, non-Central American raw materials, containers, and semimanufactured products.

Classified in Group C will be those enterprises which:

a) Do not satisfy the requirements indicated for Groups A and B;
b) Simply assemble, pack, cut up, or dilute products; or
c) Belong to the industries expressly enumerated in Annex 1 to this Agreement.

For the purpose of applying this article, use shall be made of the definitions established in Annex 2 of this Agreement. For the purpose of classifying the enterprises in Group A, subheading (a), use shall be made of the list of capital goods and of raw materials of industrial origin which will be adopted, for this purpose, by the Executive Council of the General Treaty of Central American Economic Integration, within a period of thirty days from the date the present Agreement enters into force.

Article 6   On obtaining a favorable technical opinion from the Permanent Secretariat of the General Treaty, based on studies requested from the Central American Institute of Industrial Research and Technology, the national administrative authority shall be empowered to classify in Group A those enterprises which satisfy the requirements of Group B and which, by employing efficient industrial processes, make direct use of manpower whose cost represents a high proportion of the total cost of production.

The general procedure established in Article 29 of the present Agreement will be equally applicable to the executive orders or decrees on classification which may be issued by the national administrative authorities on the basis of this article.

Article 7   The industrial enterprises in Groups A and B shall be classified as belonging to new or existing industries.

Classified as new industries will be those manufacturing articles which:

a) Are not produced in the country; or
b) Are produced in the country by rudimentary methods of manufacture, provided that the new plant satisfies the two following conditions:
   i) It fills an important part of the unsatisfied demand in the market of the country; and
   ii) It introduces radically different technical processes of manufacture which change the existing structure of the industry and lead to an improvement in productivity and a reduction in costs.

In order to determine whether an enterprise fulfills the requirements enumerated in section (b), it will be necessary for the authorities charged with the application of this Agreement in each country, before classifying one of these enterprises as belonging to the group of new industries, to request and receive a favorable technical opinion of the Permanent Secretariat of the General Treaty.

All other industries not included under the headings (a) and (b) above shall be classified as belonging to the group of existing industries.

Chapter V

FISCAL BENEFITS

Article 8 The fiscal benefits which will be granted in accordance with this Agreement are the following:

I. Total or partial exemption from customs duties and other related charges (including the consular fees but not charges for specific services) which are levied on the importation of the articles mentioned below when the latter are indispensable for the establishment or operation of the enterprises and cannot be taken care of by adequate Central American substitutes:

a) Machinery and equipment;
b) Raw materials, semimanufactured products, and containers;
c) Fuels strictly for the industrial process, except gasoline. This exemption will not be granted to industrial enterprises for their transport operations, nor for the generation of their own power when there already exists an adequate supply from public service plants.

II. Exemption, for the enterprise and its owners, from the tax on income and on profits with respect to revenues derived from qualified activities. The exemption will not be granted when these enterprises or their owners are subject in other countries to taxes which would make this exemption ineffective.

III. Exemption from taxes on assets and on net worth payable by the enterprise or its owners or stockholders by reason of qualified activities.

Article 9 Every enterprise which has been classified in accordance with this Agreement will have the right, during the time it is in force, to deduct from its profits subject to the tax on income, or on profits, the amount reinvested in machinery and equipment in order to increase the productivity or the productive capacity of the enterprise and of the industrial branch involved, in the Central American area. The amount reinvested in each year will be deductible only from the profits obtained during the same year in the qualified activities.

Article 10 If any of the member States reimburses the amount of the charges paid on the importation of raw materials, semimanufactured products, and containers used in products exported to countries outside Central America, this amount will be considered to be adjusted to the terms of this Agreement.

Chapter VI

GRANTING OF BENEFITS

Article 11   Enterprises classified in Group A as belonging to new industries will receive the following benefits:

a) Total exemption from customs duties and other related charges, including consular fees, for ten years, on the importation of machinery and equipment;

b) Exemption from customs duties and other related charges, on the importation of raw materials, semimanufactured products and containers, as follows: one hundred percent during the first five years; sixty percent during the three following years; and forty percent during the two years then following;

c) Total exemption from customs duties and other related charges, including consular fees, for five years, on the importation of fuels strictly for the industrial process, except gasoline;

d) Total exemption from taxes on income and profits for eight years; and

e) Total exemption from taxes on assets and on net worth for ten years.

Article 12   Enterprises classified in Group A as belonging to existing industries will receive the following benefits:

a) Total exemption from customs duties and other related charges, including consular fees, for six years on the importation of machinery and equipment;

b) Total exemption from taxes on income and profits for two years; and,

c) Total exemption from taxes on assets and on net worth for four years.

Article 13   Enterprises classified in Group B as belonging to new industries will receive the following benefits:

a) Total exemption from customs duties and other related charges, including consular fees, for eight years, on the importation of machinery and equipment;

b) Exemption from customs duties and other related charges, including consular fees, on the importation of raw materials, semimanufactured products, and containers, as follows: one hundred percent during the first three years and fifty percent during the two following years;

c) Exemption from customs duties and other related charges, including consular fees, on the importation of fuels strictly for the industrial process, except gasoline, as follows: one hundred percent during the first three years and fifty percent during the two following years;

d) Total exemption from taxes on income and profits during six years; and

e) Total exemption from taxes on assets and on net worth for six years.

Article 14 Enterprises classified in Group B as belonging to existing industries will receive total exemption from customs duties and other related charges, including consular fees, on machinery and equipment for a period of five years.

Article 15 Enterprises classified in Group C will receive total exemption from customs fees and other related charges, including consular fees, on the importation of machinery and equipment for a period of three years.

Article 16 Classified enterprises which produce raw materials or capital goods and which during the period of their concession utilize or come to utilize Central American raw materials which represent at least fifty percent of the total value of the raw materials will enjoy the benefit of total exemption from the taxes referred to by letters (d) and (e) of Article 11, and (b) and (c) of Article 12, above, of the present Agreement, for an additional period of two years.

Article 17 Qualified enterprises, which propose to install plants in an industry in which other enterprises of the same country are enjoying fiscal benefits corresponding to new industries in accordance with this Agreement, will have a right to the same benefits in return for fulfilling equivalent commitments and obligations, but only for the time elapsing before the expiration of the benefits corresponding to the first concession granted.

Once the period referred to in the preceding paragraph is over, and if this period is shorter than that corresponding to existing industry, the enterprises shall receive the benefits of existing industries, but only for the time that must elapse to complete the time period of the latter, in accordance with the terms of their executive order or decree of classification.

Article 18 The period of exemption for the tax on income or profits will begin to be counted from the tax period in which the classified industry begins its production, or, if it had already been in production, from the tax period in which the order or decree of classification enters into effect.

The first year of the period of exemption for taxes on assets or net worth will be that in which the order or decree of classification was published.

Article 19   The period of exemptions on customs duties and other related charges, in the case of machinery and equipment, will begin on the date on which the first importation is made of any of these goods.

The period of custom exemption for raw materials, semimanufactured products, containers, and fuels will begin to be counted from the date on which the first importation of any of these articles is effected.

After the presentation of an application, and before the order or decree of classification enters into effect, the contracting States will be empowered to permit the importation of products subject to exemption from customs, provided that the interested parties guarantee, by bond or deposit, the amount of the import charges applicable.

Article 20   Qualifiable enterprises which propose to invest in the expansion of their industrial plants will receive exemption from customs on the importation of machinery and equipment, and exemption from taxes on assets and on net worth, both for the amounts and periods corresponding to the classification group applicable to them. The exemption from taxes on assets and on net worth will be applied, in each case, only to the additional investment.

Chapter   VII

COORDINATION

Article 21   The States signatory to this Agreement obligate themselves to apply it in a coordinated manner among themselves, and to take the measures necessary to prevent the granting of fiscal privileges and exemptions from leading to situations of competitive disparity which could obstruct or distort the process of Central American trade on an economic basis of integration.

Article 22   The application of this Agreement will be made at the national level by the competent administrative authority.

Article 23   In accordance with Article XIX of the General Treaty of Central American Integration, the Executive Council will be the coordinating organ, at the regional level, in the application of this Agreement. In this character, it will study and resolve any problem or conflict to which the application thereof may give rise among the contracting Parties.

Article 24 The application of this Agreement, in respect to the qualification and classification of industries, will be made on an entirely Central American basis by no later than the end of the seventh year the present Agreement is in force.

When the classification of an enterprise has been made on an entirely Central American basis in accordance with this article, the governments of the contracting States will not be empowered to apply the provisions of Article 25 of this Agreement.

Article 25 During the first seven years the present Agreement is in force, the enterprises which propose to dedicate themselves to industries which already exist in one or more of the countries, but not in others, may be classed in the latter as new industries, being granted the benefits corresponding to this condition and to the classification assigned to them within the three groups referred to in Article 5 of this Agreement.

Article 26 Those exemptions on the importation of raw materials, semimanufactured products and containers, granted to an enterprise in any of the member States in conformity with this Agreement or with national laws, which may affect competitive relations existing in the Central American common market, may be granted, wholly or partially, for the time elapsing until the expiration of these exemptions, provided that, in addition, the following conditions are present simultaneously:

a) The amount of the import taxes on the raw materials, semimanufactured products, and containers utilized must represent a proportion of the total cost of manufacture which is precisely the determining factor in the change registered in competitive conditions; and

b) There must be a favorable judgment by the Executive Council of the General Treaty, establishing that the granting of the exemptions on raw materials, semimanufactured products, and containers to the existing plants in other countries will restore, or tend to restore, the competitive relation that must exist in the common market.

The judgment of the Council will be made at the request of the interested government or governments and in accordance with cost data referring to a determined period of effective production, and not to estimates contained in production plans. It will have validity with respect to the petitioning State or States. When it is favorable, the granting of the exemptions will have an optional character.

Article 27 When the application presented in one country for an enterprise for developing an industrial investment project has been rejected by the national administrative authority, and the rejection is confirmed by the Executive Council, no enterprise shall be qualified or classified in any of the other States with respect to the same investment project.

Article 28   When a contracting State believes that in another of the countries an enterprise has been put into a classification group different from that corresponding to terms of this Agreement, it may submit the case to the Executive Council within a period of three months, counting from the publication of the decree or order of classification. The Executive Council will determine the classification group which would be applicable to the enterprise and will make its decision known to the national administrative authority. The latter will be obligated to modify accordingly the terms of said decree or order.

Chapter VIII

PROCEDURES

Article 29   Request to take advantage of this Agreement shall be presented to the national administrative authority, and shall contain at least the following information:

a) Name, address, and nationality of the applicant, and, when companies are involved, the name of the managing director, the kind of company, and, where appropriate, the names of the members of the board of directors;

b) Amount and composition of the capital, origin thereof, investment plans, and projected productive capacity;

c) Location of the plant;

d) Description of the products;

e) Dates on which it is planned to begin and end the installation of plant and to begin production;

f) Raw materials, semimanufactured products, containers, machinery, and equipment which the enterprise plans to import during the first five years, with or without exemptions, and estimate of consumption of these raw materials per unit produced.

Article 30   In addition to the data mentioned in the preceding article, the applicant shall present to the administrative authority a technical and economic study which should contain at least the following information:

a) The market conditions for the industry involved, especially with respect to the productive capacity already installed, present level of imports, and the effects of the new production on the balance of payments;

b) The economic adequacy of the investment for the type of industry and enterprise involved;

c) Labor that it will employ;

d) Raw materials that it will use, indicating, in case they come from outside Central America, their origin and the possibility of replacing them by Central American production, as well as the value added in the industrial process;

e) Value, quality, and kind of installations, machinery, and equipment that will have to be used, and, in general, the efficiency of the manufacturing processes that will be used;

f) The uses, characteristics, costs, and estimated prices of the final product; and

g) The capacity of the enterprise to operate economically after the period of benefits has expired.

Article 31 There shall be published in the official gazette or newspaper and in a newspaper of large circulation a summary of the application, which shall contain the name or the trade name of the applicant, enumeration of the products, kind of industry, and the classification asked for. On the basis of this publication, any natural or legal person may oppose the classification and the granting of the benefits requested, according to the circumstances of the case, and in accord with the procedures established in the Regulations of this Agreement and in national laws.

Article 32 The administrative authority will make an evaluation of the project which is the object of the application. The evaluation, the application, and the technical and economic study will be considered by a national advisory committee. This committee will present an opinion to the administrative authority in which it will indicate the classification which, in its judgment, fits the applicant enterprise.

Article 33 The order or decree of classification issued by the administrative authority will begin to have effect when it is accepted in writing by the applicant and is published in the official gazette or newspaper.

Article 34 The order or decree shall specify, among other data, the following:

a) The classification of the enterprise and the products which it will manufacture;

b) The benefits granted, including a list of all the articles which may be imported free of customs duties, classified according to the corresponding headings of NAUCA (the common customs nomenclature agreed upon by the Central American countries);

c) The period stipulated for the beginning and the end of the installation of the plant;

d) The period for the beginning of production, which shall not
exceed two years from the effective date of the order or decree
of classification but which may be extended for exceptional reasons for a period not greater than three years;

e) The other obligations of the enterprise.

Article 35   The Permanent Secretariat shall submit monthly reports
to the governments concerning the applications presented and the orders and decrees of classification issued. To this end, the administrative
authorities will provide the Secretariat in good time with the necessary
information, including information on the applications that have been
rejected, as well as an annual report, of a general nature, on the application of the Agreement.

Article 36   The fiscal benefits established in the present Agreement
may be granted only to the persons or enterprises that are to make the
industrial investment, and not to mere intermediaries.

These benefits may be transferred to other persons or enterprises,
provided that the latter satisfy the same requisites fulfilled by the first
beneficiaries. The application for transfer must be presented to the national administrative authority, which will subject it to the procedures
called for.

Chapter IX

CONTROL

Article 37   The national administrative authority will maintain a
periodic control over the fulfillment of the commitments of enterprises
classified in accordance with this Agreement. For this purpose, and especially for the purpose of supervision with respect to the use of exemptions, the enterprises will be required to provide all the information and data which the national administrative authority may request,
and to permit such inspections as may be necessary.

The information provided by each enterprise will be treated by the
national administrative authority as confidential.

Chapter X

SANCTIONS

Article 38   Any improper use of the articles imported under this
Agreement with exemptions from customs duties will be sufficient
ground for applying to the exempted enterprise a fine of from three to
ten times the total amount of the customs duties and other related

charges not paid on them, and/or for canceling the order or decree of classification, without prejudice to other legal provisions in force in each country.

The transfer or change of destination of any article imported with exemptions will be permitted, provided payment is made of the customs duties and other related charges from which exemption has been given.

If permission has previously been obtained from the national administrative authority, these articles may also be transferred without having to pay the taxes and other charges still to be collected because of the exemptions, whenever the transfer is made to a country outside Central America or whenever the one acquiring the articles enjoys the privilege of importing the same articles with exemption from customs.

When five years have elapsed since machinery or equipment was imported with exemptions, it may be transferred or its destination may be changed freely.

Article 39   The administrative authority shall declare the cancelation of the order or decree of classification whenever the enterprise fails to fulfill the obligation to begin production within the period referred to in Article 34, section (d), the enterprise being obligated to pay to the fiscal authorities the amount of the taxes from which they have been exempted.

Article 40   If the beneficiary fails to fulfill any of the other obligations to which it is subject in accordance with this Agreement and with the decree or order of classification, the administrative authority may cancel the latter.

Article 41   It will be considered a practice of unfair competition to export to another Central American country any product whose cost has been reduced by virtue of improper use of the fiscal benefits granted or of an order or decree of classification which is not adjusted to the terms of this Agreement. Such practices will be subject to the procedures and sanctions established in Chapter III of the General Treaty of Central American Economic Integration.

Chapter XI

PREFERENCE TO CENTRAL AMERICAN PRODUCTS

Article 42   Governments, autonomous or decentralized state institutions, municipalities, and all the public agencies of the contracting Parties shall give preference, in their purchases, to products of Central American industry, provided that the price of the products is equal to or below the price of imported products, and that their quality is comparable. For the purpose of comparing prices, fifty percent of the import charges, related duties, and other costs of entry shall be considered to be components of the price of the non-Central American product, even when the entity acquiring the product is exempt from paying such import charges.

Chapter XII

FINAL PROVISIONS

Article 43   This Agreement shall be submitted for ratification to each contracting State, in conformity with its constitutional or legal norms, and will enter into force eight days after the date on which the fifth instrument of ratification is deposited.

Article 44   The General Secretariat of the Organization of Central American States shall be the depository of the present Agreement, and shall send certified copies thereof to the ministry of foreign affairs of each of the Central American States, and to the Permanent Secretariat of the General Treaty, all of which it will notify immediately of the deposit of each of the instruments of ratification. On the Agreement's entering into force, it will also send a certified copy thereof to the General Secretariat of the United Nations, for the purpose of registration as indicated by Article 102 of the United Nations Charter.

Article 45   The duration of the present Agreement will be contingent upon that of the General Treaty of Central American Economic Integration.

Article 46   The present Agreement repeals provisions, contained in general and special laws, which are in opposition to it.

Article 47   The contracting States shall adopt a uniform regulation to this Agreement within a period not longer than thirty days from the date on which the present instrument enters into force. This regulation will be drawn up by the Executive Council.

Chapter XIII

TRANSITIONAL PROVISIONS

First Transitional   Enterprises which are classified under national laws of industrial development will continue to enjoy the fiscal benefits which had been granted to them by said laws, except for the provisions established in the following paragraphs of this article. In addition, they may be granted benefits equal to the greatest which were being enjoyed by other enterprises producing the same articles under national concessions granted in any other Central American country, but only for the time elapsing before the termination of the concession of these benefits.

Concessions for the importation of construction materials granted by virtue of national laws of industrial development will cease to have effect thirty days after this Agreement enters into force. The exemptions for the importation of machinery and equipment, raw materials, semimanufactured products, containers, and fuels which may have been granted by virtue of national laws remain subject to the provisions of Article IX of the General Treaty of Central American Economic Integration.

No legal effect will attach to concessions granted by means of general or special national laws for the development of manufacturing industries to those enterprises which, within a period of one year beginning with the date of the order or decree of classification, or of six months from the date this Agreement enters into force, whichever is longer, would not have made use of any of the exemptions granted.

Second Transitional Enterprises which, at the date this Agreement enters into force, are enjoying fiscal exemptions by virtue of national laws, will have the right to be reclassified in accordance with this Agreement within a period of six months. In case they are reclassified, they will be granted the corresponding benefits, deducting from the periods of benefit that part which will have elapsed of the periods granted in accordance with the national law.

Third Transitional Enterprises included under national laws to which would apply a classification in Group C according to this Agreement, which will not have been reclassified in accordance with the preceding article and which export their products to any other Central American country, will be considered to be favored by export subsidies. As a consequence, such exports will be subject to the procedure with respect to bonding and the other provisions of Article XI of the General Treaty, except that contained in paragraph four of said article.

Fourth Transitional The governments may extend to the enterprises which are classifiable in accordance with this Agreement benefits equal to the greatest that were being enjoyed, in their country or in another Central American country, by enterprises producing the same articles by virtue of national concessions, during the time these concessions are in effect. When these concessions will have been terminated, the enterprises will receive the benefits envisaged in this Agreement for the time elapsing before the completion of the corresponding period.

Fifth Transitional For the purpose of applying the principle of balanced development among the Central American countries, the Central American States agree that the national administrative authority of the Republic of Honduras may grant for two years, and that of the Republic of Nicaragua for one year, exemption from taxes on income or profits, assets, and net worth to enterprises which, in accordance with this Agreement, they classify as belonging to new industries in Groups A and B. These additional benefits shall be granted during the first ten years this Agreement is in force.

Sixth Transitional   The contracting States will sign a protocol to this Agreement stipulating the regime of fiscal incentives which will be applied to enterprises producing pharmaceutical and medicinal articles. Until the aforementioned protocol enters into effect, these enterprises will be classified, and will receive the corresponding benefits, in accordance with this Agreement.

Seventh Transitional   The contracting States undertake to sign, within a period no longer than a year from the date this instrument goes into effect, an additional protocol to this Agreement in which will be established the regime of fiscal incentives applicable to assembly activities. In this protocol will be specified, among other factors:

a) The assembly activities that shall be acceptable;
b) The system of fiscal incentives that will be applied to assembly enterprises, including, among other things, the requirements of qualification and classification, the amount and the duration of the fiscal benefits and the methods of regional coordination;
c) The requirements and obligations to which the assembly enterprises shall be subject with respect to the production and utilization of parts of regional origin;
d) The conditions of trade to which the respective articles assembled will be subject within the Central American common market.

Until the aforementioned protocol goes into effect, assembly activities accepted under this provision will receive exemptions, for three years only, on the importation of machinery and equipment, and everything established in the clauses applicable to them.

Eighth Transitional   For the purposes of classifying the enterprises included in Group A, subheading (a), of Article 5 of this Agreement, and until the Executive Council of the General Treaty has drawn up the list of capital goods and of industrial raw materials to which the last paragraph of said article refers, the contracting Parties will observe exclusively the definitions established in Annex 2 of the present Agreement.

IN TESTIMONY WHEREOF, the respective Plenipotentiaries sign the present Agreement in the city of San José, capital of the Republic of Costa Rica, on the thirty-first day of the month of July, nineteen hundred sixty-two.

For the Government of Guatemala:

> *Jorge L. Caballeros*
> Minister of Economy
>
> *Julio Prado García Salas*
> Minister for Coordination of
> Central American Integration

For the Government of El Salvador:

> *Salvador Jáuregui*
> Minister of Economy

For the Government of Honduras:

> *Jorge Bueso Arias*
> Minister of Economy and Finance

For the Government of Nicaragua:

> *Juan José Lugo Marenco*
> Minister of Economy
>
> *Gustavo A. Guerrero*
> Vice Minister of Economy

For the Government of Costa Rica:

> *Raúl Hess Estrada*
> Minister of Economy

Annex 1

LIST OF PRODUCTS OF INDUSTRIES CLASSIFIABLE IN GROUP C

For the purposes of industrial classification indicated in Article 5 of this Agreement, a classification of Group C will be assigned to qualified enterprises which devote themselves to the cutting and making of clothing, the manufacturing of leather shoes, and to those which manufacture the products enumerated in this Annex.

Industry or productive activity	Uniform tariff classification (NAUCA)
1. *Beverages*	
Mineral waters	111–01–01
Carbonated water, with or without flavor	111–01–02
Nonalcoholic beverages (not previously specified)	111–01–03
Choice wines	112–01–02
Champagne	112–01–03
Other sparkling wines (not previously specified)	112–01–04

Industry or productive activity	Uniform tariff classification (NAUCA)
Other wines, including grape juice (n.p.s.)	112–01–05
Beer and other cereal beverages, fermented	112–03–00
Aromatic bitter extracts, liquid, such as angostura bitters, and similar items	112–04–01

2. *Manufactured tobacco*

Cigars, made from tobacco produced outside Central America	112–01–00
Cigarettes	112–02–00
Processed tobacco in a form not previously specified	112–03–00

3. *Perfumery, cosmetics, and toilet preparations (except soaps and dentifrices)*

Perfumes	552–01–01
Lotions, eau de cologne and toilet waters	552–01–02
Cosmetics	552–01–03
Toilet powders	552–01–04
Dyes, tonics, pomades, shampoos and other preparations for the hair	552–01–05
All other toilet preparations, not previously specified, including shaving creams, depilatories, etc.	552–01–07
Sprays, fumigators, and other preparations for perfuming the surroundings, and deodorants for houses	552–01–08

Annex 2

For the purposes of the provisions of Article 5 of this Agreement, the following definitions apply:

Industrial raw materials   Goods produced by manufacturing industry which have been processed with materials in their primary stages, modifying their form or nature and incorporating in them a high proportion of added value, and which are destined to be used in further industrial processes.

For the purpose of classification in Groups A and B with reference to the use of raw materials of regional origin, consideration will be given, in addition to those appearing in the list which the Executive Council will prepare in conformity with the foregoing definition, to the components forming part of these industrial raw materials as well as the primary products entering into their processing.

Capital goods   are those utilized to process or transform other products, or to provide a service of a productive character, which are not used up in a single cycle of production.

PROTOCOL TO THE CENTRAL AMERICAN AGREEMENT ON FISCAL INCENTIVES TO INDUSTRIAL DEVELOPMENT

(Protocol on Preferential Treatment for Honduras)

(Signed at Managua, Nicaragua, September 23, 1966)

WHEREAS one of the aims of the economic integration program is to encourage a balanced growth of the Central American countries; and

IN VIEW of the fact that the Economic Cooperation Committee and the Central American Economic Council have recommended the signing of an instrument that will permit the Republic of Honduras to grant to industrial enterprises that may be established in its territory greater benefits than those contemplated in the Central American Agreement on Fiscal Incentives to Industrial Development, signed in San José, Costa Rica, on July 31, 1962,

The Governments of the Republics of Guatemala, El Salvador, Honduras, Nicaragua, and Costa Rica

HAVE DECIDED to conclude this Protocol, for which they have named their respective Plenipotentiaries, to wit:

[Here follow the names of the delegates]

who, after having communicated their respective full powers and found them to be in good and due form, agree to the following:

Article 1   By means of this Protocol the contracting States agree to establish a preferential juridical regime, as an exception to the Central American Agreement on Fiscal Incentives to Industrial Development (hereinafter called simply the "Agreement"), which the Republic of Honduras shall apply during the period fixed below, to the establishment or expansion of manufacturing industries within its territory, pursuant to the following provisions.

Article 2   Industrial enterprises that may be established in Honduras shall receive the benefits granted under the terms of this Protocol.

Industrial enterprises already established in Honduras that expand their activities shall receive the benefits indicated in Article 8 of this Protocol. Expansion is defined as an increase in machinery and/or equipment that increases the installed production capacity of the plant to an amount specified in the Regulations of the Agreement, that incorporates new developments in the productive process, or that modernizes those in existence; in the latter cases the increase in investment may not be less than that established in the Regulations cited.

Article 3 Enterprises classified in Group A belonging to new industries shall receive the following benefits:

a) Total exemption from customs duties and other related charges, including consular fees, for twelve years, on the importation of machinery and equipment.

b) Exemption from customs duties and other related charges, including consular fees, on the importation of raw materials, semi-manufactured products, and containers, as follows:

   i) For enterprises established during the first year this Protocol is in effect, one hundred percent during the first five years and seventy percent for the five years following;

   ii) For those established during the second year, one hundred percent for the first five years, seventy percent for the subsequent four years, and fifty percent for the remaining year;

   iii) For those established during the third year, one hundred percent for five years, seventy percent for the subsequent three years, and fifty percent for the last two years;

   iv) For those established during the fourth year, one hundred percent for the first five years, seventy percent for the succeeding two years and fifty percent for the last three years;

   v) For those installed during the fifth year, one hundred percent during the first five years, seventy percent for the following year, and fifty percent for the subsequent four years.

The foregoing benefits appear in the table shown in Appendix No. 1 that forms an integral part of this Protocol.

c) Total exemption from customs duties and other related charges, including consular fees, for five years, on imports of fuel strictly for the industrial process, except gasoline;

d) Total exemption from taxes on income and profits for ten years;

e) Total exemption from taxes on assets and on net worth for twelve years.

Article 4 Enterprises classified in Group A belonging to existing industries, shall receive the following benefits:

a) Total exemption from customs duties and other related charges, including consular fees, for eight years, on the importation of machinery and equipment;

b) Total exemption from taxes on income and profits, for four years;

c) Total exemption from taxes on assets and on net worth for six years.

Article 5 Enterprises classified in Group B belonging to new industries shall receive the following benefits:

a) Total exemption from customs duties and other related charges, including consular fees, for ten years, on the importation of machinery and equipment;

b) Exemption from customs duties and other related charges, including consular fees, on the importation of raw materials, semi-manufactured products and containers, as follows:

  i) For enterprises installed during the first year this Protocol is in force, one hundred percent for the first three years and seventy percent during the two years following;

  ii) For those established during the second year, one hundred percent for the first three years, seventy percent for the following year, and fifty percent for the remaining year;

  iii) For enterprises installed during the third year, one hundred percent for the first three years and fifty percent in the two remaining years;

  iv) For those installed during the fourth year, one hundred percent for the first two years, eighty percent for the following year, and fifty percent for the remaining two years;

  v) For enterprises installed during the fifth year, one hundred percent for the first year, eighty percent for the next two years, and fifty percent for the last two years.

  The foregoing benefits appear in the table of Appendix No. 2 which forms an integral part of this Protocol.

c) Exemption from customs duties and other related charges, including consular fees, on the importation of fuel strictly for the industrial process, except gasoline, as follows: one hundred percent during the first three years and fifty percent during the two years following;

d) Total exemption from taxes on income and profits for eight years; and

e) Total exemption from taxes on assets and on net worth for eight years.

Article 6 Enterprises classified in Group B belonging to existing industries shall receive the following benefits:

a) Total exemption from customs duties and other related charges, including consular fees, on machinery and equipment for a period of six years;

b) Total exemption from taxes on income and profits for two years; and

c) Total exemption from taxes on assets and on net worth for three years.

Article 7 Enterprises classified in Group C shall receive the following benefits:

a) Total exemption from customs duties and other connected charges, including consular fees, on imports of machinery and equipment, for a period of five years;

b) Total exemption from taxes on income and profits for two years; and

c) Total exemption from taxes on assets and on net worth for two years.

Article 8 Classifiable enterprises that propose to invest in the expansion of their industrial plants shall receive customs exemptions on imports of machinery and equipment, and exemption from taxes on assets and on net worth, both in the amounts and for the periods corresponding to the classification group that would be applicable under this Protocol. The tax exemption on assets and on net worth shall be applicable, in its case, only to the additional investment.

Article 9 The Government of Honduras may grant to enterprises classified in Groups A and B belonging to new industry, as additional benefits to those indicated in Articles 3 and 5, the free use for ten years, of industrial buildings that the State may have available, or their sale at fifty percent of their value.

Article 10 The Government of Honduras may authorize any industrial enterprise, classified or not, that expands its installations, to deduct from its profits subject to income tax, the amount of the reinvestment made in industrial buildings, machinery and equipment. Such authorization may also be granted to any taxpayer who invests in the installation of industrial enterprises.

Article 11 Paragraph (b) of Article 11 of the Agreement is amended to read as follows:

"b) Exemption from customs duties and other related charges, on the importation of raw materials, semimanufactured products, and containers, as follows: eighty percent for the first five years and fifty percent during the five years then following."

Article 12 Paragraph (b) of Article 13 of the Agreement is amended to read as follows:

"b) Exemption from customs duties and other related charges, including consular fees, on the importation of raw materials, semimanufactured products, and containers, as follows: eighty percent during the first three years and fifty percent during the two following years."

Article 13 Article 26 of the Agreement is amended and rewritten as follows:

"Whenever one enterprise believes that the competitive ratio it had been enjoying with another enterprise has been broken, in any Central American country, in respect of exemptions or reductions in taxes on the importation of raw materials, semimanufactured products, and containers, by reason of the exemptions granted to this other enterprise, the former may request the competent authorities of its country to grant exemptions on raw materials, semimanufactured products, and containers to the extent that may be necessary to reestablish the competitive ratio.

The administrative authority of that country must submit the case for consideration by SIECA, so that it may issue an appropriate decision, which should be rendered not more than thirty days after the request was submitted. When it has rendered its decision, SIECA must convoke the Executive Council to take cognizance of the matter. If the Council does not issue a resolution within ninety days, the question shall be considered resolved in accordance with the decision of SIECA. However, during the course of the periods indicated, the administrative authority may grant the exemptions if this is deemed advisable, through the posting of bond for the amount of the exempted customs duties.

The SIECA report must take into account, above all:

a) The level of the tariff rates on the raw materials, semimanufactured products, and containers that are concerned;
b) The ratio of the cost of these products to the total cost of the finished article; and
c) The price of the article in question on the market concerned."

The provisions of this article shall also be applicable to situations that may arise as a consequence of the preferential treatment granted to Honduras in this Protocol in respect of the customs exemptions on raw materials, semimanufactured products, and containers.

Article 14 The Governments of the signatory States undertake not to grant exemptions for the importation of any article that is produced in Central America under adequate conditions.

Even though a country may consider that the conditions are not adequate, such exemptions may not be granted until this fact has been proved by an opinion rendered by SIECA, which it shall prepare in collaboration with ICAITI and which it must render within thirty days.

If any of the interested parties does not agree with the opinion rendered by SIECA, it shall give notice thereof within fifteen days, so that the matter may be submitted to the Executive Council at its next meeting, in order that steps deemed pertinent may be taken. If the Council does not issue its opinion within ninety days, the question is thereby decided in accordance with the opinion rendered by SIECA. Nevertheless, during the course of the periods indicated, the administrative authority may grant the exemptions, if this is deemed advisable, through the posting of bond for the amount of the exempted customs duties.

Article 15 The provisions of the first paragraph of Article 3 of the Agreement shall not affect the powers or rights that are granted to the

Republic of Honduras by this Protocol. Consequently, in no case shall it be held that acts executed by the authorities of that country in accordance with the present instrument contravene or in any way prejudice the provisions of the paragraph cited.

Article 16 Whenever in applying the Second Transitory Article of the Agreement, any enterprise established in Honduras asks to be reclassified, it may receive only the benefits of the Agreement in the form specified therein and not those of this Protocol.

Article 17 This Protocol rescinds the most favorable treatment granted to industrial enterprises in Honduras pursuant to the Fifth Transitory Article of the Agreement.

Article 18 Matters not covered by this Protocol shall be governed by the provisions of the Central American Agreement on Fiscal Incentives to Industrial Development.

Article 19 This Protocol shall have a duration of five years counted from the date it comes into force. This period, however, may be extended if so determined by the Central American Economic Council, after an evaluation of the results obtained by virtue of the provisions of this Protocol.

The amendments made to Articles 11, 13, and 26 of the Agreement shall be considered as incorporated in that instrument and shall be in force with it.

Article 20 This Protocol shall be submitted for ratification in each contracting State, in conformity with their respective constitutional or legal rules, and shall take effect eight days from the date of deposit of the fifth instrument of ratification.

Article 21 The General Secretariat of the Organization of Central American States shall be the depository of this Protocol and shall transmit certified copies thereof to the Foreign Office of each of the contracting States, and to the Permanent Secretariat of the General Treaty of Central American Economic Integration, and shall give notice to them immediately of the deposit of each instrument of ratification. When this Protocol comes into force, it shall also transmit a certified copy thereof to the General Secretariat of the United Nations, for purposes of registration pursuant to Article 102 of its Charter.

IN WITNESS WHEREOF, the respective plenipotentiaries sign this Protocol in the city of Managua, Republic of Nicaragua, on September 23, 1966.

For the Government of Guatemala:

Isidro Lemus Dimas
Minister of Economy

For the Government of El Salvador:
>*Victor Manuel Cuéllar Ortíz*
>Under Secretary of Economic Integration
>and International Trade

For the Government of Honduras:
>*Manuel Acosta Bonilla*
>Minister of Economy and Finance

For the Government of Nicaragua:
>*Silvio Argüello Cardenal*
>Minister of Economy

For the Government of Costa Rica:
>*Manuel Jiménez de la Guardia*
>Minister of Industry and Commerce

APPENDIX No. 1

AMOUNT OF THE EXEMPTIONS ON RAW MATERIALS, SEMIMANUFACTURED PRODUCTS AND CONTAINERS
GROUP A NEW INDUSTRIES

Year	1st year		2nd year		3rd year		4th year		5th year		6th year		7th year		8th year		9th year		10th year	
	Rest of C.A.	Hond.	Rest of C.A.	Hond.	Rest of C.A.	Hond.	Rest of C.A.	Hond.	Rest of C.A.	Hond.	Rest of C.A.	Hond.	Rest of C.A.	Hond.	Rest of C.A.	Hond.	Rest of C.A.	Hond.	Rest of C.A.	Hond.
	%	%	%	%	%	%	%	%	%	%	%	%	%	%	%	%	%	%	%	%
I	80	100	80	100	80	100	80	100	80	100	50	70	50	70	50	70	50	50	50	70
II	80	100	80	100	80	100	80	100	80	100	50	70	50	70	50	70	50	50	50	70
III	80	100	80	100	80	100	80	100	80	100	50	70	50	70	50	70	50	50	50	50
IV	80	100	80	100	80	100	80	100	80	100	50	70	50	70	50	50	50	50	50	50
V	80	100	80	100	80	100	80	100	80	80	50	70	50	70	50	50	50	50	50	50

APPENDIX No. 2

AMOUNT OF THE EXEMPTIONS ON RAW MATERIALS, SEMIMANUFACTURED PRODUCTS AND CONTAINERS
GROUP B NEW INDUSTRIES

Year	1st year		2nd year		3rd year		4th year		5th year	
	Rest of C.A.	Hond.	Rest of C.A.	Hond.	Rest of C.A.	Hond.	Rest of C.A.	Hond.	Rest of C.A.	Hond.
I	80	100	80	100	80	100	50	70	50	70
II	80	100	80	100	80	100	50	70	50	50
III	80	100	80	100	80	100	50	50	50	50
IV	80	100	80	100	80	80	50	50	50	50
V	80	100	80	80	80	80	50	50	50	50

Financial Regime

AGREEMENT ESTABLISHING THE CENTRAL AMERICAN BANK FOR ECONOMIC INTEGRATION

(Signed at Managua, Nicaragua, December 13, 1960)

The Governments of the Republics of Guatemala, El Salvador, Honduras, and Nicaragua agree to create, by virtue of the present Agreement, the Central American Bank for Economic Integration, in accordance with the following provisions:

Chapter I

NATURE, PURPOSE AND HEADQUARTERS

Article 1 The Central American Bank for Economic Integration is an international juridical person, and shall perform its functions in conformity with the present Agreement and with its Regulations.

Article 2 The purpose of the Bank shall be to promote the economic integration and balanced economic development of the member countries. In pursuance of this objective, its activities shall be primarily designed to meet the needs of the following investment sectors:

a) Infrastructure projects to complete existing regional systems or counterbalance disparities in basic sectors which hinder the balanced economic development of Central America. Consequently, the Bank shall not finance infrastructure projects of purely local or national scope which will not contribute to the completion of the said systems or to the counterbalancing of significant disequilibriums as between the member countries;

b) Projects for long-term investment in industries of a regional character or of importance for the Central American market, which will help to increase the supply of goods available for intra-Central American trade, or for such trade and the export sector. The Bank's activities shall not include investment in essentially local industries;

c) Coordinated agricultural projects aiming at the improvement or expansion of farms or the replacement of less economic by more

143

economic farms conducive to Central American regional self-sufficiency;

d) Projects for the financing of enterprises that need to expand their operations, modernize their processes or change the structure of their production in order to improve their efficiency and their competitive capacity within the common market with a view to facilitating free trade among the Central American countries;

e) Projects for financing services vital to the operation of the common market;

f) Other productive projects calculated to create economic complementarity among the member countries and to expand intra-Central American trade.

Article 3   The Bank shall have its headquarters and head office in the city of Tegucigalpa, in the Republic of Honduras, and shall be empowered to establish branch offices, agencies, and correspondents.

Chapter II

CAPITAL, RESERVES AND RESOURCES

Article 4   The Bank's initial authorized capital shall be a sum equivalent to sixteen million United States dollars, to which each of the member States shall subscribe four million dollars, payable in its national currency.

One half of the capital subscribed by each member State shall be paid as follows: the equivalent of one million dollars within sixty days from the date of entry into force of the present Agreement, and the equivalent of one million dollars within fourteen months of the said date.

The rest of the capital subscribed shall be payable as and when called in by decision of the Board of Governors, with the concurring vote of at least one governor from each member State.

The Bank shall be empowered to augment its capital if all the members of the Board of Governors adopt a unanimous decision to that effect.

Article 5   The shares of the member States in the capital of the Bank shall be represented by stock certificates issued in favor of the States concerned. These certificates shall confer upon their holders equal rights and obligations, shall not yield interest or dividends and shall not be taxable or transferable.

Such net profits as may accrue to the Bank in the course of its operation shall be deposited in a capital reserve fund.

The responsibility of the members of the Bank, as such, shall be confined to the amount of their capital subscription.

The capital contributed in national currency by each of the member States shall enjoy a guarantee of free convertibility at the official exchange rate most favorable to the Bank.

Each of the member States engages to maintain the value in United States dollars of the capital contribution which it has disbursed to the Bank. Should a change take place in the external official exchange rate for any of the national currencies concerned, the Bank's resources in that currency shall be adjusted in the exact proportion required to maintain their value in United States dollars.

Article 6   In addition to its own capital and reserves, the resources of the Bank shall include the proceeds from loans and credits obtained in capital markets and any other resources received in any legal form.

Chapter III

OPERATIONS

Article 7   The capital, capital reserves, and other resources of the Bank shall be used solely for the fulfillment of the purpose set forth in Article 2 of the present Agreement. To this end, the Bank shall be empowered:

a) To study and promote the investment opportunities created by the economic integration of the member States, duly programming its activities and establishing the necessary financing priorities;

b) To make or participate in long- and medium-term loans;

c) To issue bonds of its own, which may or may not be guaranteed by means of sureties, pledges, or mortgages;

d) To participate in the issuance and placing of credit documents of all kinds, related to the fulfillment of its purpose;

e) To obtain loans, credits, and guarantees from Central American, international, and foreign financial institutions;

f) To act as intermediary in the concerting of loans and credits for the Governments, public institutions, and established enterprises of the member States, to which end it shall institute such arrangements for cooperation with other Central American, international, and foreign institutions as it may deem expedient in that connection, and shall be empowered to take part in the preparation of the specific projects concerned;

g) To guarantee the commitments of public institutions or private enterprises up to such amounts and for such periods as the Board of Governors may determine;

h) To obtain guarantees from the member States for the purpose of securing loans and credits from other financial institutions;

    i) To provide, using its own resources or those it may obtain for the purpose, executive, administrative, and technical advisory services for the benefit of applicants for credit;

    j) To conduct all such additional business as may be necessary, under the terms of the present Agreement and its Regulations, for the furtherance of its purpose and operation.

Article 8 The Bank shall finance only economically sound and technically feasible projects and shall refrain from making loans or assuming any responsibility whatsoever for the payment or refinancing of earlier commitments.

Chapter IV

ORGANIZATION AND ADMINISTRATION

Article 9 The Bank shall have a Board of Governors, a Board of Directors, a President, and such other officials and employees as may be deemed necessary.

Article 10 All the powers of the Bank shall be vested in the Board of Governors. Each member country shall provide two Governors, who shall be absolutely independent in the exercise of their functions and shall have separate votes; one of them shall be the Minister of Economy or his equivalent, and the other shall be the president or manager of each country's central bank, or his equivalent. From among the Governors the Board shall elect a President, who shall remain in office until the next regular meeting of the Board.

Article 11 The Board of Governors shall be at liberty to delegate all its powers to the Board of Directors, except those relating to the following procedures:

    a) Calling-in of capital contributions;

    b) Augmentation of the authorized capital;

    c) Determination of capital reserves on the basis of proposals made by the Board of Directors;

    d) Election of the President and determination of his emoluments;

    e) Determination of the emoluments of the Directors;

    f) Examination of the interpretations placed upon the present Agreement by the Board of Directors and ruling thereon in case of appeal;

    g) Authorization of the conclusion of general agreements relating to cooperation with other agencies;

    h) Appointment of outside auditors to check financial statements;

    i) Adoption and publication, following auditor's report, of the overall balance-sheet and the statement of profits and losses;

j) Adoption of decisions, in the event of the Bank's terminating its operations, with respect to the distribution of its net assets.

Article 12   The Board of Governors shall retain full control over all the powers which, in accordance with Article 11, it may delegate to the Board of Directors.

Article 13   The Board of Governors shall meet in regular session once a year. It shall also be at liberty to meet in special session whenever it so determines or whenever it is convened by the Board of Directors. The Board of Directors shall convene the Board of Governors whenever one of the member States so requests.

Article 14   At the meetings of the Board of Governors one half the total number of Governors plus one shall constitute a quorum. In all cases except that provided for in Article 4, decisions shall be made by the concurring votes of one half of the total number of Governors plus one.

Article 15   The Board of Directors shall be responsible for the conduct of the operations of the Bank, and to this end shall be entitled to exercise all the powers delegated to it by the Board of Governors.

Article 16   There shall be one Director for each State member of the Bank, elected by the Board of Governors. The Directors shall be appointed for a term of five years and shall be eligible for re-election for successive periods. They shall be citizens of the member States and persons of acknowledged capacity and wide experience in economic, financial, and banking affairs.

Article 17   The Directors shall remain in office until their successors are appointed or elected. When a Director's post becomes vacant, the Governors shall appoint a substitute for the remainder of the period.

In the event of a Director's absence for legitimate reasons, the Board of Directors shall be empowered to appoint his temporary substitute.

Article 18   The Directors shall work full time in the Bank and shall, in addition, discharge such functions as the President may assign to them.

Article 19   The Board of Directors shall be of a permanent character and shall function at the headquarters of the Bank.

The Board of Directors shall determine the basic organization of the Bank, including the number of major administrative and professional posts and the general responsibilities attaching, shall adopt the budget, and shall lay before the Board of Governors a proposal for the establishment of reserves.

Article 20   The Board of Governors shall elect from among the Directors the President of the Bank, who shall be its legal representative. Similarly, it shall appoint the person who, should the President himself be prevented from so doing, shall exercise his authority and his functions. The President shall take the chair at the meetings of the Board of Directors and shall conduct the ordinary business of the Bank. His vote shall carry the same weight as that of the other members, except in the event of a tie, in which case he shall have two votes.

Article 21   There shall be an Executive Vice President who shall be appointed by the Board of Directors on the proposal of the President of the Bank. He shall exercise the authority and discharge the administrative functions determined by the Board of Directors.

The Executive Vice President shall attend the meetings of the Board of Directors, but without the right to vote.

Article 22   In the discharge of their functions, the President, officers, and employees of the Bank shall be answerable to it alone and shall acknowledge no other authority. The member States shall respect the international character of this obligation.

Article 23   The primary consideration to be borne in mind by the Bank in appointing its staff and determining their conditions of service shall be the need to ensure the highest possible degree of efficiency, competence, and integrity. Staff shall also be recruited with regard to the equitable geographical distribution.

Article 24   The Bank, its officers, and its employees—with the exception of the Governors in their respective countries—shall be debarred from taking active part in political affairs.

Chapter V

INTERPRETATION AND ARBITRATION

Article 25   Any difference of opinion as to the interpretation of the provisions of the present Agreement which may arise between any member and the Bank or among member States shall be submitted for a ruling to the Board of Directors.

Any member State shall be entitled to demand that the solution proposed by the Board of Directors in accordance with the first paragraph of this article shall be submitted to the Board of Governors, whose decision shall be final. Pending the Board's decision, the Bank shall be empowered to take such action as it may deem necessary on the basis of the decision reached by the Board of Directors.

Article 26   Should any disagreement arise between the Bank and a State which has ceased to be a member, or between the Bank and one of its members after it has been agreed that the operations of the institution shall be terminated, the controversy shall be submitted for arbitration to a tribunal composed of three persons. The Bank and the State concerned shall each appoint one of the arbiters, and shall jointly appoint a third and disinterested party. Should agreement not be reached with respect to the last-mentioned appointment, the third member shall be chosen by lot from among the Presidents of the Supreme Courts of Justice of the member States, with the exception of that of the country concerned.

The third arbiter shall be empowered to decide upon all questions of procedure in cases where the parties are not in agreement.

Chapter VI

IMMUNITIES, EXEMPTIONS, AND PRIVILEGES

Article 27 The Bank, in the discharge of its functions and in conformity with its purposes, shall enjoy in the territory of the member States the immunities, exemptions, and privileges which are set forth in this chapter or which may be otherwise granted to it.

Article 28 Actions may be brought against the Bank only in a court of competent jurisdiction in the territories of a member State in which the Bank has an office, has appointed an agent for the purpose of accepting service or notice of process, or has issued or guaranteed securities.

Article 29 The Bank's property and other assets, wheresoever situated and by whomsoever held, shall enjoy immunity from attachment, sequestration, embargo, distraint, auction, adjudication, or any other form of seizure or alienation or forfeiture, so long as no definitive judgment has been pronounced against the Bank.

The property and other assets of the Bank shall be deemed to be international public property, and shall enjoy immunity in respect of investigation, requisition, confiscation, expropriation, or any other form of seizure or forfeiture by executive or legislative action.

The Bank's property and other assets shall be exempt from restrictions, regulations, controls, and moratoria of every kind, except as otherwise provided in the present Agreement.

Article 30 The files and records of the Bank shall be inviolable and shall enjoy absolute immunity.

Article 31 In territories of the member States the Bank's communications shall be entitled to the same ranking privileges as are granted to official communications.

Article 32   The personnel of the Bank, whatever their category, shall enjoy the following privileges and immunities:

a) Immunity in respect of judicial, administrative, and legislative proceedings relating to acts performed by them in their official capacity, unless the Bank waives such immunity;

b) In the case of non-nationals of the member State concerned, the same immunities and privileges in respect of immigration restrictions, registration of aliens and military service requirements, and other facilities relating to exchange and travel regulations, which the State grants to other member States in respect of personnel of comparable rank.

Article 33

a) The Bank, its income, property, and other assets, as well as any operations and transactions which it may effect in accordance with the present Agreement, shall be exempt from taxes of every kind and from customs duties and other charges of similar nature. The Bank shall likewise be exempt from all responsibility in connection with the payment, withholding, or collection of any tax, import, or duty;

b) The bonds or securities issued or guaranteed by the Bank, including dividends or interest thereon, whosoever be their holder, shall not be subject to duties or taxes of any kind;

c) The salaries and emoluments paid by the Bank to its personnel of whatsoever category shall be exempt from taxation.

Chapter VII

REQUIREMENTS FOR OBTAINING GUARANTEES OR LOANS

Article 34   It is hereby established that the members of the Bank shall not be entitled to obtain guarantees or loans from the said institution unless they have previously deposited the instruments of ratification of the following international agreements:

General Treaty on Central American Economic Integration, signed on the same date as the present Agreement;

Multilateral Treaty of Free Trade and Central American Economic Integration, signed on June 10, 1958;

Agreement on the System of Central American Integrated Industries, signed on June 10, 1958;

Central American Agreement on the Equalization of Import Charges, signed on September 1, 1959, and the *Protocol* signed on the same date as the present Agreement.

Chapter VIII

ACCESSION OF NEW MEMBERS

Article 35 Central American States not signatories to the present Agreement shall be entitled to adhere to it at any time.

Chapter IX

DISSOLUTION AND LIQUIDATION

Article 36 The Bank shall be dissolved:

a) By unanimous decision of the member States; or
b) When only one of the parties continues to uphold the present Agreement.

In the event of dissolution, the Board of Governors shall determine the conditions under which the Bank shall terminate its operations, liquidate its obligations, and distribute among the member States the surplus capital and reserves remaining after the discharge of the obligations in question.

Chapter X

GENERAL PROVISIONS

Article 37 The present Agreement shall be of unlimited duration and cannot be denounced earlier than twenty years from the date of its entry into force. Denunciation shall become effective five years after its presentation. The Agreement shall remain in force if at least two countries continue to uphold it.

Article 38 The present Agreement shall enter into force as from the date on which the third instrument of ratification is deposited with the General Secretariat of the Organization of Central American States. For Central American States adhering to it subsequently, it shall enter into force from the date of deposit of the pertinent instrument with the said Secretariat.

Article 39 In the event of a signatory State's separation from the Bank, the State shall continue to be responsible for its obligations to the Bank, whether direct or deriving from loans, credits, or guarantees obtained prior to the date on which the State ceases to be a member. However, it shall not be responsible in respect of loans, credits, or guarantees effected subsequent to its withdrawal.

The rights and obligations of the withdrawing State shall be determined in conformity with the Special Liquidation Balance Sheet which shall be drawn up for the purpose on the date on which the State's separation becomes effective.

Article 40   The Bank shall be empowered to make its facilities available for the organization and operation of a clearing house on behalf of the Central Banks if and when they so request.

Article 41   The General Secretariat of the Organization of, Central American States shall be the depository of the present Agreement and shall transmit certified copies thereof to the Ministry of Foreign Affairs of each of the Contracting States, which it shall immediately notify of the deposit of each of the instruments of ratification, as well as of any denunciation which may be presented. On the entry into force of the Agreement, it shall also transmit a certified copy thereof to the United Nations Secretariat for registration purposes in conformity with Article 102 of the United Nations Charter.

Article 42   The Bank constituted by virtue of the present Agreement is the institution referred to in resolution 84 and 101 of the Central American Economic Cooperation Committee, and, in founding it, Guatemala, El Salvador, and Honduras are complying with the provisions respecting the establishment of the Development and Assistance Fund laid down in the *Economic Association Treaty* and the *Protocol* concluded by them on June 8, 1960.

Provisional Article   The amounts advanced by the governments for the initial expenditure arising from the establishment of the Bank shall be deemed to constitute part of their capital contributions to the Bank.

Provisional Article   The first meeting of the Board of Governors of the Bank shall be convened by the Ministry of Foreign Affairs of the Republic of Honduras at the earliest opportunity and not later than sixty days from the date of entry into force of the present Agreement.

In witness whereof the respective plenipotentiaries sign the present Agreement in the city of Managua, capital of the Republic of Nicaragua, this thirteenth day of the month of December, nineteen hundred sixty.

For the Government of Guatemala:

> *Julio Prado García Salas*
> Minister for Coordinating Central
> American Integration
> *Alberto Fuentes Mohr*
> Head of the Economic Integration Bureau

For the Government of El Salvador:

> *Gabriel Piloña Araujo*
> Minister of Economy
> *Abelardo Torres*
> Under-Secretary for Economy

For the Government of Honduras:

> *Jorge Bueso Arias*
> Minister of Economy and Finance

For the Government of Nicaragua:

> *Juan José Lugo Marenco*
> Minister of Economy

AGREEMENT ESTABLISHING THE CENTRAL AMERICAN CLEARING HOUSE

(Signed at Tegucigalpa, Honduras, July 28, 1961)

The Central Bank of Costa Rica, the Central Reserve Bank of El Salvador, the Bank of Guatemala, the Central Bank of Honduras and the Central Bank of Nicaragua, by the present Agreement hereby establish the Central American Clearing House, in accordance with the following stipulations:

Chapter I

PURPOSE AND HEADQUARTERS

Article 1 The purpose of the Clearing House shall be to promote the use of Central American currencies among the countries of the Isthmus as a means of speeding up their economic integration. It shall have its headquarters at the main office of the Central American Bank for Economic Integration.

Chapter 2

WORKING CAPITAL

Article 2 Each central bank shall contribute an amount equivalent to THREE HUNDRED THOUSAND DOLLARS United States currency to comprise the working capital with which the Clearing House will operate.

This contribution shall be made as follows:

a) 25 percent in United States dollars; and
b) 75 percent in its own currency.

Article 3 The amount of the contribution payable in United States dollars shall serve to establish the Guaranty Fund, and the amount of the contributions payable in the currency of each country shall serve to establish the Current Operations Fund.

Article 4 The first three banks that ratify this Agreement shall make their contribution within eight days following the first meeting of the Board of Directors of the Clearing House referred to in the transitory article of this Agreement. The remaining banks shall do so within thirty days following the respective ratification.

Article 5 The contribution in the national currency of each country shall be operated by the Clearing House as a bookkeeping unit to be known as the "Central American Peso" ($C.A.), equivalent to $1.00 US currency and at the rate of exchange which each central bank declares as of the date this Agreement is ratified.

Article 6 Any change or changes that may be made in the declared rate of exchange referred to in the preceding article must be reported immediately by the respective central bank to the Clearing House and to the other member banks.

Article 7 If a country changes its rate of exchange, the respective central bank must readjust its balances in local currency in order to maintain invariable the working capital of the Clearing House.

Article 8 The central banks guarantee the convertibility into United States dollars of their balances registered in the Clearing House in excess of the contribution in their own currencies, at the latest declared rate of exchange.

Chapter 3

AGENCIES

Article 9 The Clearing House shall have as agents the member central bank in each of the respective countries for the purpose of clearing the documents which cover intra-Central American transactions and to handle all other matters relating to the functioning of the Clearing House.

Chapter 4

OPERATIONS

Article 10 The Clearing House shall operate the Guaranty Fund account in Central American Pesos as follows:

a) Debits
   1) Initial contribution in dollars;
   2) Replacement in United States dollars of the debtor banks by transfers to creditor banks;
   3) Semiannual settlement in United States dollars of debtor balances;
   4) Interest derived from investments;
   5) Other debit operations.

b) Credits
   1) Transfers in dollars at the request of creditor banks;
   2) Semiannual settlement in United States dollars of creditor balances;
   3) Distribution of interest derived from investments;
   4) Cancellation by withdrawal;
   5) Other credit operations.

The Clearing House shall carry an account for each member bank, in the Guaranty Fund.

Article 11 The Clearing House shall operate the accounts making up the Current Operations Fund, in Central American Pesos, with notices received from the central banks, as follows:

a) Debits
   1) Initial contribution in local currency;
   2) Remittances that a Bank receives, in its own currency, from the other member banks;
   3) Interest on debtor balances;
   4) Allotments for administrative expenses;
   5) Receipts from semiannual settlement of balances;
   6) Readjustments of contributions in local currencies;
   7) Other debit operations.

b) Credits
   1) Remittances that a member makes in currencies of other countries;
   2) Interest on creditor balances;
   3) Repayment of allotments for administrative expenses;
   4) Expenditures for annual settlement of balances;
   5) Readjustment of contributions in local currencies;
   6) Cancellation by withdrawal;
   7) Other credit operations.

The Clearing House shall keep separate accounts for each bank.

Article 12 The Clearing House shall make payments in United States dollars chargeable to the Guaranty Fund at the request of any bank whose contribution in national currency has become exhausted and to which credits have been granted in excess of the established limit. The maximum payment in United States dollars shall be the equivalent of the amount of the excess.

Article 13   In order to regularize the Guaranty Fund in respect of the payments in United States dollars to which the preceding article refers, the Clearing House shall immediately demand of debtor banks proportional reimbursement in the same currency and they must make such reimbursement not later than eight days after receiving notice of the demand.

Article 14   The Clearing House shall charge or pay interest at the close of each fiscal period, at a uniform rate for all member banks, on the daily differences in excess of or below the contribution in local currency, as the case may be. This rate shall be equal to the average interest rate earned by investments of the Guaranty Fund.

Article 15   In computing the interest referred to in the foregoing article, no account shall be taken of changes in position of the banks in the Clearing House which were incurred by changes in exchange rates as indicated in Article 6 of this Agreement or by the repayment of funds by receiving banks.

Article 16   Debtor central banks shall make payments in United States dollars of amounts charged to them as shown in the semiannual settlement statements submitted by the Clearing House; such payments shall be made not later than eight days after the statement has been received. Amounts received by the Clearing House under this heading shall be transferred to the creditor banks in order to reestablish their initial position.

Article 17   For purposes of payment, the banks shall consider as correct the settlement statement referred to in the preceding article. In the event of disagreement, the banks shall have a period of fifteen days in which to submit a claim, counted from the date on which the statement was received.

Article 18   The Clearing House shall maintain its available funds in dollars, invested in first-class and immediately negotiable securities, in accordance with the investment policy decided upon by the Board of Directors.

Chapter 5

ORGANIZATION AND FUNCTIONING

Article 19   The Clearing House shall have a Board of Directors composed of one representative from each member bank and one representative of the Central American Bank for Economic Integration.

Article 20   The Board of Directors shall elect a Chairman from among the representatives of the central banks, in rotation. The Chairman shall hold office until the subsequent regular meeting.

Article 21   The Board of Directors shall meet if three of the representatives are present regularly once a year and extraordinarily whenever convoked by the Chairman on his own initiative or at the request of a majority of the members. The Chairman shall make known to the member banks the purpose of an extraordinary meeting at least fifteen days in advance.

Article 22   Decisions of the Board of Directors shall be adopted by majority vote. Each Director shall have one vote and in case of a tie the Chairman shall decide. The Director representing the Central American Bank for Economic Integration shall participate in discussions of the Board of Directors with the right to speak but not to vote.

Article 23   The powers and duties of the Board of Directors are as follows:

a) To interpret the provisions of this Agreement;
b) To issue regulations to govern the activities of the Clearing House;
c) To authorize the annual budget of receipts and expenditures of the Clearing House;
d) To determine the investment policy;
e) To approve the financial statements and reports on the work of the Clearing House submitted by the Central American Bank for Economic Integration;
f) To appoint each year an auditing committee to examine the operations of the Clearing House;
g) Others within its competence not included in the foregoing items.

Article 24   The powers and duties of the Chairman are:

a) To convoke the regular and extraordinary meetings of the Board of Directors and preside over meetings; and
b) Any others assigned to him by the Board of Directors.

Article 25   Operation of the Clearing House shall be entrusted to the Central American Bank for Economic Integration, pursuant to Article 40 of the Agreement establishing the Bank and the Agreement concluded between the Board of Directors of the Clearing House and the Bank indicated.

Article 26   The expenses of administration of the Clearing House shall be borne by the member central banks in the manner determined by the Board of Directors of the Clearing House, after submission of the annual budget adopted by the Board.

Chapter 6

WITHDRAWAL AND DISSOLUTION

Article 27 If a central bank decides to withdraw from the Clearing House it must give notice thereof to the Clearing House and to the other member banks thirty days in advance and shall make immediate payment in dollars of the balance charged to it shown by the settlement statement submitted by the Clearing House on the date of withdrawal.

In the event that there is a balance in favor of the withdrawing bank, the Clearing House shall pay such balance in dollars within thirty days following the withdrawal, according to the statement of settlement.

Article 28 The Clearing House shall be dissolved:

a) By unanimous decision of the member central bank; or
b) If only two of them remain adhered to this Agreement.

In the event of dissolution the Board of Directors shall determine the conditions by which the Clearing House shall liquidate its operations.

Chapter 7

GENERAL PROVISIONS

Article 29 The central banks of the countries which have exchange restrictions shall adopt measures in accord with their control to facilitate the functioning of the Clearing House. Such measures shall be made known immediately to the Clearing House and to the other banks, which shall be obligated to take direct action in accord with their better effectiveness and to cooperate in seeing that the measures are enforced in their respective countries.

Article 30 Each central bank may include in its international monetary reserves its net position with the Clearing House.

Article 31 The central banks agree to encourage a greater use of the Central American currencies.

Article 32 Each central bank undertakes to submit to the Clearing House all available information relating to the misuse of checks and moneys.

The Clearing House should immediately transmit such information to the other central banks.

Article 33 The Clearing House shall study and work for the unification of legislation relating to documents and funds subject to clearance.

Article 34 This Agreement shall come into force immediately following the last ratification of three central banks, communicated to the President of the Central American Bank for Economic Integration.

Transitory Article

1. This Agreement shall not affect the force of Agreements already signed by two or more banks that are members of the Clearing House.

2. The first meeting of the Board of Directors shall be convoked by the President of the Central Bank for Economic Integration as soon as possible and within a period not to exceed thirty days from the date this Agreement comes into force. The Clearing House shall begin its operations not later than sixty days after this Agreement comes into force.

Due note is hereby made that the representatives of the Central Banks of Costa Rica, El Salvador, and Nicaragua sign this Agreement *ad referendum.*

Tegucigalpa, Honduras, July 28, 1961

CENTRAL BANK OF COSTA RICA
BANK OF GUATEMALA
CENTRAL RESERVE BANK OF EL SALVADOR
CENTRAL BANK OF HONDURAS
CENTRAL BANK OF NICARAGUA

NOTES ON AGREEMENTS AMENDING THE ORIGINAL ORGANIZATION OF THE CENTRAL AMERICAN CLEARING HOUSE

The Central American Clearing House was established in July 1961, by the Central Banks of Guatemala, El Salvador, Honduras, Nicaragua, and Costa Rica and has been subject to significant changes since its establishment, through agreements made by its Board of Directors composed of delegates of the abovementioned banks.

Its operations have shown considerable growth during the years 1962, 1963 and 1964. At the present time eighty percent of the payments resulting from intra-Central American trade are channeled through the Clearing House. February 25, 1964 saw the culmination of the efforts to link the central banks of the Isthmus, on a technical as well as an executive level, when these banks, through their Boards of Directors, signed the Agreement for the Establishment of the Central American Monetary Union. This agreement permits the functioning of a system of executive and advisory organs, including the Central American Clearing House itself, for the purpose of gradually and progressively bringing about a Monetary Union in Central America.

New Activities and Change in Organization   For practical reasons, at the end of 1962 the central banks, as members of the Clearing House, decided to make additions and changes in the Agreement, among those of importance being the programming of new activities and a change in organization. These changes took effect on January 16, 1963. The Clearing House operates by means of the following organization: (a) the Committee on Exchange and Clearing Policy, created by the Agreement for the Establishment of the Central American Monetary Union, which is entrusted with carrying out the present Agreement; (b) the coordination, execution, and supervision of the activities of the Clearing House are entrusted to the Executive Secretary. There is also a Chief of Clearing House, who is in charge of recording its operations. The Committee is to appoint an Auditing Committee each year, which will periodically review the operations of the Clearing House. The Central Bank of Honduras acts as the legal representative of the Clearing House.

Abolishment of the Guaranty Fund and the Working Capital   In order to make the clearing system more workable and expeditious, the Board of Directors of the Clearing House, in August 1963, proposed substantial changes in the original agreement, the most important of which is the abolishment of the Guaranty Fund and the Working Capital, replacing the latter by the establishment in each member bank of a line of credit equivalent to US $500,000 as a minimum. These changes came into force on January 1, 1964, thus virtually bringing about a new agreement. In addition, certain activities subject to determination by joint policies in the monetary field were discontinued; these activities are included in the Agreement for the Establishment of a Central American Monetary Union, as powers of its action and advisory committees.

Uniformity of Exchange Restrictions   In December 1961, the Central Banks of El Salvador, Guatemala, and Honduras signed a supplementary accord to the Clearing House Agreement, to facilitate the operating rules in respect of the Savaldorian colón, in view of the exchange restrictions adopted by El Salvador, all based on Article 29 of the original agreement. In June 1963 the central banks signed a new agreement which kept transactions in quetzales and Salvadorian colones subject to exchange restrictions. Since that time this uniform system has functioned for all the member banks, and central banks, in countries where exchange control exists, may operate through the clearing system without any difficulty.

Creation of the Central American Check In June 1962, an agreement was signed by the Central American banks establishing an interbank check to be known as the "Central American Check". However, due to practical problems of application, the Central American Monetary Council, in July 1964, voted to suspend the part referring to the "Central American Check" and recommended that the banks in the Clearing House apply the name of Central American Check to cashier's checks (*de caja* or *de gerencia*).

Purpose, Seat, and Denominations This agreement established a multilateral machinery for clearance and reciprocal credits among the Central American banks, the purposes of which are to facilitate payments and encourage the use of the currencies of the region in Central American transactions. The agreement further provided that the Central American Clearing House shall have its main office in the Central Bank of Honduras. That bank will have charge of all matters connected with the collection, handling, and liquidation of Clearing House funds. In addition it shall see that operations are carried out in conformity with the agreement, with pertinent regulations, and with resolutions of the Council and of the Committee. It may also sign documents and contracts relating to this agreement, as proposed to it by the Council or the Executive Secretary, and it shall perform any other functions entrusted to it by the Council, within the limits of the agreement.

Bookkeeping Unit, Parity, and Guaranties All operations of the Clearing House shall be stated in a bookkeeping unit termed the Central American Peso ($C.A.), equivalent to $1.00 U.S. currency, at the parity which each bank declares and guarantees for its respective currency.

Credits and Operations Each bank shall extend a credit in its own currency to the other banks, up to the equivalent of five hundred thousand United States dollars ($500,000), which may be increased on the initiative of each bank or at the proposal of the Central American Monetary Council.

AGREEMENT ON THE ESTABLISHMENT OF A CENTRAL AMERICAN MONETARY UNION

(Signed at San Salvador, El Salvador, February 25, 1964)

The Central Bank of Costa Rica, the Central Reserve Bank of El Salvador, the Bank of Guatemala, the Central Bank of Honduras, and the Central Bank of Nicaragua,

CONSIDERING:

First:

That the General Treaty of Central American Economic Integration, in Article X commends to the Central Banks of the Member States, the cooperation necessary "to prevent currency speculations which might affect the exchange rates and so as to maintain the convertibility of the currencies of the respective countries on a basis which, under normal conditions, guarantees freedom, uniformity, and stability of exchange";

Second:

That the Central American Economic Council, at its Second Extraordinary Meeting on August 16, 1962, agreed "To declare that it is of interest to the Program of Central American Economic Integration to establish the means and machinery which will ensure the continuous and permanent coordination of the monetary and exchange policies of the Member States, including the expansion and improvement of the present system of multilateral clearance of payments" and "To request the Central Banks of the Member States to make an early study of the machinery referred to in the preceding point and to submit to the Executive Council of the General Treaty concrete projects as to what agreements it may be necessary to sign in order to fully accomplish the indicated objectives";

Third:

That the Presidents of the Central American States, meeting in San José, Costa Rica on March 19, 1963, agreed in the name of their peoples "to establish a monetary union and a common policy in fiscal, economic, and social matters under the Program of Economic Integration"; and

Fourth:

That the agreements and statements of the Central American governments, to which reference has been made, and the progress achieved under the Program of Central American Economic Integration within the machinery of cooperation established by the central banks, as well as the monetary conditions prevailing in the countries of the region, point to the need and the opportunity for adopting measures designed to accomplish the monetary integration of Central America by stages,

Undertake to conclude and formalize the following

AGREEMENT FOR THE ESTABLISHMENT OF THE
CENTRAL AMERICAN MONETARY UNION

Article I The purpose of the present Agreement is to promote the coordination and harmonization of the monetary, exchange, and credit policies of the Central American countries, and to create progressively the bases for a Central American Monetary Union.

To this end, the Central American central banks have set the following goals:

1) To promote a uniformity in the exchange systems, as well as stability and convertibility of the Central American currencies;
2) To broaden the Central American system of multilateral clearing and encourage the use of national currencies in transactions between Central American countries;
3) To promote financial assistance, with the aim of correcting temporary maladjustments in the balance of payments and preventing adverse trends in the exchange systems of the Central American countries;
4) To obtain a high degree of uniformity in legislation and in the monetary, exchange, and credit structures and conditions in the Central American countries;
5) To create conditions which will encourage coordination of monetary policy and fiscal policy; and
6) To establish a permanent system of information and consultation, with the aim of harmonizing the course of action and the instruments relating to monetary, exchange, and credit policy.

Article II The goals of monetary integration fixed by this Agreement are to be achieved gradually and progressively, through the following courses of action:

1) Exchange of information, undertaking of specific research, and regular concerted mutual consultation in the monetary, exchange, and credit fields;
2) Technical research in matters relating to legislation, institutional structure, conditions for development, and the nature of instruments to govern the monetary, exchange, and credit policy of the Central American countries;
3) Consultation on a high executive and technical level, on a voluntary and strictly confidential basis, concerning the domestic and foreign policy of the Central American Central Banks;
4) Specific machinery designed to provide adequate financial assistance to prevent unfavorable trends in the exchange systems, to soften the effects of temporary malajustments in the balance of payments, and to promote a free movement of capital in Central America; and

5) Consultation and studies seeking to obtain favorable conditions for coordinating monetary policy with fiscal policy.

On the basis of the progress that may be attained, the proper time will be determined for formulating and proposing the agreements that may be required to create adequate machinery for finally achieving the organization and functioning of the Central American Monetary Union.

Article III   The execution of this Agreement shall be entrusted to the System of Central American Central Banks, under the following organs:

1) The Central American Monetary Council;
2) The advisory or working committees; and
3) The Executive Secretariat.

Article IV   The Central American Monetary Council shall consist of the presidents of the Central Banks of El Salvador, Guatemala, Honduras, and Nicaragua, and the manager of the Central Bank of Costa Rica, as proprietary members.

Each central bank shall appoint a permanent alternate member of the Council from among their high-ranking executive officers.

Article V   The Central American Monetary Council shall have the following powers and duties:

1) To hold periodic consultations concerning the general aspects of the monetary, exchange, and credit policies of the Central American countries and to agree upon or recommend appropriate measures for their coordination and harmonization;
2) To maintain the necessary relationships and hold consultations with the governmental authorities of the Central American countries, for the purpose of coordinating and harmonizing monetary policy and fiscal policy;
3) To determine the scope and the procedures to be carried out to accomplish the program outlined in this present Agreement;
4) To agree on measures for expanding and improving the Central American system of multilateral clearing;
5) To set up the advisory or working committees that are considered necessary for carrying out the duties relating to the accomplishment of the program outlined in this Agreement. The Council itself shall determine the powers and duties of these committees;
6) To appoint the Executive Secretary;
7) To approve the regulations for the committees and for the Executive Secretariat;
8) To approve the budget of the organs of the System of Central American Central Banks;

9) To propose draft agreements that it may be necessary to conclude on the governmental level in order to achieve the Central American Monetary Union;

10) To interpret the terms of the present Agreement; and

11) Any others that may be necessary for carrying out the purposes of this Agreement.

Article VI The Council shall elect a president from among its members, annually in rotation.

Meetings of the Council shall be governed by the following rules:

1) One regular meeting shall be held each year, and special meetings whenever called by the Council or the President, or whenever requested by one of its members.

2) Resolutions of the Council shall be adopted by a majority vote of all the members, with the understanding that an adopted resolution is binding only on the central banks whose representatives signed it or subsequently adhered to it.

3) The Executive Secretary shall take part in the discussions of the Council, with the right to speak but not to vote. The alternate members of the Council may also participate in that way.

Article VII The following committees, at the least, shall be named:

1) Committee on Monetary Policy;

2) Committee on Exchange Policy and Clearings;

3) Committee on Financial Operations; and

4) Committee on Legal Studies.

The Council shall install the committees that have been created or that may be created in the future, as circumstances require.

Article VIII Each of the Central American central banks shall take part in every committee, for which purpose one proprietary and one alternate representative are to be appointed.

Article IX The Executive Secretariat is to be in charge of a Secretary, who shall be a Central American official, elected by the Monetary Council for a term of two years, with the right to reelection. He must be a person of recognized professional competence in matters of central banking and international finance.

The Executive Secretary shall be exclusively responsible to the Central American Monetary Council.

Article X The Executive Secretariat shall be entrusted with the preparation of the technical studies that may be desirable and the co-ordination of the activities of the different committees. In addition, it shall provide secretariat services at the conferences and meetings of the System of the Central Banks. It shall be subject to this Agreement, to the regulations and to the resolutions adopted by the Central American Monetary Council.

The Executive Secretary shall have a rotating headquarters, for periods of two years, among the Central American central banks, in the manner determined by the Monetary Council.

Article XI The officials and employees of the Executive Secretariat must be nationals of one of the Central American countries.

Article XII The funds to defray the expenses incurred by the organs of the System shall be contributed in the manner determined by the Central American Monetary Council.

Article XIII The organs of the System, through the Executive Secretary, shall maintain and develop a close collaboration and coordination of activities with other agencies and bodies in the Program of Central American Economic Integration.

Article XIV This Agreement shall be of indefinite duration. It may be amended by unanimous decision of the Central American central banks.

Article XV This Agreement shall be subject to ratification by the Central American central banks. The ratification of each one shall be communicated to the Permanent Secretariat of the General Treaty of Central American Economic Integration and at the same time to the other central banks.

Article XVI This Agreement shall come into force eight days after the date of notification of the third ratification. It shall take effect only for those central banks that have ratified it.

Article XVII The Committee on Exchange Policy and Clearing referred to in Article VII shall have the status of an advisory body on the subject of exchange policy and, when this Agreement has been ratified by the five Central American central banks, it shall also be responsible for carrying out the Agreement on the Central American Clearing House, as well as any other agreements on clearing or credits concluded with countries outside Central America.

Article XVIII The Central American Monetary Council shall hold its first meeting within sixty days from the date that this Agreement comes into force. It shall be convoked by the Central Reserve Bank of El Salvador, in consultation with the other central banks.

At that meeting appropriate steps shall be taken to organize and install the different organs of the System.

IN WITNESS WHEREOF, the representatives of the Central American central banks hereby sign this instrument in five copies of the same text, in the city of San Salvador, Republic of El Salvador, on February 25, 1964.

For Costa Rica

Carlos M. Escalante
President of the Board of Directors
of the Central Bank of Costa Rica

Alvaro Castro Jenkins
Manager of the Central Bank of Costa Rica

For El Salvador

Francisco Aquino Jr.
President of the Central Reserve Bank of El Salvador

For Guatemala

Gustavo Herrera Orellana
President ad int. Bank of Guatemala

Francisco Fernández Rivas
Manager, Bank of Guatemala

For Honduras

Roberto Ramírez
President, Central Bank of Honduras

For Nicaragua

Francisco J. Laínez
President, Central Bank of Nicaragua

AGREEMENT ON CLEARANCE AND RECIPROCAL CREDITS BETWEEN THE CENTRAL BANKS MEMBERS OF THE CENTRAL AMERICAN CLEARING HOUSE AND THE BANK OF MEXICO

(Signed at Mexico City, Mexico, August 27, 1963)

The Central Bank of Costa Rica, the Central Reserve Bank of El Salvador, the Bank of Guatemala, the Central Bank of Honduras, and the Central Bank of Nicaragua, comprising the Central American Clearing House, and the Bank of Mexico,

CONCLUDE the following Agreement:

Chapter I

PURPOSE

Article 1   The present Agreement is for the purpose of establishing a system of clearance and reciprocal credits between the central banks, members of the Central American Clearing House, and the Bank of Mexico, and to promote the use of national currencies in monetary and banking transactions between the Central American countries and Mexico.

Chapter II

ITEMS FOR CLEARANCE

Article 2   The items that may be cleared pursuant to this Agreement are: banknotes, checks in general subject to final collection, settlements derived from documentary credits, orders for payment, and circular letters of credit, stated in the currencies of the countries of the signatory Central Banks.

Chapter III

CLEARANCE SYSTEM AND ESTABLISHMENT OF RECIPROCAL CREDITS

Article 3   To accomplish the stated purpose of this Agreement, the Central American central banks and the Bank of Mexico undertake to receive for clearance, from their banking systems, the items indicated in Article 2 and stated in the currency of the signatory central banks.

Article 4   The Bank of Mexico shall grant to the signatory Central American central banks, a credit without interest, for ordinary clearance settlements up to THREE MILLION DOLLARS and for extraordinary clearance settlements up to TWO MILLION DOLLARS.

This credit for ordinary and extraordinary clearance settlements shall be distributed by the Bank of Mexico among the indicated central banks in the equitable proportion agreed upon by these banks, which is to be specified every three months by the Central Bank of Honduras, as administrator of the Central American Clearing House. Likewise, each of the signatory Central American central banks shall grant a reciprocal credit for ordinary and extraordinary clearance settlements, without interest, to the Bank of Mexico, for the same amount as was proportionally granted to them by the latter institution.

Article 5   Each of the signatory Central American central banks shall open in its books, in its own currency, an account designated as "Bank of Mexico–Mexican–Central American Clearance Agreement" in which shall be recorded operations that can be cleared with the Mexican banking system. Likewise, the Bank of Mexico shall open in its books an account for each of the signatory Central American central banks in its own currency, designated as "Central Bank of . . .

—Mexican–Central American Clearance Agreement" which shall record operations for clearance performed with the banking system of the central bank to which the account pertains.

Article 6   The Central American Clearing House shall act as Agent of this System of Clearance and Reciprocal Credit.

In its capacity as Agent it shall keep an accounting ledger which will show all operations performed and the status of the accounts of each of the signatory central banks. The ledger accounts kept by the Clearing House will show the position of each Central American bank with the Bank of Mexico.

Article 7   All clearing operations shall be recorded on the basis of the declared parity of each national currency with respect to the United States dollar. This declaration shall be communicated to the signatory central banks among themselves and to the Central American Clearing House on the date of ratification of this Agreement. The Clearing House, in turn, shall immediately inform the other signatory central banks of the parity that each central bank has declared.

Article 8   Any change in the parity fixed in accordance with the preceding article must be reported immediately by the respective central bank to the other signatory central banks and to the Central American Clearing House. The change shall become effective at the close of operations on the business day on which the notification is received and the corresponding central bank and the Central American Clearing House shall readjust the balances in national currency, as of that date, for accounts relating to this Agreement, in order that these balances shall be maintained invariable in terms of United States dollars.

The banks must immediately notify the signatory parties and the Central American Clearing House of existing balances to which the preceding paragraph refers.

Article 9   Each signatory central bank guarantees to the other central banks the convertibility of the balances represented by clearance items in cash and remittances in transit, at the latest parity declared in accordance with this Agreement. Whenever the declared parity is changed, the previous parity will be recognized for balances derived from clearance items in cash and remittances in transit in the hands of the banking systems of the other signatory central banks, at the close of operations on the business day on which the change becomes known.

Article 10   The signatory central banks shall negotiate documents and clearance items among themselves, at the same time transmitting a copy of the remittance notice to the Central American Clearing House.

Article 11   The Clearing House shall transact the clearing accounts on the basis of the confirmation notices of remittances received from the signatory banks. The Administrative Committee of the Clearing House shall determine the period within which confirmation notices must be sent. After this period has expired the Clearing House shall act on its own.

Article 12   The Central American Clearing House shall keep all clearing accounts in its own accounting unit, termed the "Central American Peso" ($C.A.) equivalent to one dollar in United States currency, using, for conversion for currencies to be cleared, the parities declared or changed by the central banks pursuant to Article 8.

Article 13   Whenever a Central American central bank exceeds the share granted by the Bank of Mexico for ordinary settlement of credits, it may avail itself of its share for extraordinary settlements in clearing operations.

The Bank of Mexico may demand from such Central American bank, through the Clearing House, a payment in United States dollars or other convertible currency acceptable to it, the share of the credit for extraordinary settlement. This payment must be effected within a maximum period of thirty days, counting from the date on which the excess began.

Moreover, whenever the Bank of Mexico exceeds the share for ordinary settlement of credit that was granted to it by any Central American central bank, it may avail itself of the share granted to it for extraordinary settlements, for clearing operations. The Central American central bank, in turn, may demand from the Bank of Mexico, through the Clearing House, payment in United States dollars or other convertible currencies acceptable to the creditor Central American bank, of the amount due for extraordinary credit settlement. This payment must be effected within a maximum period of thirty days, counting from the date on which the excess began.

Article 14   Whenever a Central American central bank exceeds its total credit for ordinary and extraordinary clearance settlements granted to it by the Bank of Mexico, the latter may demand payment immediately, through the Central American Clearing House, in United States dollars or other convertible currencies acceptable to it, of the amount in excess of the total credit granted. The same right pertains to the Central American central banks whenever the Bank of Mexico exceeds the total credit for ordinary and extraordinary settlements granted by any of the said banks. The Clearing House shall calculate the amount to be paid and notify both debtor and creditor central banks, within a period of five days.

Article 15   Payments that creditor central banks demand from debtor central banks for credits granted in excess of the share for ordinary settlements or for ordinary and extraordinary settlements, must be made not later than eight days after receipt of the demand notice sent by the Clearing House. Debtor central banks shall make payments directly to creditor central banks, at the same time giving notice thereof to the Clearing House.

Chapter IV

ORDINARY SETTLEMENTS

Article 16   The Central American Clearing House shall make ordinary settlements of all clearing accounts resulting from operations covered by this Agreement, on June 15 and December 15 of each year.

Article 17   For purposes of payments resulting from ordinary settlements, the signatory central banks shall use as a basis the settlement submitted by the Clearing House.

Article 18   Debtor central banks shall submit their objections or make payment in United States dollars, or other convertible currencies acceptable to the creditor central bank, of the amount charged to them as a result of an ordinary settlement, not later than eight days after receiving the statement of the respective settlement. Payments shall be made directly to the creditor central banks, at the same time giving notice thereof to the Clearing House.

Article 19   In the event of disagreement with the statement of ordinary settlement submitted by the Clearing House, the central banks shall have a period of fifteen days, without extension, following receipt of the statement, to come to an agreement on the items objected to. Upon expiration of that period, the banks must pay, within the next eight days, without prejudice to rights pertaining to them as interested banks.

Chapter V

ADMINISTRATION

Article 20   Administration of this present Agreement shall be entrusted to an Administrative Committee, composed of the Board of Directors of the Central American Clearing House and a representative of the Bank of Mexico.

Article 21   The Committee shall elect a Chairman in rotation who shall serve for one year.

Article 22   The Committee shall meet with a representative of the

Bank of Mexico and at least three members of the Board of Directors of the Clearing House, regularly every six months within thirty days after the date of an ordinary clearance settlement, and in special session when convoked by the Chairman of the Committee at the request of any member.

The Chairman shall make known the purpose of a special meeting at least fifteen days in advance.

Article 23   To take effect, resolutions of the Administrative Committee must be ratified by all the signatory central banks.

Article 24   The Central American Clearing House shall be the Permanent Secretariat of the Administrative Committee. The Manager of the Clearing House shall participate in the discussions of the Committee, with voice but without vote.

Article 25   The powers of the Administrative Committee shall be:

a) To interpret the terms of this Agreement;
b) To issue administrative and operational regulations which will facilitate their execution;
c) To approve the financial statements and reports on activities that are to be submitted to it at least every six months by the Central American Clearing House; and
d) Any others that are compatible with the proper administration of this Agreement.

Article 26   Administrative expenses incurred from the operation of this Agreement shall be divided in equal parts among the signatory banks.

Chapter VI

GENERAL PROVISIONS

Article 27   The signatory central banks may invest, according to their judgment and their respective laws, in securities issued in the countries of the said banks, for the purpose of offsetting the movements of funds originating from operations covered by this Agreement.

Article 28   Each signatory central bank undertakes to provide the Clearing House and the other signatory central banks, as soon as possible and with necessary specifications, all information in its possessions relating to improper use of items for clearance in the respective countries.

Article 29   The auditing of the operations resulting from this Agreement shall be entrusted to the Committee of Auditors appointed annually by the Central American Clearing House. The Bank of Mexico may audit the same operations through its auditors.

Chapter VII

WITHDRAWAL AND DISSOLUTION

Article 30   Any signatory bank that decides to denounce the present Agreement must notify the other central banks and the Central American Clearing House. The denunciation shall take effect thirty days from the date on which such notification is received. The Clearing House will undertake an extraordinary settlement to determine the debtor or creditor position of the denouncing bank. The corresponding payment shall be made in accordance with the provisions of Articles 18 and 19 of this Agreement.

Article 31   This Agreement shall cease to be in effect by a unanimous decision of the signatory central banks, by decision of the Bank of Mexico, or when less than three central banks that are members of the Central American Clearing House remain parties thereto.

Article 32   The final liquidation shall be effected by the Central American Clearing House, along lines indicated by the Administrative Committee on the basis of the provisions of Articles 18, 19, and 30 of this Agreement. If within a period of thirty days no acceptable agreement is reached among the parties, the liquidation will be undertaken at the level of the presidents, directors, or managers of the central banks.

Chapter VIII

RATIFICATION AND VALIDITY

Article 33   This Agreement shall come into force when it has been ratified by the Bank of Mexico and by at least three of the central banks that are members of the Central American Clearing House.

Article 34   Each signatory central bank must notify the Central American Clearing House of the ratification of this Agreement, and the Clearing House shall in turn notify the other central banks as soon as possible, indicating also the date that operations are to commence.

SPECIAL PROVISIONS

Article 35   Each central bank shall notify the other signatory banks and the Clearing House of any restrictions and requirements for validity to which the clearance items mentioned in Article 2 of this Agreement are subject, which originate from its respective banking system.

IN WITNESS WHEREOF the present Agreement is signed by the representatives of the Central Bank of Costa Rica, of the Central Reserve Bank of El Salvador, of the Bank of Guatemala, of the Central Bank of Honduras, of the Central Bank of Nicaragua, and of the Bank of Mexico, in Mexico City, D.F., on August 27, 1963.

(Signed for the six banks, the Central Bank of Honduras signing also as administrator of the Central American Clearing House).

Other Instruments

REGULATIONS OF THE EXECUTIVE COUNCIL OF THE GENERAL TREATY OF CENTRAL AMERICAN ECONOMIC INTEGRATION

Permanent Secretariat of the General Treaty of Central American Economic Integration

(Approved by the Executive Council at its First Meeting, July 9–12, 1962, held in Guatemala City. Approval by the Economic Council is pending.)

Chapter I

ORGANIZATION

Article 1 The Executive Council created by Article XXI of the General Treaty of Central American Economic Integration is a permanent organization.

Article 2 The Executive Council is composed of one proprietary Representative and one alternate for each of the member countries of that treaty.

The proprietary Representatives and their alternates shall be appointed by the governments of the respective States and shall perform their functions permanently as long as they are not replaced.

In the absence of a proprietary Representative, his place shall be filled by the respective alternate. If there is no alternate, a special appointment shall be required of the interested State, in order that it may be represented on the Council.

Article 3 The Representatives on the Executive Council may be accompanied at meetings by such special consultants and advisers as deemed desirable, such persons having the right to speak but not to vote.

Article 4 The special consultants and advisers of the Representatives on the Executive Council must be accredited to each meeting by

175

an appointment issued by their government or by a written notification from the Representative to the Secretary General.

Chapter II

POWERS AND DUTIES

Article 5   In order to ensure the proper application and administration of the General Treaty of Central American Economic Integration, the Executive Council shall have the following powers and duties:

a) To adopt such measures as are necessary to achieve the fulfillment of the undertakings set forth in the General Treaty and all other agreements on economic integration signed by or that may be signed by the member states of the Treaty;

b) To carry out the commitments called for by the Central American Trade Commission under the Multilateral Treaty of Free Trade and Central American Economic Integration and under the Central American Agreement on the Equalization of Import Charges; the commitments to the Central American Commission on Industrial Integration under the Agreement on the System of Central American Integrated Industries; and those of the Joint Commissions under the bilateral treaties in force between the contracting parties;[1]

c) To carry out all action and work, consistent with the treaties, that are designed to put into practice the economic union of Central America, and to propose to the governments the conclusion of multilateral treaties that may be required additionally in order to achieve the aims of the economic integration of the region, including a Customs Union;

d) To study and to approve, when feasible, at the request of any of the member states of the General Treaty, or at the initiative of the Permanent Secretariat, administrative procedures that will tend to facilitate free trade among the parties;

e) To determine whether export subsidies or unfair practices exist in Central American trade, in accordance with provisions of the General Treaty and other agreements on economic integration;

f) To study, in collaboration with the central banks of the member states, problems of payments that may arise and to recommend solutions in conformity with the maintenance of free trade, as provided in Article X of the General Treaty;

g) To study and rule upon, in accordance with Article IX of the General Treaty, the granting of customs exemptions on imports

---

[1] The pertinent provisions of the abovementioned instruments, in which these commitments are established, appear as an Appendix to these Regulations.

that are authorized by the governments of the member states, as well as imports made by the governments that are not for their own use or for the agencies;

h) To coordinate the application of the fiscal incentives to industrial development in the member states of the General Treaty;

i) To establish the procedures to be followed to determine the origin of goods covered by the General Treaty and to verify such origin when necessary, until such time as the member states form the Customs Union to which Article I of the Treaty refers;

j) To answer requests for advice made by the contracting parties prior to the conclusion of new treaties that may affect free trade among them, in accordance with Article XXVIII of the General Treaty;

k) To settle, in accordance with Article XXV of the General Treaty, questions raised by the governments concerning the conclusion of agreements to regulate their commercial relations with third countries or groups of countries;

l) To assign to the Permanent Secretariat such studies and tasks as are deemed necessary;

m) To settle any other problems that may arise concerning the interpretation and the application of the provisions of the General Treaty on Central American Economic Integration and of the other agreements on economic integration signed by the contracting parties.

Article 6 The Executive Council may delegate functions to the Permanent Secretariat, as provided for in Article XXIV of the General Treaty.

Article 7 In solving the problems that may arise concerning the interpretation and application of the General Treaty and other integration agreements concluded or that may be concluded, the following procedure is to be followed:

a) The problem may be dealt with directly between the countries concerned, if so agreed, in which case a technical opinion from the permanent Secretariat may be requested, to be issued within thirty days following the date of the request.

   If no satisfactory result is attained, or if direct action was not taken, the Permanent Secretariat, at the request of an interested party, shall submit the problem to the Executive Council, with a report containing the pertinent technical opinion and the background features of the matter, for its decision;

b) If the Executive Council is unable to reach a decision, the matter shall be submitted to the Central American Economic Council for final decision, for which the Permanent Secretariat must transmit all material on the case;

c) If no decision is reached because of lack of agreement within the Economic Council, the parties may resort to arbitration in accordance with the procedure outlined in Article XXVI of the General Treaty.

Chapter III

MEETINGS

Article 8   The Executive Council shall meet at the request of any of the member states of the General Treaty, at the initiative of the Secretariat, or whenever the Council itself considers it desirable. In all cases the convocation shall be transmitted through the Secretariat. When a meeting is about to end, the Council shall fix the date and place of the next meeting, in agreement with the Secretariat. The decision on this matter, however, may be changed after consultation among the Representatives on the Council and the Secretariat.

Article 9   In order that a meeting of the Council may be held, the presence of a majority of the Representatives thereon is necessary, unless it is otherwise provided in an economic integration agreement. Decisions are to be taken by a majority of the votes of all the members of the Council, and each State shall be entitled to one vote. In case of a tie or abstentions which prevent a decision, the matter is to be submitted to the Central American Economic Council, in accordance with the procedure outlined in section (b) of the foregoing Article 7.

Article 10   The Council shall elect a Director of Debates at each of its meetings; the debating and voting procedure shall be governed by the usual parliamentary rules.

Article 11   At the close of each meeting the Permanent Secretariat shall prepare minutes containing a resumé of the discussions and the texts of resolutions adopted. The original thereof is to be signed by the Representatives of each State and shall be kept in the custody of the Permanent Secretariat, which shall transmit a certified copy to each of the governments of the member states and to their respective Representatives, for subsequent purposes.

Article 12   When a resolution has been adopted by the Executive Council its observance shall be compulsory on the part of the member states. In case of noncompliance, any member state may request the Council to declare such noncompliance in order that the difference may be settled by the Central American Economic Council, or if necessary, by arbitration.

Article 13 The Permanent Secretariat of the General Treaty of Central American Economic Integration shall serve in the same capacity for the Executive Council, in accordance with Article XXIII of that Treaty. The secretariat functions of the meetings shall be entrusted to an official of the Permanent Secretariat designated in each case by the Secretary General.

In addition, the Secretary General—or his special representative—must attend the meetings of the Executive Council, and at any meeting he may make oral or written observations on any matter that is being discussed.

Article 14 The Permanent Secretariat shall be in charge of the organization and preparation of the meetings of the Council. During periods of adjournment, it shall see that the Representatives are kept informed of the progress of action or work that is being undertaken.

Chapter IV

GENERAL PROVISIONS

Article 15 The members of the Council may travel between the territories of the member states for the purpose of attending its meetings or to study in the field matters within their concern, and the pertinent authorities must offer such facilities as are within the scope of their duties.

Article 16 In order to carry out specific functions of a regional character, the Executive Council shall have special appropriations in the Budget of the Permanent Secretariat.

Article 17 In performing its functions, the Executive Council may seek the advice of such Central American and international agencies as it may consider desirable.

Article 18 The Executive Council shall decide matters not provided for in these Regulations.

Article 19 These Regulations must be submitted for approval to the Central American Economic Council, which may amend them by its own decision or at the initiative of the Executive Council.

Article 20 These Regulations, as well as any amendments that may be agreed upon, shall be adopted by a decree or order of the Executive Branch of each of the member states of the General Treaty of Central American Economic Integration, and they shall take effect as soon as the respective decree or order comes into force.

Appendix to the Regulations

MULTILATERAL TREATY OF FREE TRADE AND CENTRAL AMERICAN ECONOMIC INTEGRATION[1]

Article XIX The functions of the Central American Trade Commission shall be as follows:

a) To propose to the contracting Parties measures conducive to the development and improvement of the Central American free trade zone referred to in the Treaty as well as measures designed to attain the objectives of Central American economic integration, and to prepare a specific plan for such purposes, including a customs union and the establishment of a Central American common market;

b) At the request of one or several governments to study questions and matters relating to the development of intra-Central American trade, in particular those connected with the application of this Treaty, and to propose measures for the solution of any problem which may arise;

c) To study production and trade in the signatory States, to recommend additions to the appended schedule, and to take appropriate measures to ensure:

    i) the standardization of customs tariffs and regulations;

    ii) the establishment of a single fiscal system for articles under state monopoly and for goods subject to production, sales, and consumption taxes;

    iii) the conclusion of agreements designed to avoid double taxation in the matter of direct taxes;

    iv) the improvement of intra-Central American transportation through the conclusion of appropriate agreements;

    v) The application of the decimal metric system of weights and measures.

d) To collect and analyze statistics and other data relating to trade between the signatory States.

In fulfilling these functions, the Commission shall avail itself of the reports and studies made by other Central American and international organizations and agencies.

The Central American Trade Commission shall give priority attention to the problem of equalizing customs tariffs and shall submit to the Economic Council of the Organization of Central American States, for consideration at its regular sessions, draft contractual agreements covering the greatest possible number of products.

---

[1] Signed at Tegucigalpa, Honduras on June 10, 1958. See the complete text on pp. 3–14.

CENTRAL AMERICAN AGREEMENT ON THE EQUALIZATION OF IMPORT CHARGES[1]

Article XI The following shall be the terms of reference of the Central American Trade Commission:

a) To recommend to the contracting Parties measures conducive to the establishment of the Central American customs tariff referred to in this Agreement;

b) To study, at the request of one or more governments, topics or matters relating to the development of tariff equalization and in particular to the implementation of the present Agreement, and to propose the measures that should be adopted in order to solve such problems as may arise;

c) To study production and trade activities in the signatory States and recommend additions to Schedules A and B;

d) To act as the agency responsible for coordinating tariff equalization, taking into special consideration the progress made in this field by virtue of bilateral treaties signed between Central American countries, with a view to submitting early proposals for standard duties and charges and endeavoring to promote their adoption by all the contracting Parties. In this connection, the Parties undertake to notify the Commission of bilateral tariff equalization agreements as soon as these are negotiated;

e) To study the various aspects of the maintenance of uniformity in the application of the Standard Central American Tariff Nomenclature and to recommend to the contracting Parties such amendments as may seem advisable in the light of experience and from the standpoint of increased diversification of production in Central America;

f) To take steps calculated to establish and maintain uniformity in customs regulations.

In the discharge of its functions, the Commission shall utilize the studies carried out by other Central American international bodies.

[1] Signed at San José, Costa Rica on September 1, 1959, See complete text on pp. 79–86.

AGREEMENT ON THE CENTRAL AMERICAN SYSTEM OF INTEGRATED INDUSTRIES[1]

Article II The contracting States declare their interest in the development of industries with access to a common Central American market. These shall be designated Central American integrated industries and shall be so declared jointly by the contracting States, through

[1] Signed at Tegucigalpa, Honduras on June 10, 1958. See complete text on pp. 89–94.

the agency of the Central American Industrial Integration Commission established in conformity with Article VIII of this Agreement.

The contracting States shall regard as Central American integrated industries those industries which, in the judgment of the Central American Industrial Integration Commission, comprise one or more plants which require access to the Central American market in order to operate under reasonably economic and competitive conditions even at minimum capacity.

Article V   In conformity with the provisions of Article IV of the multilateral treaty of free trade and Central American economic integration, the Central American Trade Commission shall give priority consideration to the equalization of the customs duties and other charges levied upon imports of commodities that are similar to or substitutes for the commodities produced by the Central American integrated industries covered by the additional protocols to this Agreement, as well as upon imports of raw materials and of the containers necessary for their production and distribution.

Article VII   Except in cases of emergency, the governments of the contracting States shall not grant customs duty exemptions or reductions below the Central American common tariff on any imports from countries outside Central America of goods which are equal or similar to or substitutes for goods manufactured in any of the Central American countries by plants of industrial integrated industries, nor shall they apply to such imports preferential exchange rates equivalent to such exemptions or reductions.

The governments and other state bodies shall also give preference in their official imports to the products of the Central American integrated industries.

Article VIII   In order to ensure due application of this Agreement and of the additional protocols, the signatory States agree to establish a Central American Industrial Integration Commission, to which each of the contracting States shall appoint a special representative; the Commission shall meet as frequently as its work may require or at the request of any of the participating States.

The Commission or any of its members may travel freely in the contracting States in order to study matters within the Commission's competence in the field, and the authorities of the contracting States shall provide them with whatever information and facilities may be necessary for the proper discharge of their functions.

The Commission shall have a permanent secretariat which shall be under the responsibility of the General Secretariat of the Organization of Central American States.

The Commission shall adopt its rules of procedure unanimously and shall prescribe the regulations relating to the conduct of matters within its competence, in particular the regulations relating to the conditions and form in which, in each specific case, the views of private enterprise shall be heard.

Article IX Individuals or legal entities desiring the incorporation of a given plant into the present System shall present an application to that effect to the Secretariat of the Central American Industrial Integration Commission and accompany it with the required information.

When the Secretariat has sufficient information available, it shall advise the Commission of the application. If the Commission finds that the project meets the aims of this Agreement, the application shall be referred for an opinion to the Central American Institute of Industrial Research and Technology or to any other person or body that the Commission considers competent. Such opinion shall take into account the technological and economic aspects of the project and, in particular, the market prospects, and the costs incurred shall be borne by the interested parties.

The Commission shall decide on the project on the basis of the said opinion, and if it finds the project capable of being realized, shall make whatever recommendations it considers pertinent to the governments of the contracting States on the conclusion of the protocol covering the industry concerned and on the conditions to be stipulated.

When the project refers to a plant which forms part of an industry already covered by a protocol, the Commission may, in conformity with the terms of the relevant protocol and of this article, declare that the plant shall be admitted to the benefits of the present System and advise the governments of the contracting States to that effect.

Article X The Central American Industrial Integration Commission shall submit an annual report on its activities to the contracting States.

The Commission shall periodically carry out studies with a view to enabling the governments to evaluate the results of the application of the present System.

The Commission may propose to the contracting States measures favorable to the development of the Central American integrated industries and to the efficient functioning of their plants. The Commission may also propose to the governments any measures necessary to resolve any problems arising from the application of this Agreement.

TREATY OF FREE TRADE BETWEEN EL SALVADOR AND NICARAGUA
(Signed in Managua on March 9, 1951)

Article XIX The Governments of the two States shall appoint delegations, which shall include one or more representatives of the respective National Commissions, to comprise a Joint Trade Commission which shall meet at least once every six months and shall have the following functions:

a) To analyze and reconcile the statistics and other data relating to trade between the two States;

b) To discuss and propose to the signatory governments measures which in its opinion should be adopted in order to solve the problems that may arise over the application of this Treaty; and

c) To discuss and recommend increases, reductions, or modifications in the annexed List and the provisions that may be advisable to promote the economic integration of the two countries and the unification of their tariffs, with the aim of gradually achieving the customs union they propose to establish.

TREATY OF FREE TRADE AND ECONOMIC INTEGRATION BETWEEN GUATEMALA AND EL SALVADOR

(Signed in San Salvador on December 14, 1951 and amplified by additional Protocols signed on February 5, 1957 and April 15, 1959)

Article XVI   The Joint Trade Commission shall have the following functions:

a) To analyze and seek to reconcile the statistics and other data relating to trade between the two States;

b) To study, at the request of one or both governments, the measures that should be adopted to solve the problems that arise from its application; and

c) To study the activities of production and trade in both States, and recommend increases, reductions, and modifications in the annexed List, as well as action conducive to:

    1) the unification of customs tariffs and regulations;

    2) the establishment of a single fiscal system for state monopoly articles and goods subject to production, sales, or consumption taxes;

    3) the conclusion of agreements designed to prevent double taxation in respect to direct taxes;

    4) the application of the decimal metric system for weights and measures;

    5) a customs union and general economic integration of the two countries.

TREATY OF FREE TRADE AND ECONOMIC INTEGRATION BETWEEN EL SALVADOR AND COSTA RICA

(Signed in San Salvador on October 5, 1953)

Article XVI   The Joint Trade Commission shall have the following functions:

a) To analyze and reconcile statistics and other data relating to trade between the two States;

b) To study, at the request of one or both governments, subjects and matters relating to this Treaty, and to propose measures that should be adopted to settle problems that may be caused by its application; and

c) To study the activities of production and trade of interest to both countries and to recommend increases, reductions, and modifications in the annexed List, as well as action conductive to:

  1) the unification of customs tariffs and regulations;

  2) the establishment of a single fiscal system for state monopoly articles and goods subject to production, sales, or consumption taxes;

  3) the conclusion of agreements designed to prevent double taxation in respect to direct taxes;

  4) the application of the decimal metric system for weights and measures;

  5) development of the customs union and general economic integration of the two countries.

TREATY OF FREE TRADE AND ECONOMIC INTEGRATION BETWEEN GUATEMALA AND HONDURAS

(Signed at Guatemala City on August 22, 1956)

Article XVI   The Joint Trade Commission shall have the following functions:

a) To analyze and seek to reconcile statistics and other data relating to trade between the two States;

b) To study, at the request of one or both governments, subjects or matters relating to this Treaty, and to propose measures that should be adopted in order to solve the problems that may arise from its application; and

c) To study the activities of production and trade in both States, and recommend increases, reductions, and modifications in the annexed List, as well as action conducive to:

  1) the unification of customs tariffs and regulations for products in free trade or their raw materials;

2) the establishment of a single fiscal system for state monopoly products and for goods subject to production, sales, or consumption taxes;

3) the conclusion of agreements designed to prevent double taxation in respect to direct taxes;

4) the application of the decimal metric system for weights and measures; and

5) a customs union and economic integration coordinated with the customs union and economic integration of the countries that formed the Central American Federation, and directed toward that end.

TREATY OF FREE TRADE AND ECONOMIC INTEGRATION BETWEEN EL SALVADOR AND HONDURAS

(Signed in El Amatillo, a frontier point of El Salvador and Honduras, on February 16, 1957)

Article XIII The signatory States agree to form a Joint Trade Commission, consisting of an equal number of delegates of each party, which shall meet whenever deemed advisable and at least once a year, the first meeting to be held in San Salvador and the subsequent meetings alternately in each capital.

The Commission may travel freely in the contracting countries to study in the field matters within its competence, and the authorities of the two States must furnish any information and facilities that may be required in fulfilling its duties.

The Joint Trade Commission shall have the following duties:

a) To analyze and seek to reconcile the statistics and other data relating to trade between the two States;

b) To study, at the request of either government, subjects and matters relating to this Treaty, and to propose measures that should be adopted to solve problems that arise over its application; and

c) To study activities of production and trade in both States, and recommend increases and modifications in the annexed Lists, as well as action conducive to:

1) The unification of customs tariffs and regulations;

2) The establishment of a single fiscal system for state monopoly products and for goods subject to production, sales or consumption taxes;

3) The conclusion of agreements designed to prevent double taxation;

4) Application of the decimal metric system to weights and measures;

5) A customs union and general economic integration of the countries that formed the Central American Federation; and

6) Verification of the declarations contained in customs forms for articles covered by this Treaty.

The Permanent Secretariat is an Organ established by Article XXIII of the General Treaty of Central American Economic Integration.

NOTES ON PRIVILEGES AND IMMUNITIES

The rules on privileges and immunities which are accorded to international officials who perform tasks in the various Central American organizations, are determined by the provisions on the subject contained in the documents that established such organizations. Consequently there is no one common system but rather a special one for each type or class of organization. The following instruments contain provisions concerning privileges and immunities:

Multilateral Treaty of Free Trade and Central American Economic Integration (Art. XVIII)

Central American Agreement on the Equalization of Import Charges (Art. X)

Agreement on the System of Central American Integrated Industries (Art. VIII)

Agreement Establishing the Central American Bank for Economic Integration (Arts. 27 to 33 inclusive)

General Treaty of Central American Economic Integration (Art. XXIII)

The rules established vary from a simple right of freedom of transit among the contracting countries to the recognition or granting of diplomatic privileges and immunities, such as are enjoyed by the Secretary General and Secretariat of SIECA. It is of interest to note that officials of SIECA are entitled only to diplomatic immunity whereas the Secretariat and the Secretary General are also entitled to diplomatic privileges. In order to establish a special system in the country which is the headquarters of the Secretariat (Guatemala) negotiations are in progress with the government at the present time to conclude a special accord, following the basic principles of this class of agreements.

NOTES ON THE CENTRAL AMERICAN REGIONAL AGREEMENT FOR THE TEMPORARY IMPORTATION OF VEHICLES BY HIGHWAY; THE CENTRAL AMERICAN AGREEMENT ON HIGHWAY TRAFFIC; AND THE CENTRAL AMERICAN AGREEMENT ON UNIFORM ROAD SIGNS

THE CENTRAL AMERICAN REGIONAL AGREEMENT FOR THE TEMPORARY IMPORTATION OF VEHICLES BY HIGHWAY

Within a general plan to regulate traffic and transportation problems, the countries comprising the Central American common market on November 8, 1956 signed in San Salvador the Regional Agreement for the Temporary Importation of Vehicles by Highway, which is now in force between Guatemala, El Salvador, Nicaragua, and Costa Rica, not having been ratified as yet by Honduras. The preamble of the Agreement states that one objective of the Central American republics animated by the desire to increase the links that tend toward greater economic integration, is to increase the interchange of persons and goods through their respective territories. To this end, they agree (Art. 2) to admit under a temporary exemption, without any financial guarantee of payment of import duties and charges, vehicles registered in any of the territories of the parties, provided the terms of the Agreement are met and they are brought in by persons who reside in any such territory. The duration of the exemption is thirty days, unless the state authorizes a longer period. If the vehicle has not been removed from that territory when the period has expired, payment of the pertinent import duties and charges may be required (Art. 3). In order to facilitate the temporary importation procedure, the Central American states joined in establishing a single customs certificate which is valid for one journey to another specified territory. It is very possible that in the near future it will be decided to extend the certificate to other territories and/or for several journeys, following the experience that the countries comprising Benelux have had. Another provision (Art. 6) states that the Agreement shall also apply to vehicles destined for commercial traffic that are "in transit" in the territory of a contracting state, with the limitation that while a vehicle remains in that territory it may not load, unload, or transfer goods that it carries (including passengers), with the exception of those vehicles that have special international concessions. The Agreement is in effect for an indefinite period and is open to adherence by the Republic of Panama at any time.

CENTRAL AMERICAN AGREEMENT ON HIGHWAY TRAFFIC

This Agreement was signed in Tegucigalpa, on June 10, 1958 and is currently in force among the signatories, Guatemala, El Salvador, Honduras, Nicaragua, and Costa Rica. Its fundamental purpose is the same as the Agreement previously described, with the added feature that its adoption should facilitate the adherence of the states to the Convention on Highway Traffic, opened for signature in Geneva on September 19, 1949, the purpose of which is the improvement and safety of international traffic. The points specifically covered by this Central American Agreement are the following: Title I, Provisions of a general nature (definition of the terms highway, street, route, crossing, driver, automotive vehicle, etc.). Title II, General provisions relating to highway traffic and applicable to all users. This refers to the driving of vehicles and animals, speed, meeting and passing, road crossings, right of way, use of the horn, parking, lights and signals, and similar questions. Title III contains provisions concerning weight, dimensions, freight, brakes, etc., of both automotive vehicles and "articulated vehicles" or those hauling trailers or semitrailers. Titles IV to VIII refer to motorcycles and sidecars, bicycles, motorbicycles and their sidecars; to vehicles drawn by animals or pushed by manpower; to pedestrians and herders of unhitched animals; to farm vehicles and machinery and equipment for the public works. The Final Provisions (as in the preceding Agreement) establish an indefinite duration for this Agreement and the right of Panama to adhere to it at any time. Appendixes include rules for safety and comfort for vehicles used in public transportation, rules concerning licenses or registration, and concerning drivers' licenses.

CENTRAL AMERICAN AGREEMENT ON UNIFORM ROAD SIGNS

This instrument was signed at the same time as the Central American Agreement on Highway Traffic (Tegucigalpa, June 10, 1958) and is in effect among all the signatory parties, Guatemala, El Salvador, Honduras, Nicaragua, and Costa Rica. Its purpose, as stated in the preamble, is "to contribute to highway traffic safety and to unify as far as possible the system of traffic signs." The instrument contains only a few articles, in one of which (Art. 1) the parties accept the uniform system of road signs contained in the Appendix entitled "Manual of Road Signs," covering all technical specifications. Part One of the Manual refers to road signs; Part Two to traffic lights; and Part Three covers pavement markings. Article 2 of the Agreement provides that the contracting parties shall authorize their respective competent authorities to consult with each other periodically and to prepare additions or revisions in the Manual whenever necessary. The instrument is of unlimited duration and remains open for signature by Panama.

AGREEMENT ON THE ESTABLISHMENT OF THE CENTRAL AMERICAN INSTITUTE OF INDUSTRIAL RESEARCH AND TECHNOLOGY (ICAITI)

The Governments of Costa Rica, El Salvador, Guatemala, Honduras and Nicaragua

PURSUANT TO Resolution No. 6 (CCE) of the Committee on Economic Cooperation of the Central American Isthmus of the Economic Commission for Latin America of the United Nations, dated May 7, 1955;

BY VIRTUE OF the basic agreements on technical assistance signed by the Government of Costa Rica on February 26, 1953, by the Government of El Salvador on February 26, 1951, by the Government of Guatemala on March 10, 1954, by the Government of Honduras on December 29, 1952, and by the Government of Nicaragua on December 16, 1952, with the United Nations;

BY VIRTUE OF the Guiding Principles and Observations contained in Annex 1 of Resolution 222A(IX) of the Economic and Social Council of the United Nations of August 15, 1949;

FOR THE PURPOSE OF advancing its collaboration in the solution of common economic, social, and administrative problems, particularly those relating to economic integration; and

FOR THE PURPOSE OF advancing the collaboration of the governments in carrying out regional plans for technical assistance,

HAVE AGREED TO conclude this Agreement for the Establishment of the Central American Institute of Industrial Research and Technology (ICAITI), and have so authorized their Representatives, who have agreed to the following:

1. The Central American Institute of Industrial Research and Technology (ICAITI) is hereby established.

2. The Institute is established for the following purposes:

a) To undertake studies on the production, preparation, and use of local raw materials in existence or obtainable in the future, in order to discover or propose new products, manufacturing processes, or uses. To this end, the Institute may set up research centers and laboratories and experiment stations.

b) To develop, improve, and test processes, methods, tools, implements, equipment, and materials for new industries, for farm production, mining, household industries, handicrafts, and for the allied activities of handling, conservation, storage, packaging, transportation, and maintenance and repair services.

c) To undertake studies of existing producer enterprises in order to resolve technical problems, reduce costs of production, improve techniques, discover useful by-products, eliminate or reduce risk, and establish better methods for determining and regulating quality.

d) To take charge, with or without remuneration, of research work entrusted to it by government institutions, industrial organizations, private enterprises or individuals who wish to utilize the services of the Institute.

e) To undertake or participate in the preparation, publication and distribution in a practical way, of technical information useful to the producers of the region.

f) To assist in any other way in the progress of the technology of production and research, and of technical knowledge.

g) To collaborate with pertinent offices of the governments of the Central American Isthmus, universities, technical organizations, and other entities, whether governmental or otherwise, to promote scientific and industrial research and the training of researchers and technical experts, artisans, and skilled workers.

3. To attain the objectives of the foregoing article the Institute may:

a) Buy and sell, acquire or transfer title to real and personal property;

b) Borrow and contract services, and obtain loans;

c) Accept gifts and legacies;

d) Solicit, purchase, or receive by assignment or in any other form, in accordance with the laws of any country, any patents, concessions, or permits which may or may not confer exclusive rights to the knowledge, use, or appropriation of any invention, discovery or manufacturing process. To complete, use, exercise, assign, transfer, sell, or grant licenses or permits concerning ownership or acquired rights or for making use of such rights in any other way;

e) To organize companies for purposes of the Institute;

f) To perform any legal acts that may be necessary or incidental to carrying out its purposes;

g) To be a party to judicial proceedings, with the right to waive immunities whenever considered advisable.

Organs

4. The organs of the Institute are the Committee on Economic Co-operation of the Central American Isthmus and the Director.

The Committee

5. The Institute shall operate under the direction of the Committee on Economic Cooperation of the Central American Isthmus (herein-after the Committee). The Committee shall act in representation of the governments, without prejudice to its functions as a subsidiary organ of the Economic Commission for Latin America of the United Nations. The Committee shall decide questions of substance by a unanimous vote of its members. Questions of procedure shall be decided by major-ity vote. A unanimous vote is necessary to decide whether a question is one of substance or of procedure. The Committee may vote by cor-respondence, through its Chairman, whenever it is not in session.

6. The powers and duties of the Committee are:

a) To determine the policy of the Institute regarding scientific, technical, functional, and administrative matters;
b) To approve plans for research and make decisions concerning supplementary activities of the Institute;
c) To adopt the budget, determine financial needs, and keep the accounts of the Institute;
d) To approve the appointment of the Director of the Institute;
e) To exercise the rights referred to in Article 3;
f) To delegate to the Director any powers deemed desirable;
g) To conclude regional technical assistance agreements with inter-national organizations;
h) To establish an administrative board whenever considered neces-sary and to specify its powers and duties and regulations. It may also establish a technical advisory committee for giving advice to the Director and other organs in line with the aims of the Institute.

The Director

7. The functions of the Director are:
a) Under the direction of the Committee, to organize and direct the administration of the Institute;
b) With the approval of the Committee, to appoint the administra-tive, technical, and scientific staff of the Institute and specify the service requirements of these officials;
c) To enforce the decisions of the Board in respect of the policies of the Institute in scientific, technical, functional, and administra-tive matters;

d) With the approval of the Committee, to draw up the regulations for the staff and for the handling of funds of the Institute;

e) To propose a budget for the Committee and to estimate annual resources;

f) To report periodically to the Committee on the activities of the Institute.

Privileges and Immunities

8. In the territory of each member the Institute shall have the privileges, immunities, and exemptions established in the Agreement on Privileges and Immunities of the United Nations. The Institute shall be entitled to the postal franking privilege. The Institute may waive all or any of its privileges, immunities, and exemptions whenever it is deemed desirable. The governments undertake to exempt from taxes gifts made by individuals to the Institute and, specifically, they will permit such gifts to be deducted by individuals from their taxable income.

Provisional Article

9. a) During the period of organization the positions of Director and of his collaborators shall be held by experts from the Technical Assistance Administration of the United Nations on terms to be established by agreement between the Committee and that organization.

b) It is a duty of the Director to propose to the Committee at the proper time a plan for the establishment of a Board of Administration and a Technical Advisory Committee to assist him in his functions. The latter Committee may include representatives from the universities and research institutes and from industry in the countries of the Central American Isthmus.

Final Clauses

10. This Agreement shall come into force on the date it has been signed by all the duly authorized representatives of the respective governments.

11. This Agreement shall remain in force for a period of five years, after which it shall automatically be extended for an indefinite time. When the period that it is obligatorily in force has expired and in the event that any government desires to withdraw from the Institute, this Agreement may be denounced, such denouncement to take effect one year from the date of such notification. In the event that three participating governments denounce this Agreement, the Institute shall be liquidated and its assets will be distributed pro rata among the participating governments.

IN WITNESS WHEREOF, the undersigned Plenipotentiaries sign this Agreement at the place and on the date indicated next to their signatures.

	Date of Signature
Costa Rica	July 23, 1955
El Salvador (with reservations)	September 27, 1955
Guatemala	July 21, 1955
Honduras (with reservations)	July 22, 1955
Nicaragua	July 23, 1955
Panama	Adherence

NOTES ON THE COMMITTEE ON ECONOMIC COOPERATION OF THE CENTRAL AMERICAN ISTHMUS AND THE ADVANCED SCHOOL OF PUBLIC ADMINISTRATION, CENTRAL AMERICA (ESAPAC)

The Committee on Economic Cooperation of the Central American Isthmus was established at the meeting held by the Committee on Economic Cooperation of the Ministers of Economy of the Central American Isthmus, in Tegucigalpa, August 23 to 28, 1952, under the auspices of the Economic Committee for Latin America (ECLA) of the United Nations. The Committee was created as a permanent agency of ECLA, entrusted with studying and promoting economic progress and with stimulating the process of economic integration in the Central American Isthmus. The terms of reference of the Committee, as stated in Resolution XI, are as follows (It should be noted that its original name was "Committee on Economic Cooperation of the Ministers of Economy of the Central American Isthmus"):

Resolution XI

Powers and Duties of the Committee on Economic Cooperation of the Ministers of Economy of the Central American Isthmus

WHEREAS:

Resolution 9(IV) of the Economic Commission for Latin America, adopted June 16, 1951, indicated the functions of the Committee in a general way, and, at the time of holding its first sessions it is well to specify these powers and duties in precise form so that its future tasks may be duly carried out according to rules,

THE COMMITTEE ON ECONOMIC COOPERATION
OF THE MINISTERS OF ECONOMY OF THE
CENTRAL AMERICAN ISTHMUS

RESOLVES:

a) To propose to the respective governments specific measures tending toward a gradual and progressive integration of the economies of the Central American countries and the coordination of national programs of economic development.

b) To provide for research and studies supporting the aims indicated in the preceding point.

c) To channel and direct the utilization of technical assistance in matters pertaining to the integration of the Central American economies; to coordinate requests for technical assistance that are submitted to the governments; to see to the proper development and execution of the work of the technicians; and to examine the studies and reports that they submit.

d) To set up subcommittees to deal with matters relating to the economic integration of Central America and to sponsor meetings of specialists.

The Committee shall meet regularly once a year and the Ministers shall attend personally, except that when this is impossible any Minister may be represented by a delegate. In addition, the Committee may hold other meetings with Ministers or their delegates present whenever the continuity of the work merits such a meeting.

The Committee may invite observers or representatives from the Specialized Agencies of the United Nations or other entities to be present at its meetings, in order to obtain their advice.

The Committee shall decide on the places for holding its meetings, when possible in accordance with an adequate rotation among the Central American countries, without prejudice to having them coincide with sessions of the Economic Commission for Latin America whenever feasible.

Up to the present time the Committee has held numerous meetings, having been the principal promoter of the advanced stage in which Central American economic integration now finds itself.

The Advanced School of Public Administration, Central America (ESAPAC)[1] was founded on March 10, 1954 by virtue of a Basic Agreement on Technical Assistance between the United Nations and the Governments of Costa Rica, Guatemala, Nicaragua, Honduras, and El Salvador. In 1961 the Government of the Republic of Panama ad-

---

1. On February 17, 1967, the name was changed to Central American Institute of Public Administration (ICAP) and a Plan of Operations was approved and signed by the General Board.

hered to this Basic Agreement. The School operates in San José, Costa Rica. As its name indicates, the fundamental purpose of this institution is the training of technicians in the field of public administration, as an indispensable requirement for a proper execution of plans for the development of economic integration.

Its administrative structure is not complicated, its most important organ being the General Board which is composed of the Ministers of Economy of the Central American countries. The Board appoints its chairman and also the director of the School selected from a list of candidates submitted by the United Nations. The teaching staff is recruited through the United Nations in cooperation with the chairman of the General Board and the Director of the School. Financial needs are met by contributions from the several countries, contributions from the United Nations and help from other national and international organizations.

The work accomplished up to the present time by the Advanced School has been particularly impressive. In the period 1954-1963 approximately 700 scholarships have been granted to Central American officials, along with travel allowances and stipends so that they might attend general courses, seminars, and short courses.

Because of the growing needs of the Central American economic integration movement, the work schedules of the School for the period 1963-1966 have placed special emphasis on the following studies: customs administration, fiscal administration, administration for development, and collaboration with the universities of the Central American Isthmus for improving and broadening their study programs in the field of public administration. The Advanced School possesses an excellent specialized library, and it has developed an intensive publishing activity so as to provide Central American students with material needed for this specialty. Since 1961, the Director of the School has been Dr. Wilburg Jiménez Castro, a Costa Rican.

TREATY ON TELECOMMUNICATIONS BETWEEN THE REPUBLICS OF NICARAGUA, EL SALVADOR, GUATEMALA, AND HONDURAS

(Signed at Managua, Nicaragua, April 26, 1966)

WHEREAS it is their manifest desire to give effective support to the fulfillment of the noble ideal of Central American Union;

WHEREAS they should unite their efforts toward intensifying a close relationship and mutual cooperation among the signatory countries, efforts which should be coupled with the tasks of Central American Integration;

WHEREAS one of the means of achieving these goals is facility in radiotelegraphic and radiotelephonic communications for which an effective system and trustworthy service should exist.

The Governments of Nicaragua, El Salvador, Guatemala, and Honduras have agreed to conclude a treaty on telecommunications, for which they have designated their respective Plenipotentiaries, to wit:

[Here follow the names of the delegates]

who, after presenting their respective Full Powers found to be in due form, have agreed on the following:

Article I   The Governments of the Republics of Nicaragua, El Salvador, Guatemala, and Honduras, agree to establish a modern telecommunications service which will connect the cities of Managua, San Salvador, Guatemala, and Tegucigalpa. This service will receive first-class equipment which shall have an adequate capacity of telephonic channels (960 as a minimum).

Article II   The contracting parties undertake separately to pay the costs of construction and conservation, in their respective territories, of the public works that are considered necessary to ensure the normal functioning of the radio-network that shall unite the capitals and, also, the costs of the installation, operation, and maintenance of the equipment which will be put in service initially, as well as that to be added whenever an extension of the system is agreed upon.

Article III   The technical specifications needed to put the present Treaty into practice, the aim of which is the formation of a Central American Telecommunications Network, shall be based on a study prepared by the French Mission, with such modifications as may be agreed upon by the interested countries.

Article IV   The preparation of the bases and technical specifications for the bids that will be required for the purchase of equipment and materials; the request for bids; and the study of bids received and the adjudication and negotiation of the respective contracts shall be done jointly by the signatory States, through the authorities designated by them.

Article V   In order to facilitate the execution and administration of this Treaty, a Regional Technical Telecommunications Commission is established, composed of the directors general, presidents, or others responsible for telecommunications in the contracting countries.

The Commission shall have broad powers to coordinate all the work that must be undertaken pursuant to this Treaty and to adopt pertinent resolutions.

This Commission shall be a juridical person under international law.

Article VI For the radiotelephonic and radiotelegraphic service between the capitals the rates shall be the same in both directions and no one of the signatory countries may change them without the previous consent of the others.

Article VII The rates to be charged for telephonic communications between capitals, or for telegraphic messages from one capital to any place in the territory of another contracting country, shall be the same as in the country of origin, except in the case of messages sent to San Pedro Sula, Honduras, which shall have a surcharge of 90% over the rate for Tegucigalpa-San Pedro Sula, and the indicated surcharge will be credited to the Honduran administration.

Article VIII The teletype service for individuals between capitals shall be charged at both ends, according to their rates, and if there is a request for the service to be extended to another place in a contracting country, the subscriber shall pay in addition the local rate in effect in the country of destination.

Article IX During the first five days of each month, the contracting parties shall make an adjustment in accounts and those that show a debit balance must reimburse the others within ten days after that date.

Article X Whenever one signatory country requests another for telephone or telegraph service outside Central America, the requesting country shall pay the corresponding charge.

Article XI In order to facilitate the proper application of the provisions of this Treaty, an additional Protocol will be prepared.

Article XII The instruments of ratification of this Treaty should be deposited in the General Secretariat of the Organization of Central American States.

The Treaty shall come into force eight days from the date on which the second instrument of ratification is deposited for the first two to ratify and, for the others, on the date of deposit of their respective instruments.

Article XIII The duration of this Treaty shall be ten years, counted from the date it comes into force, and it will be extended for successive equal periods, by tacit renewal, if none of the parties express a desire to the contrary by giving notice six months in advance of the date the initial period or subsequent periods will expire. A denunciation shall take effect two years after the General Secretariat of the Organization of Central American States has been notified.

Article XIV The General Secretariat of the Organization of Central American States shall be the depository of this Treaty and shall transmit certified copies thereof and of each instrument of ratification as well as any denunciation that may be submitted to each Foreign Office. When the Treaty comes into force it shall also transmit a certified copy thereof to the General Secretariat of the United Nations for registration purposes as prescribed in Article 102 of the Charter of the United Nations.

Transitory Article   This Treaty is open to adherence by the Republic of Costa Rica at any time.

IN WITNESS WHEREOF, the respective Plenipotentiaries sign the present Treaty in the city of Managua, Nicaragua, on April 26, 1966.

For the Government of Nicaragua

Francisco J. Medal
Director General of Communications

For the Government of El Salvador

Mario Guerrero
President of the National Administration
of Telecommunications

For the Government of Guatemala

Joaquín Olivares
Minister of Communications
and Public Works

For the Government of Honduras

Ramón Lovo Sosa
Minister of Public Works
and Communications

Costa Rica adhered to this treaty on January 18, 1968.

CHARTER OF THE ORGANIZATION OF CENTRAL AMERICAN STATES (ODECA) (1962)

WHEREAS:

It is necessary to provide the five States with a more effective instrument by establishing organs which assure their economic and social progress, eliminate the barriers which divide them, improve constantly the living conditions of their peoples, guarantee the stability and expansion of industry, and strengthen Central American solidarity,

THEREFORE:

The Governments of Costa Rica, Nicaragua, Honduras, El Salvador, and Guatemala decide to replace the Charter signed on October 14, 1951, in San Salvador, Republic of El Salvador, by the following CHARTER OF THE ORGANIZATION OF CENTRAL AMERICAN STATES:

PURPOSES

Article 1 Costa Rica, Nicaragua, Honduras, El Salvador, and Guatemala are an economic-political community which aspires to the integration of Central America. For this purpose the Organization of Central American States (ODECA) has been established.

ORGANS

Article 2 To achieve the purposes of the Organization of Central American States, the following Organs are established:

a) The Meetings of Heads of State;
b) The Conference of Ministers of Foreign Affairs;
c) The Executive Council;
d) The Legislative Council;
e) The Central American Court of Justice;
f) The Central American Economic Council;
g) The Cultural and Educational Council; and
h) The Council for Central American Defense.

Article 3 The Meeting of Heads of State is the Supreme Organ of the Organization.

The Conference of Ministers of Foreign Affairs is the Principal Organ.

The Executive Council is the Permanent Organ of the Organization. Its seat shall be in the city of San Salvador.

PRINCIPAL ORGAN

Article 4 The Conference of Ministers of Foreign Affairs shall meet ordinarily once each year, and extraordinarily whenever at least three of them deem it necessary.

Article 5 At the Conference of Ministers of Foreign Affairs each Member State shall have only one vote.

Decisions on substantive questions must be adopted unanimously. If there is doubt as to whether a decision is substantive or procedural, it shall be resolved by unanimous vote.

Article 6 The Conference of Ministers of Foreign Affairs may create the subsidiary organs which it considers appropriate for the study of the different problems.

The seat of the different subsidiary organs shall be designated in accordance with an equitable geographic distribution and with the needs that determined their creation.

EXECUTIVE COUNCIL

Article 7   The Executive Council shall be composed of the Ministers of Foreign Affairs or their specially accredited representatives. It shall be the legal representative of the Organization.

Article 8   The Executive Council shall be presided over by one of its members. The Presidency shall rotate annually among the States Members of the Organization. The Council shall meet ordinarily once a week and extraordinarily when convoked by its President.

Article 9   The function of the Executive Council is to direct and coordinate the policy of the Organization for the fulfillment of its objectives. For the proper functioning of the offices charged with executing administrative tasks, the Council shall designate a Secretary and the necessary personnel. For this purpose it shall adopt the respective regulations to determine their obligations.

The Council shall be the means of communication between the Organs and the Member States.

LEGISLATIVE COUNCIL

Article 10   The Legislative Council is composed of three representatives from each of the Legislative Powers of the Member States.

This Council shall act as advisor and organ of consultation in legislative matters. Likewise, it shall study the possibilities of unifying the legislation of the Central American States.

Article 11   The Council shall establish the working Committees which it deems convenient, in accordance with its own regulations.

Article 12   The Legislative Council shall meet ordinarily once each year starting September 15, and extraordinarily whenever the Executive Council convokes it at the request of at least two governments of Member States.

Article 13   For the adoption of the resolutions and recommendations of the Council, a favorable vote of the majority of its members shall be required.

CENTRAL AMERICAN COURT OF JUSTICE

Article 14   The Central American Court of Justice is composed of the Presidents of the Judicial Powers of each of the Member States.

Article 15   The functions of the Central American Court of Justice are:

a) To decide the conflicts of a legal nature which arise among the Member States and which the latter agree to submit to it;

b) To prepare and render opinions on projects for the unification of Central American Legislation, when so requested by the Conference of Ministers of Foreign Affairs or the Executive Council.

Article 16 The Central American Court of Justice shall meet whenever it deems it necessary or it is convoked by the Executive Council.

CENTRAL AMERICAN ECONOMIC COUNCIL

Article 17 The Central American Economic Council is composed of the Ministers of Economy of each of the Member States and shall be charged with the planning, coordination, and execution of the Central American economic integration.

All the agencies of Central American economic integration shall form part of the Council.

Article 18 The Economic Council shall make annually a full report of its activities to the Executive Council, for the information of the Conference of Ministers of Foreign Affairs, based on the reports of the various agencies connected with the Program of Central American Economic Integration.

CULTURAL AND EDUCATIONAL COUNCIL

Article 19 The Cultural and Educational Council shall be composed of the Ministers of Education of the Member States or their representatives.

Article 20 The functions of the Cultural and Educational Council are:

a) To promote educational, scientific, and cultural interchange between the Member States;

b) To undertake studies concerning the status of education, science, and culture in the region;

c) To coordinate the efforts to achieve the uniformity of the educational systems in Central America;

d) To render a report of its activities to the Conference of Ministers of Foreign Affairs through the Executive Council of the Organization.

DEFENSE COUNCIL

Article 21 The Defense Council is composed of the Ministers of Defense or of the heads of equivalent departments, corresponding to them in rank or functions in the respective Member States.

Article 22   The Defense Council shall act as Organ of Consultation in matters of regional defense and shall watch over the collective security of the Member States. It shall report on its activities to the Conference of Ministers of Foreign Affairs through the Executive Council.

GENERAL PROVISIONS

Article 23   Any Member State may propose, through the Executive Council, a meeting of the Organs or of Ministers of other departments to deal with matters of Central American interest.

Article 24   The operation of the Organization shall not interfere with the internal regime of the States and none of the provisions of the present Charter shall affect the respect for and fulfillment of the constitutional norms of each of them, nor may it be interpreted in such a way as to impair the rights and obligations of the Central American States as members of the United Nations and of the Organization of American States, nor the particular positions which any of them may have assumed through specific reservation in treaties or agreements in force.

Article 25   The present Charter shall be ratified by the Central American States in the shortest possible time in accordance with their respective constitutional procedures.

It shall be registered with the General Secretariat of the United Nations in compliance with Article 102 of its Charter.

Article 26   Each of the Organs originating in the present Charter shall prepare its own regulations.

Article 27   The Organs shall meet at the seat of the Organization unless they decide otherwise.

Article 28   The original of the present Charter shall be deposited in the Office of the Organization, which shall forward a true certified copy to the Ministers of Foreign Affairs of the Member States.

The instruments of ratification shall be deposited in the Office of the Organization, which shall notify the Chancelleries of the Member States of the deposit of each of said instruments.

Article 29   The present Charter shall enter into force the day on which the instruments of ratification of the five Member States are deposited.

Article 30   This Agreement on the Organization of Central American States shall maintain the name of "Charter of San Salvador."

TRANSITIONAL PROVISIONS

Article 1   The present Agreement remains open to the Republic of Panama so that it may adhere at any time to this Charter and form part of the Organization of Central American States.

Article 2   Until the Republic of Panama adheres to this Charter and forms part of the Organization of Central American States, it may join any of the subsidiary agencies already established or which may be established in the future, signing for this purpose the Protocol or Protocols which may be necessary.

Article 3   The financial resources for the functioning of the Organization shall be the object of a special protocol between the Member States, and for this purpose the Central American Economic Council is entrusted with carrying out the corresponding studies.

Until the plan for financing ODECA goes into effect in definitive form and the necessary funds for this purpose can be counted upon, the Member States shall continue to contribute to the budget of the Organization with quotas proportional to the coefficients established in the distribution of quotas of the United Nations.

In case said coefficients should be modified, the Executive Council shall adjust the quotas of the Member States in accordance with these modifications.

Article 4   Within thirty days after the date of the deposit of the last instrument of ratification of the present Charter, the Ambassadors of the Member States accredited to ODECA shall form an *ad hoc* Committee to receive by inventory the assets of the Organization as well as the rendering of accounts by the General Secretariat.

Article 5   When the present Charter enters into force and the Executive Council is constituted, the latter shall elect its first President by drawing lots.

IN WITNESS WHEREOF:

The Ministers of Foreign Affairs of the Central American Republics sign this document in Panama City, Republic of Panama, on the twelfth day of December, Nineteen Hundred and Sixty-two.

THE LATIN AMERICAN
FREE TRADE ASSOCIATION

TREATY ESTABLISHING A FREE TRADE AREA AND INSTITUTING THE LATIN AMERICAN FREE TRADE ASSOCIATION (MONTEVIDEO TREATY)
(Including the Relevant Protocols)

(Signed at Montevideo, Uruguay, February 18, 1960)

The Governments represented at the Inter-Governmental Conference for the Establishment of a Free Trade Area among Latin American countries,

Persuaded that the expansion of present national markets, through the gradual elimination of barriers to intra-regional trade, is a prerequisite if the Latin American countries are to accelerate their economic development process in such a way as to ensure a higher level of living for their peoples,

Aware that economic development should be attained through the maximum utilization of available production factors and the more effective coordination of the development programs of the different production sectors in accordance with norms which take due account of the interests of each and all and which make proper compensation, by means of appropriate measures, for the special situation of countries which are at a relatively less advanced stage of economic development,

Convinced that the strengthening of national economies will contribute to the expansion of trade within Latin America and with the rest of the world,

Sure that, by the adoption of suitable formulas, conditions can be created that will be conducive to the gradual and smooth adaptation of existing productive activities to new patterns of reciprocal trade, and that further incentives will thereby be provided for the improvement and expansion of such trade,

Certain that any action to achieve such ends must take into account the commitments arising out of the international instruments which govern their trade,

Determined to persevere in their efforts to establish, gradually and progressively, a Latin American common market and, hence, to continue collaborating with the Latin American Governments as a whole in the work already initiated for this purpose, and

Motivated by the desire to pool their efforts to achieve gradually

207

complementary and integrated national economies on the basis of an effective reciprocity of benefits, decide to establish a Free Trade Area and, to that end, to conclude a Treaty instituting the Latin American Free Trade Association; and have, for this purpose, appointed their plenipotentiaries who have agreed as follows:

Chapter I

NAME AND PURPOSE

Article 1   By this Treaty the contracting Parties establish a Free Trade Area and institute the Latin American Free Trade Association (hereinafter referred to as "the Association"), with headquarters in the city of Montevideo (Eastern Republic of Uruguay).

The term "Area", when used in this Treaty, means the combined territories of the contracting Parties.

Chapter II

PROGRAM FOR TRADE LIBERALIZATION

Article 2   The Free Trade Area, established under the terms of the present Treaty, shall be brought into full operation within not more than twelve (12) years from the date of the Treaty's entry into force.

Article 3   During the period indicated in Article 2, the contracting Parties shall gradually eliminate, in respect of substantially all their reciprocal trade, such duties, charges, and restrictions as may be applied to imports of goods originating in the territory of any contracting Party.

For the purposes of the present Treaty the term "duties and charges" means customs duties and any other charges of equivalent effect—whether fiscal, monetary or exchange—that are levied on imports.

The provisions of the present article do not apply to fees and similar charges in respect of services rendered.

Article 4   The purpose set forth in Article 3 shall be achieved through negotiations to be held from time to time among the contracting Parties with a view to drawing up:

a) National Schedules specifying the annual reductions in duties, charges and other restrictions which each contracting Party grants to the other contracting Parties in accordance with the provisions of Article 5; and

b) A Common Schedule listing the products on which the contracting Parties collectively agree to eliminate duties, charges and other restrictions completely, so far as intra-Area trade is concerned, within the period mentioned in Article 2, by complying with the minimum percentages set out in Article 7 and through the gradual reduction provided for in Article 5.

Article 5 With a view to the preparation of the National Schedules referred to in Article 4, sub-paragraph (a), each contracting Party shall annually grant to the other contracting Parties reductions in duties and charges equivalent to not less than eight (8) per cent of the weighted average applicable to third countries, until they are eliminated in respect of substantially all of its imports from the Area, in accordance with the definitions, methods of calculation, rules and procedures laid down in the Protocol.

For this purpose, duties and charges for third parties shall be deemed to be those in force on 31 December prior to each negotiation.

When the import regime of a contracting Party contains restrictions of such a kind that the requisite equivalence with the reductions in duties and charges granted by another contracting Party or other contracting Parties is unobtainable, the counterpart of these reductions shall be complemented by means of the elimination or relaxation of those restrictions.

Article 6 The National Schedules shall enter into force on 1 January of each year, except that those deriving from the initial negotiations shall enter into force on the date fixed by the contracting Parties.

Article 7 The Common Schedule shall consist of products which, in terms of the aggregate value of the trade among the contracting Parties, shall constitute not less than the following percentages, calculated in accordance with the provisions of the Protocol:

Twenty-five (25) per cent during the first three-year period;
Fifty (50) per cent during the second three-year period;
Seventy-five (75) per cent during the third three-year period;
Substantially all of such trade during the fourth three-year period.

Article 8 The inclusion of products in the Common Schedule shall be final and the concessions granted in respect thereof irrevocable.

Concessions granted in respect of products which appear only in the National Schedules may be withdrawn by negotiation among the contracting Parties and on a basis of adequate compensation.

Article 9 The percentages referred to in Articles 5 and 7 shall be calculated on the basis of the average annual value of trade during the three years preceding the year in which each negotiation is effected.

Article 10 The purpose of the negotiations—based on reciprocity of concessions—referred to in Article 4 shall be to expand and diversify trade and to promote gradually complementary economies for the countries in the Area.

In these negotiations the situation of those contracting Parties whose levels of duties, charges, and restrictions differ substantially from those of the other contracting Parties shall be considered with due fairness.

Article 11   If, as a result of the concessions granted, significant and persistent disadvantages are created in respect of trade between one contracting Party and the others as a whole in the products included in the liberalization program, the contracting Parties shall, at the request of the contracting Party affected, consider steps to remedy these disadvantages with a view to the adoption of suitable, nonrestrictive measures designed to promote trade at the highest possible levels.

Article 12   If, as a result of circumstances other than those referred to in Article 11, significant and persistent disadvantages are created in respect of trade in the products included in the liberalization program, the contracting Parties shall, at the request of the contracting Party concerned, make every effort within their power to remedy these disadvantages.

Article 13   The reciprocity mentioned in Article 10 refers to the expected growth in the flow of trade between each contracting Party and the others as a whole, in the products included in the liberalization program and those which may subsequently be added.

Chapter III

EXPANSION OF TRADE AND COMPLEMENTARY ECONOMIES

Article 14   In order to ensure the continued expansion and diversification of reciprocal trade, the contracting Parties shall take steps:

a) To grant one another, while observing the principle of reciprocity, concessions which will ensure that, in the first negotiation, treatment not less favorable than that which existed before the date of entry into force of the present Treaty is accorded to imports from within the Area;

b) To include in the National Schedules the largest possible number of products in which trade is carried on among the contracting Parties; and

c) To add to these Schedules an increasing number of products which are not yet included in reciprocal trade.

Article 15   In order to ensure fair competitive conditions among the contracting Parties and to facilitate increasing economic integration and complementary economies, particularly with regard to industrial production, the contracting Parties shall make every effort—in keeping with the liberalization objectives of the present Treaty—to reconcile their import and export regimes, as well as the treatment they accord to capital, goods, and services from outside the Area.

Article 16   With a view to expediting the process of integration and complementary economies referred to in Article 15, the contracting Parties:

a) Shall endeavor to promote progressively closer coordination of the corresponding industrialization policies, and shall sponsor for this purpose agreements among representatives of the economic sectors concerned; and
b) May negotiate mutual agreements on complementary economies by industrial sectors.

Article 17   The complementary economy agreements referred to in Article 16, sub-paragraph (b), shall set forth the liberalization program to be applied to products of the sector concerned and may contain, *inter alia,* clauses designed to reconcile the treatment accorded to raw materials and other components used in the manufacture of these products.

Any contracting Party concerned with the complementary economy programs shall be free to participate in the negotiation of these agreements.

The results of these negotiations shall, in every case, be embodied in protocols which shall enter into force after the contracting Parties have decided that they are consistent with the general principles and purposes of the present Treaty.

Chapter IV

MOST-FAVORED-NATION TREATMENT

Article 18   Any advantage, benefit, franchise, immunity, or privilege applied by a contracting Party in respect of a product originating in or intended for consignment to any other country shall be immediately and unconditionally extended to the similar product originating in or intended for consignment to the territory of the other contracting Parties.

Article 19   The most-favored-nation treatment referred to in Article 18 shall not be applicable to the advantages, benefits, franchises, immunities, and privileges already granted or which may be granted by virtue of agreements among contracting Parties or between contracting Parties and third countries with a view to facilitating border trade.

Article 20   Capital originating in the Area shall enjoy, in the territory of each contracting Party, treatment not less favorable than that granted to capital originating in any other country.

Chapter V

TREATMENT IN RESPECT OF INTERNAL TAXATION

Article 21 With respect to taxes, rates, and other internal duties and charges, products originating in the territory of a contracting Party shall enjoy, in the territory of another contracting Party, treatment no less favorable than that accorded to similar national products.

Article 22 Each contracting Party shall endeavor to ensure that the charges or other domestic measures applied to products included in the liberalization program which are not produced, or are produced only in small quantities, in its territory, do not nullify or reduce any concession or advantage obtained by any contracting Party during the negotiations.

If a contracting Party considers itself injured by virtue of the measures mentioned in the previous paragraph, it may appeal to the competent organs of the Association with a view to having the matter examined and appropriate recommendations made.

Chapter VI

SAVING CLAUSES

Article 23 The contracting Parties may, as a provisional measure and providing that the customary level of consumption in the importer country is not thereby lowered, authorize a contracting Party to impose nondiscriminatory restrictions upon imports of products included in the liberalization program which originate in the Area, if these products are imported in such quantities or under such conditions that they have, or are liable to have, serious repercussions on specific productive activities of vital importance to the national economy.

Article 24 The contracting Parties may likewise authorize a contracting Party which has adopted measures to correct its unfavorable overall balance of payments to extend these measures, provisionally and without discrimination, to intra-Area trade in the products included in the liberalization program.

The contracting Parties shall endeavor to ensure that the imposition of restrictions deriving from the balance-of-payments situation does not affect trade, within the Area, in the products included in the liberalization program.

Article 25 If the situations referred to in Articles 23 and 24 call for immediate action, the contracting Party concerned may, as an emergency arrangement to be referred to the contracting Parties, apply the measures provided for in the said articles. The measures adopted must immediately be communicated to the Committee mentioned in Article 33, which, if it seems necessary, shall convene a special session of the Conference.

Article 26 Should the measures envisaged in this chapter be prolonged for more than one year, the Committee shall propose to the Conference, referred to in Article 33, either *ex officio* or at the request of any of the contracting Parties, the immediate initiation of negotiations with a view to eliminating the restrictions adopted.

The present article does not affect the provisions of Article 8.

Chapter VII

SPECIAL PROVISIONS CONCERNING AGRICULTURE

Article 27 The contracting Parties shall seek to coordinate their agricultural development and agricultural commodity trade policies, with a view to securing the most efficient utilization of their natural resources, raising the standard of living of the rural population, and guaranteeing normal supplies to consumers, without disorganizing the regular productive activities of each contracting Party.

Article 28 Providing that no lowering of its customary consumption or increase in antieconomic production is involved, a contracting Party may apply, within the period mentioned in Article 2, and in respect of trade in agricultural commodities of substantial importance to its economy that are included in the liberalization program, appropriate nondiscriminatory measures designed to:

a) Limit imports to the amount required to meet the deficit in internal production; and

b) Equalize the prices of the imported and domestic product.

The contracting Party which decides to apply these measures shall inform the other contracting Parties before it puts them into effect.

Article 29 During the period prescribed in Article 2 an attempt shall be made to expand intra-Area trade in agricultural commodities by such means as agreements among the contracting Parties designed to cover deficits in domestic production.

For this purpose, the contracting Parties shall give priority, under normal competitive conditions, to products originating in the territories of the other contracting Parties, due consideration being given to the traditional flows of intra-Area trade.

Should such agreements be concluded among two or more contracting Parties, the other contracting Parties shall be notified before the agreements enter into force.

Article 30 The measures provided for in this chapter shall not be applied for the purpose of incorporating, in the production of agricultural commodities, resources which imply a reduction in the average level of productivity existing on the date on which the present Treaty enters into force.

Article 31 If a contracting Party considers itself injured by a reduction of its exports attributable to the lowering of the usual consumption level of the importer country as a result of measures referred to in Article 28 and/or an antieconomic increase in the production referred to in the previous article, it may appeal to the competent organs of the Association to study the situation and, if necessary, to make recommendations for the adoption of appropriate measures to be applied in accordance with Article 12.

Chapter VIII

MEASURES IN FAVOR OF COUNTRIES AT A RELATIVELY LESS ADVANCED STAGE OF ECONOMIC DEVELOPMENT

Article 32 The contracting Parties, recognizing that fulfillment of the purposes of the present Treaty will be facilitated by the economic growth of the countries in the Area that are at a relatively less advanced stage of economic development, shall take steps to create conditions conducive to such growth.

To this end, the contracting Parties may:

a) Authorize a contracting Party to grant to another contracting Party which is at a relatively less advanced stage of economic development within the Area, as long as necessary and as a temporary measure, for the purposes set out in the present article, advantages not extended to the other contracting Parties, in order to encourage the introduction or expansion of specific productive activities;

b) Authorize a contracting Party at a relatively less advanced stage of economic development within the Area to implement the program for the reduction of duties, charges, and other restrictions under more favorable conditions, specially agreed upon;

c) Authorize a contracting Party at a relatively less advanced stage of economic development within the Area to adopt appropriate measures to correct an unfavorable balance of payments, if the case arises;

d) Authorize a contracting Party at a relatively less advanced stage of economic development within the Area to apply, if necessary and as a temporary measure, and providing that this does not entail a decrease in its customary consumption, appropriate nondiscriminatory measures designed to protect the domestic output of products included in the liberalization program which are of vital importance to its economic development;

e) Make collective arrangements in favor of a contracting Party at a relatively less advanced stage of economic development within the Area with respect to the support and promotion, both inside and outside the Area, of financial or technical measures designed to bring about the expansion of existing productive activities or to encourage new activities, particularly those intended for the industrialization of its raw materials; and

f) Promote or support, as the case may be, special technical assistance programs for one or more contracting Parties, intended to raise, in countries at a relatively less advanced stage of economic development within the Area, productivity levels in specific production sectors.

Chapter IX

ORGANS OF THE ASSOCIATION

Article 33   The organs of the Association are the Conference of the contracting Parties (referred to in this Treaty as "the Conference") and the Standing Executive Committee (referred to in this Treaty as "the Committee").

Article 34   The Conference is the supreme organ of the Association. It shall adopt all decisions in matters requiring joint action on the part of the contracting Parties, and it shall be empowered, *inter alia:*

a) To take the necessary steps to carry out the present Treaty and to study the results of its implementation;

b) To promote the negotiations provided for in Article 4 and to assess the results thereof;

c) To approve the Committee's annual budget and to fix the contributions of each contracting Party;

d) To lay down its own rules of procedure and to approve the Committee's rules of procedure;

e) To elect a Chairman and two Vice Chairmen for each session;

f) To appoint the Executive Secretary of the Committee; and

g) To deal with other business of common interest.

Article 35   The Conference shall be composed of duly accredited representatives of the contracting Parties. Each delegation shall have one vote.

Article 36   The Conference shall hold: a) a regular session once a year; and b) special sessions when convened by the Committee.

At each session the Conference shall decide the place and date of the following regular session.

Article 37   The Conference may not take decisions unless at least two thirds ($\frac{2}{3}$) of the contracting Parties are present.

Article 38   During the first two years in which the present Treaty is in force, decisions of the Conference shall be adopted when affirmative votes are cast by at least two thirds ($\frac{2}{3}$) of the contracting Parties and providing that no negative vote is cast.

The contracting Parties shall likewise determine the voting system to be adopted after this two-year period.

The affirmative vote of two thirds ($\frac{2}{3}$) of the contracting Parties shall be required:

a) To approve the Committee's annual budget;
b) To elect the Chairman and two Vice Chairmen of the Conference, as well as the Executive Secretary; and
c) To fix the time and place of the sessions of the Conference.

Article 39   The Committee is the permanent organ of the Association responsible for supervising the implementation of the provisions of the present Treaty. Its duties and responsibilities shall be, *inter alia:*

a) To convene the Conference;
b) To submit for the approval of the Conference an annual work program and the Committee's annual budget estimates;
c) To represent the Association in dealings with third countries and international organs and entities for the purpose of considering matters of common interest. It shall also represent the Association in contracts and other instruments of public and private law;
d) To undertake studies, to suggest measures and to submit to the Conference such recommendations as it deems appropriate for the effective implementation of the Treaty;
e) To submit to the Conference at its regular sessions an annual report on its activities and on the results of the implementation of the present Treaty;
f) To request the technical advice and the cooperation of individuals and of national and international organizations;
g) To take such decisions as may be delegated to it by the Conference; and
h) To undertake the work assigned to it by the Conference.

Article 40   The Committee shall consist of a Permanent Representative of each contracting Party, who shall have a single vote.

Each Representative shall have an Alternate.

Article 41   The Committee shall have a secretariat headed by an Executive Secretary and comprising technical and administrative personnel.

The Executive Secretary, elected by the Conference for a three-year term and eligible for reelection, shall attend the plenary meetings of the Committee without the right to vote.

The Executive Secretary shall be the General Secretary of the Conference. His duties shall be, *inter alia:*

a) To organize the work of the Conference and of the Committee;
b) To prepare the Committee's annual budget estimates; and
c) To recruit and engage the technical and administrative staff in accordance with the Committee's rules of procedure.

Article 42   In the performance of their duties, the Executive Secretary and the secretariat staff shall not seek or receive instructions from any government or from any other national or international entity. They shall refrain from any action which might reflect on their position as international civil servants.

The contracting Parties undertake to respect the international character of the responsibilities of the Executive Secretary and of the secretariat staff and shall refrain from influencing them in any way in the discharge of their responsibilities.

Article 43   In order to facilitate the study of specific problems, the Committee may set up Advisory Commissions composed of representatives of the various sectors of economic activity of each of the contracting Parties.

Article 44   The Committee shall request, for the organs of the Association, the technical advice of the secretariat of the United Nations Economic Commission for Latin America (ECLA) and of the Inter-American Economic and Social Council (IA-ECOSOC) of the Organization of American States.

Article 45   The Committee shall be constituted sixty days from the entry into force of the present Treaty and shall have its headquarters in the city of Montevideo.

Chapter X

JURIDICAL PERSONALITY—IMMUNITIES AND PRIVILEGES

Article 46   The Latin American Free Trade Association shall possess complete juridical personality and shall, in particular, have the power:

a) To contract;
b) To acquire and dispose of the movable and immovable property it needs for the achievement of its objectives;
c) To institute legal proceedings; and
d) To hold funds in any currency and to transfer them as necessary.

Article 47 The representatives of the contracting Parties and the international staff and advisers of the Association shall enjoy in the Area such diplomatic and other immunities and privileges as are necessary for the exercise of their functions.

The contracting Parties undertake to conclude, as soon as possible, an Agreement regulating the provisions of the previous paragraph in which the aforesaid privileges and immunities shall be defined.

The Association shall conclude with the Government of the Eastern Republic of Uruguay an Agreement for the purpose of specifying the privileges and immunities which the Association, its organs, and its international staff and advisers shall enjoy.

Chapter XI

MISCELLANEOUS PROVISIONS

Article 48 No change introduced by a contracting Party in its regime of import duties and charges shall imply a level of duties and charges less favorable than that in force before the change for any commodity in respect of which concessions are granted to the other contracting Parties.

The requirement set out in the previous paragraph shall not apply to the conversion to present worth of the official base value (*aforo*) in respect of customs duties and charges, providing that such conversion corresponds exclusively to the real value of the goods. In such cases, the value shall not include the customs duties and charges levied on the goods.

Article 49 In order to facilitate the implementation of the provisions of the present Treaty, the contracting Parties shall, as soon as possible:

a) Determine the criteria to be adopted for the purpose of establishing the origin of goods and for classifying them as raw materials, semimanufactured goods or finished products;

b) Simplify and standardize procedures and formalities relating to reciprocal trade;

c) Prepare a tariff nomenclature to serve as a common basis for the presentation of statistics and for carrying out the negotiations provided for in the present Treaty;

d) Determine what shall be deemed to constitute border trade within the meaning of Article 19;

e) Determine the criteria for the purpose of defining "dumping" and other unfair trade practices and the procedures relating thereto.

Article 50 The products imported from the Area by a contracting Party may not be reexported save by agreement between the contracting Parties concerned.

A product shall not be deemed to be a reexport if it has been subjected in the importer country to industrial processing or manufacture, the degree of which shall be determined by the Committee.

Article 51 Products imported or exported by a contracting Party shall enjoy freedom of transit within the Area and shall only be subject to the payment of the normal rates for services rendered.

Article 52 No contracting Party shall promote its exports by means of subsidies or other measures likely to disrupt normal competitive conditions in the Area.

An export shall not be deemed to have been subsidized if it is exempted from duties and charges levied on the product or its components when destined for internal consumption, or if it is subject to drawback.

Article 53 No provision of the present Treaty shall be so construed as to constitute an impediment to the adoption and execution of measures relating to:

a) The protection of public morality;
b) The application of security laws and regulations;
c) The control of imports or exports of arms, ammunition, and other war equipment and, in exceptional circumstances, of all other military items, in so far as this is compatible with the terms of Article 51 and of the treaties on the unrestricted freedom of transit in force among the contracting Parties;
d) The protection of human, animal and plant life and health;
e) Imports and exports of gold and silver bullion;
f) The protection of the nation's heritage of artistic, historical, and archaeological value; and
g) The export, use, and consumption of nuclear materials, radioactive products or any other material that may be used in the development or exploitation of nuclear energy.

Article 54 The contracting Parties shall make every effort to direct their policies with a view to creating conditions favorable to the establishment of a Latin American common market. To that end, the Committee shall undertake studies and consider projects and plans designed to achieve this purpose, and shall endeavor to coordinate its work with that of other international organizations.

Chapter XII

FINAL PROVISIONS

Article 55 The present Treaty may not be signed with reservations nor shall reservations be admitted at the time of ratification or accession.

Article 56   The present Treaty shall be ratified by the signatory States at the earliest opportunity.

The instruments of ratification shall be deposited with the Government of the Eastern Republic of Uruguay, which shall communicate the date of deposit to the Governments of the signatory and successively acceding States.

Article 57   The present Treaty shall enter into force for the first three ratifying States thirty days after the third instrument of ratification has been deposited; and, for the other signatories, thirty days after the respective instrument of ratification has been deposited, and in the order in which the ratifications are deposited.

The Government of the Eastern Republic of Uruguay shall communicate the date of the entry into force of the present Treaty to the Government of each of the signatory States.

Article 58   Following its entry into force, the present Treaty shall remain open to accession by the other Latin American States, which for this purpose shall deposit the relevant instrument of accession with the Government of the Eastern Republic of Uruguay. The Treaty shall enter into force for the acceding State thirty days after the deposit of the corresponding instrument.

Acceding States shall enter into the negotiations referred to in Article 4 at the session of the Conference immediately following the date of deposit of the instrument of accession.

Article 59   Each contracting Party shall begin to benefit from the concessions already granted to one another by the other contracting Parties as from the date of entry into force of the reductions in duties and charges and other restrictions negotiated by them on a basis of reciprocity, and after the minimum obligations referred to in Article 5, accumulated during the period which has elapsed since the entry into force of the present Treaty, have been carried out.

Article 60   The contracting Parties may present amendments to the present Treaty, which shall be set out in protocols that shall enter into force upon their ratification by all the contracting Parties and after the corresponding instruments have been deposited.

Article 61   On the expiration of the twelve-year term starting on the date of entry into force of the present Treaty, the contracting Parties shall proceed to study the results of the Treaty's implementation and shall initiate the necessary collective negotiations with a view to fulfilling more effectively the purposes of the Treaty and, if desirable, to adapting it to a new stage of economic integration.

Article 62   The provisions of the present Treaty shall not affect the rights and obligations deriving from agreements signed by any of the contracting Parties prior to the entry into force of the present Treaty.

However, each contracting Party shall take the necessary steps to reconcile the provisions of existing agreements with the purposes of the present Treaty.

Article 63   The present Treaty shall be of unlimited duration.

Article 64   A contracting Party wishing to withdraw from the present Treaty shall inform the other contracting Parties of its intention at a regular session of the Conference, and shall formally submit the instrument of denunciation at the following regular session.

When the formalities of denunciation have been completed, those rights and obligations of the denouncing Government which derive from its status as a contracting Party shall cease automatically, with the exception of those relating to reductions in duties and charges and other restrictions, received or granted under the liberalization program, which shall remain in force for a period of five years from the date on which the denunciation becomes formally effective.

The period specified in the preceding paragraph may be shortened if there is sufficient justification, with the consent of the Conference and at the request of the contracting Party concerned.

Article 65   The present Treaty shall be called the Montevideo Treaty.

IN WITNESS WHEREOF the undersigned Plenipotentiaries, having deposited their full powers, found in good and due form, have signed the present Treaty on behalf of their respective Governments.

DONE in the City of Montevideo, on the eighteenth day of the month of February in the year One Thousand Nine Hundred and Sixty, in one original in the Spanish and one in the Portuguese language, both texts being equally authentic. The Government of the Eastern Republic of Uruguay shall be the depositary of the present Treaty and shall transmit duly certified copies thereof to the Governments of the other signatory and acceding States.

For the Government of Argentina: *Diógenes Taboada*

For the Government of Brazil: *Horacio Lafer*

For the Government of Chile: *Germán Vergara Donoso*

For the Government of Mexico: *Manuel Tello*

For the Government of Paraguay: *Raúl Sapena Pastor*
Pèdro Ramón Chamorro

For the Government of Peru: *Hernán Bellido*
Gonzalo L. de Aramburu

For the Government of Uruguay: *Horacio Martínez Montero*
                                   Mateo Magariños de Melo

The signatory governments deposited their instruments of ratification on May 2, 1961. Subsequently, the following governments adhered on the dates indicated

Colombia	September 30, 1961
Ecuador	November 3, 1961
Venezuela	September 1, 1966
Bolivia	January 31, 1967

Protocol No. 1

ON NORMS AND PROCEDURES FOR NEGOTIATIONS

On the occasion of the signing of the Treaty establishing a Free Trade Area and instituting the Latin American Free Trade Association (Montevideo Treaty), the signatories, thereunto duly authorized by their Governments, hereby agree upon the following Protocol:

TITLE I

Calculation of Weighted Averages

1. For the purposes of Article 5 of the Montevideo Treaty, it shall be understood that, as a result of the negotiations for the establishment of the National Schedules, the difference between the weighted average of duties and charges in force for third countries and that which shall be applicable to imports from within the area shall be not less than the product of eight per cent (8%) of the weighted average of duties and charges in force for third countries multiplied by the number of years that have elapsed since the Treaty became effective.

2. The reduction mechanism shall therefore be based on two weighted averages: one corresponding to the average of the duties and charges in force for third countries; and the other to the average of the duties and charges which shall be applicable to imports within the Area.

3. In order to calculate each of these weighted averages, the total amount that would be represented by the duties and charges on aggregate imports of the goods under consideration shall be divided by the total value of these imports.

4. This calculation will give a percentage (or *ad valorem* figure) for each weighted average. It is the difference between the two averages

that shall be not less than the product of the factor 0.08 (or eight per cent) multiplied by the number of years elapsed.

5. The foregoing formula is expressed as follows:

$$t \leqslant T\,(1 - 0.08n)$$

in which t = weighted average of the duties and charges that shall be applicable to imports from within the area; T = weighted average of duties and charges in force for third countries; n = number of years since the Treaty entered into force.

6. In calculating the weighted averages for each of the contracting Parties, the following shall be taken into account:

a) Products originating in the territory of the other contracting Parties and imported from the area during the preceding three-year period and further products included in the National Schedule concerned as a result of negotiations;

b) The total value of imports, irrespective of origin, of each of the products referred to in subparagraph a), during the three-year period preceding each negotiation; and

c) The duties and charges on imports from third countries in force as on 31 December prior to the negotiations, and the duties and charges applicable to imports from within the Area entering into force on 1 January following the negotiations.

7. The contracting Parties shall be entitled to exclude products of little value from the group referred to in subparagraph a), provided that their aggregate value does not exceed five per cent (5%) of the value of imports from within the Area.

TITLE II

Exchange of Information

8. The contracting Parties shall provide one another, through the Standing Executive Committee, with information as complete as possible on:

a) National statistics in respect of total imports and exports (value in dollars and volume, by countries both of origin and of destination), production and consumption;

b) Customs legislation and regulations;

c) Exchange, monetary, fiscal and administrative legislation, regulations and practices bearing on exports and imports;

d) International trade treaties and agreements whose provisions relate to the Treaty;

e) Systems of direct or indirect subsidies on production or exports including minimum price systems; and

f) State trading systems.

9. So far as possible, these data shall be permanently available to the contracting Parties. They shall be specially brought up to date sufficiently in advance of the opening of the annual negotiations.

TITLE III

Negotiation of National Schedules

10. Before June 30 of each year, the contracting Parties shall make available to one another, through the Standing Executive Committee, the list of products in respect of which they are applying for concessions and, before August 15 of each year (with the exception of the first year, when the corresponding final date shall be October 1), the preliminary list of items in favor of which they are prepared to grant concessions.

11. On September 1 of each year (with the exception of the first year, when the corresponding date shall be November 1), the contracting Parties shall initiate the negotiation of the concessions to be accorded by each to the others as a whole. The concessions shall be assessed multilaterally, although this shall not preclude the conduct of negotiations by pairs or groups of countries, in accordance with the interest attaching to specific products.

12. Upon the conclusion of this phase of the negotiations, the Standing Executive Committee shall make the calculations referred to in Title I of this Protocol and shall inform each contracting Party, at the earliest possible opportunity, of the percentage whereby its individual concessions reduce the weighted average of the duties and charges in force for imports from within the Area, in relation to the weighted average of duties and charges applicable in the case of third countries.

13. When the concessions negotiated fall short of the corresponding minimum commitment, the negotiations among the contracting Parties shall be continued, so that the list of reductions of duties and charges and other restrictions to enter into force as from the following January 1 may be simultaneously published by each of the contracting Parties not later than November 1 of each year.

TITLE IV

Negotiation of the Common Schedule

14. During each three-year period and not later than on May 31 of the third, sixth, ninth, and twelfth years from the time of the Treaty's entry into force, the Standing Executive Committee shall supply the contracting Parties with statistical data on the value and volume of the products traded in the Area during the preceding three-year period,

indicating the proportion of aggregate trade which each individually represented.

15. Before June 30 of the third, sixth, and ninth years from the time of the Treaty's entry into force, the contracting Parties shall exchange the lists of products whose inclusion in the Common Schedule they wish to negotiate.

16. The contracting Parties shall conduct multilateral negotiation to establish, before November 30 of the third, sixth, ninth, and twelfth years, a Common Schedule comprising goods whose value meets the minimum commitments referred to in Article 7 of the Treaty.

TITLE V

Special and Temporary Provisions

17. In the negotiations to which this Protocol refers, consideration shall be given to those cases in which varying levels of duties and charges on certain products create conditions such that producers in the Area are not competing on equitable terms.

18. To this end, steps shall be taken to ensure prior equalization of tariffs or to secure by any other suitable procedure the highest possible degree of effective reciprocity.

IN WITNESS WHEREOF the respective representatives have signed the Protocol.

DONE in the City of Montevideo, this eighteenth day of the month of February in the year One Thousand Nine Hundred and Sixty, in one original in the Spanish and one in the Portuguese language, both texts being equally authentic.

The Government of the Eastern Republic of Uruguay shall act as depositary of the present Protocol and shall send certified true copies thereof to the Governments of the other signatory and acceding countries.

Protocol No. 2

ON THE ESTABLISHMENT OF A
PROVISIONAL COMMITTEE

On the occasion of the signing of the Treaty establishing a Free Trade Area and instituting the Latin American Free Trade Association (Montevideo Treaty), the signatories, thereunto duly authorized by their Governments, taking into consideration the need to adopt and coordinate measures to facilitate the entry into force of the Treaty, hereby agree as follows:

1. A Provisional Committee shall be set up, composed of one representative of each signatory State. Each representative shall have an alternate.

At its first meeting the Provisional Committee shall elect from among its members one Chairman and two Vice Chairmen.

2. The terms of reference of the Provisional Committee shall be as follows:

a) To draw up its rules of procedure;

b) To prepare, within sixty days from the date of its inauguration, its work program and to establish its budget of expenditures and the contributions to be made by each country;

c) To adopt the measures and prepare the documents necessary for the presentation of the Treaty to the contracting Parties of the General Agreement on Tariffs and Trade (GATT);

d) To convene and prepare for the first Conference of contracting Parties;

e) To assemble and prepare the data and statistics required for the first series of negotiations connected with the implementation of the liberalization program provided for in the Treaty;

f) To carry out or promote studies and research, and to adopt whatsoever measures may be necessary in the common interest during its period of office; and

g) To prepare a preliminary draft agreement on the privileges and immunities referred to in Article 47 of the Treaty.

3. In technical matters, the Provisional Committee shall be assisted in an advisory capacity by the United Nations Economic Commission for Latin America (ECLA) and the Inter-American Economic and Social Council (IA-ECOSOC), of the Organization of American States, in accordance with the relevant Protocol.

4. The Provisional Committee shall appoint an Administrative Secretary and other requisite staff.

5. The Provisional Committee shall be inaugurated on April 1, 1960, and its quorum shall be constituted by not less than four members. Up to that date, the Offices of the Inter-Governmental Conference for the Establishment of a Free Trade Area among Latin American Countries shall continue to discharge their functions, for the sole purpose of establishing the Provisional Committee.

6. The Provisional Committee shall remain in office until the Standing Executive Committee, provided for in Article 33 of the Treaty, has been set up.

7. The Provisional Committee shall have its headquarters in the city of Montevideo.

8. The Officers of the abovementioned Conference are recommended to request the Government of the Eastern Republic of Uru-

guay to advance the necessary sums to cover the payment of staff salaries and the installation and operational expenses of the Provisional Committee during the first ninety days. These sums shall be subsequently reimbursed by the States signatories of the present Treaty.

9. The Provisional Committee shall approach the signatory Governments with a view to obtaining for the members of its constituent delegations, as well as for its international staff and advisers, such immunities and privileges as may be needful for the performance of their duties.

IN WITNESS WHEREOF the respective representatives have signed the present Protocol.

DONE in the City of Montevideo, this eighteenth day of the month of February in the year One Thousand Nine Hundred and Sixty, in one original in the Spanish and one in the Portuguese language, both texts being equally authentic. The Government of the Eastern Republic of Uruguay shall act as the depositary of the present Protocol and shall send certified true copies thereof to the Governments of the other signatory and acceding countries.

Protocol No. 3

ON THE COLLABORATION OF THE UNITED NATIONS ECONOMIC COMMISSION FOR LATIN AMERICA (ECLA) AND OF THE INTER-AMERICAN ECONOMIC AND SOCIAL COUNCIL (IA-ECOSOC) OF THE ORGANIZATION OF AMERICAN STATES

On the occasion of the signing of the Treaty establishing a Free Trade Area and instituting the Latin American Free Trade Association (Montevideo Treaty), the signatories, thereunto duly authorized by their Governments, hereby agree as follows:

1. With reference to the provisions of Article 44 of the Treaty and in view of the fact that the secretariats of ECLA and of IA-ECOSOC have agreed to assist the organs of the Latin American Free Trade Association with advice on technical matters, a representative of each of the secretariats in question shall attend the meetings of the Standing Executive Committee of the abovementioned Association when the business to be discussed is, in the Committee's opinion, of a technical nature.

2. The appointment of the representatives referred to shall be subject to the prior approval of the members of the said Committee.

IN WITNESS WHEREOF the respective representatives have signed the present Protocol.

DONE at the City of Montevideo, this eighteenth day of the month of February in the year One Thousand Nine Hundred and Sixty, in one original in the Spanish and one in the Portuguese language, both texts being equally authentic. The Government of the Eastern Republic of Uruguay shall act as the depositary of the present Protocol and shall send certified true copies thereof to the Governments of the other signatory and acceding countries.

Protocol No. 4

ON COMMITMENTS TO PURCHASE OR SELL PETROLEUM AND PETROLEUM DERIVATIVES

On the occasion of the signing of the Treaty establishing a Free Trade Area and instituting the Latin American Free Trade Association (Montevideo Treaty), the signatories, thereunto duly authorized by their Governments, hereby agree:

To declare that the provisions of the Montevideo Treaty, signed on February 18, 1960, are not applicable to commitments to purchase or sell petroleum and petroleum derivatives resulting from agreements concluded by the signatories of the present Protocol prior to the date of signature of the abovementioned Treaty.

IN WITNESS WHEREOF the respective representatives have signed the present Protocol.

DONE at the City of Montevideo, this eighteenth day of the month of February in the year One Thousand Nine Hundred and Sixty, in one original in the Spanish and one in the Portuguese language, both texts being equally authentic.

The Government of the Eastern Republic of Uruguay shall act as depositary of the present Protocol and shall send certified true copies thereof to the Governments of the other signatory and acceding countries.

Protocol No. 5

ON SPECIAL TREATMENT IN FAVOR OF BOLIVIA AND PARAGUAY

On the occasion of the signing of the Treaty establishing a Free Trade area and instituting the Latin American Free Trade Association (Montevideo Treaty), the signatories, thereunto duly authorized by their Governments, hereby agree:

To declare that Bolivia and Paraguay are at present in a position to invoke in their favor the provisions in the Treaty concerning special treatment for countries at a relatively less advanced stage of economic development within the Free Trade Area.

IN WITNESS WHEREOF the respective representatives have signed the present Protocol.

DONE in the City of Montevideo, this eighteenth day of the month of February in the year One Thousand Nine Hundred and Sixty, in one original in the Spanish and one in the Portuguese language, both texts being equally authentic.

The Government of the Eastern Republic of Uruguay shall act as depositary of the present Protocol and shall send certified true copies thereof to the Governments of the other signatory and acceding countries.

Resolutions on the Functions and Organization of the Latin American Free Trade Association

REGULATIONS OF THE CONFERENCE OF THE CONTRACTING PARTIES
Resolution 35(II), Resolution 159(VI)

Chapter I

PARTICIPANTS IN THE CONFERENCE

Article 1 The Conference shall consist of the delegations of the contracting Parties that have been accredited by their respective governments.

Article 2 The chairman of each delegation and such members as the respective governments consider desirable must be vested with full powers.

Article 3 Each delegation shall have a chairman. In case of absence or impediment, the chairman of the delegation shall be represented by a member of his delegation designated by him. The delegations may be represented at both plenary sessions and on committees by any of their members.

Article 4 The Secretary General of the Conference shall participate in its discussions.

Article 5 Representatives of the organizations mentioned in Article 44 of the Montevideo Treaty may participate in the Conference as advisers.

Article 6 Representatives of countries and of specialized international organizations that have been invited by the Standing Executive Committee may attend plenary sessions of the Conference as observers.

Chapter II

SESSIONS OF THE CONFERENCE

Article 7 The Conference shall hold regular sessions once a year and special sessions whenever it is convoked by the Committee.

Chapter III

AGENDA OF THE CONFERENCE

Article 8[1] The Committee shall prepare the provisional agenda for each session of the Conference, which shall be transmitted to the contracting Parties not later than forty-five days prior to the opening of the corresponding session.

In the case of special sessions, this period may be reduced to a minimum of twenty days prior to the opening of the session.

Article 9 The agenda of the session of the Conference shall be adopted at the first plenary session. For a special session no topics may be introduced in the agenda other than those for which the meeting was convoked.

Article 10 After the agenda has been adopted, the Conference may change it only at the request of at least five member States.

Chapter IV

OFFICIAL LANGUAGES

Article 11 The official languages of the Conference are Spanish and Portuguese.

Chapter V

AUTHORITIES OF THE CONFERENCE

Article 12 The Conference shall have a Chairman and two Vice Chairmen elected from among the heads of the delegations at the first plenary session. The Executive Secretary of the Standing Executive Committee shall be its Secretary General.

Article 13 The Chairman and the Vice Chairmen shall be elected by an affirmative vote of at least two thirds of the contracting Parties.

---

[1] As modified by Resolution 159(VI).

Article 14   The duties of the Chairman are:

a) To preside over the plenary sessions of the Conference;
b) To install the committees of the Conference;
c) To determine the order of the day for the plenary sessions, in conformity with paragraph 2 of Article 20;
d) To take any steps necessary to maintain order and to enforce the Regulations; and
e) Any others established in the Regulations.

Article 15   If the Chairman does not attend a session or leaves while it is in progress, the chair shall be occupied by one of the Vice Chairmen. If the Chairman fails to attend another session the other Vice Chairman shall preside, the two alternating in succession in alphabetical order of countries. In the event that the Chairman and the Vice Chairmen cannot attend, the chair shall be occupied *ad interim* by the remaining heads of delegations in alphabetical order of countries.

Article 16   The Chairman of each session of the Conference shall be the provisional Chairman of the following session. In case of an impediment he shall be replaced by the Vice Chairmen in the order indicated in Article 15.

Article 17   In plenary sessions the Chairman cannot serve as a delegate at the same time. In the event that the Chairman of the Conference wishes to act as a delegate he must be replaced in his presiding functions in the manner indicated in Article 15.

Article 18   The Secretary General shall organize, direct, and coordinate the Secretariat of the Conference. In performing these functions he shall:

a) Direct the preparation of the minutes;
b) Serve as rapporteur of plenary sessions of the Conference;
c) Appoint the secretaries of the committees and other officials who are to serve on them, on subcommittees and working groups, and specify their duties;
d) Answer official correspondence addressed to the Conference, according to directives of the Chairman when pertinent;
e) Conduct public and press relations;
f) Perform any other functions assigned by the Conference.

Chapter VI

COMMITTEES OF THE CONFERENCE

Article 19   There shall be a Coordinating Committee, a Committee on Credentials, a Committee on Negotiations, and any other working committees that the Conference may deem necessary.

Article 20   The Coordinating Committee shall be composed of the chairmen of the delegations or their substitutes, and the Secretary General of the Conference shall act as its secretary. The chief representatives of the organizations named in Article 5 of the Regulations may participate in the work of this committee.

Article 21   The Coordinating Committee shall coordinate the work of the Conference and seek to harmonize the points of view of the several delegations and rule on matters submitted to it by the Chairman of the Conference and the chairmen of committees and delegations. The Coordinating Committee shall determine the order in which the topics of the agenda shall be taken up by the Conference.

Article 22   The Committee on Credentials shall be composed of members of the delegations of the contracting Parties designated at the first plenary session. It shall examine the full powers and credentials of the members of the delegations, of the representatives mentioned in Article 5 of the Regulations, and of observers in attendance, and submit its report to the Conference.

Article 23   The Committee on Negotiations shall be composed of members from all the delegations. It shall deal with questions relating to the establishment and application of the rules and procedures for negotiations, as well as rules and criteria for determining the origin of goods; it shall coordinate the action of the several delegations in respect of the method and order for conducting negotiations; and it shall study other matters connected with these subjects.

Article 24   The other working committees shall be composed of members of all delegations. Their function is to study the topics of the agenda assigned to them by the Conference and to present the corresponding reports and projects.

Article 25   The committees, with the exception of the Coordinating Committee, may also include members representing the organizations referred to in Article 5 of the Regulations.

Article 26   Each committee shall have a chairman and a rapporteur, such positions to be held by representatives of delegations so designated. Each committee may name such subcommittees and working groups as it considers advisable.

Article 27   The committees shall present their conclusions at the plenary sessions through their rapporteurs, who shall be limited to an objective presentation of the facts and of the results obtained.

Chapter VII

MEETINGS

Article 28   The Conference shall hold plenary sessions and committee meetings.

Article 29   The plenary sessions shall be public, unless the Conference decides otherwise, and they shall be convoked by the Chairman of the Conference on his own initiative or at the request of any delegation.

Article 30   At plenary sessions, in addition to performing the duties assigned him by other provisions of the Regulations, the Chairman shall:

a) Open and adjourn the sessions;
b) Direct the discussion and submit for consideration the matters listed in the order of the day;
c) Grant the floor to delegates in the order in which they have requested it;
d) Rule points of order in accordance with the provisions of Article 31;
e) Call for votes and announce the results thereof; and
f) Submit to a vote motions for postponing or ending discussion, at the time they are offered.

Article 31   During the discussion of a subject, any delegate may raise a point of order, and in such event the Chairman shall rule immediately as to whether the question is proper. If his ruling is appealed, the Chairman shall immediately submit the case to the Conference, and the ruling shall prevail unless it is rejected by a majority of the members.

Article 32   In plenary sessions the Chairman may limit the number of times that each delegation may speak on the same subject.

Article 33   No project or proposal may be considered in a plenary session unless a report has been submitted by the pertinent committee, unless the Conference decides to the contrary.

Article 34   The order of the day of plenary sessions shall be prepared by the Chairman, with the help of the Secretary General. Changes in the order of the day may be proposed only through the Coordinating Committee.

Article 35   The meetings of committees, subcommittees, and working groups shall be private, and only members of the delegations of the contracting Parties, representatives of the advisory organizations indicated in Article 5 of the Regulations, and members of the staff of the Secretariat of the Conference may attend. Committees may authorize exceptions to this rule, if duly justified. The committees shall be convoked by their chairmen, on their own initiative or at the request of any delegation.

Article 36 The committees shall adopt for their meetings whatever rules are considered most convenient, in accordance with the provisions of the Regulations.

Chapter VIII

QUORUM AND VOTING

Article 37 In order that a plenary session may be held a majority of the delegations accredited to the Conference must be present. However, no proposal of any kind may be voted on unless at least two thirds of the contracting Parties are present.

Article 38 Unless the contracting Parties establish some other system of voting, decisions taken at a plenary session shall require an affirmative vote of at least two thirds of the contracting Parties and providing there is no negative vote, except in those cases covered by Article 39 of the Treaty.

Article 39 In order that a committee meeting be held a majority of the delegations composing it must be present.

Article 40 Decisions of committees shall be adopted by an affirmative vote of a majority of the contracting Parties represented thereon.

Article 41 Only delegations accredited to the Conference may take part in the voting.
Each delegation is entitled to one vote.
A roll call vote may be requested by any delegate.

Article 42 At plenary sessions, at the request of any delegate, the voting on any motion or draft resolution may be divided into parts. If this is done, the text resulting from the partial votes shall then be voted on as a whole.

Article 43 Whenever an amendment modifies a proposal, or adds or suppresses concepts, the amendment itself shall be voted on first, and if this is approved, the proposal as amended shall then be voted on.

Article 44   If two or more amendments to a proposal are submitted, the one that departs the most from the substance of the original proposal shall be voted on first, and secondly, if necessary, the one that departs the most from the proposal after the first amendment was added, and thereafter successively until there has been a vote on all amendments.

Chapter IX

MINUTES AND DOCUMENTS

Article 45   A formal record shall be kept of plenary sessions and minutes shall be kept of committee meetings.

Article 46   The record of a plenary session shall reproduce the discussions accurately. In respect of the committees, the minutes may summarize the discussions and the conclusions reached shall be included. By decision of the Conference or of a committee, and when the subject dealt with so requires, a stenographic version of specific sessions may be taken.

Article 47   The order of the day and the documents to be used in plenary sessions shall be distributed to the delegations at least 24 hours in advance of the meeting concerned or within a shorter period if the Chairman of the Conference so decides.

Article 48   Whenever appropriate, agreements and protocols may be concluded, and the official texts in Spanish and Portuguese must be signed by all the contracting Parties.

Article 49   A Record of Negotiations shall be kept in accordance with the rules and procedures governing this matter, and in this shall be recorded the results and the decisions approved by the contracting Parties for carrying them out. The Record shall include the National Lists to which Article 4 of the Montevideo Treaty refers.

Article 50   The Final Act of the Conference shall contain the Record of Negotiations and any agreements, accords, protocols, resolutions, and other decisions adopted by the Conference. This instrument shall be drawn up in Spanish and in Portuguese, both official texts to be equally valid. The Secretariat of the Standing Executive Committee shall transmit a certified copy of the Final Act to each of the contracting Parties.

Article 51   The Standing Executive Committee shall be the depository of all instruments signed at a Conference.

REGULATIONS OF THE STANDING EXECUTIVE COMMITTEE

Resolution 152 (VI)

(Approved November 18, 1966)

IN VIEW OF Article 39, section (d) of the Treaty,
The Conference of the contracting Parties, at its Sixth Regular Session

RESOLVES

To approve the following:

REGULATIONS OF THE STANDING EXECUTIVE COMMITTEE

Chapter I

ORGANIZATION AND AUTHORITIES

Article 1 The Standing Executive Committee (henceforth called the Committee) is the permanent organ of the Latin American Free Trade Association entrusted with overseeing the application of the provisions of the Treaty of Montevideo (henceforth called the Treaty).

Article 2 The Committee shall consist of one Permanent Representative of each contracting Party.

The persons designated as Permanent Representatives shall present their credentials to the Chairman of the Committee.

Article 3 Each Permanent Representative shall have an alternate, who shall be accredited by him to the Chairman of the Committee. An alternate Representative shall replace his principal in the event of the absence or impediment of the latter, with the same functions and duties. Each delegation may have other members in whatever number and of whatever kind deemed desirable by each contracting Party, any of whom may be accredited by written notice from the principal Representative to replace the alternate Representative.

Article 4 The Committee shall select a Chairman and two Vice Chairmen from among the Permanent Representatives, the Vice Chairmen to replace the Chairman alternately, by alphabetical order of countries, in the event of his absence or impediment.

Whenever the Chairman and Vice Chairmen are all absent or under impediment, an interim chairman shall be selected alternately from among the Permanent Representatives in alphabetical order of countries.

Article 5   The Chairman and Vice Chairmen shall be elected for a term of one year by rotation and in alphabetical order of countries.

In the event of a vacancy of either office a new Representative shall be elected to complete the term.

Chapter II

FUNCTIONS AND REPRESENTATION

Article 6   The Committee has the following duties:

a) To convene the Conference in regular and special sessions;
b) To submit the annual work program for the approval of the Conference;
c) To submit the annual budget estimates for the approval of the Conference and see that it is carried out in accordance with the rules established by the Conference;
d) To submit to the Conference as its regular sessions an annual report on its activities and on the results of the implementation of the Treaty;
e) To perform functions of liaison and coordination between the organs of the Association and between the contracting Parties, in all matters bearing a relation with the Treaty and all other instruments making up the legal structure of LAFTA;
f) To issue the organic regulations for the Secretariat of the Committee;
g) To designate the high-ranking officials of the Association for the purpose of carrying out the provisions of the protocols to which Resolutions 6(I) and 7(I) of the Conference refer;
h) To represent the Association in matters within its competence and of mutual interest, between:
   i) The contracting Parties through the Permanent Representatives or directly in pertinent cases;
   ii) Third countries;
   iii) International organs or agencies;
i) To represent the Association in contracts and other instruments of public and private law;
j) To undertake studies, make recommendations to the Conference, and suggest measures considered desirable for implementing the Treaty;
k) To request the technical advice or cooperation of individuals and of national or international organizations;
l) To take decisions on matters delegated to it by the Conference;
m) To perform the tasks entrusted to it by the Conference;
n) To attend to all other matters included within the objectives of

the Treaty, unless they have been specifically assigned to the Conference; and

o) To perform all other tasks and carry out the other functions entrusted to it by the Treaty and related international instruments.

Article 7   The Committee acts as representative of the Association, and such representation may be delegated to the Chairman, to another of its members, to the Executive Secretary, or to anyone considered advisable, as determined in each case.

Chapter III

SECRETARIAT

Article 8   The Committee has a Secretariat headed by an Executive Secretary and comprised of the technical and administrative staff.

The Secretariat shall be organized in accordance with its organic regulations.

Article 9   The Executive Secretary shall be responsible to the organs of the Association for the proper conduct of business by the Secretariat.

Article 10   The Committee, by a vote of two thirds of the contracting Parties, may suspend the Executive Secretary from his duties and propose his removal to the Conference if he has committed serious acts or omissions which affect the progress of the Association.

Article 11   In case of a temporary impediment or absence of the Executive Secretary, he shall be replaced by the highest-ranking official of the Secretariat.

Article 12   In case of vacancy the duties of the Executive Secretary shall be performed by the highest-ranking official of the Secretariat until the Conference of the contracting Parties appoints a new Executive Secretary.

Article 13   In selecting the staff of the Secretariat account shall be taken, as a primary consideration, of the need for assuring the highest degree of efficiency. Likewise due consideration shall be given to contracting personnel in such a way as to have as broad a geographical representation as possible.

The selection shall be made on the basis of background and tests of competency as provided in the Regulations of the Secretariat.

Article 14   In the performance of their duties, the Executive Secretary and members of the staff of the Secretariat may not request or receive instructions from any government nor from any national or international entity, and they must refrain from any acts incompatible with their status as officials of an international organization.

The staff of the Secretariat shall be responsible to the Executive Secretary.

Chapter IV

FUNCTIONS OF THE EXECUTIVE SECRETARY

Article 15   The Executive Secretary shall have the following functions:

a) To propose to the Committee the annual work program;
b) To organize the work of the Committee and of the Conference;
c) To prepare the annual budget estimates and propose to the Committee measures deemed pertinent for carrying it out;
d) To offer suggestions to the Committee designed to improve the work of the Association;
e) To prepare a draft of the annual report of the activities of the Association and to submit a report annually to the Committee on the activities of the Secretariat;
f) To participate in meetings of the Committee without the right to vote;
g) To serve as Secretary General of the Conference;
h) To contract for and remove members of the staff and advisers on specific matters, in accordance with the provisions of these Regulations and the Organic Regulations of the Secretariat;
i) To organize, direct, and supervise the functioning of the Secretariat;
j) To maintain a working contact with other technical international organizations on the Secretariat level;
k) To assemble the information required for carrying out the tasks of the Secretariat;
l) To authenticate the documents issued by the Committee whenever necessary;
m) To perform any other functions conferred on him by the organs of the Association and the Organic Regulations of the Secretariat.

Chapter V

MEETINGS

Article 16   Whenever it is deemed necessary, the Committee may hold meetings which only the Permanent Representatives and persons specially authorized in each case may attend.

Article 17 The Permanent Representatives or their alternates and the Executive Secretary shall participate in the meetings. In all cases whenever it is considered desirable, the Representatives and the Executive Secretary may be assisted by other officials of the delegations or the Secretariat, respectively.

Article 18 Representatives of advisory international organizations which are recognized as such by the Association may participate with the right to speak in meetings of the Committee at which, in its judgment, matters of a technical nature are to be considered. They may also participate in working groups.

Article 19 The Committee may authorize the attendance at meetings of observers from Latin American governments that are not members of the Association.

Article 20 Meetings are to be convoked by the Chairman on his own initiative or at the request of any representative.

At the request of a representative, they may be suspended by the Chairman provided this is agreed to by a simple majority of the others.

Article 21 The provisional order of the day for meetings shall be prepared and made known by the Executive Secretary at least 24 hours in advance, except in special cases. By agreement of the Committee, at the request of any representative, other matters not expressly included in the order of the day may be dealt with.

Article 22 At the request of a representative, the Committee may postpone any discussion or voting for a specified period of time.

Article 23 The Chairman has the following duties:

a) To preside over, open, and adjourn the meetings;
b) To direct the discussion and submit matters for consideration, as they are listed in the order of the day;
c) To grant the floor to representatives in the order it is requested;
d) To rule on points of order as provided in Article 28 of these Regulations;
e) To call for a vote and announce the results.

Article 24 At meetings one person may not simultaneously perform the functions of Chairman of the Committee and those of a representative. In the event that the Chairman wishes to act as a representative, he must be replaced in the manner established in Article 4 of these Regulations.

Article 25 The Committee may hold a meeting if two thirds of the representatives are present.

Article 26   Each representative has the right to one vote. Resolutions of the Committee shall be adopted by an affirmative vote of at least two thirds of all the representatives, unless it is acting in accordance with powers delegated by the Conference, in which case it is required that there shall be no negative vote. The Committee shall endeavor to see that its resolutions reflect the consensus of opinions of all representatives.

In cases of a roll-call vote, the representatives shall cast their votes as affirmative, as negative, or as abstaining, stating their intention clearly.

In any case, a delegation may request that its vote be considered at the end of the voting.

Article 27   At the beginning of each year, in the first meeting it holds, the Committee shall establish by lot the order in which the representatives shall cast their votes during that year.

Article 28   The decisions and recommendations of the Committee shall be adopted in the form of Resolutions, which shall be numbered consecutively, except in those cases in which the Committee deems it sufficient that the decisions be merely recorded in the minutes.

Article 29   During a meeting, any representative may raise a point of order, and in such a case the Chairman must rule on it at once if the question is in order. If his ruling is appealed, the Chairman shall immediately submit the matter to the Committee, which may revoke it by a two-thirds vote of the members present.

Article 30   During the discussion of any matter, the Chair, with the consent of the majority of the delegations, may limit the length and number of speeches of each representative.

Article 31   Any representative may offer a proposal or motion, as well as request that a matter submitted to a decision of the Committee be voted on in parts. If this is done, the text resulting from the respective votes shall afterwards be voted on as a whole.

Article 32   Whenever an amendment modifies a proposal, or adds or eliminates concepts, the amendment itself shall first be voted on and, if it is approved, the proposition thus amended shall be voted on.

Article 33   Whenever two or more amendments to a proposal are offered, the one that departs most from the substance of the original proposal shall be voted on first. In the event that this amendment is not approved, a vote shall be taken next on the amendment that, after the one defeated, departs most from the original proposal and thus successively until all the amendments submitted have been voted on.

Article 34   Any representative may request, with reasons, the consideration of a matter as urgent. The Committee shall decide, without discussion, in the same meeting at which the request is submitted, or in the next meeting at the latest, whether it shall be granted such character and at the same time fix the period within which its decision on the matter must be reached.

Article 35 In special cases, the Committee may receive or request the visit of representatives of countries, of international organizations, or of private enterprise.

Chapter VI

ADVISORY COMMITTEES

Article 36 To facilitate the study of specific problems, the Committee may establish Advisory Committees composed of representatives of the various sectors of public or private economic activities, from each of the contracting Parties.

Article 37 The Committee shall determine the aims, rules of procedure, composition, and meeting place of the Advisory Committees and shall provide them with adequate facilities. The Advisory Committees shall elect their chairman and vice chairmen and fix their work schedules.

Article 38 Members of the delegations making up the Committee may take part in the discussions of an Advisory Committee, without the right to vote, as may officials of the Secretariat and of advisory international organizations and, when appropriate, persons and representatives from the organizations referred to in Article 39, section (f), of the Treaty.

Chapter VII

RELATIONS WITH NATIONAL AND INTERNATIONAL ORGANIZATIONS AND INSTITUTIONS

Article 39 The relations of the Association with national and international organizations, institutions, and associations, whose collaboration the Committee considers desirable for achieving the aims of the Treaty, shall be regulated in accordance with the following categories:

A. Advisory international organizations, including:

   i) The advisory international organizations mentioned in Article 44 of the Treaty, and those that have been or may be assigned the same status, by organs of the Association; and

   ii) Organizations which with the approval of the Committee have signed or may sign agreements for permanent collaboration with the Secretariat.

The relations with the first group shall be subject to the provisions of the Protocol annexed to the Treaty and, with the second group, they shall be governed by the pertinent agreement of collaboration.

B. Public international organizations: This includes intergovernmental institutions and associations not included in category A, as well as those established by state or semi-governmental organizations recognized as such by the Committee with competence in the basic sectors of economic activity closely linked with the process of integration. In the latter case, the Committee shall consider them as technical advisers in their respective fields in accordance with the terms of Article 39, section (f), of the Treaty.

C. Private regional associations: This includes those that the Committee recognizes as representative of the respective activity. The official recognition implies an invitation to participate, with the right to speak, in activities of a technical nature that the Association may organize in the corresponding specialty. Such recognition shall imply, on the part of the institution concerned, an engagement to respect, insofar as pertinent, the decisions of the Association and its organs.

D. Other international, regional, or national organizations: This includes those which it is not pertinent to include in the foregoing categories, and relations with them shall have whatever characteristics the Committee may establish in each case.

Article 40   The Committee, whenever it deems it desirable, may request the advisory international organizations and the other organizations covered by Article 39 to prepare special studies and work necessary for the better progress of the Association.

Chapter VIII

OFFICIAL LANGUAGES

Article 41   The official languages of the Committee are Spanish and Portuguese.

Chapter IX

FINAL CLAUSE

Article 42   This Resolution replaces Resolution 19(I) of the Conference.

TRANSITORY

The provisions of Article 5 shall apply as soon as each of the permanent representatives of the contracting Parties has occupied the chairmanship of the Committee in accordance with the election procedure established in the foregoing regulations. At that time a representative shall be chosen by lot, after which the rotation by alphabetical order of countries shall be established.

NOTES ON PRIVILEGES AND IMMUNITIES OF LAFTA IN THE MEMBER STATES

The system governing the privileges and immunities of LAFTA is provided for in Article 47 of the Montevideo Treaty by virtue of which the contracting Parties as well as international officials and advisers of the Association shall be entitled within the area to diplomatic immunities and privileges and any others necessary for the performance of their functions.

This system governing privileges and immunities has been covered in detail by Resolutions 6(I) and 7(I) of the Conference. The first of these contains the "Agreement concerning the privileges and immunities of the Latin American Free Trade Association in the territory of the member States"; it is a general agreement that is applicable to all the contracting Parties. The second resolution cited contains the "Agreement between the Government of Uruguay and the Latin American Free Trade Association concerning privileges and immunities within Uruguayan territory"; this is a special agreement which governs privileges and immunities within Uruguayan territory only, the headquarter country of LAFTA.

Provisions concerning privileges and immunities may also be found in other LAFTA instruments. Among these should be noted Protocol No. 2 appended to the Treaty concerning the establishment of a Provisional Committee, and Resolution 101 of the Standing Executive Committee which contains the organic regulations of the Secretariat.

REPLIES BY PARTICIPATING GOVERNMENTS OF THE LATIN AMERICAN FREE TRADE ASSOCIATION TO THE QUESTIONNAIRES SUBMITTED BY THE CONTRACTING PARTIES OF THE GENERAL AGREEMENT ON TARIFFS AND TRADE (GATT)

Three questionnaires, containing questions submitted by the contracting Parties of the General Agreement on Tariffs and Trade, were transmitted to the participating governments of LAFTA by the Executive Secretary of GATT. In submitting their replies, the signatory countries of the Montevideo Treaty commented as follows:

The States which are signatories to the Montevideo Treaty have collected in one single document, which they hereby submit to the CONTRACTING PARTIES, the answers to the three questionnaires which have been transmitted on different dates by the Executive Secretary.

In accordance with the information furnished in due time to the CONTRACTING PARTIES (document L/1230 of 4 June 1960), the signatory States have amended the answers to the first questionnaire (document L/1201), having arrived at a better understanding of these questions after a minute examination of the subsequent questionnaires addressed to them in documents L/1177/Add. 1 and Add. 2.

Part I

INTRODUCTION

The Montevideo Treaty represents a considerable effort by the signatory States in order to reduce trade barriers. It is hoped that the progressive intensification of intra-area trade which would result therefrom will make for a better utilization of the available economic resources of the Area, a resulting increase in the per capita income levels of its peoples, and the expansion of trade with the rest of the world. Bearing these objectives in mind, the signatory States when elaborating the Treaty have always taken into account not only the characteristics of their intra-area trade but also their important economic relations with third countries which they wish to maintain and develop.

The Treaty, which is specially adapted to the conditions and the problems of the countries in the Area, also takes into account the existing disparities between the levels of economic development in the signatory States so as to meet the imperative requirements of an economic expansion to which they are all entitled and which they are endeavoring to achieve jointly.

At this stage, the signatory States wish to reaffirm, as they have already done in the Preamble to the Treaty, their readiness to achieve these objectives, while strictly observing their international commitments. To that effect, those members which are members of the GATT stress their firm intention always to proceed, within the framework of the Association or in their relations with third countries, in conformity with the provisions of the General Agreement, to which the letter and the spirit of the Montevideo Treaty conform.

Chapter I

NAME AND PURPOSE

Article 1

Question 1 Do the Member States propose that the Latin American Free Trade Association be considered as the kind of free-trade area covered by Article XXIV of the GATT?

Answer Yes.

Question 2 Do the Member States consider that the Montevideo Treaty constitutes an "interim agreement" leading to the formation of a free-trade area or an agreement establishing such an area?

Answer The Montevideo Treaty is a final agreement establishing a free-trade area within the period and in accordance with the conditions set forth in the Treaty.

Question 3 On what percentage of the trade between the Member States in products originating in their territories will duties be eliminated?

Answer Article 7 provides that substantially all the trade between the members shall be between 75 per cent and 100 per cent of such trade. The signatory States intend to achieve the highest possible level.

Question 4 Would Member States indicate how the percentage stated in answer to the preceding question is arrived at, indicating whether account has been taken of the removal of monetary charges (arising from multiple exchange rates, prior deposits of import payments, import surcharges, and other non-tariff payments required of importers) levied on imports?

Answer The percentage indicated in the preceding answer will be computed on the basis of the total value of imports into the Member States originating in the Area, taking into account the elimination of the charges resulting from the specific practices referred to in the question.

Question 5 Since four signatory governments of the Montevideo Treaty are parties to the GATT, is it the intention of the Member States to request the CONTRACTING PARTIES to the GATT to approve the formation of the Free Trade Area in accordance with the provisions of Article XXIV:10 of the GATT?

Answer In view of the fact that the Treaty is in conformity with the provisions of Article XXIV, paragraphs 5–9 of the GATT, and considering that the provisions of the Treaty are mandatory upon the members of the Association, we are of the opinion that Article XXIV, paragraph 10, of the General Agreement need not be resorted to.

Question 6 Does acceptance of the Treaty entail, for the Member States which are not parties to the GATT, any obligations toward third countries similar to those arising out of Article XXIV of the GATT for other members of the Association?

Answer   Although the Treaty only covers commitments undertaken by the Member States as between one another, the members
which are contracting parties to the General Agreement are under the
obligation to ensure that the operation of the Free Trade Area will
conform to Article XXIV and in their relations with the Member
States which are not contracting parties to the General Agreement
they will endeavor to ensure that the implementation of the Treaty is in
conformity with the rules of Article XXIV.

Question 127   Having regard to Articles 15, 54 and 61 and to the
seventh paragraph of the Preamble to the Montevideo Treaty, is it the
opinion of the Member States that the Treaty may be considered as
constituting an "interim agreement" with a view to the formation of a
customs union?

Answer   No.

Chapter II

PROGRAM FOR TRADE LIBERALIZATION

Articles 2–13

Question 128
a) Are any duties, charges, or restrictions in respect of exports imposed by Member States?
b) If so, how do Member States intend to reduce and finally eliminate such duties and restrictions?
c) Can such duties, charges, and restrictions be maintained or be
   introduced as between Member States in respect of goods listed
   in the Common Schedule?

Answer
a) Yes, in certain cases some countries impose export duties
   and/or restrictions.
b) The export systems applied by the signatory States are of a
   liberal and nondiscriminatory nature. In view of the fact that the
   export charges or restrictions applied by the Member States are
   of little significance or are due to very special reasons, for instance, to the need to ensure internal supplies and to carry out
   international agreements, it did not appear necessary to adopt
   special provisions in this respect.
c) Yes. However, it is clear that the Member States will endeavor
   to avoid that the application of such measures should operate to
   impair or nullify the liberalization program.

Article 2

Question 7   The provisions of the Montevideo Treaty are to be
brought into full operation by the end of a twelve-year period. Would
the Member States agree:

a) To keep the CONTRACTING PARTIES to the GATT informed of the progress made in the implementation of the provisions of the Treaty?

b) To keep the CONTRACTING PARTIES to the GATT informed *in advance* of all important developments and afford an opportunity for discussions of any important issues before final decisions are taken by the institutions of the Association?

Answer

a) Yes.

b) When the institutions of the Association consider it to be appropriate.

Question 129 Is it intended under this Article that the period within which the Free Trade Area is to be brought into full operation may in no case exceed twelve years from the date of the Treaty's entry into force?

Answer The signatory States intend strictly to comply with the liberalization program within the period set forth in Article 2.

Articles 3–8

Question 130 Is it intended that for new intra-area trade, negotiations on the lines of Articles 4, 5, 6, and 7 will take place after the twelve-year transition period? (Article 13 also refers.)

Answer Negotiations on the lines of Articles 4, 5, 6, and 7 are to take place during the transition period. For the subsequent stage, the Member States will determine what procedures are necessary to secure the best possible implementation of the objectives of the Treaty.

Question 131 Would the Member States give a full explanation of the methods and processes proposed for drawing up the National Schedules and the Common Schedule?

Answer Articles 4 to 9 inclusive of the Treaty and the Protocol relating to rules and procedures for negotiations contain a detailed explanation of proposed methods and procedures for the establishment of the National Schedules and of the Common Schedule.

Question 132 The second paragraph of Article 8, which refers to "products which appear only in the National Schedules," gives the impression that products can appear in both a National and the Common Schedule at the same time. Is this correct?

Answer Yes, this interpretation is correct.

Question 133

a) Is the Common Schedule made up of items which appear in all the National Schedules?

b) Is it the intention that the products listed in National Schedules will have been entirely transferred to the Common Schedule at the end of the four three-year periods?

Answer

a) Not necessarily during the transition period. At the end of the twelve-year period, the products included in the Common Schedule will, of necessity, have to be included in each National Schedule.

b) Not necessarily entirely transferred, but a number equivalent to substantially all the intra-area trade.

Question 134 Could the Member States undertake to make available to the CONTRACTING PARTIES to the GATT all National Schedules and Common Schedules as and when they are compiled, together with information about any measures taken concerning them.

Answer The signatory States have no objection to providing the CONTRACTING PARTIES with all possible information concerning the negotiations and the results thereof.

Article 3

Question 8 Will the restrictions, duties, and other charges imposed by the Member States on goods not subject to the complete elimination of restrictions, duties, and other charges at the end of the transition period (and thus not in the Free Trade Area) be nondiscriminatory among Member States and with regard to third countries? If this is not the case, how do the Member States reconcile this discrimination with Article 18 of the Montevideo Treaty and Article I of the GATT?

Answer They will not be discriminatory within the Area. *Vis-à-vis* third countries, each Member State will have to take account of its international commitments.

Question 9 Would the Member States indicate whether "substantially all their reciprocal trade" in this Article means "substantially all the trade between the constituent territories" of the Free Trade Area?

Answer Yes. (See answer to question 4.)

Question 10 Would the Member States supply all available information concerning "other charges of equivalent effect", indicating those which are actually in force in the Member States?

Answer Such information will be supplied in due time.

Question 11 Are prior deposits covered by the term "restrictions"? If so, do the parties to the Treaty envisage a time when products of the Area will be imported into Member States free of deposit, while imports from outside the Area will be subject to prior deposits?

Answer No; prior deposits, as regards their financial implications, which are considered to be charges as per Article 3, paragraph 2 of the Treaty, are not covered by the term "restrictions".

Question 12 In Mexico, importers in certain circumstances have to produce evidence of compensating exports. Is it envisaged that importers in Mexico of goods from the Area will be relieved of these obligations?

Answer   Yes, when they have equivalent effects to duties, charges or other restrictive regulations.

Question 13   Can it be assumed that the obligation to eliminate duties, charges, etc., does not affect the exchange auction system in Brazil?

Answer   This obligation does not affect the exchange auction system in Brazil as such (see answer to question 135 (a)).

Question 14   Do the provisions of this Article apply to quantitative restrictions now maintained by Member States for the purpose of safeguarding their balances of payments?

Answer   Yes, this Article provides for the elimination of restrictions, irrespective of their nature or purpose, in respect of substantially all intra-area trade.

Question 15   What protection could a Member State expect from the Treaty against deflections of trade resulting from the fact that the Member State concerned was maintaining quantitative restrictions toward countries outside the Area, while applying the provisions of this Article to other Member States only?

Answer   One of the objectives of the Latin American Free Trade Association is to expand trade as between the Member States. If there is any deflection of trade which is deemed to affect any Member States, the provisions of the Treaty relating to difficulties in the conduct of general trade will be applied.

Question 16
a) Will Member States, acting in conformity with the provisions of this Article, be required to accomplish the gradual elimination of "restrictions" other than customs duties and other charges even though these restrictions may have been permitted under Articles XI, XII, XIII, XIV, XV, or XX of the GATT?
b) If so, is it intended that such restrictions be eliminated in the case of imports from other contracting parties to the GATT as well as from parties to the Montevideo Treaty? If not, what restrictions now maintained will be eliminated pursuant to this Article, and to what extent will this elimination be extended to imports from other contracting parties to the GATT as well as from parties to the Montevideo Treaty?

Answer
a) Yes, with the exception provided for under Article 53.
b) The Treaty does not cover this point. In conformity with Article XXIV of GATT, the Free Trade Area provides essentially for the elimination of such restrictions as between the Member States. *Vis-à-vis* third countries, the signatory States will conform to their obligations arising out of international agreements.

Question 17   Member States of the Montevideo Treaty who are members of the International Monetary Fund or contracting parties to the GATT have broad international obligations for the removal of quantitative restrictions and the elimination of discrimination in the application of such restrictions:

a) Would it be appropriate conduct for such a contracting party to relax quantitative import restrictions, including import prohibitions, on intra-area trade without at the same time relaxing such restrictions on trade with third countries?

b) Is it anticipated that the provision for gradual elimination of such quantitative import restrictions under this Article could inhibit a Member State from removing immediately quantitative restrictions inconsistent with that Member State's broader international commitments?

Answer

a) We are of the opinion that this would be appropriate to the extent that the reasons which have justified the imposition of restrictions were persisting.

b) No.

Question 135

a) Does the phrase "such duties, charges, and restrictions" in the first paragraph of this Article cover multiple exchange practices?

b) Is it to be inferred that, in the case of a country in which a multiple exchange system is practiced, the exchange differentials would have to be eliminated and a single rate system adopted?

c) If so, would the Member State concerned be free to continue to apply a multiple exchange system in respect of countries outside the Area?

Answer

a) This phrase does not cover multiple exchange practices as such, but that part of their effects which is equivalent to "such duties and charges" or "restrictions as may . . ." is covered.

b) and c) The Treaty does not include any agreement to that effect.

Question 136

a) What are the "fees and similar charges" referred to in the third paragraph of this Article?

b) What are the "services" to which this provision is applicable?

Answer a) and b) Those which are generally accepted as such in international practice.

Question 221 This Article provides that the Member States shall eliminate gradually, on substantially all their reciprocal trade, duties, charges, and restrictions of any kind on imports originating in the territory of any Member State. Are there any particular products or groups of products in respect of which it is not expected that customs duties will be eliminated?

Answer Any product can be included in the liberalization program. It is not possible at present to indicate what are the items in respect of which customs duties will not be eliminated at the end of the twelve-year period.

Article 4

Question 18 Does the Montevideo Treaty contain provisions which the Member States consider constitute a "plan and schedule" complying with the provisions of the GATT? If not, is it the intent of the Member States to supply to the CONTRACTING PARTIES to the GATT such a "plan and schedule"?

Answer Chapter II of the Treaty includes a schedule, the implementation of which will ensure the full establishment of the Free Trade Area.

Question 19 How will the Member States ensure that there will be a progressive, regular reduction, within the period mentioned in Article 2, in duties, charges, and other restrictions affecting intra-area trade in products listed in the Common Schedule?

Question 20 Does the clause in sub-paragraph (b) of this Article which reads "through the gradual reduction provided for in Article 5", constitute a commitment on the part of each of the Member States to include annually in their respective National Schedules commodities listed in the Common Schedule? If not, what assurance is there that there will be progressive and regular reductions in duties, charges, and other restrictions on commodities listed in the Common Schedule during the twelve-year period mentioned in Article 2?

Question 21 Does the Treaty contemplate the gradual addition to the Common Schedule of items appearing on the National Schedules?

Answer to questions 19, 20, and 21 The National Schedules and the Common Schedules are independent from one another but their coordinated operation will secure the achievement of the liberalization program.

The National Schedules incorporate the fulfillment of individual commitments to eliminate duties, charges, and other restrictions on substantially all imports into the territory of each member from other members in the Area.

The Common Schedule incorporates products which, at the expiry of the twelve-year period, must be entirely free from duties, charges, and other restrictions.

At the expiry of the twelve-year period all the products included in the Common Schedule must be included in each National Schedule.

Question 22 Will the Member States inform the CONTRACTING PARTIES to the GATT of the results of the periodic negotiations provided for in this Article?

Answer Yes.

Question 137 Article 5 refers to rules, methods of calculation, and procedures for a gradual yearly reduction in "duties and charges" imposed by the Member States. No similar provision is specified in respect of a reduction in "restrictions". How do the Member States propose to achieve the gradual elimination of such restrictions, and how, in particular, can they ensure that reductions in such restrictions will not be deferred from year to year during the twelve-year period?

Answer   As we are dealing here with measures which cannot easily be assessed quantitatively, the Treaty provided for their elimination during the period for the full establishment of the Area without setting forth any minimum undertakings. Furthermore, the negotiations provided for under Article 4 for the purposes of Article 5:3 and Article 7 will in many cases involve the elimination or reduction of such restrictions so that it does not seem appropriate to presume that the corresponding reductions might be deferred from year to year.

Question 138   Is there not a danger that the benefits which are expected to be derived from a gradual integration of the economies of the Member States may be curtailed or delayed due to uncertainty resulting from the lack of a complete and detailed plan for trade liberalization?

Answer   Chapter II includes a plan which is considered appropriate for the purposes of the Treaty.

Article 5

Question 23   Since the duties and charges levied by each Member State on its imports from the others is to constitute a decreasing percentage of duties and charges currently applicable to third parties, could not a part of the required decrease in this percentage be achieved by raising duties applicable to third parties? What assurances are there that the Montevideo Treaty will conform with Article XXIV: 5 (b) of the GATT, concerning the level of duties and other restrictive regulations applicable to the trade of countries outside the Treaty Area?

Answer   The Treaty stipulates that duties and charges and other restrictions which affect substantially all intra-area trade shall be gradually eliminated. As regards the policy which each Member State will adopt concerning customs duties and other regulations in their respective trade with third countries, see answer to question 6.

Question 24   Is the "weighted average applicable to third countries" obtained by dividing 1) the total duties and charges which would have been collected on three years' imports from all sources of the relevant commodities had these duties and charges been assessed at rates in force on 31 December prior to the negotiations by 2) the total value of these imports from all sources in the three-year period?

Answer   This interpretation is correct.

Question 25   In performing the computations required by this Article, how will "charges" (fiscal, monetary, or other) which are distinct from rates of duty be computed?

Answer In conformity with the criteria to be laid down by the institutions of the Association.

Question 26 What are the plans of the Member States with regard to discussions with the IMF of measures to be taken under the Treaty (e.g. Articles 3–5) insofar as the provisions of the Treaty are applicable to multiple exchange rates or other measures subject to the Articles of Agreement of the IMF?

Answer This point relates to the relations of each Member State with the International Monetary Fund.

Question 27 What kinds of restrictions would be subject to the provisions of the third paragraph of this Article? Would the relaxation or the elimination of these restrictions be extended to all Member States on a nondiscriminatory basis?

Answer

1. This provision refers to restrictive regulations of any type which are not included in the concept of duties and charges referred to in paragraph 2 of Article III.
2. Yes.

Question 28 Is it anticipated that, under the provisions of the third paragraph of this Article, a Member State that is a member of the IMF or a contracting party to the GATT would relax quantitative import restrictions toward countries inside the Area without extending similar treatment to third countries?

Answer Yes, for the reasons given in the answer to question 16 (b).

Question 139 Would the Member States provide an example showing how the weighted average is actually arrived at?

Question 140 The method of calculation of the reduction in duties and charges on the basis of the weighted average of duties and charges applicable in respect of third countries, referred to in the first paragraph of this Article, does not provide the means of ascertaining the extent of the reduction on individual products, particularly as the products affected by the reduction are not known in advance. In order to facilitate a clearer understanding of the reduction mechanism, would the Member States provide a few examples?

Answer to questions 139 and 140

Weighted average of duties and charges on trade with third countries			*Weighted average of duties and charges on intra-area trade*		
V1 x T1 :		P1	V1 x t1 :		p1
V2 x T2 :		P2	V2 x t2 :		p2
V3 x T3 :		P3	V3 x t3 :		p3
... ...		...	... ...		...
Vn x Tn :		Pn	Vn x tn :		pn
$\frac{\Sigma P}{\Sigma V}$ Weighted average for third countries			$\frac{\Sigma p}{\Sigma V}$ Weighted average for the Area		

V—Yearly average of the aggregate import value for a specific item during the three-year period prior to each negotiation.

T—Existing duties and charges on this product in respect of third countries as of 31 December prior to each negotiation.

t—Duties and charges on this product resulting from the concession accorded to other Member States during the last negotiations.

n—Last product in the series, which comprises:
  a) products included in the list of imports from the Area during the three-year period prior to the year when the negotiation took place, whether or not concessions have been granted in respect of such items, and
  b) products which are not included in the list referred to in the preceding paragraph but which have been included in the liberalization program in the course of the negotiations.

Σ—Total of "V", "P", and "p".

Question 141   More detailed information appears to be required concerning the envisaged elimination of duties and charges. For instance, is it correct to assume that, for products listed in a schedule for the last three-year period, all duties and charges are to be eliminated in those three years?

Answer   If the question refers to the Common Schedule: yes. If it refers to a National Schedule: not necessarily.

Question 142   The time factor which enters into the calculation of the reduction in duties and charges entails, for countries acceding to the Montevideo Treaty at a later date, the necessity of implementing, with immediate effect from the date the Treaty becomes applicable to them, a tariff reduction on all goods amounting to 8 per cent of the weighted average multiplied by the number of years that have elapsed since the entry into force of the Treaty:
  a) Assuming that a country accedes six years after the entry into force of the Treaty, would it be required to lower its customs duties on the goods concerned by 48 per cent at one and the same time?
  b) If so, is it the opinion of the Member States that such a far-reaching reduction is a practical possibility?

Answer
a) Yes, under Article 59 of the Montevideo Treaty.
b) Obviously, yes.

Question 143
a) With reference to the second paragraph of this Article and on the assumption that the Montevideo Treaty enters into force in the course of 1960, will the application of the contemplated reductions be based on the duties and charges in effect as at 31 December 1959?
b) What is the reason for using a different base year each time the annual calculations are made?

Answer

a) Yes.

b) The intention is to impart dynamism to the liberalization of substantially all intra-area trade, by adapting the negotiations to the annual variations in the composition and value of imports.

Question 144   What are the methods and the pace envisaged for the elimination of existing quantitative restrictions on imports in each of the Member countries? What is the exact scope of the third paragraph of this Article?

Answer

1. This will be determined by negotiation in each case, on the occasion of annual negotiations.
2. To ensure the reciprocity of concessions.

Question 145

1. Is it the intention that the Member State concerned should gradually eliminate all the restrictions referred to in the third paragraph of this Article?
2. Or is the relaxation of such restrictions to be effected only to the extent considered necessary to obtain the requisite equivalence with the reductions in duties and charges granted by other Member States?

Answer

1. Yes, for substantially all imports of products originating in the Area.
2. See answer to paragraph 1 of this question.

Article 7

Question 29   What percentage of the aggregate value of trade between themselves do the Member States consider would have to be liberalized to achieve liberalization of "substantially all of such trade" as referred to in this Article?

Answer   Article 7 provides that substantially all the trade shall mean a proportion between 75 and 100 per cent of the total volume of trade; this objective is to be achieved during the fourth three-year period.

Question 30   This Article provides for inclusion of products on a Common (liberalized) Schedule equivalent to "substantially all of such trade" within the fourth three-year period of the transition period. If some duties, charges, or restrictions are permitted to be retained, how and when will the permissible extent of these be determined in respect of each Member State?

Answer   As far as products included in the Common Schedule are concerned, at the expiry of the twelve-year period, no duties, charges, or other restrictions will be maintained, with the exception of the "other restrictions" referred to in Chapters VI and VIII in the Treaty.

Question 31   Does the "aggregate value of the trade among the contracting Parties" mentioned in this Article mean the total value of all trade between the Member States regardless of the origin of the products traded or does it refer merely to the trade between the Member States in products originating in their territories?

Answer   Article 7 refers to the aggregate value of trade in products originating in the Area.

Question 32   How do the Member States plan to reconcile the commitment in Article 7 to free an increasing proportion (ultimately "substantially all") of trade among Member States with actions which may be taken under the Saving Clauses (Articles 23–26), the Special Provisions Concerning Agriculture (Articles 27–31), and the Measures in Favor of Countries at a Relatively Less Advanced State of Economic Development (Article 32) in the event of a conflict between the commitment of Article 7 and these actions?

Answer   The restrictions mentioned will always be of a temporary nature and will not hinder the fulfillment of the liberalization program.

Question 33   Do the Member States intend to eliminate duties and other restrictive regulations of commerce on substantially all the trade between their constituent territories in products originating in such territories, not only on commodities actually traded, but with respect to substantially all *actual and potential* trade in products originating in their territories? If so, how do the Member States propose to ensure the incorporation in the liberalization program set forth in Articles 2–13 of the Montevideo Treaty of substantially all products originating in their constituent territories and potentially tradeable among them?

Answer   Yes, by means of annual negotiations.

Question 146   Is it intended that, during the fourth three-year period, products representing *at least* 75 per cent of the aggregate value of trade among the Member States will be included in the Common Schedule? In the absence of any mention of a percentage for the fourth three-year period can it be inferred that, in the view of the Member States, the criterion referring to "substantially all the trade" is not only of a quantitative but also of a qualitative nature?

Answer

1. Yes.
2. The basic notion is a quantitative one. The formation of the Area is not limited to specific items or branches of production. (See Article 14 of the Treaty and answer to question 221.)

Question 147

a) Will the Common Schedule and the relevant obligations (*inter alia* the obligation relating to the irrevocability of concessions on products included in the Common Schedule) remain in force after the end of the period of twelve years referred to under Article 2?

b) If so, would additions be made to the Schedule in the event that, as a result of altered conditions in trade, substantially all intra-area trade is no longer covered?

Answer

a) Yes.

b) As from the expiry of the twelve-year period, the Common Schedule will always cover substantially all intra-area trade.

Question 148 Are the percentages referred to in this Article to be applied to the total imports of the Member States as a whole or to the total imports of each Member State individually?

Answer To the total value of the intra-area imports of the Member States.

Question 149 Will agricultural products be included in the percentages referred to in this Article?

Answer Yes.

Article 4–7

Question 34 What measures would Member States agree to in order to prevent sudden changes in Area treatments of goods originating in third countries unduly affecting normal trade channels?

Answer The Treaty does not contain any provisions which could operate so as to affect unfavorably trade channels between the Member States and third countries.

Article 8

Question 35 May a product included in the Common Schedule be subject to the restrictions permitted by Articles 23, 24 and 25? If so, how is such action reconciled with the "irrevocable" nature of the Common Schedule as described in this Article?

Answer This "irrevocable" nature refers to the withdrawal of concessions but not to the temporary suspension of their practical effects in cases of emergency.

Question 36

1. In what circumstances is it envisaged that withdrawal would take place?
2. Would withdrawal of a National Schedule concession preclude its final incorporation in the Common Schedule?

Answer

1. The Treaty does not provide explicitly what kind of circumstances could be invoked to request the withdrawal of concessions. The Member States will deal with individual cases as and when they arise.
2. The rescinding of concessions included in the National Schedules does not prevent subsequent inclusion in the Common Schedule.

Question 37 Could the expression "adequate compensation" in the second paragraph of this Article include reimposition or intensification of quantitative import restrictions by the country with respect to which concessions are withdrawn? If so, would such measures be consistent with a country's obligations under the GATT or the IMF?

Answer No. "Adequate compensation" refers to the substitution of a concession by a concession or concessions of equivalent value.

Question 150 The fact that, under the second paragraph of this Article, a Member State may withdraw concessions granted in respect of products which appear in its National Schedule constitutes an element of uncertainty. How, for example, would the following case be dealt with?:

Country X has developed standardized, large-scale production and intensified its exports of a particular product, because of its being included in the National Schedule of Country Y. Country Y wants to withdraw this article from its Schedule; Country X opposes this, and no agreement can be reached between them.

Answer In practice, the assumption made in this question could hardly materialize. If it did, the case would be considered jointly by the Member States.

Question 151 Do the Member States consider that the retention of the National Schedules, to a substantial extent, until the end of the transition period, is consistent with the relevant rules of the GATT?

Answer Yes. The National Schedules merely record the implementation by each individual Member State of the undertaking to eliminate duties, charges, and other restrictive regulations. At the expiry of the twelve-year period the National Schedules considered jointly will, of necessity, cover essentially all the reciprocal trade covered by the Common Schedule and possibly part of the residual trade.

Question 222 This Article provides that withdrawal of tariff reductions may be permitted as long as these items are not included in the Common Schedule. Accordingly, there would seem to be a danger that, for the more sensitive items, there will not be a progressive reduction in the tariff barriers to trade during the transition period. What measures do Member States contemplate so as to prevent the accumulation of a hard core of items where very substantial tariff reductions will have to be made at the end of the transition period if the Free Trade Area objectives are to be attained?

Answer The application of Articles 5, 7, and 8 taken jointly, removes the possibility entertained in this question.

Article 10

Question 38
a) What is the phrase "shall be considered with due fairness" intended to mean?
b) What criteria will be used in determining the concept of "fairness" in considering the situations of those Member States whose levels of duties, charges and restrictions differ substantially from those of others?

Answer
a) In the usual sense.

b) The criteria to be used for the determination of the concept of "fairness" will be laid down in due time by the institutions of the Association.

Question 152

1. What is the exact meaning and scope of paragraph 2 of this Article?

2. Could the Member States give examples?

Answer 1. and 2. It means that during each negotiation the advantages and disadvantages resulting for each country and for the Area as a whole from the existence of substantially different levels of duties, charges, and other restrictive regulations will be duly weighed. The concept of fairness is intended to avoid that such difference should, as a result of the negotiations, have trade effects contrary to the objectives of the Treaty.

Article 11

Question 154 Does the expression "products included in the liberalization program" refer to products listed in the Common Schedule or in a National Schedule?

Answer The phrase "products included in the liberalization program" refers to products included in the Common Schedule or in a National Schedule.

Question 155 Would the Member States explain whether the phrase "suitable, nonrestrictive measures designed to promote trade at the highest possible levels" refers to intra-area trade only?

Answer Yes. The phrase refers only to intra-area trade.

Question 223 Would the Member States confirm that steps to remedy the difficulties envisaged in this Article would not involve derogations from the obligations regarding the elimination of tariff barriers to trade within the Area?

Answer Yes.

Articles 11 and 12

Question 39 When drafting these Articles, what had the parties to the Treaty in mind?

Answer In the case of Article 11, the intention was to ensure that the concessions granted should not result in a situation involving serious and persistent injury as between the Member States. As regards Article 12, the intention was to safeguard the Area against possible similar situations resulting from factors independent from the liberalization program.

Question 40 What criteria are contemplated for determining "significant and persistent disadvantages" under the provisions of these Articles?

Answer The criteria to determine whether there is a case of serious and persistent disadvantage shall be defined in due time by the institutions of the Association.

Question 41 How will injury arising from concessions (Article 11) be distinguished from injury arising from other circumstances (Article 12)?

Answer As a result of an analysis of the situation which would arise.

Question 42
  a) What are the kinds of "nonrestrictive measures" and remedies contemplated under these Articles?
  b) Would such measures be nonrestrictive not only of intra-area trade but also of trade with contracting parties to the GATT not signatories to the Montevideo Treaty?
  c) Would such measures in any way affect products in the Common Schedule?

Answer
  a) Basically, an extension of the concessions.
  b) Only in respect of intra-area trade.
  c) The only foreseeable effect would be to speed up the liberalization process.

Question 43 Could the implementation of Article 12 result in an intensification of discrimination against third countries?

Answer No.

Question 44 Does the making of "every effort within their power," referred to in Article 12, include the taking of measures which would otherwise be inconsistent with a) the Montevideo Treaty and/or b) the GATT?

Answer No.

Question 153 What type of measures are envisaged in these Articles which are not covered by Articles 23 to 26?

Answer The measures provided for under Articles 11 and 12 are not covered by Articles 23 to 26, as they will always be of a nonrestrictive nature.

Article 12

Question 156 Would the Member States explain fully the nature of the other circumstances referred to in this Article?

Answer Circumstances arising out of unfavorable economic situations which do not result from the implementation of the liberalization program. Those that could be most easily defined would be natural circumstances such as droughts, floods, earthquakes, etc.

Question 157 Are the measures envisaged by the phrase "every effort within their power" in this Article intended to include quantitative import restrictions as well as tariff measures, such as for example the

withdrawal of tariff concessions granted under the liberalization program? Could the Member States give examples of the type of measures
that might be used?

Answer

1. No, because this Article deals with nonrestrictive measures.
2. In particular, financial and technical assistance.

Article 13

Question 45   Should a Member State find it impossible to comply
with the provisions of Article 5 and 7 on the basis of concessions
intended to result in reciprocity as defined in this Article, what procedure is envisaged to ensure its full participation in a free trade area in
which duties and restrictive regulations of commerce have been removed
with respect to substantially all its trade with other participants in the
area in products of territories of the area?

Answer   We do not see how in practice the case under reference
could occur. The undertakings subscribed by the parties of Articles 3,
5, and 7 of the Treaty are fundamental and mandatory. Article 13 refers
to the principles on which the negotiations provided for under the Treaty
will be based.

Question 46   If a Member State has removed duties and other restrictive regulations with respect to substantially all trade with the
other Member States in the Area in products originating in the territories of the Area, how will it then be possible for the principle of
reciprocity to guide any further negotiations between that country and
the other Member States under the provisions of Articles 5 and 7?

Question 47   Given the above situation, could those Member States
still short of achieving the required trade liberalization refuse or obstruct
the offering of what they might consider as "unilateral" concessions to
the Member State which had achieved the required liberalization on
the grounds that reciprocity of concessions was not possible?

Answer to question 46 and 47   There is little likelihood that the assumption referred to in questions 46 and 47 would materialize. However,
the principle of reciprocity will be applicable in the negotiations which
will take place at any stage during the period leading to the full establishment of the Area.

Question 48

a) How are the Member States to measure the "expected growth in
the flow of trade"?
b) Is the "expected growth" defined as the expectation of individual
Member States or of the Committee of the Association?

Answer

a) By assessing at the time of the negotiations the foreseeable trade
effects of the concessions granted and received.
b) As the expectation of each individual Member State.

Chapter III

EXPANSION OF TRADE AND COMPLEMENTARY ECONOMIES

Article 14

Question 49   What steps are contemplated to attain the objectives set forth in subparagraphs b) and c) of this Article?

Answer   By means of annual negotiations.

Question 158   In view of the fact that the Montevideo Treaty provides for the gradual elimination of duties, charges, and restrictions of all kinds, would the Member States provide more detailed information with regard to the scope of subparagraph a) of this Article?

Answer   The progressive nature of the elimination of duties, charges, and other restrictive regulations provided for under the Treaty is no reason why the members of the Association should not proceed in accordance with Article 14 (a) in view of the fact that the Treaty undertakings are minimum undertakings. It will always be open to the Member States, subject to the principle of reciprocity, to speed up the liberalization program in respect of specific products.

For that reason and having regard to the objectives of the Treaty, the Member States have deemed it appropriate to make every endeavor in order to ensure during the first negotiation that products imported from the Area should receive no less favorable treatment than that existing prior to the entry into force of the Treaty.

Question 159   Can the inference be drawn from the provisions of subparagraph a) of this Article that some of the Member States might intend to raise, between the date of entry into force of the Treaty and the initial series of negotiations provided for in Article 4, the level of duties, charges, and restrictions imposed by them?

Answer   The signatory States do not intend to resort to the procedures referred to in this question.

Question 160   What is the reason for not making it mandatory to ensure that imports from within the Area are accorded, from the initial negotiation, treatments not less favorable than that which existed before the entry into force of the Treaty?

Answer   The full and immediate extension at multilateral level, of existing favorable treatments might create distortions in intra-area trade.

Article 15

Question 50   What is meant by the term "reconcile" in this Article?

Answer   To reduce the most significant disparities.

Question 51   In order to ensure fair competition among themselves, particularly with regard to industrial production, the Member States are to endeavor "to reconcile their import and export regimes, as well as the treatment they accord to capital, goods, and services from outside the Area". Does this mean:

a) that a Member State which has no local production to protect will have to raise its duties to the level of those levied by Member States which have local industries to protect? How will this apply to products subsequently added to the Schedules?

b) that all Member States will adopt a common policy in their investment laws, terms of credit for imports, etc.?

c) that the Member States propose to adopt a uniform policy as regards the treatment to be given to foreign shipping services?

Answer

a) No.

b) and c) The CONTRACTING PARTIES will endeavor to the greatest extent possible to reconcile treatment accorded to capital, goods, and services from outside the Area in accordance with the criteria to be fixed in due time by the institutions of the Association.

Question 52 Will the implementation of this Article result in the imposition of quantitative restrictions?

Answer No.

Question 53 If Member States are considering moving towards uniform tariff rates, would they be willing to move towards the lowest rather than the highest rates of duty?

Answer The reconciliation provided for under Article 15 does not necessarily imply that customs duties will be made uniform. Every endeavor will be made to carry out this process of reconciliation in accordance with the most liberal criteria.

Question 54 Is there any possibility that, in the process of reconciling their import and export systems, Member States might be required to reconcile their import systems and might such reconciliation or other action under this Article mean that barriers to the trade of third countries would be increased and discrimination against such countries intensified?

Question 55 Do the Member States intend to use their import system in such a way as to preserve the expansion of trade with outside countries, especially with those whose imports of Latin American products as well as exports of goods important for industrial development show an increasing trend?

Question 56 By what means will the measures taken with respect to import and export regimes and the treatment accorded to goods from outside the Area be so implemented as to be consistent with the provisions of the GATT?

Answer to questions 54, 55, and 56 One of the objectives of the Treaty is to expand the trade of the Member States with the rest of the world. The intention therefore is not that restrictions should be intensified *vis-à-vis* third countries.

Question 161   If this Article means that the Member States will, to a greater or lesser degree, reconcile their external tariffs, will the reconciliation apply to tariffs on agricultural products in view of the emphasis on industrial production in the Article?

Answer   The reconciliation provided for under Article 15 does not exclude agricultural products. On the other hand, the Treaty does not lay down any specific obligation to reconcile external tariffs.

Question 162   Does the "reconciliation" envisaged in this Article mean that quota measures in respect of countries outside the Area will be brought to a uniform level?

Answer   No.

Question 163   Are there at present any plans concerning the elimination of quantitative restrictions etc. toward third countries?

Answer   Although the Treaty does not contain any provisions in this respect, it should be pointed out that the signatory States are making considerable individual efforts in this direction, as is shown by the reforms of the external trade systems which most of them have carried out in recent years.

Question 224   Would the Member States confirm that the provisions of this Article will not preclude them from maintaining the reciprocal tariff concessions negotiated under the GATT?

Answer   Each signatory State which is a contracting party to GATT will act in conformity with its GATT obligations.

Article 16

Question 57   Subparagraph a) of this Article envisages the formulation of agreements among representatives of economic sectors in order to promote closer coordination of industrialization. In the light of this provision, are any measures contemplated in order to prevent restrictive business practices frustrating the benefits expected from the reduction or removal of trade barriers between Member States?

Answer

1. Subparagraph a) does not refer to agreements but to arrangements between the economic sectors concerned for the purpose of facilitating the coordination of the industrialization policies of the Member States.
2. The Treaty contains provisions intended to prevent practices which might impair normal competitive conditions.

Question 58   Would the complementarity agreements provided for in this Article have the effect of confining the number of competing plants in an industry? How would this achieve the objective in Article 15 of ensuring "fair competitive conditions" among the Member States?

Answer   This is not the intention. Such complementarity agreements are not intended to limit the number of competing undertakings in a given industrial sector. In their implementation, every effort will be made to avoid any impairment to fair competitive conditions between the Member States.

Question 59   Will the Member States explain fully the anticipated nature of the "mutual agreements on complementary economies by industrial sectors" authorized by this Article?

Answer   These are agreements intended to speed up the process of liberalization relating to products included in the relevant sector.

Question 60   How will the agreements contemplated by this Article affect customs duties and other regulations of commerce applied by Member States to products of a) other parties to the Montevideo Treaty, and b) third countries?

Answer   The complementarity agreements entered into in respect of various industrial sectors will not be of a discriminatory nature as between the countries in the Area. As far as third countries are concerned, their only effects will be those resulting from the process of liberalization provided for in the Treaty.

Question 61   What is the anticipated duration of the complementarity agreements?

Answer   The period of validity of such agreements will be determined in each individual case.

Articles 16 and 17

Question 62   Do those Articles mean that the Member States propose to try and plan investment in the Area as a whole, and that before any foreign projects may be undertaken in the territories of any one of the Member States, approval of the project must be given by all the Member States?

Answer   No.

Question 63   Will the agreements contemplated in the provisions of these Articles be consistent with the provisions of Articles 18 and 20 of the Montevideo Treaty?

Answer   Yes, in view of the provisions of the last paragraph of Article 17.

Question 64   Are the agreements under these Articles to be regarded as an integral part of the Association arrangements for the purposes of the consideration of the arrangements by the CONTRACTING PARTIES to the GATT?

Question 65   Will the Member States undertake to submit to the CONTRACTING PARTIES to the GATT, pursuant to Article XXIV:7 of the GATT, any agreements which may be concluded pursuant to the provisions of these Articles of the Montevideo Treaty?

Answer to questions 64 and 65   The establishment of complementarity agreements in respect of individual industrial sectors is an integral part of the Association arrangements. Such agreements constitute mechanisms intended to facilitate the achievement of the objectives of the Association as promptly as possible. It is not therefore considered necessary to submit such agreements to the CONTRACTING PARTIES to GATT. However, the signatory States have no objection to the relevant information being furnished to the CONTRACTING PARTIES.

Question 164 As a result of expediting the closer coordination of industrial policies, it would appear that conditions of self-sufficiency may be built up within the Free Trade Area. Is it not possible that, in such circumstances, the Member States will be led to discriminate against imports from third countries?

Answer This is not a process intended to promote self-sufficiency in the Area. However, in view of the fact that the regional production would be increased, the implementation of the Treaty can bring about a decline in imports of certain products from third countries, although this will not imply a decline in the total import figure. In the case under consideration, there would only be a change in the import pattern. On the other hand, it is foreseen that the increase in the purchasing power resulting from the economic development of the Member States will generate an intensification of the demand for other goods and services which will ensure an expansion of trade with the rest of the world.

Question 165 How would the liberalization program for commodities covered by the complementarity agreements relate to Articles 4, 5, and 7?

Is it envisaged that the removal of tariffs, other import charges and quantitative restrictions would proceed at a different pace?

Answer The complementarity agreements constitute mechanisms supplementing the program of liberalization provided for in the Treaty; they may envisage an accelerated pace for the reduction of duties, charges, and other restrictive regulations.

Question 166 Can third countries expect that their present ability to obtain raw materials will not be impaired by agreements of the kind envisaged in these Articles?

Answer There is no doubt that this ability will not be impaired.

Question 167 What kind of "sponsorship" is it envisaged the Member States might undertake in terms of subparagraph a) of Article 16?

Answer In particular, by promoting the setting up of the advisory commissions referred to in Article 43.

Article 17

Question 66 Will the liberalization program applied to the products of the sector concerned contemplate the inclusion of these products in the Common Schedule and the complete elimination of duties, charges, and other restrictions, insofar as intra-area trade in these products is concerned, within the period mentioned in Article 2 of the Montevideo Treaty?

Answer   Yes, if the Member States so agree, subject to the time-limit set forth in Article 2 of the Treaty.

Question 67   By what means will "clauses designed to reconcile the treatment accorded to raw materials and other components" be so implemented as to be consistent with the GATT?

Answer   Reconciliation will be directed towards a reduction of the most important differences and the avoidance of any additional restrictions on trade with third countries.

Chapter IV

MOST-FAVORED-NATION TREATMENT

Article 18

Question 168   What is the reason for not incorporating in the Montevideo Treaty all of the provisions of paragraph 1 of Article I of the GATT regarding the most-favored-nation clause?

Answer   Article 18 is a synthesis of all the provisions of Article I, paragraph 1, of the General Agreement on Tariffs and Trade.

Question 169   Is it intended that the preferential tariff treatment accorded by some of the Member States shall be extended to all countries within the Area from the date of entry force of the Treaty?

Answer   Yes.

Chapter V

TREATMENT ON INTERNAL TAXATION

Article 21

Question 170   Can it be expected that the elimination of any discriminatory element in internal taxation will be applicable to imports from any country which is a contracting party to the GATT (in accordance with Article III of the GATT)?

Answer   In this respect every member will act in conformity with its international commitments.

Chapter VI

ESCAPE CLAUSES

Articles 23–26

Question 225

a) What would be the nature of the negotiations envisaged in Article 26 relating to restrictions which may be imposed under Article 23 of the Treaty?

b) What arrangements are there to ensure that the use of quantitative restrictions envisaged under Article 23 will not be such as to result in the postponement of the economic objectives required to permit the full establishment of the Free Trade Area?

Answer

a) These would be joint negotiations.
b) The interim nature of such restrictions and the obligation to carry out fully the liberalization program within the time-limit set forth in the Treaty.

Article 23

Question 68   How would restrictions applied pursuant to this Article be justified under the GATT?

Answer   Being always of an interim nature, such restrictions would not prevent the achievement of the objectives of the Treaty.

Question 69   What specific criteria are contemplated for identifying and determining the existence or threatened existence of "serious repercussions on specific productive activities of vital importance to the national economy"?

Answer   They will be determined in each individual case by the institutions of the Association.

Question 70   Would quantitative import restrictions applied under the provisions of this Article be nondiscriminatory as between countries outside the Area as well as towards those inside the Area?

Answer   The restrictions referred to in Article 23 only cover products from the Area which are included in the liberalization program. Such restrictions would be applied without discrimination between the Member States.

Question 71   What obligations under the Treaty does a country have with respect to relaxing and removing such quantitative import restrictions?

Answer   Those that had been determined in granting the authorization and, if the case arises, the provisions of Article 26 of the Treaty.

Question 72   Could such quantitative import restrictions be relaxed toward countries inside the Area and not toward third countries?

Answer   The case envisaged in this question is not conceivable, in view of the provisions of Article 23 of the Treaty.

Question 171

a) In the circumstances envisaged in this Article would restrictions be imposed upon like products originating outside the Area?
b) If so, could the Member States undertake to notify the CONTRACTING PARTIES to the GATT of any measures taken in pursuance of this Article by Member States who are contracting parties to the GATT?

Answer

a) Such restrictions will not necessarily be applied to like products originating outside the Area. However, if and when the case arises, due account will be taken of the interests of third countries.

b) Each Member State which is a contracting party to GATT will act in this respect in accordance with its obligations under the General Agreement.

Question 172   In a case where the interests of another contracting party to the GATT is involved, would a Member State wishing to take action under this Article first have resort to the relevant provisions of the GATT?

Answer   Each Member State will act in conformity with its international commitments.

Question 173   Will this Article continue to apply after the end of the period of twelve years referred to in Article 2?

Answer   Yes.

Article 24

Question 73   What criteria will the Member States follow in determining whether to authorize a Member State to extend to intra-area trade in products included in the liberalization program measures adopted to correct its overall balance of payments?

Answer   The criteria will be fixed in due time by the institutions of the Association.

Question 74

a) Will import restrictions applied by a Member State under this Article for balance-of-payments reasons in relation to Member States and to other members of GATT accord with Articles XIII and XIV of the GATT?

b) If it is intended that restrictive measures to correct an unfavorable balance of payments should be applied first against third countries and only later, if at all, to other Member States, how would Member States reconcile such action with their commitments under the IMF and the GATT?

Answer

a) Yes, to the extent that the application of such provisions does not impair the implementation of the liberalization program referred to in Chapter II of the Treaty.

b) Yes, there is no incompatability whatever between such provisions and the international commitments undertaken by some Member States within the framework of the IMF or of GATT, because the elimination of such restrictions inside a free trade area is an inherent feature of such an area.

Question 75

a) What procedure will be followed to ensure that a country imposing quantitative import restrictions under this Article will relax them as its balance-of-payments position improves?

b) Could a country relax such quantitative import restrictions toward countries inside the Area but not likewise toward third countries?

Answer

a) The procedure which had been fixed in the authorization.

b) Yes.

Question 174   Although this Article states that authorization *may* be given by the Member States to a Member State to extend restrictions in intra-area trade, does not the Article as a whole imply that balance-of-payments restrictions should not apply to members of the Free Trade Area?

Answer   This interpretation is correct.

Question 175   Would it be permissible, under this Article, for a Member State merely to reinstate quantitative restrictions previously removed in pursuance of Article 3 in respect of Member States only, if the Member State concerned felt that the deterioration in its balance-of-payments situation was attributable to measures which it had had to take under the provisions of the Treaty?

Answer   Yes, if this was the adequate solution.

Question 176   What is the reason why the provisions of the second paragraph of this Article do not likewise apply to intra-area trade in products which are not in the liberalization program?

Answer   Paragraph 2 of Article 24 is intended to prevent to the greatest extent possible that the liberalization program should be impaired as a result of the imposition of balance-of-payments import restrictions.

Question 226   There would appear to be a danger that the obligations under Article 24 could result in the failure of the Member States to make the most effective use of their limited foreign exchange availabilities in relation to their import requirements. How do the Member States envisage avoiding this kind of difficulty?

Answer   The signatory States are aware of the need to avoid such a situation. However it should be pointed out that Article 24 is intended to correct any balance-of-payments disequilibrium and that Article 24 will therefore be so applied as not to raise additional difficulties to the correction of such disequilibrium.

On the other hand, the Member States are those which are most interested in using their foreign exchange availabilities in the most efficient manner.

Article 26

Question 76   Would negotiations foreseen under this Article deal only with the elimination of restrictions within the Area?

Answer Yes.

Question 77 Could the outcome of negotiations foreseen under this Article result in more rapid relaxation of quantitative import restrictions toward countries in the Area than toward third countries?

Answer Yes.

Chapter VII

SPECIAL PROVISIONS CONCERNING AGRICULTURE

Articles 27–31

Question 177 With regard to the application of the provisions of Chapter VII of the Montevideo Treaty, is the Conference empowered to decide which products shall be considered as being "agricultural commodities"?

Answer Yes.

Question 178

a) Is information available showing the distribution as between Member and nonMember States of imports of such agricultural products as are expected to be included in the liberalization program from the outset?

b) Is similar information available with respect to such agricultural products as may be included in the liberalization program only at a later stage?

Answer a) and b) The inclusion, by stages, of products in the liberalization program has not been provided for. This can give rise to negotiations in any year during the transition period. It cannot, therefore, be said that agricultural products would be included from the outset or at subsequent stages.

Article 27

Question 179 The Montevideo Treaty gives no indication as to the nature of measures which might be contemplated for the purpose of coordinating agricultural commodity trade policies as provided for in this Article. Are any such measures contemplated by the Member States?

Answer Such measures would be the object of decisions made in due time by the institutions of the Association.

Article 28

Question 78 This Article provides for the maintenance in certain circumstances of certain restraints on competition in trade between Member States in agricultural products during the transitional period. Is it intended to require complete removal of these restraints at the end of the twelve-year period and to require complete free trade within the Area on agricultural goods? If this is the case, what arrangments, if any, exist to ensure the progressive removal of these restraints during the twelve-year period? If Member States cannot at present give the CONTRACTING PARTIES to the GATT an assurance that these restraints will all be removed at the end of the twelve-year period and that trade in agricultural products will then be free do they agree that the CONTRACTING PARTIES will need to know their plans before being able finally to determine that the requirements of Article XXIV: 8 (b) have been fulfilled?

Answer   The provisions of Article 28 are not applicable after the expiry of the twelve-year period for the full establishment of the Area. The Treaty does not envisage the removal of these restraints during the twelve-year period.

Question 79   How would the measures applied pursuant to this Article be justified under the GATT?

Answer   These measures are justified because being applicable only during the transition period they do not impede the implementation of the liberalization program, neither do they have unfavorable effects on the treatment accorded to third countries.

Question 80   What is meant by the term "antieconomic" used in this Article and in Article 31?

Answer   This refers to situations resulting from a decline in the average level of productivity referred to in Article 30.

Question 81   What criteria are contemplated for determining whether an "increase in antieconomic production" is involved in measures a Member State might decide to apply pursuant to the provisions of this Article?

Answer   The situation will be examined in each individual case by the institutions of the Association.

Question 82   What is the definition of "agricultural commodities"? Will rubber, raw cotton, and the more highly processed foodstuffs (e.g. packaged foodstuffs) be covered by this definition?

Answer   The institutions of the Association will provide a definition in due time.

Question 83   What criteria are contemplated for determining "those agricultural commodities which are of substantial importance" under the provisions of this Article?

Answer   These will be determined in each individual case by the institutions of the Association.

Question 84   What proportion of intra-area trade do the Member States anticipate will be excluded by this Article from the regular trade liberalization program during the transitional period defined in Article 2?

Answer   It is not possible at this stage to estimate the proportion of intra-area trade which would be affected by a possible application of Article 28.

Question 85   How and when is it intended that the products affected by measures applied pursuant to this Article at the end of the transition period will be subject to the provisions of Articles 3, 4, 5, 7, and 8?

Answer   The measures provided for under this Chapter do not involve the exclusion of those products from the liberalization program but only the temporary suspension, on an exceptional basis, of some of the effects of this program.

Question 86   May the measures permissible under this Article be applied to a product in the Common Schedule?

Answer   Yes.

Question 87

a) How would imports be limited under the provisions of this Article?

b) Is it envisaged that imports would be controlled by means of quantitative restrictions? If so, how would such restrictions be justified under the GATT?

Answer

a) Mainly by means of quantitative restrictions.

b) Not necessarily. As regards the compatibility with the General Agreements, see answers to questions 79 and 85.

Question 88   Where Member States limit the import of certain commodities from other Member States under Article 23 or 28, will they be expected or required to limit the import of these commodities from third countries? If so, will the Member States inform the GATT before these measures are put into effect?

Answer   Not necessarily (see answer to question 171).

Question 89   Would the measures applied pursuant to the provisions of this Article be nondiscriminatory not only as between Member States but also as between them and contracting parties to the GATT?

Answer   As far as relations between the Member States are concerned, such measures will be applied on a nondiscriminatory basis. As regards their relations with third countries, the Member States will adapt the application of such measures to their respective international commitments.

Question 180   To what extent will agricultural products come within the provisions of Articles 2 to 13?

Answer   Agricultural products are included in the liberalization program.

Question 181   Will the assessment of whether there is "antieconomic production" be on a world-wide basis of comparison, or only by comparison with costs of production within the Area?

Answer   For the purpose of determining whether there is any "antieconomic production," the provisions of Chapter VII take into account the level of productivity existing in each Member State prior to the entry into force of the Treaty.

Question 182

1. Will the nondiscriminatory measures referred to in this Article cease to be effective at the end of the period prescribed in Article

2, or could they be maintained in force by the Conference beyond that period?

2. Assuming the first alternative, how do the Member States propose to ensure that, at the end of that period, such measures could effectively be abolished?

Answer

1. As is clearly laid down in Article 28, the provisions of this Article will only apply "within the period mentioned in Article 2".

2. The obligation undertaken under Article 28 means that each Member State which applies such restrictions will take the necessary steps in order to be in a position to eliminate them at the expiry of the twelve-year period referred to in Article 2.

Question 183

a) What measures are envisaged in order to equalize the prices of the imported and the domestic product?

b) Where such measures are introduced, will these apply also to items where duties are bound under the GATT?

Answer

a) Such measures as may be necessary in each case and in respect of each country.

b) If necessary. In such a case, a Member State which is a contracting party to GATT will act in conformity with its GATT obligations.

Question 184   What arrangements do the Member States have in mind for the periodic review of measures applied pursuant to this Article during the transition period?

Answer   The Treaty does not contain any specific provisions in this field. However, paragraph 2 of Article 28 provides that the Member States receive prior notification. This implies that the intention is to examine the conditions in which such measures will be applied.

Article 29

Question 90   This Article provides that an attempt shall be made to expand intra-area trade in agricultural commodities by such means as agreements:

a) What is the nature of the agreements envisaged in this Article?

b) What safeguards exist that the conclusion of such agreements will not increase the barriers to trade of countries outside the Area?

c) Will the Member States undertake to submit to the CONTRACT-ING PARTIES to the GATT, pursuant to Article XXIV:7 of the GATT, details of such agreements?

Answer

a) Mainly long-term purchases and sales agreements, provided however that normal channels of trade shall not be disrupted.

b) Such agreements cannot conceivably affect such countries considering that under this Article they will operate in normal competitive conditions.

c) Although Article XXIV:7 is not considered to be applicable, the signatory States have no objection to any relevant information being furnished.

Question 91 Are agreements under this Article to be regarded as an integral part of the Association arrangements for the purpose of the consideration of the arrangements by the CONTRACTING PARTIES to the GATT?

Answer The signatory States are of the opinion that the provisions of this Article are an integral part of the Association arrangements. Agreements resulting from the implementation of this Article constitute mechanisms which are intended to facilitate the achievement of its objectives.

Question 92 Would the agreements contemplated under the provisions of this Article result in discrimination between countries within the Area or between the countries inside and those outside the Area? Should there be discrimination within the Area, how would it be reconciled with the provisions of Article 18?

Answer There does not appear to be any reason why there should be any discrimination.

Question 93 What assurances are there that these agreements would be consistent with the provisions of the GATT and the policies and decisions of the CONTRACTING PARTIES to the GATT or the IMF regarding bilateralism?

Answer The provisions of Article 29 do not necessarily lead to bilateral agreements. On the other hand, in considering this Article due account must be taken of the multilateral trade objectives on which the Treaty is based. As regards systems of payments, the Treaty does not contain any provision.

Question 94 Will products included in the agreements permitted by this Article be excluded from the provisions of Articles 3, 4, 5, 7, and 8 during the transition period of Article 2? If so, how and when will these products be made subject to the provisions of Articles 3, 4, 5, 7, and 8?

Answer No.

Question 185 How do the Member States who are also contracting parties to the GATT reconcile this Article with their obligations under the GATT, especially in view of Article XXIV:4 of the GATT, which states that "the purpose of a customs union or of a free-trade area should be to facilitate trade between the constituent territories and not to raise barriers to the trade of other contracting parties with such territories"?

Question 186 May it be assumed that the Member States, in pursuing the aim set out in the first paragraph of this Article, will give due consideration not only to the traditional flow of intra-area trade but also to traditional imports from countries outside the Area?

Answer to questions 185 and 186   The provisions of this Article do not raise obstacles to trade with other contracting parties to the General Agreement in view of the fact that priority will be granted only in normal competitive conditions, and because the great bulk of imports of agricultural and livestock products has been coming traditionally from within the Area.

Question 187   Is it intended that the agreements referred to in this Article shall apply exclusively to agricultural commodities which are not included in the program for liberalization of intra-area trade?

Answer   No. Such agreements can be applied to any agricultural product.

Question 188   Is it contemplated that the agreements envisaged in this Article may continue in force after the end of the period prescribed in Article 2?

Answer   No.

Question 189

   a) Would the agreements envisaged in this Article mean that a Member State would replace normal commercial importations, necessary to meet deficits in domestic production, by long-term arrangements with other Member States?

   b) If so, do the Member States envisage that this could mean the exclusion of imports from outside countries, especially in view of the obligation to give priority, under normal competitive conditions, to products originating in the territories of the other Member States?

Answer

   a) and b) Not necessarily, because in such circumstances encouragement to the substitution of imports from third countries by products originating in the area could be given only in respect of part of such imports.

Question 190   What does "priority" under normal competitive conditions mean?:

   1. Does it mean that, all else being equal, priority shall be given to Member States?

   2. Or does it mean that priority can be given to Member States even though sources outside the Area can supply at lower prices?

Answer

   1. Yes.

   2. No.

Question 191   Can the agreements referred to in this Article consist of sales/purchase contracts between importing and exporting countries?

Answer   Yes.

Question 227   Apart from the reference to "due consideration being given to the traditional flows of intra-area trade" in this Article, in what way do the Member States envisage that distortions in the development of the agricultural economy of the Area can be avoided through negotiation of agreements between Member States on agricultural commodities?

Answer   Mainly by means of the other provisions of this Chapter.

Article 30

Question 95   Could the Member States give an example of the type of situation to which the provisions of this Article would apply?

Answer   The provisions of Article 30 are intended to prevent a Member State from applying restrictions in order to stimulate production increases where such restrictions would bring about a decline in the average level of productivity existing prior to the date of the entry into force of the Treaty.

Question 96   What criteria will be followed in determining whether the measures provided for in Chapter VII of the Treaty are applied for the purpose of incorporating, in the production of agricultural commodities, resources which imply a reduction in the average level of productivity?

Answer   The institutions of the Association will examine each case individually.

Question 192   Considering that Article 27 calls for policies aimed at securing the most efficient utilization of the natural resources of Member States and that Article 28 rules out any increase in antieconomic production, may it be assumed that the purpose of this Article is to prevent Member States from employing an increasing number of workers in the production of a given volume of argicultural output? If not, what is the specific purpose of this Article?

Answer   The intention is to prevent the utilization of resources of all kinds (land, capital, labor, know-how, etc.) in antieconomic undertakings.

Article 31

Question 193   Is the term "reduction of its exports" intended to mean a reduction in absolute value or a reduction in relation to the volume of exports which would have been reached had the measures referred to in Article 28 not been instituted?

Answer   This phrase refers to a decline in the volume of exports as a result of a reduction in regular consumption levels of an antieconomic increase of productive activities in the importing country, in the circumstances referred to in Article 31.

Chapter VIII

MEASURES IN FAVOR OF COUNTRIES IN A RELATIVELY LESS ADVANCED STAGE OF ECONOMIC DEVELOPMENT

Article 32

Question 97 Are measures authorized under this Article to be regarded as an integral part of the Association arrangements for the consideration of the arrangements by the CONTRACTING PARTIES to the GATT?

Answer Yes.

Question 98 Will the Member States undertake to submit to the CONTRACTING PARTIES to the GATT pursuant to Article XXIV:7 of the GATT any measures authorized pursuant to this Article of the Montevideo Treaty?

Answer When the institutions of the Association deem it appropriate.

Question 99 What criteria are used to determine whether a Member State may benefit from the provisions of this Article?

Answer Under the Protocol of 18 February 1960, the governments which are signatories to the Treaty have agreed that Bolivia and Paraguay are at present in a position to claim the special treatment provided for in Chapter VIII. In future cases, it will be incumbent upon the institutions of the Association to lay down the criteria to be followed for the purpose of determining whether a Member State is entitled to the benefit of the provisions of Article 32 of the Treaty.

Question 100 Is it envisaged that quantitative import restrictions would be applied under the provisions of this Article (subparagraphs a, b, c, and d)?

   a) If so, could such restrictions be applied or relaxed so as to discriminate in favor of countries in the Area and against third countries?

   b) How would it be determined when a country shall cease to apply such restrictions?

Answer Yes, as far as paragraphs c) and d) are concerned.

   a) Yes; in this case each Member State would have to act in conformity with its international commitments.

   b) This will be determined in each individual case by the institutions of the Association.

Question 101 What is the nature of the "advantages" contemplated in subparagraph a) of this Article and what special arrangements are envisaged?

Answer A Member State may grant another Member State in a relatively less advanced stage of economic development in the Area concessions which will not be extended to other members.

Question 102 Could the "advantages" contemplated under the provisions of subparagraph a) of this Article be retained after the termination of the period cited in Article 2? If so, how could such action be reconciled with Article 18 of the Treaty of Montevideo and Article I of the GATT?

Answer Article 32 is an exception to the rule of Article 18 of the Treaty. If the assumption referred to in the first part of the question did materialize the Member States would adapt such situations to their international commitments.

Question 103 Are measures affecting imports or exports envisaged under subparagraph a) of this Article? If so, what kind of measures? Is there an upper limit to the duration for which a measure may be applied?

Answer The Treaty does not cover exports. The measures referred to are intended to apply to products originating in countries in a relatively less advanced stage of economic development in the Area. The nature of these measures will depend upon the circumstances of each individual case, and will be of an interim nature.

Question 104 What are the "more favorable conditions" contemplated under subparagraph b) of this Article?

a) Could the liberalization program be applied in a discriminatory fashion?

b) Would the program still provide for the reduction of duties, charges, and other restrictions within twelve years, or could it be extended beyond that period?

c) To what extent would the program for the reduction of duties be made more favorable and would there, nevertheless, be a final time-limit for achieving a free trade area?

Answer

a) No.

b) and c) The matter shall be the object of a decision by the institutions of the Association. Although the provisions considered permit certain Member States to reduce duties, charges, and other restrictive regulations "under more favorable conditions", the firm intention is to comply strictly with the general obligation of Article 7. This is possible in view of the fact that the shares of the Member States in total intra-area trade are different.

Question 105 How do the provisions of subparagraph c) of this Article differ from those of Article 24?

Answer The difference arises from the fact that the measures provided for under Article 24 are subject to the limitation laid down in paragraph 1 of Article 26.

Question 106 What criteria are contemplated for determining an "unfavorable balance of payments" under the provisions of subparagraph c) of this Article?

Answer   The criteria which are usually applicable.

Question 107   In order for the provisions of subparagraph c) of this Article to become operative would a country's balance of payments have to be "unfavorable" simply with countries in the Area or with the world as a whole?

Answer   What is involved here is the overall balance of payments.

Question 108   If the measures under subparagraph c) of this Article take the form of import restrictions, would they be operated in the manner provided for in Article XVIII, XIII, and XIV of the GATT?

Answer   To the extent that this was appropriate.

Question 109   How will the authorizations under subparagraph d) of this Article be controlled?

Answer   By the institutions of the Association.

Question 110

a) May the measures permissible in subparagraph d) of this Article be applied after the end of the transition period?

b) Would such measures be consistent with the GATT, particularly Article I thereof?

Answer

a) Yes.

b) Yes, because the exceptional measures permissible under these provisions will be of an interim nature and will not prevent the attainment of the objectives of the Treaty.

Question 111

1. Are measures affecting imports or exports envisaged under subparagraph d) of this Article?

2. If so, what kind of measures?

Answer

1. Only measures affecting imports by countries enjoying the benefit of the provisions of this Article.

2. *Inter alia* quantitative restrictions.

Question 112

a) Are the products which may benefit from the provisions of subparagraph d) of this Article to be excluded from the provisions of Article 3, 4, 5, 7, and 8 during the transition period of Article 2?

b) If so, how and when will these products be made subject to the provisions of Article 3, 4, 5, 7, and 8?

Answer   a) and b) No. The application of the provisions of paragraph d) does not interrupt the implementation of the liberalization program. It only results in some of its effects being temporarily suspended.

Question 194   Are the measures in favor of countries in a relatively less advanced stage of economic development to be regarded as general exceptions to the program of trade liberalization with the consequence that such measures could likewise be initiated or maintained after the end of the twelve-year period?

Answer The measures covered by Chapter VIII constitute an exception to the Treaty which does not prevent the fulfillment of the liberalization program, and they can be applied after the end of the twelve-year period.

Question 195 Would it be correct to assume that steps taken under this Article will not have the effect of injuring the interests of third countries?

Answer Yes.

Question 196 Does this Article imply that even antieconomic production of agricultural products would be countenanced, together with limitation of imports, in spite of the exception to it in Article 28?

Answer No. The purpose of this Chapter is to raise the average level of productivity of those countries.

Question 197 Do the collective arrangements referred to in subparagraph e) of this Article refer also to help in expanding the agricultural development of less-developed Member States and the promotion of their external trade in agricultural products?

Answer They are intended to bring about an expansion in productive activities in general.

Question 198 Would the special technical assistance program referred to in subparagraph f) of this Article cover agricultural production?

Answer Agricultural production is not excluded.

Question 199 Is it intended that there should be some review of the special provisions of this Article, so as to take account of any improvements in economic development and so gradually lessen any internal differences of treatment?

Answer The interpretation is that this question does not refer to a modification of the Article proper but to a review of its effects.

In this case, the imposition of the measures envisaged in Article 32 will be the object of a joint authorization which implies that the terms and conditions of the authorization will include adequate provisions to ensure that such measures are applied only to the extent necessary.

Question 228 Would the Member States confirm that the special arrangements envisaged in subparagraph a) of this Article relate to Bolivia and Paraguay exclusively, and that this special provision would not be available to other Member States?

Answer The Member States will determine in each individual case what are the countries to which the provisions of this Article will apply.

Question 229 To what extent is it envisaged that Member States will resort to the provisions of subparagraph a) of this Article to assist the less-developed Member States rather than through other forms of assistance envisaged under this Article?

Answer   The institutions of the Association will determine in each individual case what provisions are most suitable for the attainment of the objectives pursued.

Chapter XI

MISCELLANEOUS PROVISIONS

Article 48

Question 200   With reference to the first paragraph of this Article, will there be a similar guarantee for third countries that changes made will not imply a level of duties and charges less favorable than that in force before the changes?

Answer   In its relations with third countries, each Member State will act in conformity with its international commitments.

Article 49

Question 113   What are the criteria to be adopted for the purpose of determining the origin of goods and for their classification?

Answer   The criteria will be determined in due time by the institutions of the Association.

Question 114   In adopting criteria for the purpose of determining the origin of goods, will the Member States make special provisions to facilitate the use of raw materials normally imported from outside the Area in goods deemed to originate within the Area?

Answer   Yes, in all likelihood.

Question 201   In view of the far-reaching significance of the rules governing criteria for determining the origin of goods in a free trade area, full information on the criteria adopted or to be adopted in the Latin American Free Trade Area would be very useful in assessing the practical scope of the Treaty:

a) Is it the intention of the Member States to make available to the CONTRACTING PARTIES to the GATT the text of any rules which they might adopt concerning the origin of goods?

b) Are they at this stage in a position to give information on such rules?

Answer

a) Yes.

b) No.

Question 202   What are the means envisaged by the Member States to protect themselves against deflections of trade? Is it intended to require a certificate of origin for all goods or only for specific categories of goods?

Answer   The question will be examined in due time by the institutions of the Association.

Question 203   What criteria for determining the origin of goods will be applied during the intermediary period which may elapse before the rules on origin enter into force?

Answer   The criteria applicable to intra-area trade. It is intended that the final criteria will be fixed as soon as possible.

Question 204   With reference to subparagraph c) of this Article, is it the intention of the Member States to adopt the Brussels Nomenclature or to establish a distinct tariff nomenclature of their own?

Answer   The provisional committee of Montevideo has recommended to the governments of the signatory States that they adopt the Brussels Nomenclature.

Question 205   With reference to subparagraph e) of this Article, is it the intention of the Member States to establish criteria different from those contained in the General Agreement with regard to "dumping" and other unfair trade practices?

Answer   For the purpose of such studies the criteria referred to in Article VI of the GATT will be taken into account.

Article 50

Question 115   Under what provision of the GATT do the Member States justify the restrictions on exports set forth in this Article?

Answer   The provisions of this Article do not run counter to the spirit of the General Agreement. The signatory States intend to apply this Article only in cases where differences between the systems of external trade could give rise to operations involving disruptions of natural trade channels.

Question 206   What are the reasons which have prompted the Member States to introduce a procedure of prior approval for the reexport of products imported by a Member State from the Area?

Answer   Reexportation will be authorized only where no deflection of trade flows likely to injure a Member State is threatened.

Question 207   Could the Member States provide information concerning the "degree of industrial processing or manufacture" which the Committee will determine for the purposes of the second paragraph of this Article?

Answer   Not at present. The criteria will be determined as soon as possible by the institutions of the Association in pursuance of Article 49 a).

Article 52

Question 208
1. Can it be assumed that this Article applies to agricultural products as well as industrial products? and that
2. Production relying on subsidies would be classified as uneconomic for the purposes of Article 28?

Answer

1. Yes.
2. Not necessarily. It should be pointed out, however, that the provisions of Article 52 do not cover production subsidies.

Question 209

a) Does this Article also relate to the subsidization of exports to countries outside the Area?
b) If not, what rules will apply to the subsidization of such exports?

Answer

a) No.
b) In its relation with third countries, each Member State will act in conformity with its international commitments.

Question 210   Are the provisions of this Article to be construed as debarring goods which are subsidized from being exported to the Area when such goods are also produced in other countries of the Area?

Answer   No.

<h2 style="text-align:center">Chapter XII</h2>

<h3 style="text-align:center">FINAL CLAUSES</h3>

Article 58

Question 211   This Article provides that accession to the Treaty will be open to all Latin American countries. Will any countries other than Latin American countries be considered for full or partial membership?

Answer   No. The Treaty will be open for accession by Latin American countries only.

Article 60

Question 116   Will the Member States undertake to submit to the CONTRACTING PARTIES to the GATT, pursuant to Article XXIV: 7 of the GATT, amendments to the Montevideo Treaty presented pursuant to the provisions of this Article?

Answer   Yes.

Article 62

Question 117   Does this Article apply to international agreements such as the GATT and the IMF?

Answer   In view of the provisions of paragraph 1 of Article 62, the Montevideo Treaty will not affect the agreements entered into by the signatory States under the General Agreement or with the International Monetary Fund.

Paragraph 2 does not apply to such cases in view of the fact that there is no incompatibility between the Montevideo Treaty on the one hand, and the General Agreement and the IMF on the other.

Question 118 Does the second paragraph of this Article imply that the Member States must reconcile conflicts between the Montevideo Treaty and existing agreements in favor of the former?

Answer Under paragraph 2 of Article 62 each signatory State undertakes to renegotiate its agreements so that the provisions of such agreements should not hinder the application of the Montevideo Treaty or the attainment of its objectives.

Question 212 In the case of those Member States which are also contracting parties to the GATT, which provisions of the Montevideo Treaty are considered to be inconsistent with the GATT and in what ways will the Member States concerned seek to reconcile the provisions of the Treaty with the provisions of the GATT?

Answer The Member States which are contracting parties to the General Agreement are of the opinion that the provisions of the Montevideo Treaty have been duly adjusted to the rules laid down in the General Agreement.

Question 213 What attitude will the Member States adopt in respect of agreements signed with countries outside the Area, due consideration being given to the second paragraph of this Article?

Answer The Member States will take the necessary steps in order to harmonize the provisions of such agreements with the objectives of the Treaty.

Protocol No. 1

Question 119 Paragraph 7 of this Protocol provides that the Member States shall be entitled to exclude products of little value from the group subject to tariff reduction provided that their aggregate value does not exceed 5 per cent of the value of imports for the Area. Are the products to be excluded left entirely within the discretion of the importing Member? What safeguard is there that this Member will not exclude products produced in the Area in which there has hitherto been little trade because of high import barriers? What does the expression products "of little value" mean?

Answer For practical reasons, these products are excluded from statistical computations but this does not mean that they are excluded from the liberalization program.

The Standing Executive Committee will be called upon to furnish statistical evidence.

Question 120 Does paragraph 18 of Title V of this Protocol imply the procedure for securing "the highest possible degree of effective reciprocity" may involve restrictive measures which would favor reciprocity at the expense of inhibiting the highest possible trade levels?

Answer No.

Question 121 If Member States are considering the equalization of tariff rates, would they be willing to move toward the lowest rather than the highest rates of duty?

Question 122   How will Member States ensure that measures taken pursuant to paragraph 18 of Title V of this Protocol will be consistent with Article XXIV: 5 of the GATT?

Answer to question 121 and 122   These provisions are not directed towards the establishment of a common external tariff. They merely incorporate the rules which are intended to serve as a basis for specific negotiations in which the advantages and disadvantages of the situation of each item will be weighed.

Question 214

1. Would it be possible for the individual Member States to provide a rough estimate of the values which "t" and "T" in the formula set out in paragraph 5 of Title I of this Protocol are likely to assume at the time of the inauguration of the program for trade liberalization?
2. Would an increase in "T" be considered as a step towards the fulfillment of the obligations of a Member State?

Answer

1. The signatory States which are contracting parties to GATT are prepared to furnish such information in due time.
2. No, if an increase in "T" is attributable to an increase in the general tariff or to other practices, contrary to the provisions of the Treaty.

Question 215   Could the Member States also supply all contracting parties to the GATT with the information called for under subparagraphs a) to f) of paragraph 8 of Title II of this Protocol?

Answer   Yes, in due time.

Question 216

1. What are the meaning and scope of paragraph 17 of Title V of this Protocol?
2. Is it contemplated that duties, charges, and other restrictions should be eliminated at a faster rate or to a greater extent in the case of Member States which impose duties, charges, and restrictions substantially higher or more severe than those in force in other countries of the Area? Could examples be quoted?

Answer

1. See answer to question 152.
2. For the purposes of paragraph 17 of Title V of Protocol I, one of those measures could be the measure referred to in the question.

Question 217   What is meant by "prior equalization" in paragraph 18 of Title V of this Protocol?

Answer   This phrase refers to a comparison of the various tariffs prior to the negotiations so as to assess the value of possible concessions in order to assure reciprocity.

Protocol No. 4

Question 123 What proportion of inter-area trade is represented by the exclusion of petroleum and petroleum derivatives, as qualified by the second paragraph of the Protocol, from the provisions of the Treaty?

Answer Trade in petroleum and petroleum derivatives is not excluded from the system of liberalization instituted under the Treaty.

The second paragraph of this Protocol merely refers to certain commitments arising out of purchases and sales contracts entered into by Member States prior to the signature of the Treaty.

The actual value of the trade resulting from such commitments is not significant.

Question 218 Are the Member States in a position to give information on the main provisions of the agreements relating to commitments to purchase and sell petroleum and petroleum derivatives referred to in this Protocol, also on the period of duration of such commitments and on the value of total trade involved?

Answer Information will be supplied upon request.

Resolution I

Question 124 Apart from Resolution I, the Treaty contains no references to provisions for invisible transactions and credits. Are Member States contemplating preferential area arrangements for such transactions? If not, are nonmember countries right in assuming that invisible transactions and transfers will continue to be on a nondiscriminatory basis?

Answer No preferential treatment is contemplated for such transactions.

General Questions

Question 125 Will Member States be free without restriction to reduce their external tariffs in negotiation with other GATT contracting parties or otherwise?

Answer Yes, in view of the provisions of Articles 5 to 13 inclusive of the Montevideo Treaty.

Question 126 Are existing special regimes for free zones and ports to be retained?

Answer The Treaty does not deal with this matter.

Question 219 The Preamble emphasizes that the expansion of trade with the rest of the world is to follow after "the strengthening of national economies". Do not Member States consider that the improvement of their trade links with third countries is necessary to the progressive establishment of the Free Trade Area and that more consideration should have been given to this aspect in the Treaty?

Answer The main objective of the liberalization program is to speed up the economic development of the countries in the Area as a prerequisite to an increase in their external trade in general.

Question 220

a) To what extent will state-traded commodities come within the scope of the Free Trade Area?

b) Are any special arrangements in mind to cover these commodities?

Answer a) and b) Products coming under state trading are not excluded from the liberalization program provided for in the Treaty.

PART II

INTRODUCTION

On 1 and 3 June 1960 there was a meeting of the Working Party appointed by the CONTRACTING PARTIES at the meeting of 27 May 1960 comprising representatives from the Federal Republic of Germany, Australia, Austria, Belgium, Brazil, Canada, Chile, Cuba, the United States, France, India, Israel, Italy, Japan, Peru, the United Kingdom, Sweden, Switzerland, Czechoslovakia, and Uruguay, with the task of examining the Montevideo Treaty in the light of the provisions of the General Agreement on Tariffs and Trade and subsequently reporting to the CONTRACTING PARTIES at their seventeenth session.

The Working Party, having begun its discussions on 1 June 1960, the spokesman of the members of the Latin American Free Trade Associations (LAFTA) gave a preliminary and general explanation of the Treaty which was appreciated by the representatives of the contracting parties present.

Being requested to give information of a legal and technical nature as to whether the Treaty was a provisional or a constituent agreement for the area, the Executive Secretary of GATT stated:

> "One of the advantages of Article XXIV lies in the fact that it allows the contracting parties a waiver in respect of the most-favored nation clause and other provisions of the General Agreement in connection with not only the formation of a customs union or of a free trade area, but also the interim arrangements intended to lead to such formation. In order, however, to comply with the requirements of Article XXIV the 'interim' agreement must provide a plan and schedule for the formation of such a customs union or of such a free trade area within a reasonable length of time.
>
> "Failing such provision, the waiver would not be authorized until the customs union or the free trade area was an accomplished fact.

In other words, as the Montevideo Treaty does not provide for the *immediate* elimination of restrictions on trade between signatories, it would not, in the absence of the facilities allowed in the case of an 'interim' agreement, meet the necessary requirements for consideration under Article XXIV. From the point of view of GATT, the Treaty of Rome and the Treaty of Stockholm constitute 'interim' agreements within the meaning of Article XXIV; it therefore seems to me essential that the parties to the Montevideo Treaty should obtain the same approval for their own arrangements pending the full achievement of the free trade area at the end of the transitional period."

Subsequently members of the Working Party requested information about various Protocols and Articles of the Montevideo Treaty.

The questions asked and the replies given which have already been circulated, together with the three GATT questionnaires to which replies were given by countries members of LAFTA, are considered to form part of the present document.

Finally it was agreed that the Working Party would resume its meetings on 17 October, after consulting the countries concerned, and that on this occasion it would not only study the replies to the second and third questionnaires but that it could revert to the points dealt with at the previous meetings.

Questions asked during meetings of the Working Party on 1 and 3 June 1960 and replied to by representatives of signatories of the Montevideo Treaty at the meetings.

Chapter I

NAME AND PURPOSE

Article 1

Question 230 Could the Member States explain what measures they intend to take to liberalize trade in accordance with the provisions of Article XXIV of the General Agreement?

Answer The purpose of the Montevideo Treaty is to promote trade liberalization as a means of facilitating the economic development of the region. In progressively eliminating charges and barriers of all sorts on intra-area trade, Member States will take due account of the objective of the Treaty to expand and diversify trade within the Area as well as international trade in general. In establishing the Free Trade Area, Member States will act in accordance with their commitments under other international agreements. The Montevideo Treaty is designed to conform both in letter and in spirit with the provisions of Article XXIV of the General Agreement.

Question 231   Does the Treaty affect only trade between Member States or will Member States also follow a common commercial policy *vis-à-vis* other countries?

Answer   The Montevideo Treaty only covers intra-area trade. Member States will remain free to determine their commercial policy towards third countries. In doing this they will, of course, take account of their commitments under the Montevideo Treaty and other international agreements.

Chapter II

PROGRAM FOR TRADE LIBERALIZATION

Article 3

Question 232   Could the Member States supplement the information given in the reply to question 12 concerning the requirement that importers of certain products in Mexico have to produce evidence of compensating exports?

Answer   Article 3 provides that the Member States shall "gradually eliminate, in respect of substantially all their reciprocal trade, such duties, charges, and restrictions as may be applied to imports of goods originating in the territory of any contracting Party". If the requirement for compensatory exports causes an increase in the price of the imported commodity, this requirement will be considered as a "charge" in the sense of Article 3 of the Treaty. It is understood that the Mexican Government in imposing or maintaining such requirements will apply them in accordance with its obligations under the Treaty and in accordance with other international commitments.

Quesion 233   What are the other international commitments of Mexico referred to in the reply to question 232?

Answer   Mexico is not a contracting party to the General Agreement on Tariffs and Trade; it is, however, a signatory to the International Monetary Fund Agreement and is bound by the provisions of that Agreement. There is no discriminatory tariff treatment in Mexico as a result of bilateral agreements.

Question 234   Could the Member States expand on their reply to question 13 relating to the effect which the obligation under the Treaty to eliminate duties, charges, etc., would have on the operation and maintenance of the exchange auction system in Brazil?

Answer   In cases where the use of different auction rates causes an increase in the price of imported products the practice of applying different exchange auction rates may be construed as a charge in the sense of Article 3 of the Montevideo Treaty, and may thus have to be eliminated.

Question 235   Will the application of any of the provisions of the Treaty have the effect of preventing an individual Member State from reducing or eliminating balance-of-payments restrictions as and when its balance-of-payments and external reserve position improves?

Answer The Treaty does not relieve Member States of their obligation to reduce and eliminate restrictions as required by the GATT or the IMF.

Question 236 Does the Treaty require the abolition of all restrictions regardless of their purpose or will it be possible for Member States to retain restrictions in certain circumstances or in respect of certain goods?

Answer The objective of the Member States under the Treaty is to eliminate all restrictions. The approval of the Member States is required for any deviation from the program of trade liberalization.

Articles 4 to 8

Question 237

a) The Treaty provides for the gradual elimination of duties, charges, and restrictions through the negotiation of National Schedules and a Common Schedule. How are National Schedules and the Common Schedule to be negotiated and how will they be coordinated?

b) Is it correct to assume that at the end of the transitional period all items included in the National Schedules will also be included in the Common Schedule and that the rate of duty applying to trade between Member States will be nil?

c) What provision has been made for including in the Schedules items which, although not at present moving between Member States, are items which can potentially be traded between the countries of the Free Trade Area?

Answer The Treaty provides for a flexible approach to the gradual but progressive elimination of duties, charges, and restrictions on substantially all the trade during the twelve-year period. Duties, charges, and other restrictions for all products included in the Common Schedule will have been eliminated at the latest by the time the transitional period expires, as provided for in paragraph b) of Article 4 of the Treaty. Annual reductions in duties and charges concerning items to be included in the National Schedules equivalent to not less than 8 per cent of the weighted average applicable to third countries will be made through annual negotiations between Member States. The level of these duties and charges shall, as provided for in Article 5, be based on the level of those duties and charges in force *vis-à-vis* third countries on 31 December prior to each negotiation. Under Article 14 c) Member States will take the necessary steps to add to these Schedules each year an increasing number of products which are not yet included in reciprocal trade. Common Schedules will be negotiated every three years and Member States are obliged under Article 7 to include in the Common

Schedule not less than 25, 50, and 75 per cent of the aggregate value of trade among the Member countries during the first, second, and third three-year periods respectively. During the fourth three-year period substantially all the intra-area trade will have been included in the Common Schedules. While substantially all the trade will move freely between member countries, it is possible that a limited number of items may continue to be subject to certain duties, charges, or restrictions. If this is the case, it will be necessary for Member States to reexamine at the end of the transitional period the measures that will have to be taken to deal with these items. In arriving at a decision Member States will take into account the international obligations of member countries, as well as the particular circumstances affecting trade in these commodities.

Question 238 In proceeding with the reduction of duties and charges by a given percentage each year, will it be possible for Member States to reduce or eliminate duties and charges on certain products while maintaining them on other products?

Answer The Member States undertake in Article 5 to reduce annually duties and charges equivalent to not less than 8 per cent of the weighted average applicable to third countries until such duties and charges are eliminated in respect of substantially all of their imports from the Area. It is left to the Member States to decide the items to be negotiated each year and the extent to which duties and charges will be reduced on specific items, subject only to the provision that the reduction is not less than 8 per cent per year of the average.

Question 239 Will Member States which are not signatories to the General Agreement follow a commercial policy which is consistent with the international obligations of other Member States?

Answer Member States which are not contracting parties to the General Agreement will, of course, not be under any legal obligation to comply with the provisions of that Agreement. It can be assumed, however, that such Member States will take into consideration the effects of policies pursued by them on other Member States which have to observe the provisions of the General Agreement. Note may be taken of the fact that all signatories to the Montevideo Treaty have accepted that the obligations of Member States under the Treaty should not be inconsistent with the obligations of those Member States which are signatories to the GATT.

Articles 11 and 12

Question 240 These Articles provide for action by Member States to remedy "significant and persistent disadvantages" which might result from the implementation of the liberalization program. a) What kind of action is envisaged by the Member States for dealing with these problems and what different circumstances are envisaged which would lead to action under Article 12 rather than Article 11? b) Will action under Article 12 also be implemented in a way permitting the maintenance of trade at the highest possible level or will measures applied under this Article take the form of import restrictions?

Answer   The provisions of these Articles are designed to contribute to the balanced development of the economies of the countries in the region by permitting Member States, primarily through the negotiation of additional concessions, to counteract persistent and significant disadvantages which may result from the implementation of the liberalization measures negotiated between the Member States. Although the type of action most appropriate to deal with a given case will depend on the particular cirumstances of the case, the overriding objective of the Treaty of expanding trade will not be lost sight of. The provisions of Article 12, although essentially similar to those of Article 11, have been included in the Treaty as an additional safeguard for the interests of the relatively less-developed Member States.

Chapter III

Article 15

Question 241   In reply to question 51 c) Member States have indicated that they do not envisage the adoption of a uniform policy in their treatment of foreign shipping services. What are the services from outside the Area envisaged in Article 15 on which Member States may want to reconcile their respective policies?

Answer   The use of the term "services" in the Treaty corresponds to the definition and use of this term by the International Monetary Fund. Although shipping is one of the items included in this definition the Member States have not contemplated the adoption of a uniform policy towards foreign shipping services under the provisions of Article 15. This does not preclude the possibility of other suitable action under the GATT or other international agreements, and the introduction of defense measures against discrimination in shipping rates affecting the export and import trade of Latin American countries. This kind of discrimination has been experienced in recent years and because of its adverse effects on the trade of the Area it is a matter of particular concern to the countries in the region.

Question 242   Will the provisions of Article 15 be implemented in such a way as to prevent the imposition of new barriers and the withdrawal of reciprocal tariff concessions negotiated under the GATT?

Answer   The Treaty does not affect the freedom of individual Member States to determine and maintain tariffs and charges *vis-à-vis* imports from third countries. However, in the process of establishing the Free Trade Area, Member States will bear in mind the common objectives of the Treaty. There is no intention on the part of the Member States to take any action which will lead to the abrogation of their international commitments or to a reduction of trade with countries outside the Area.

Articles 16 and 17

Question 243 In the reply to question 64, it is stated that "complementarity agreements constitute mechanisms intended to facilitate the achievement of the objectives of the Association as promptly as possible." Can it be assumed that the complementarity agreements will be terminated by the end of the transitional period, by which time the liberalization program is supposed to have been completed?

Answer It is thought that it should be possible to terminate the complementarity agreements, which aim at promoting the expansion of production and trade, by the end of the transitional period. Any extension of the period of operation of such agreements, if considered desirable, will be subject to review at the expiration of the transitional period.

Chapter VI

ESCAPE CLAUSES

Article 23

Question 244 Will the application of the escape clauses of Article 23 be limited to the transitional period?

Answer Escape clauses, by their very nature, could be applied after the transitional period.

Chapter VII

SPECIAL PROVISIONS CONCERNING AGRICULTURE

Article 28

Question 245 In reply to question 82, concerning the commodities to be considered under the Treaty as "agricultural commodities", it has been stated that the institutions of the Latin American Free Trade Association will provide a definition of this term in due time. Have the Member States agreed on such a definition and will the definition be communicated to the CONTRACTING PARTIES?

Answer The Member States have not yet decided what commodities will be covered by this term. A definition will, however, be submitted to the CONTRACTING PARTIES in due time.

Article 29

Question 246 This Article provides that Member States shall give priority "... under normal competitive conditions to products originating in the territories of the other contracting parties, due consideration being given to the traditional flows of intra-area trade". Will due consideration also be given to the maintenance of traditional flows of trade with countries outside the Area?

Answer The purpose of the agreements envisaged in Article 29 is to enlarge and consolidate the flows of trade within the Area so as to facilitate the adjustment towards the free exchange of agricultural products within the Area after the end of the transitional period. The agreements are not intended to mitigate against trade between Member States and third countries.

Chapter VIII

MEASURES IN FAVOR OF COUNTRIES AT A RELATIVELY LESS ADVANCED STAGE OF ECONOMIC DEVELOPMENT

Article 32

Question 247 What are the special considerations which prompted the inclusion in the Treaty of special provisions for relatively less developed Member States?

Answer In order to deal with the emergency situation at the end of the war and in the early postwar years, it was necessary for Latin American countries to rely upon import restrictions to protect their balance of payments. Many of these countries, although still in balance-of-payments difficulties, have in recent years undertaken comprehensive measures to simplify their import control systems. Moreover, in accordance with their obligations under international agreements, they have taken steps to reduce and eliminate nontariff barriers in general. However, some of the relatively less developed countries in the region have found it difficult to adjust their import control systems as rapidly as the more developed countries of the region. Having regard to the beneficial effects of the free trade area arrangement on trade not only within the Area but also with third countries, the Treaty endeavors to make it easier for such less developed countries to participate by enabling them to make the necessary adjustments in their pattern of trade and their structure of productions in accordance with their particular circumstances.

Question 248 Will Bolivia be entitled to avail itself of the provisions of Article 32 and of Protocol No. 5 if that country signs the Treaty?

Answer It is hoped that Bolivia will soon be in a position to sign the Treaty. In that event, Bolivia will be entitled to invoke the provisions of Article 32 and Protocol No. 5 of the Treaty.

Question 249 In the reply to question 101 it is stated that a Member State may grant another Member State which is at a relatively less advanced stage of economic development advantages which it may not necessarily extend to other members. How can this be reconciled with the reply to question 104 a) that the liberalization program as provided for in Article 32 will not be implemented in a discriminatory fashion? Will the CONTRACTING PARTIES be informed of special measures applied under Article 32?

Answer   The provisions of this Article are designed to deal with special circumstances affecting certain countries. If identical conditions warranting the granting of "more favorable conditions" for the implementation of the liberalization program are to be found in more than one Member State, identical treatment will be given to all Member States qualifying for this special consideration. Any measures which will be applied under this Article will be communicated to the CONTRACTING PARTIES.

Question 250   Does Article 32 provide for the extension of special tariff concessions or special State-trading concessions to Member States which are relatively less developed?

Answer   The provisions of this Article are designed to give Member States at a relatively less developed stage of economic development an opportunity to activate their respective economies. The type of measures applied under these provisions will depend on the particular circumstances of the country involved. It is not contemplated, however, that a country invoking the provisions of Article 32 will be permitted to discriminate between countries in the Area.

Chapter XI

MISCELLANEOUS PROVISIONS

Article 49

Question 251   In the reply to question 113 the Member States have indicated that in due time the criteria for the establishment of rules of origin and for the classification of goods will be decided by the institutions of the Association. Have these criteria been determined and will they be communicated to the CONTRACTING PARTIES?

Answer   The Member States have set up a Commission for the purpose of determining these criteria. Rules thus formulated will be submitted to the first conference of the Latin American Free Trade Association, to be convened in Montevideo after the ratification of the Treaty; once established they will be made public, and will certainly be communicated to the CONTRACTING PARTIES.

General Questions

Question 252   Since the Treaty does not deal with the maintenance of the existing regimes for free zones and ports, can it be assumed that these will be continued as at present?

Answer   The existing special regimes for free zones and ports will not be affected by the Treaty and the operation and maintenance of these will continue to be determined by individual Member States. It is expected, however, that Member States will operate them in a manner which is compatible with the terms of the Treaty.

VOTING SYSTEM AT THE LAFTA CONFERENCE

Resolution 68(III)

IN VIEW OF Article 38 of the Montevideo Treaty;

WHEREAS the Treaty having been in force for two years, a system of voting should be established for the Conference of the Contracting Parties to be in effect hereafter;

Experience in the application of the Treaty recommends the gradual elimination of the requirement that there can be no negative vote for the Conference to make a decision.

The Conference of the Contracting Parties at its Third Meeting

RESOLVES:

First   Unless there is an express provision to the contrary, decisions of the Conference shall continue to be taken by an affirmative vote of at least two thirds of the contracting Parties, and provided there is no negative vote.

Second   The contracting Parties shall establish, to the extent considered necessary, cases that are to be added to those indicated in sections a), b), and c) of Article 38 of the Treaty, in relation to which decisions shall be taken by an affirmative vote of at least two thirds of the contracting Parties.

NOTE ON THE DRAFT RESOLUTIONS CONCERNING THE VOTING SYSTEM FOR THE CONFERENCE OF THE CONTRACTING PARTIES

Provisions of the Montevideo Treaty

1. In the Montevideo Treaty there are separate rules concerning the formation of a "quorum" and the voting system at a Conference of the Contracting Parties.

2. In respect of the formation of a quorum, Article 37 of the Treaty provides the definitive rule that "The Conference may not take decisions unless at least two thirds ($\frac{2}{3}$) of the contracting Parties are present."

3. On the other hand, in regard to the voting system, the rule stated in Article 38 of the Treaty is not definitive. It is expressly provided that the rule shall govern "During the first two years in which the present Treaty is in force" and it is added further that "The Contracting Parties shall likewise determine the voting system to be adopted after this two-year period."

4. The fundamental part of the current rule provides that "Decisions of the Conference shall continue to be taken by an affirmative vote of at least two thirds of the contracting Parties, and provided there is no negative vote."

5. Two aspects should be noted in this rule, that is:

a. The *percentage* that defines a decision of the Conference, which is at least two thirds of the contracting Parties, and
b. The *condition* that there may be no negative vote.

6. It appears necessary to point out the distinction, bearing in mind that when the contracting Parties decide to make some change in the voting system, possibly the aspect that should be changed is not so much the percentage as the condition that there may be no negative vote.

In regard to the condition that there may be no negative vote, under the system currently in effect, the Treaty indicates only the three exceptions precisely enumerated in the last part of Article 38:

The affirmative vote of two thirds ($\frac{2}{3}$) of the contracting Parties shall be required:

a. To approve the Committee's annual budget;
b. To elect the Chairman and two Vice-Chairmen of the Conference, as well as the Executive Secretary;
c. To fix the time and place of sessions of the Conference.

PROGRAM OF ECONOMIC INTEGRATION AND COMPLEMENTARY ECONOMIES

Resolution 100(IV)

(Fourth Regular Session, Bogotá, December 8, 1964)

HAVING SEEN the Report of the Special Committee created by Resolution 75 (III) at its meeting held in Montevideo in September 1964 (Doc. ALALC/CE/I/Informe), and

CONSIDERING that the conclusions of the Special Committee and the various initiatives of the Delegations to the Fourth Regular Session offer precise guidelines for the development of the process of integration of the economies of the contracting Parties directed toward achieving the objective of Article 54 of the Treaty, and allow for the establishment of a program of action designed to attain the co-ordination of economic policies contemplated by Resolution 75 (III) of the Conference,

THE CONFERENCE OF THE CONTRACTING PARTIES, in its Fourth Regular Session

DECLARES:

That the fundamental objective of the Montevideo Treaty is to pro-mote in a harmonious way the economic and social development of the contracting Parties by the progressive establishment of complementary and integrated economies;

That to advance the aims envisioned in the foregoing paragraph, in addition to carrying out the Liberation Program of the Treaty, the con-tracting Parties shall put into effect, as soon as possible, rules de-signed to:

1. Attain an equitable distribution of the results of the integration process; and

2. Ensure equitable conditions of competition;

That the program of coordination of economic policies and har-monization of the instruments for regulating foreign trade put under way by Resolution 75 (III) shall be directed toward the creation of conditions favorable to the establishment of a Latin American common market, in accordance with the provisions of Article 54 of the Treaty; and

That it is indispensable to give special attention to the problems which affect the countries with relatively less economic development in order to arrive at solutions which will guarantee their effective and immediate participation in the benefits of free trade and of the indus-trialization of the region.

RESOLVES:

To adopt the following Basic Directives of Economic Policy and Program of Action:

I. BASIC DIRECTIVES OF ECONOMIC POLICY

A. Foreign Trade

First The program contemplated by Resolution 75 (III) is di-rected toward the coordination of the foreign trade policies of the con-tracting Parties and toward harmonizing the respective instruments, with the aim of applying the machinery adopted therein on a common basis.

Second Pursuant to the provisions of the foregoing article, the greatest possible equalization shall be sought for the charges and restrictions applicable to imports from third countries in order to prevent distortions that might aggravate the differences in treatment that now exist. Within this general program, in the work that is being undertaken, the possibility of establishing a common foreign tariff is under analysis.

Third The program, insofar as foreign trade policies are concerned, is to be based on the following points:

1. The program for harmonizing the instruments for regulating foreign trade is intimately linked with the coordination of economic policies, which is the essential objective of Resolution 75 (III).

Consequently, the common instrumentation that may be adopted and the establishing of the treatments relating to third countries should help toward a balanced economic development of the region and the achievement of the goals stated in the Preamble of the Treaty and in the declaration contained in the present Resolution.

2. Creation of conditions which will permit the establishment of a common market (Article 54 of the Treaty).

3. The program for harmonizing the instruments for regulating foreign trade will be closely linked with the progressive elimination of the barriers in intraregional trade, not only with respect to the correlation that should exist in the speed of the two processes but also with respect to the creation of equitable conditions of competition which should facilitate the carrying out of the Liberation Program.

4. The common instruments on foreign trade must meet the need for:

   i) Stimulating greater productivity within the region, by avoiding the development of nonprofitable production that is supported by exaggerated protection; and

   ii) Establishing effective protection in behalf of the production of the region, as an adequate defense against possible excessive competition from outside the region.

5. The harmonized instruments of foreign trade must ensure the possibility that the contracting Parties will have adequate provision for confronting the particular problems of each country in its trade with third countries.

6. In the tasks to be undertaken to achieve the greatest possible equalization in the treatment applied to imports coming from third countries, and eventually, to formulate a common foreign customs

tariff, account shall be taken of the possibility and desirability of attaining a gradual harmonization by sectors of production or groups of products, giving priority to those that are of greatest importance to the economic development of the region.

B. Industrial Development

Fourth In the first stage of the work directed toward the formulation of a regional policy of industrial development the following bases shall be taken into account:

1. The problems of industrial development that are involved in the process of economic development being pursued by the contracting Parties of the Montevideo Treaty must be approached by taking into account both the utilization of the expanded market as well as the idea of achieving a greater and better use of the resources of the region and of seeking a distribution of the benefits of integration that duly considers the interests of each and every one of the member countries.

2. In a process of integration industrial development must be considered in the light of its interdependence with the other sectors of production and within the context of the general economic policies of the member countries of the Montevideo Treaty.

3. Industrial complementation must be considered and stimulated as an important instrument for the harmonious economic growth of the region. The countries should not hope to attain a certain level of development in a given sector in order to begin its complementation.

4. In order to achieve an effective advance in economic integration there must be immediate stimulation of the examination, the installation, and the development of industries of a regional character which will be of real significance to the industrial structure and the economic growth of the region.

5. The programming of the industrial development of the region must be based on the intention to preserve the legitimate interests of the contracting Parties, reconciling the degree of employment that is attained and the best possible utilization of capital goods and technological capacity with the aim of achieving a greater rationalization in production.

6. The establishment of equitable conditions of competition among the products of the region will stimulate the gradual industrial reorganization in the countries of the area.

7. In order to achieve an equitable distribution of the benefits of integration and because of the different structures and levels of develop-

ment of the countries of LAFTA, it is necessary that the location of industries be undertaken jointly and by plan.

8. In order to speed up the economic growth of the countries classed as relatively less economically developed and of those mentioned in Resolution 71 (III) of the Conference, the search for and assignment of concrete industrial projects of a regional nature for those countries should be encouraged.

9. The planned locating of industries of a regional nature in specified countries implies the adoption of a common policy in the production sector under consideration.

10. The locating of industries of a regional nature must be based on criteria of profitability and/or productivity, considering also the necessity for all the contracting Parties, because of their participation in these industries, to obtain equitable benefits from the integration.

11. To the extent that technical and economic conditions permit, participation of the greatest possible number of countries should be sought in the production of sectors developed or to be developed regionally.

12. To ensure the fulfillment of the common sectorial policy, the countries in which the installation of industries declared to be of regional interest may be proposed, must grant incentives to attain the location of such industries in their territories. At the same time, the other contracting Parties shall undertake not to adopt measures of any kind that will undo the aims being pursued. In the studies of projects of location there should be included the incentives that are deemed necessary for the sector concerned, and the aspects of the inequality in the internal regional development of each country should also be borne in mind.

13. Among the means and incentives to be used, the contracting Parties should consider not only the elimination of charges and restrictions on intraregional imports but also all those that are involved in a process of sectorial industrial integration.

Fifth The studies and undertakings concerning regional industrial development should be subject to the following criteria, among others:

1. Special importance should be assigned to sectorial integration as a means of promoting the economic development of the region. In applying this concept account must be taken of the possibilities of complementation and of identification of industries of a regional character, that is, of those that are of real significance to the structure and economic growth of the region. Sectorial integration presupposes the

development of the industrial activity of the pertinent sector in accordance with the outline of the joint programming that has been established.

2. In order to achieve industrial complementation pursuant to paragraph 3 of Article Four, all possible forms of complementation in the field of industrial production should be utilized, without being limited to the provisions of Article 16 of the Treaty.

3. In the studies directed toward speeding up the industrial development of the region through the utilization of the regional market, special attention must be given to those productive activities that are undeveloped or that are in a very early stage of evolution, taking into account the possibilities that this field offers to the installation of industries of a regional nature, on bases that will allow the access of all the contracting Parties to the opportunities resulting from the process of integration.

4. In the case of industries that offer scant possibilities of complementation on a basis of joint planning, equitable conditions of competition should be established which will ensure the most orderly utilization possible of the expanded market.

5. In the systematic program of studies by sectors with a view to their regional integration, priorities should be established that insofar as possible will consider the overall expectations of all the contracting Parties, especially those that are relatively less economically developed and those mentioned in Resolution 71 (III) of the Conference.

6. In sectorial integration the participation of all the member countries should be sought, with the aim of reaching insofar as possible the whole regional market.

C. Agricultural-Livestock Development

Sixth The objective of the Association in respect of agriculture and stock raising is to attain, in the shortest time possible, the coordination and harmonization of the several policies of the contracting Parties and the setting up of standards for trade in such products. To this end the following basic aspects are to be taken into account:

1. An increase in agricultural and livestock productivity through a better utilization of available resources.

2. The social and economic conditions of each country of the region.

3. Replacement of imports of agricultural and livestock products originating outside the region, by increasing the production of the region in accordance with the trend of demand and priority of access for

the region's agricultural and livestock products by means of effective preferential treatment.

4. The right of any contracting Party to apply, even after the expiration of the transition period and in accordance with rules now in effect, adequate measures designed to limit the importation of agricultural and livestock products originating in the region, whenever they cause or threaten to cause serious disturbances in domestic production that are of a social and economic significance.

5. The desirability of assistance to increase the consumption of agricultural and livestock products.

Seventh   To carry out the provisions of the preceding article, the contracting Parties shall undertake to:

1. Examine the national programs and determine what sectors of agriculture and stock raising offer the greatest relative advantages to the contracting Parties, taking into consideration the governing social and economic aspects thereof.

2. Establish a collective collaboration, with technical and financial resources from inside and outside the region, for a possible reorganization, under the special conditions of each country, of comparatively marginal productions that might be disclosed by the abovementioned examination.

3. Evaluate the importance of the production and trade in agricultural and livestock products in balances of payments, and their relation to the financing of national programs of economic development.

4. Analyze the social and economic aspects of the domestic agriculture of each country in relation to the possibilities of expanding the markets, the diversification of the national economies, and of accelerating the processes of industrialization.

5. Analyze the possibilities for expansion and diversification of the national agricultural-livestock economies on the basis of estimates of regional supply and demand for these products and of exports of such products to world markets.

6. Establish systems designed to make effective the preferential treatments intended to stimulate regional self-sufficiency.

7. Study the granting of temporary concessions for agricultural and livestock products with the aim of meeting seasonal shortages in local production.

D. Financial and Monetary Matters

Eighth The initial objective of the Association in financial and monetary matters is to attain the maximum possible interrelationship in the several systems of the contracting Parties.

Ninth To this end, the following measures are considered necessary:

1. Establishment of a system of credits for financing trade within the region in order to alleviate the short-term difficulties of the foreign sector and facilitate the growing expansion of commercial interchange.

2. Promotion of the intensification of inter-bank relations among the contracting Parties, by stimulating direct connections between commercial banks and facilitating the establishment of reciprocal lines of credit.

3. Examination of the effects of the exchange policy of the contracting Parties on the normal development of currents of trade.

4. Establishment of procedures in financial and exchange matters directed toward obtaining from foreign investment the greatest benefits for the region as a whole, bearing in mind the objective of a balanced economic development of the contracting Parties.

5. Establishment of procedures in financial and exchange matters that will enable capital of regional origin, duly classified as such, to be placed in other countries of the area, in order to organize multinational enterprises as a means of accentuating economic complementation.

6. Facilitating the establishment of agencies or representatives of the governmental or private banks of each contracting Party in the other countries of the Association.

II. PROGRAM OF ACTION

Tenth In order to accomplish the foregoing goals, the Organs of the Association will carry out the following Program of Action in the sectors indicated.

A. Customs

Eleventh With reference to the revision of the NABALALC (LAFTA Brussels Tariff Nomenclature) in order that it may be suitable for adoption as a common tariff nomenclature the following steps are to be taken:

1. Before January 1, 1965, the contracting Parties must take action on the following aspects:

i) Determination as to whether the rules and code of the NABAL-ALC are suitable for incorporation in the draft common tariff nomenclature;

ii) Possibility of including in the draft common tariff nomenclature the CUCI-NAB (Standard International Trade Classification-Brussels Tariff Nomenclature) statistical subheadings; and

iii) Desirability of having a common tariff nomenclature that can also be used for statistical purposes.

2. The Secretariat shall prepare a draft common tariff nomenclature.

3. Allowing the Secretariat a period of six months to prepare the aforementioned draft common nomenclature, counting from the date on which it submits to the countries the comparative tables of levels of charges and restrictions in each of the contracting Parties, as indicated in item e) of Article Three of Resolution 75 (III). In preparing this draft, and in order that it may reflect the economic, commercial, and technical reality of LAFTA as faithfully as possible, the Secretariat shall take into account the following criteria, among others:

i) The comparative tables of levels of charges and restrictions;

ii) The recommendations of the Advisory Committees, particularly those of Industrial Development and of Agricultural-Livestock Matters;

iii) The NAB (Brussels Tariff Nomenclature) proposals for adoption in the customs tariffs of the contracting Parties that have been undertaken or are being undertaken in studies and projects on this subject;

iv) The suggestions made with respect to Sectorial Meetings.

4. The contracting Parties shall seek to reinforce their Permanent Delegations with trained officials who can collaborate directly in the work relating to this subject, especially in view of the magnitude of the tasks to be undertaken as already indicated and in consideration of the need to make use of the experience acquired by technicians from the countries that have worked on the preparation of the national tariffs using the Brussels Tariff Nomenclature as a basis.

5. The contracting Parties recognize the necessity of adopting the Brussels Tariff Nomenclature in their national tariffs, as quickly as possible, or of speeding up the completion of the work being undertaken to that end, in order to widen by this means the fundamental bases for harmonizing the instruments for regulating their foreign trade, which is one of the principal objectives of Resolution 75 (III). Moreover, it is considered advisable that on this subject the greatest possible technical collaboration be established between the interested contract-

ing Parties and the Secretariat in regard to the basic aspects of uniformity and consensus of criteria by which the task of adopting the Brussels Tariff Nomenclature may be accomplished.

Twelfth In relation to items b), c), and d) of Article Three of Resolution 75 (III), the following steps shall be taken:

1. Completion as quickly as possible of the preparation of the schedules of customs duties, and charges of equal effect, and of the restrictions that are applied to imports of goods.

2. Continuation of the methodology used to accomplish the aforementioned tasks, which may be covered satisfactorily by the data contained in the pilot-model for schedules concerning charges and restrictions the details of which are contained in the Final Report of the First Meeting of the Advisory Committee on Customs Matters.

3. Without prejudice to the lists of products concerning which each contracting Party is interested in knowing whether internal taxes of a national, municipal, or departmental nature exist, transmittal to the Secretariat of the list and other details of those taxes which because of their discriminatory character affect the importation of goods.

Thirteenth With respect to item e) of the third article of Resolution 75 (III) the procedure will be as follows:

1. On the basis of information contained in model schedules, the Secretariat will make the comparative study of current charges and restrictions in each of the contracting Parties with relation to each product.

2. The Secretariat will complete the chart of comparative standards within six months after it receives full information from all countries, using the schedules of charges and restrictions.

3. Without prejudice to the provisions of the foregoing paragraph, the Secretariat will continue to deliver to the contracting Parties the chapters or groups of chapters of NABALALC that it considers final.

4. The date of March 2, 1964, adopted for apportioning the data relating to charges and restrictions is confirmed. However, in view of the fact that since that date some of the contracting Parties have replaced their national customs tariffs by others based on the Brussels Tariff Nomenclature, special emphasis is placed on the importance of a note explaining the procedure followed in computing all or each one (if done in a different manner) of the charges and restrictions, which each contracting Party should transmit to the Secretariat together with the first schedules to be sent.

5. The contracting Parties that have adopted new customs tariffs and not yet sent the schedules to the Secretariat should prepare them by including the data on charges and restrictions on imports contained in the newly adopted system. In such cases, the explanatory note shall cover, in the greatest detail, the method adopted or the standards followed in the transposition of the charges that prevailed before the reform and the new ones added, in order that the comparative analysis of the levels of charges will show or indicate the readjustments that were necessary to attain the greatest precision or desired approximation.

6. For the purpose of achieving completion within the maximum time indicated, with regard to transmittal to the Secretariat of the schedules of charges and restrictions, and bearing in mind that some of the contracting Parties, basing their action especially on the provisions of Resolution 74 (III), item a), paragraph 2, of the First Article, mentioned the technical assistance that should be furnished to countries classed as less economically developed, the Secretariat shall take action thereon to send technicians to the countries that require this assistance, in order to obviate the problems and difficulties that might arise in the preparation of the schedules on charges and restrictions on imports and other aspects connected with the undertakings assumed by the contracting Parties in customs matters.

Fourteenth In the work relating to the various aspects of customs technique, it must be borne in mind:

1. That the harmonization of the treatment of imports of goods coming from third countries is closely linked to the harmonization of the customs legislation and regulations now in force in the contracting Parties.

2. That some aspects of customs technique are of greater importance than others, and that the following require the most urgent and detailed study:

   i) Customs valuation;
   ii) Rates of charges for making uniform the tax systems applicable to the importation of goods;
   iii) Special customs procedures;
   iv) Normalization and unification of customs and noncustoms documents used in import and export operations;
   v) Definitions of customs terms.

3. That the methodology employed by the Advisory Committee on Customs Matters in its work on customs techniques is appropriate and that therefore these tasks should be continued and intensified in accordance with the terms approved by that Committee.

Fifteenth   The work is to be done in the following way:

1. At its next meeting the Advisory Committee shall complete the studies that it is now making on temporary admission, and shall seek to adopt appropriate definitive criteria.

2. The studies by the Secretariat on customs valuation shall be made in the following order:

  i) The countries must send their replies to the "Questionnaire on the adoption of the Definition of the Brussels Value as a uniform concept for customs valuation in the member countries of LAFTA" (Doc. CEP/Repartido 3/9/64), before January 31, 1965;

  ii) The Secretariat shall prepare the document compiling the replies mentioned in the foregoing, and the study thereof, directed toward determining the criteria considered to be most in accord with the purposes of harmonization, before April 30 of the same year, so that the documentation may be in the hands of the contracting Parties sufficiently in advance of the meeting of the Committee; and

  iii) While holding its next meeting, the Advisory Committee shall undertake a thorough study of customs valuation on the basis of the working documents submitted by the Secretariat and with the essential aim of obtaining some concrete formula for harmonization. For this purpose the contracting Parties shall appoint delegates trained in customs valuation.

3. In the consideration of special customs procedures, and without prejudice to the content of numeral 2 of the preceding article, a combined study of the following topics shall be attempted:

  i) Temporary admission;
  ii) Drawback;
  iii) Storage of goods under a system suspending payment of duties so that they may be processed or converted and subsequently exported;
  iv) Subsidies;
  v) Reimbursement of internal taxes; and
  vi) Admission of commercial samples.

It was resolved to assign special priority to "drawback".

4. It is recommended that the subject of customs techniques as called for in Resolution 74 (III) be dealt with by furnishing technical assistance to those countries that may require it and particularly to those declared to be relatively less economically developed, either by sending technical officials from the Secretariat to give advice on the

work to be undertaken by virtue of the program indicated in the present Resolution or by granting fellowships to customs officials of the countries that ask for them, or in other ways considered more suitable and timely.

Sixteenth   On the basis of the analysis of the comparative tables of levels of charges and restrictions and of the other studies undertaken in accordance with the program of action formulated by the Advisory Committee on Customs Matters, the Secretariat shall prepare a report outlining the problems connected with the program for harmonizing the instruments for regulating foreign trade and analyzing the following aspects, among others:

i) Possibilities of applying the basic criteria discussed above;

ii) The problems of protection for domestic economic activities of a fiscal nature and balance of payments that may arise in carrying out the harmonization program;

iii) Evaluation of the advantages or disadvantages present in the different instruments for regulating foreign trade in use up to the present by the contracting Parties, in order to consider the possibility of their adoption in the common foreign trade system that may be established.

The contracting Parties should provide for the permanent participation of outstanding technical officials in the work to be undertaken by the Advisory Committee in connection with this program.

B. Industrial Matters

Seventeenth   In relation to the industrial sector action will be taken in the manner indicated below.

1. Sectorial study groups.

i) The study groups created by the Standing Executive Committee shall take into account in this work, wherever pertinent, the bases and criteria outlined in the fourth and fifth articles.

ii) The Standing Executive Committee, in consultation with the Advisory Committee on Industrial Development, shall undertake to create other study groups with the aim of intensifying the task of sectorial integration, to the extent that circumstances permit, taking into account the priorities indicated in numeral 5 of the fifth article;

iii) As a result of their work the Study Groups shall recommend concrete formulas for integration of the corresponding sector;

iv) Account shall be taken of the fact that it is important that the studies on sectorial integration be ratified by the political decision of the contracting Parties in order to attain their prompt execution.

2. The Secretariat shall undertake a study of the classification of the industrial activities of the region in order to facilitate the application of what is outlined in the fourth and fifth articles and in accordance with the following terms of reference:

i) Productive activities that have not been developed in the region or that are in an incipient stage of development;

ii) Industrial activities that offer possibilities of complementation within the framework of integration;

iii) Industrial activities that do not offer sufficient possibilities of complementation;

iv) Identification of sectors of regional interest that may become the subject of complementation agreements, by examining the actual possibilities of participation by the different countries.

3. Establishment of the bases for achieving suitable conditions of competition for those industries included in section iii) of paragraph 2.

4. Analysis of the possibilities of applying these bases and criteria and of determining their validity in the case of industrial activities mentioned in sections ii) and iii) of paragraph 2.

5. In respect of the instrumentation of the bases for the formulation of a regional policy of industrial development, consideration as of possible application all the instruments of industrial development, including those indicated in the Treaty.

C. Agricultural-Livestock Matters

Eighteenth In carrying out the provisions of the Sixth and Seventh Articles the Standing Executive Committee shall organize the activities of the Advisory Committee on Agricultural and Livestock Matters in such a way that its tasks shall be as continuous as possible and along the following lines:

1. Organization of study groups to examine the principal agricultural and livestock products or groups of products for the purpose of establishing a coordinated policy in the fields of production and trade.

2. Examination of the most suitable procedures for installing a regional operating machinery that will unite the competent organs of the contracting Parties in regard to the marketing or supplying of agricul-

tural and livestock products, with an aim of realizing the possibilities of trade within the sector.

3. Establishment of a permanent and up-to-date system of reciprocal information on estimates of production, consumption, exportable balances, and shortages in agricultural and livestock products.

D. Financial and Monetary Matters

Nineteenth   In order to achieve the initial objective indicated in the Eighth Article and to put in effect the measures leading to its success, the Association shall undertake, through pertinent organs, to work specifically on the topics enumerated below:

1. Preparation of formulas concerning systems of credit for the financing of intraregional trade.

2. Preparation of formulas for cooperation that will improve relations in commercial banking.

3. Analysis of the influence of exchange rates on intraregional trade currents.

4. Consideration of the restrictions on imports within the realm of monetary authorities, with the aim of procuring their elimination for intraregional trade and their harmonization with respect to third countries.

5. Study of the treatments applicable to foreign capital.

6. Adoption of measures necessary to facilitate the circulation of LAFTA regional capital.

7. Studies concerning payments and clearings.

8. Study of the forms of cooperation that the contracting Parties may adopt for the utilization of their own and outside financial resources, with the aim of achieving the objectives of integration as set forth in the Treaty.

9. Adoption of measures to facilitate the development of national securities markets and communication between them.

E. Raw Materials

Twentieth   The contracting Parties shall undertake studies designed to establish a policy in the field of production and trade in raw materials, especially for those pertaining to industrial sectors that the Standing Executive Committee designates for advancement of their integration. These studies shall bear in mind the following objectives:

    i) Ensuring equitable conditions of competition in the regional market for manufactured products;

    ii) Ensuring the access of consumers to sources of supply under normal conditions of quantity, quality and prices; and

    iii) Encouraging a maximum utilization of raw materials originating in the region.

F. Fiscal Matters

Twenty-first   The Organs of the Association shall begin a study of the fiscal systems of the contracting Parties for the purpose of determining their effects on the development of the program of coordination of economic policies indicated in this present resolution. In addition, fiscal aspects are to be considered in the studies relating to the industrial and agricultural-livestock sectors.

G. Labor Matters

Twenty-second   The Standing Executive Committee shall continue the tasks assigned by Resolution 58 (II), the completion of which requires the collaboration of the International Labour Organisation (ILO), by collecting information regarding labor provisions, especially concerning the cost of social security and benefits.

Labor aspects will also be considered in the studies relating to the industrial and agricultural-livestock sectors.

H. Infrastructure

Twenty-third   Because in the process of integration it is necessary to solve many problems that stand in the way of the organization of a broad Latin American market, the contracting Parties shall endeavor to obtain the collaboration of pertinent international organizations, especially the Inter-American Economic and Social Council (IA-ECOSOC), the Inter-American Committee on the Alliance for Progress (CIAP), and the Inter-American Development Bank (IDB) in the undertaking of multinational projects designed to create structural conditions that will facilitate their integration. To this end, the Standing Executive Committee shall undertake:

1. To request from CIAP, through the Executive Secretariat, the list of multinational projects examined by that organization at its meetings, as well as lists to be prepared in the future, in order to establish a mutual collaboration for their analysis and fix appropriate priorities according to the importance of such initiatives to the program of integration covered by this Resolution.

2. To seek to establish a system of periodic consultations with CIAP by means of:

i) The eventual participation of LAFTA in meetings of CIAP directed toward the evaluation and the establishment of priorities of the projects mentioned; and

ii) Regular contacts between the authorities of the two organizations.

3. To seek the financial and technical collaboration of CIAP for the development of a program of coordination of the economic policies of the Association.

Twenty-fourth   In particular, the organs of the Association shall give special attention to the following topics:

1. Transportation and communications.

i) Completing the work concerning water transportation;

ii) Establishment under the Advisory Committee on Transportation, through specialized meetings, of programs of cooperation in the field of air transportation, railway transportation, and highway transportation;

iii) Promotion of technical and financial studies of programs for main line highways that are multinational in character and of fundamental importance to regional integration; and for the completion, including paving, of such highways now under construction; and

iv) Improvement and coordination of the postal and telecommunications services between the contracting Parties, giving this immediate priority for consideration by CIAP.

2. Preparation and adoption of a Latin American Foodstuffs Code.

3. Intensification of the cooperation with the Pan American Committee on Technical Standards for the adoption of common technical standards in Latin America.

4. Preparation of homogeneous regulations to govern intellectual property and industrial property (trademarks and patents).

5. Promotion of intercommunication of electrical services of the contracting Parties, by supporting the cooperation programs of the various technical agencies.

6. Facilities for the transportation of persons.

I. National Development Programs

Twenty-fifth   In order to continue laying down the bases for the coordination of national development programs, the contracting Parties shall undertake to:

1. Include among their technical representatives on the Advisory Committees of Industrial Development and of Agricultural-Livestock Matters experts in such matters from appropriate planning agencies or offices.

2. Bring together the chiefs or directors of such agencies or offices at annual meetings for the purpose of exchanging experiences, conferring on the national development policies, and gradually arriving at bases for the effective coordination thereof, taking into account the objectives of the program of regional integration set forth in this Resolution; and

3. Request the collaboration of the Latin American Institute of Economic and Social Planning in order to accomplish the objective proposed in the first paragraph of this article.

CREATION OF THE COUNCIL OF MINISTERS OF FOREIGN AFFAIRS OF THE LATIN AMERICAN FREE TRADE ASSOCIATION

Resolution 117 (V)

(Fifth Regular Session, Montevideo, December 30, 1965)

IN VIEW OF the resolutions contained in the final act of the Meeting of Ministers of Foreign Affairs of the contracting Parties of the Montevideo Treaty, held in compliance with Resolution 112 (IV);

CONSIDERING THAT the development of the process of integration will be enhanced if the Ministers or Secretaries of State who are in charge of the foreign policy of the countries of LAFTA meet periodically to take decisions relating to the higher political conduct of affairs of the Association; and

That for this reason it is desirable to establish immediately a Council of Ministers of Foreign Affairs of LAFTA as well as to prepare the instrument by which this shall become a permanent institution,

THE CONFERENCE OF THE CONTRACTING PARTIES, at its Fifth Regular Session,

RESOLVES:

First   To create the Council of Ministers of Foreign Affairs of the Latin American Free Trade Association, for which the appropriate instrument is to be signed to make it a permanent institution.

Second   To entrust the Standing Executive Committee with preparing as quickly as possible and submitting to the governments of the contracting Parties a draft of the instrument referred to in the first article, in order that it may be considered by the Ministers of Foreign Affairs at their first meeting.

Third Until such time as the establishment of the Council of Ministers as an organ of the Association has been completed, it shall meet at least once a year as a part of the Conference of the Contracting Parties of the Montevideo Treaty, which shall be called into a special session for this purpose, on the date and at the place which the Ministers of Foreign Affairs have selected at their previous meeting and also at the initiative of the Standing Executive Committee, whenever the Parties deem this necessary.

Fourth To ask the Standing Executive Committee to proceed as indicated in the preceding article to convoke the Council of Ministers to its first meeting at the headquarters of the Association, as soon as the draft referred to in the second article has been prepared.

Fifth The contracting Parties that have assigned jurisdiction over LAFTA affairs to a Minister or Secretary of State other than that of Foreign Affairs may be represented on the Council by that Minister.

PROTOCOL INSTITUTIONALIZING THE COUNCIL OF MINISTERS OF FOREIGN AFFAIRS OF THE LATIN AMERICAN FREE TRADE ASSOCIATION

(Signed at Montevideo, Uruguay, December 12, 1966)

The representatives of the governments of the contracting Parties of the Montevideo Treaty, meeting in Council of Ministers of the Latin American Free Trade Association, in accordance with the provisions of Article 60 of the Treaty, agree on the following:

Article 1 Articles 33, 34, 35, 36, 37, 38, and 39 of the Montevideo Treaty are hereby amended to read as follows:

Article 33

The organs of the Association are the Council of Ministers of Foreign Affairs of the Contracting Parties (called in this Treaty "the Council"), the Conference of the Contracting Parties (called in this Treaty "the Conference") and the Standing Executive Committee (called in this Treaty "the Committee").

Article 34

The Council is the supreme organ of the Association and shall make the decisions concerning the conduct of its higher policy. As such it shall have the following powers:

a) To enact general rules which will permit a better achievement of the objectives of the Treaty and, especially, those which will tend to accelerate harmoniously the process of development and economic and social integration of the contracting Parties;

b) To examine the results of the tasks accomplished by the Association and establish the fundamental features that may serve as the basis for work programs of the other organs of the Association;

c) To examine and resolve matters which it considers appropriate from among those referred to it by the Conference or the Committee;

d) To fix basic rules to govern the relations of the Association with third countries, regional associations, and international organizations or entities;

e) To delegate to the Conference or the Committee the authority to make decisions on specific matters designed to permit a better achievement of the objectives of the Treaty;

f) To amend the Treaty, under the terms of Article 60;

g) To change its own system of voting and that of the Conference, in accordance with the provisions of Article 38; and

h) To establish its own regulations.

The Council shall be composed of the Ministers of Foreign Affairs of the contracting Parties. However, if any of the latter have assigned jurisdiction over the affairs of the Association to a Minister or Secretary of State other than that of Foreign Affairs, it may be represented on the Council by the respective Minister or Secretary.

Article 35

The Conference shall have the following powers:

a) To promote the negotiations provided for in Article 4 and to assess the results thereof;

b) To undertake the tasks entrusted to it by the Council;

c) To consider and resolve, within its competency, matters submitted to it by the Committee;

d) To adopt, within its competency, measures necessary for carrying out the Treaty and pertinent protocols;

e) To approve the annual work programs of the Committee as well as the budget of expenditures of the Association and fix the contributions of each of the contracting Parties;

f) To approve its regulations and those of the Committee;

g) To appoint the Executive Secretary of the Committee; and

h) To deal with all other matters of common interest that do not pertain to the conduct of the higher policy of the Association.

The Conference shall be composed of duly accredited representatives of the contracting Parties. Each delegation shall have the right to one vote.

Article 36

Both the Council and the Conference shall meet in regular sessions once a year. At each session the date and place of the next regular annual session shall be fixed, without prejudice to the right of the Committee to name a new place and date whenever supervening reasons make this necessary.

Each of these organs may meet in special sessions whenever they are convoked by the Committee.

Article 37

Both the Council and the Conference may meet and take decisions only if at least two thirds of the contracting Parties are present.

Article 38

Until the Council may establish a different system of voting, its decisions and those of the Conference shall be adopted by an affirmative vote of at least two thirds ($\frac{2}{3}$) of the contracting Parties, provided there is no negative vote.

An abstention shall not mean a negative vote. Absence at the time of voting shall be interpreted as an abstention.

However, the Council, by an affirmative vote of two thirds ($\frac{2}{3}$) of its members may:

a) Elect the Chairman and two Vice Chairmen;
b) Fix the place and date of the next regular session;

The Conference, by an affirmative vote of two thirds ($\frac{2}{3}$) of the contracting Parties may also:

a) Approve the annual budget of expenditures of the Association;
b) Elect its Chairman and two Vice Chairmen, as well as the Executive Secretary; and
c) Fix the place and date of its next regular session.

Article 39

The Committee is the permanent executive organ of the Association responsible for supervising the implementation of the provisions of the present Treaty. Its duties and responsibilities shall be, *inter alia:*

a) To convoke the Council and the Conference, in each case indicating the corresponding provisional agenda;
b) To submit for the approval of the Conference an annual work program and the Association's annual budget estimates;
c) To represent the Association in dealings with third countries and international organs and entities, for the purpose of considering matters of common interest. Likewise, it shall represent the Association in contracts and other instruments of public and private law;

d) To undertake studies, suggest measures, and submit to the Council and to the Conference such recommendations as it deems appropriate for the effective implementation of the Treaty;

e) To submit to the regular sessions of the Council and of the Conference an annual report on its activities and concerning the results of the implementation of this Treaty;

f) To seek, when considered desirable, the technical advice and the cooperation of individual persons and of national and international organizations;

g) To take such decisions as may be delegated to it by the Council or the Conference; and

h) To carry out the tasks assigned to it by the Council or the Conference and those with which it is specifically charged by provisions of this Treaty and its protocols.

Article 2   This Protocol may not be signed with reservations, nor may reservations be made at the time of ratification. The instruments of ratification shall be deposited in the Secretariat of the Standing Executive Committee of the Latin American Free Trade Association, which shall communicate the date of deposit to the governments of the States that have signed this Protocol.

Article 3   This Protocol shall come into force thirty days after the deposit of the instruments of ratification of all the contracting Parties.

IN WITNESS WHEREOF the respective duly accredited Plenipotentiaries sign this Protocol.

DONE in the city of Montevideo, on December 12, 1966, in a Spanish and Portuguese original, both texts being equally valid.
[Here follow the signatures of the Plenipotentiaries.]

ORGANIZATION OF THE TECHNICAL COMMITTEE

Resolution 118 (V)

(Fifth Regular Session, Montevideo, December 30, 1965)

IN VIEW OF the resolutions contained in the final act of the Meeting of Ministers of Foreign Affairs of the contracting Parties of the Montevideo Treaty, held in compliance with Resolution 112 (IV), and

CONSIDERING that it is desirable to adapt the working machinery of the Association to the requirements of the program of economic integration and complementary economies of the contracting Parties,

THE CONFERENCE OF THE CONTRACTING PARTIES, at its Fifth Regular Session,

RESOLVES:

First To organize a technical committee composed of four outstanding nationals of the contracting Parties appointed by the Conference and the Executive Secretary, who shall act as the coordinating member. Its members shall act without responsibility to a government and exclusively in their technical capacity.

Second The Committee shall have as its mandate the undertaking of studies, the formulation of proposals, and the submission of projects to speed up the process of economic and social integration of the contracting Parties, following the directives resulting from the Montevideo Treaty, the resolutions already adopted by the Conference, and those that may be adopted in the future by the organs of the Association.

Third The proposals and projects coming out of the Committee shall be submitted to the consideration of the Standing Executive Committee. In case they are not approved by that committee or it cannot act on them for lack of jurisdiction, they shall be forwarded by the Committee, together with its observations, to the cognizance and decision of the Conference or the Council of Ministers.

Fourth The Secretariat shall provide all facilities that the Committee may require to complete its tasks, for which it will be provided with a budget that will permit it to meet the highest expenditures that the proper application of this Resolution may require.

Fifth The Council of Ministers at its 1967 meeting shall examine the system created by this Resolution in order to confirm or amend it, in the light of experience.

AGREEMENT BETWEEN THE CENTRAL BANKS OF THE MEMBER COUNTRIES OF LAFTA

(Approved by the Council on Financial and Monetary Policy of
LAFTA, September 1965)

WHEREAS currency stability and the multilateral machinery for payments in convertible and freely transferable currencies constitutes an effective medium for increasing trade and transactions;

Greater efforts must be made to counteract inflationary pressures and correct the lack of equilibrium in balances of payments;

The restrictions, prohibitions, and surcharges of a monetary and financial nature which hinder trade within the area should also be eliminated insofar as possible;

These efforts will permit the strengthening of relations between the private financial institutions of the region and will facilitate the granting of reciprocal lines of credit among them;

It is indispensable to initiate immediately a formal multilateral cooperation among the banks of the region so as to achieve financial and monetary integration in successive stages through the formation of financial agencies which will establish a more advanced cooperation, such as a clearing house and a guaranty fund;

Until appropriate measures are adopted and legal provisions are enacted by competent organs to permit the more elaborate forms of financial and monetary cooperation, it is indispensable that initial bases or conditions be established which will at the same time prepare the road for such advances and signify important progress in this field; and

As a result of what has been indicated above it is necessary to begin cooperation in the monetary and financial field by establishing a multilateral clearing system and machinery for reciprocal credits among the central banks of the member countries of LAFTA, which will stimulate financial relations, increase the expansion of reciprocal trade, and systematize mutual consultation on currency, exchange, and payments matters,

The Central Bank of Argentina
The Central Bank of Brazil
The Central Bank of Colombia
The Central Bank of Chile
The Central Bank of Ecuador
The Bank of Mexico
The Central Bank of Paraguay
The Central Reserve Bank of Peru, and
The Bank of Uruguay

AGREE:

To create among the central banks of LAFTA a machinery for multilateral clearing and reciprocal credits, in convertible currencies, on the following operational bases:

Article 1   Each pair of central banks shall undertake to establish regular lines of reciprocal credit in United States dollars, to the maximum limits indicated in the respective agreements. Preferably these credits shall not bear interest.

Article 2   The balances remaining in regular lines of credit, in the entire system, shall be liquidated every two months in the manner and times established in the Regulations.

Article 3   The balances shown in accounts at the close of each liquidation period shall be multilaterally offset by the procedure to be established in the Regulations.

Article 4   Without prejudice to the stipulations of Article 2, any excess over the limit for regular credit in the amount of the obligations assumed by a debtor central bank, shall be paid by the latter, immediately, by cable transfer.

Article 5   As a supplement to the regular lines of credit referred to in Article 1, the central banks may mutually negotiate additional extraordinary reciprocal credits, in United States dollars.

Article 6   The additional extraordinary credits shall be liquidated in the manner to be mutually stipulated by the central banks that negotiated them.

Article 7   The central banks undertake to guarantee the convertibility of exchange that is used to cancel payments that are channeled through the system, when demanded and if they are covered in local currency by the obligor.

Article 8   United States dollars shall be utilized for the payments resulting from the liquidations referred to in Articles 2, 4, 5, and 6.

Article 9   The channeling of payments through this system is voluntary. Therefore, this Agreement shall not interfere with the payments and transfer practices that exist in each country of the region.

Article 10   The signatory central banks shall encourage insofar as possible the increasing of financial relations among the commercial banks of the region. To this end, they may utilize the credits that are granted to stimulate the opening of lines of credit between commercial banks.
Transfers of the balances resulting from reciprocal credit agreements entered into by commercial banks may be cleared through the system.

Article 11   The signatory central banks shall designate one among them to serve as Agent for the system. The Agent Bank shall be charged with assembling the information that is supplied by the central banks and shall establish and make known the positions to be cleared.

Article 12   The operating machinery between commercial banks and their respective central bank shall be governed by the internal provisions of each country and must be made known to each signatory central bank through the Agent.

Article 13   Representatives of the central banks signatory to this Agreement shall meet periodically for the purpose of examining the progress that has been made, making appropriate readjustments, and establishing bases that will permit the creation of a Clearing House and a Guaranty Fund as soon as possible.

Article 14 This present Agreement shall come into force for each central bank as of the date on which it notifies the Agent Bank that all required legal and administrative steps have been completed.

IN VIRTUE OF WHICH, the representatives of the central banks hereby sign this present Agreement on the occasion of the Second Meeting of the Council on Financial and Monetary Policy, held in Mexico City on September 22, 1965.

For the Central Bank of Argentina	*Félix G. Elizalde*
For the Central Bank of Brazil	*Denio Ch. Nogueira*
For the Bank of Colombia	*Eduardo Arias Robledo*
For the Central Bank of Chile	*Carlos Massad*
For the Central Bank of Ecuador	*Guillermo Pérez Chiriboga*
For the Bank of Mexico	*Rodrigo Gómez*
For the Central Bank of Paraguay	*César Romeo Acosta*
For the Central Reserve Bank of Peru	*Alfredo C. Ferreyros*
For the Bank of Uruguay	*Jorge Puchet*

REGULATIONS FOR THE SYSTEM OF MULTILATERAL CLEARANCE OF BALANCES BETWEEN THE CENTRAL BANKS OF THE COUNTRIES OF LAFTA

These Regulations are for the purpose of establishing rules which will ensure the functioning of the system of multilateral clearance of balances established in the Agreement between the Central Banks of the member countries of LAFTA, hereinafter called the Agreement.

I. GENERAL PROVISIONS

Paragraph 1 The purpose of clearing is to reduce to a minimum the transfers of balances between the central banks participating in the Agreement, by periodically consolidating debits and credits and establishing a net balance for each central bank.

Paragraph 2 The balances referred to in the first portion of the preceding paragraph are those that result, at the close of the liquidation periods, from the regular lines of credit agreed to between pairs of central banks.

Paragraph 3 Central banks that sign reciprocal credit agreements shall transmit a copy of each such agreement to the Agent, which shall make them known to the remaining central banks.

Paragraph 4 Not later than 48 hours following the last business day of the months of February, April, June, August, October, and December of each year, each central bank shall notify the Agent by cable of the total debits corresponding to payments actually made and recorded. The central banks must forward this information regardless of whether or not any movement has been recorded during the respective period.

Paragraph 5 The Agent shall determine the balances between pairs of central banks, taking into account the total amount of the debits to which the preceding paragraph refers.

Paragraph 6 During the second month of each liquidation period, each central bank shall transmit to the Agent and to the other central banks a weekly report on the status of its debits.

Paragraph 7 For the purposes of the multilateral clearance established by Article 3 of the Agreement, the Agent shall determine the net balances of each central bank with respect to the aggregate of all the others, using as a base the balances resulting from application of Paragraph 5 of these Regulations.

Paragraph 8 The Agent, on the business day following the close of the period established by Paragraph 4 of these Regulations, shall notify each central bank of the net balances referred to in the preceding paragraph. Any central bank or banks showing a net debit balance must place, to the order of the Agent, in the common correspondent bank which is to be selected by mutual agreement, the total amount of this debit balance, by cable transfer.

Paragraph 9 As soon as the Agent has received notice from the common correspondent bank concerning the transfers of funds made by the debtor central bank or banks, it shall immediately order the transfer to the said correspondent of the amounts corresponding to the net favorable balances of the creditor central bank or banks.

Paragraph 10 All payments derived from the final clearances to which these Regulations refer shall be made in United States dollars.

Paragraph 11 The expenses incurred by the Agent in performing its functions shall be shared in equal parts by the central banks that participate in the clearance.

II. SPECIAL PROVISIONS

Paragraph 12 In the event that the Agent does not receive the information concerning one or more central banks during the first 24 hours of the time stipulated in Paragraph 4 of these Regulations, appropriate request shall be made. If thereafter no information is received during the following 24 hours, the central bank or banks from which the information is not available shall be excluded from the multilateral clearance for the period concerned. Central banks excluded from the clearance shall pay or collect their balances, as the case may be, from each of the other central banks and shall so notify the Agent.

Paragraph 13   In the event that one or more central banks do not transfer their net debit balances to the Agent within 24 hours after the date of the communication referred to in Paragraph 9, the Agent shall thereupon return to the central bank or banks that have made transfers the amounts that were received from them. At the same time the Agent shall notify the central banks of the cancellation of the clearance and of the calculation of the resulting net balances. It shall also make known which central bank or banks have not made the transfer of their net debit balances, in order that the bilateral balances between these latter central banks and the remaining ones may be paid or collected directly between them.

Paragraph 14   After carrying out the stipulations of the preceding Paragraph, the Agent shall proceed immediately with a new clearance, eliminating therefrom the central bank or banks that have not made the appropriate transfers. When the new net debit balances have been thus established, the procedure indicated in Paragraphs 9 and 10 of these Regulations shall be followed.

DRAFT PROTOCOL FOR THE SETTLEMENT OF DISPUTES

(Approved by the Council of Ministers at its Third Special Session, Resolution 172, Montevideo, Uruguay, December 12, 1966)

The representatives of the governments of the contracting Parties, meeting in Council of Ministers of Foreign Affairs of the Latin American Free Trade Association, animated by the desire to establish a system for the settlement of disputes relating to the Montevideo Treaty, have agreed on the following:

Chapter I

Article 1   The contracting Parties shall submit to the procedures applicable in accordance with the present Protocol, all disputes that may arise between them and which refer exclusively and directly to specific and concrete cases relating to the Montevideo Treaty, its Protocols, Resolutions, and Decisions rendered by organs of the Latin American Free Trade Association and any other instruments which constitute its legal structure.

Chapter II

Article 2   In a dispute included within Article 1, the Parties shall first seek its solution by direct negotiations.

Article 3   The Parties in dispute, jointly or separately, shall report to the Standing Executive Committee on the action taken during the negotiations and the final results thereof.

Article 4   The agreements reached in the direct negotiations shall be binding on the Parties in dispute.

Article 5   If no solution is reached in the negotiations or if the dispute is only partially resolved, any of the Parties may resort to the Standing Executive Committee, for the purposes indicated in the following articles of this chapter. Parties affected by the nonfulfillment of agreements reached in the direct negotiations may resort to the same procedure.

Article 6   The Committee shall decide, as a preliminary question, by a vote of the majority of its members, whether the dispute is one to which Article 1 of this Protocol refers. The Parties in dispute shall not participate in this voting.

Article 7   If the Committee decides the preliminary question affirmatively, it shall have the authority to assist the Parties, shall make an effort to achieve their agreement on conditions acceptable to them, and it may, within a reasonable period of time, take steps aimed at settlement by the Parties themselves.

Article 8   The Committee, in carrying out its functions pursuant to Articles 6 and 7 of this Protocol, shall not render a decision on the substance of the dispute.

Chapter III

Article 9   Whenever the procedures indicated in Chapter II of this Protocol have not settled a dispute, or if the agreements reached have not been fulfilled, any of the Parties in dispute may resort to the arbitration procedure established in this Protocol.

Article 10   None of the Parties in dispute may make use of, in the arbitration procedure provided for in this Protocol, the statements, admissions of facts, or offers of agreement submitted by another Party during the stages covered by Chapter II.

Article 11   By mutual agreement, the Parties in dispute may omit the submission to the Standing Executive Committee and resort, after the direct negotiations, to the arbitration procedure.

Article 12   Each contracting Party shall name one person to be included in a list of arbitrators in order to organize the Arbitration Tribunal to which Chapter IV refers. These persons must be of high moral standing and meet the requirements for holding high judicial office in their countries or they must be jurists of recognized competence.

Each Party shall also name one other person who meets the same requirements, to replace the principal in case of the temporary impediment, excuse, or disability of the latter to serve on the Tribunal, either at the time it is formed or during the course of proceedings.

Article 13   The persons included on the list of arbitrators and their alternates shall be appointed for a term of eight years and may be reappointed, counting from the date of notification of their appointment to the Executive Secretary of the Standing Executive Committee and they shall be retained on the list until notification of the appointment of their successors has been made in the same manner.

Article 14   In the event of disability, death, or resignation of a person on the list, or of his alternate, the contracting Party that made the designation shall have the right to name another person, who shall hold the appointment for eight years.

Article 15   The Executive Secretary of the Committee shall be notified of all appointments, and he shall prepare the list of arbitrators and their alternates in alphabetical order of countries, in Spanish, and shall then make this known to the contracting Parties, as well as any subsequent changes.

Chapter IV

Article 16   The contracting Parties acknowledge as compulsory and without need of special agreement the jurisdiction of the Tribunal to hear and settle disputes that may arise in relation to the list of subjects formulated by the Council of Ministers of Foreign Affairs of the Montevideo Treaty and which the Council shall review annually for the purpose of adding new subjects.

Whenever disputes arise that do not relate to the subjects included in the list referred to in the preceding paragraph and they come within those indicated in Article 1 of this Protocol, the Parties in dispute may conclude the corresponding arbitration agreement which shall include acknowledgement of the jurisdiction of the Tribunal.

If as a consequence of the process of integration provided for in the Montevideo Treaty and supplementary provisions, the contracting Parties shall sign new agreements, they must specify therein the subjects to which the compulsory arbitration procedures of the present Protocol shall apply.

Article 17   Without prejudice to the provisions of Article 16, the contracting Parties of the Montevideo Treaty may declare at any time that they acknowledge as compulsory *ipso facto* and without need of special agreement, in respect of any contracting Party that accepts the same obligation, the jurisdiction of the Tribunal to hear and settle all disputes to which Article 1 of this Protocol refers and that they agree to comply with its decisions.

These declarations are to be deposited in the Secretariat of the Standing Executive Committee, which shall make known to the contracting Parties the terms of each declaration.

Article 18   In each case that is submitted to its cognizance, the Tribunal may be composed as follows:

a) The Parties in dispute, by mutual agreement, within a period of thirty days, shall name three arbitrators selected from the list referred to in Article 12 of this Protocol;

b) If the Parties have not reached agreement within the period indicated in the foregoing section for the appointment of one or more arbitrators, the arbitrators that are lacking to make up the Tribunal shall be selected from the list in the order established therein and following the system of rotation;

c) If the Parties in dispute do not wish to make use of the procedure indicated in section (a), the Tribunal shall be composed of three arbitrators selected from the list, in the order established therein and following a system of rotation;

d) In composing the Tribunal there shall be excluded, in the cases indicated in sections (b) and (c), the arbitrators designated by the Parties in dispute for making up the list to which Article 12 refers and, in all cases, their nationals.

Article 19   A direct or personal interest in the matter in dispute shall be grounds for disqualification from serving on the Tribunal in a specific case. The Parties must assert this ground to the Standing Executive Committee. If the challenge is accepted a replacement shall be made by the alternate, in accordance with Article 12.

Article 20   The composition of the Tribunal may not be changed after it has begun to act, except under the circumstances indicated in Article 12.

Article 21   The Tribunal shall meet at the headquarters of the Association, at least during the period for submitting evidence, the oral stage, and for the decision.

Article 22   The Parties may be represented before the Tribunal by agents and they may appoint counsel or lawyers to defend their rights and interests.

Article 23   The arbitration procedure includes a written stage, a period for presentation of evidence, and an oral stage. The Tribunal may also, on its own initiative, request from the Parties any means of proof and clarifications that it considers necessary.

Article 24   The Tribunal shall rule on all pleas and counterclaims that relate directly to the dispute.

Article 25   If one Party fails to appear or does not make use of its right, this does not presume the admission of facts alleged by the other Party nor agreement with its claims. At any stage of the proceedings the other Party may request the Tribunal to settle the points in dispute, in their order, and finally render its decision.

Article 26   Any question of procedure not covered by this Protocol or its regulations shall be settled by the Tribunal.

Article 27   The Tribunal shall settle the dispute in accordance with the Montevideo Treaty, its Protocols, Resolutions, and Decisions rendered by the organs of the Association and other instruments constituting its legal structure and, subsidiarily, according to the provisions of Article 38, section 1, of the Statute of the International Court of Justice.

Chapter V

Article 28   The Tribunal shall decide all questions by a majority vote of its members.

Article 29   The arbitration decision must be given in writing and be signed by all members of the Tribunal. The decision shall rule on all claims submitted by the Parties to the Tribunal and shall state the reasoning. The arbitrators may explain their individual votes, whether or not in agreement with the majority.

Article 30   The decision is compulsory for the Parties in dispute from the moment notification thereof has been made and it shall have the effect of *res judicata*. It must be complied with immediately, unless the Tribunal has fixed a period of time for compliance. It shall not be subject to appeal or other recourse, except as provided in Articles 30, 31, and 32 of this Protocol.

Article 31   Within thirty days after the date of notification of the decision, the Tribunal may, on petition of any Party, correct material errors in the decision.

Article 32   In the event of disagreement over the meaning, scope, or the manner of complying with the decision, the Tribunal shall interpret it upon request of any Party in dispute. This request must be presented within sixty days after notification of the decision. If the Tribunal considers that circumstances so demand, it may suspend the compliance with the decision until it rules on the clarification.

Article 33   Any of the Parties in dispute may ask for a review of the decision, based on any preexisting fact that could have decisively influenced the decision and provided that at the time it was rendered such fact was unknown to the Tribunal and to the Party requesting the review if such lack of knowledge is not due to its own negligence.

The petition for review must be presented within ninety days from the date on which the fact was discovered and, in all cases, within two years following the date the decision was rendered.

Whenever it is possible, the petition for review should be presented to the Tribunal that rendered the decision. If not possible, a new Tribunal shall be formed, in accordance with Chapter IV of this Protocol.

If the Tribunal considers that circumstances so demand, it may suspend the execution of the decision until it rules on the review.

Chapter VI

Article 34   If one of the contracting Parties fails to fulfill the obligations imposed by an arbitration decision, the other interested Party or Parties may appeal to the Conference to agree on suitable steps to be taken so that the decision will be executed.

Without prejudice to the foregoing, the contracting Party or Parties affected by the noncompliance may, with the authorization of the Conference, limit or suspend concessions from its national list or not extend concessions to the Party in default.

Resolutions of the Conference, to which this article refers, shall be adopted without the votes of Parties to the dispute.

Chapter VII

Article 35   The Parties in dispute shall share equally the expenses incurred by the functioning of the Tribunal.

Article 36   The present Protocol shall be ratified by the contracting Parties in accordance with their constitutional procedures. It shall come into force for those that have ratified it as soon as at least five contracting Parties have deposited their respective instruments of ratification with the Secretariat of the Standing Executive Committee, which shall give notice of each deposit to the contracting Parties. This notification shall be considered as an exchange of instruments of ratification.

Article 37   The present Protocol shall be in effect indefinitely and may only be denounced together with the Montevideo Treaty.

Article 38   The Standing Executive Committee shall regulate this Protocol.

Article 39   Adherence to the Montevideo Treaty by a Latin American State implies *ipso jure* adherence to this Protocol.

Article 40   The official languages in all proceedings provided for in this Protocol shall be Spanish and Portuguese.

ESTABLISHMENT OF A PROVISIONAL MACHINERY FOR SETTLEMENT OF DISPUTES BETWEEN THE CONTRACTING PARTIES OF THE MONTEVIDEO TREATY

Resolution 165 (CM-I/III-E)

(Approved December 8, 1966)

IN VIEW OF Resolution 4 of the meeting of Ministers of Foreign Affairs of the contracting Parties of the Montevideo Treaty, the third article of Resolution 121(V) of the Conference and Resolution 85 of the Standing Executive Committee,

WHEREAS the Committee is the permanent organ of the Association entrusted with overseeing the application of the provisions of the Treaty;

In carrying out its functions the Committee may request the technical advice and collaboration of persons;

The Conference has the authority to "take the necessary steps to carry out the present Treaty and to study the results of its implementation" and to "deal with other business of common interest" (Article 34, sections (a) and (g));

The Conference therefore has the power to intervene in disputes that may arise between the contracting Parties whenever the common interest so demands; and

In accordance with Article 22 of the Charter of the Organization of American States "In the event that a dispute arises between two or more American States which, in the opinion of one of them, cannot be settled through the usual diplomatic channels, the Parties shall agree on some other peaceful procedure that will enable them to reach a solution",

THE COUNCIL OF MINISTERS, meeting at the Third Special Session of the Conference of the Contracting Parties of the Montevideo Treaty,

RESOLVES:

One   The contracting Parties shall submit to the settlement procedures applicable pursuant to this Resolution, disputes which may arise between them in specific and concrete cases which refer exclusively and directly to the Montevideo Treaty, its Protocols, Resolutions, and Decisions rendered by organs of the Latin American Free Trade Association and any other instruments which constitute its legal structure.

Two   The Parties to a dispute included within Article One shall first seek a solution thereto by direct negotiations.

Three   The Parties in dispute, jointly or separately, shall report to the Standing Executive Committee on the action taken during the negotiations and the final results thereof.

Four   If no solution is reached in the negotiations or if the dispute was only partially resolved, any of the Parties may resort to the Committee for the purposes indicated in the following articles.

Parties affected by the nonfulfillment of agreements reached in the direct negotiations may resort to the same procedure.

Five   The Committee shall assist the Parties in dispute, shall make an effort to achieve their agreement on conditions acceptable to them, and shall take action, within a reasonable period fixed for this purpose, to find a solution for them. The Committee shall not render a decision on the substance of the dispute.

Six   Whenever it is deemed appropriate, the Committee may appoint a Special Commission of Jurists composed of three members, which shall rule exclusively on the precise points that the Committee submits to its cognizance and opinion. The composition of this Commission and determination of the matter in dispute shall be agreed upon by the affirmative vote of two thirds of the representatives, provided there is no negative vote. If one of the Parties in dispute casts a negative vote, it shall be understood that it will seek a solution by the means established in treaties in force between the disputing Parties.

Seven   For the purposes of the preceding article, each of the contracting Parties shall designate one person to comprise a list of jurists, from which the members of the Commission shall be elected. These persons must meet the highest qualifications of independence, impartiality, and legal knowledge.

The Committee shall issue regulations which shall indicate other rules for placing names on the list of jurists and all that is necessary for the Commission mentioned in Article Six to become organized and perform its duties.

Eight   The Commission shall receive the arguments and evidence submitted by the Parties in dispute, for which it shall have previously indicated the procedure and appropriate time limits, and it may avail itself of all the means deemed necessary for the best clarification of the dispute.

Nine   When the procedure has been completed, the Commission shall render an opinion, in conformity with law, by the vote of the majority of its members. The opinion must contain a statement of the background and considerations that served as the basis of its conclusions.

Ten The opinion shall be submitted to the Standing Executive Committee, so that it may be made known to the contracting Parties.

Eleven The expenses incurred by the functioning of the Commission shall be borne by the Parties in dispute, in the form and manner determined in the regulations issued by the Committee to comply with this Resolution.

PROTOCOL ON THE TRANSIT OF PERSONS

(Signed at Montevideo, Uruguay, December 12, 1966)

The representatives of the governments of the contracting Parties of the Montevideo Treaty, meeting in Council of Ministers of the Latin American Free Trade Association, agree on the following:

Article 1 Nationals by origin, by naturalization, or by law of the countries of LAFTA, bearing a valid passport or identity card, may enter, travel in transit through, or depart from the territory of any of the contracting Parties without the need of a visa or special permit.

Article 2 The persons mentioned in the preceding article are not exempted from the duty of obeying the laws and regulations of the country in respect of engaging in lucrative independent or paid activities.

Article 3 The stay in the country may be up to ninety days, which may be extended in accordance with regulations in force in the territory concerned. During such stay persons in transit shall not be subject to taxes or charges higher than those applicable to a national of the country concerned.

Article 4 Each of the Parties undertakes to admit again, at any time and without formalities, persons who had entered the territory of another contracting Party on the basis of the provisions of this Protocol.

Article 5 All the advantages provided for in this agreement shall be understood to be without prejudice to the domestic provisions of each contracting Party on matters of public order, police, or health.

Article 6 The present agreement shall come into force thirty days after at least three signatory Parties notify the depositary of their conformity. For the other contracting Parties the agreement shall come into force thirty days after the deposit of their notification or adherence.

Any of the Parties may temporarily suspend the force of this agreement, without the need of consent by the others, for reasons of security or public order. The suspension shall be communicated to the other States.

The instrument of notification or adherence shall be deposited in the Secretariat of the Standing Executive Committee of the Latin American Free Trade Association, which shall notify the contracting Parties of such deposit. This notification shall be regarded as an exchange of instruments of ratification.

Article 7 This agreement shall continue in force indefinitely, and it may be denounced by any of the contracting Parties, in which case it shall cease to be in effect for the denouncing Party ninety days after the formal act of denunciation.

IN WITNESS WHEREOF, the respective Plenipotentiaries, duly accredited, sign the present Protocol.

DONE in the city of Montevideo, on December 12, 1966, in a Spanish and Portuguese original, both texts being equally valid.

[Here follow the signatures of the Ministers.]

The Minister of Foreign Affairs of Peru makes the following reservation: he signs this Protocol on the Transit of Persons subject in its entirety to the internal legislation and policy of Peru.

ADVISORY COMMISSION ON MANAGEMENT AFFAIRS

Resolution 75 of the Standing Executive Committee

(December 30, 1965)

IN VIEW OF: Article 43 of the Treaty, Resolution 3 of the Meeting of Ministers of Foreign Affairs of the Contracting Parties of the Montevideo Treaty, and Resolution 121 (V) of the Conference,

The Standing Executive Committee

RESOLVES:

First To create an Advisory Commission on Management Affairs which shall be charged with analyzing the aspects and features of the process of integration and with making such recommendations to the organs of the Association as it may deem appropriate.

Second The Advisory Commission shall be composed of representatives of the management sectors of each country, who may be assisted by advisers. The representatives and advisers shall be accredited by their respective governments. For voting purposes, the delegation of each country shall have a single vote.

Third The Commission shall meet at least once a year at the call of the Committee, which shall establish the corresponding agenda.

ADVISORY COMMISSION ON LABOR AFFAIRS

Resolution 74 of the Standing Executive Committee

(December 30, 1965)

IN VIEW OF: Article 43 of the Treaty, Resolution 3 of the Meeting of Ministers of Foreign affairs of the Contracting Parties of the Montevideo Treaty, and Resolution 121 (V) of the Conference,

The Standing Executive Committee

RESOLVES:

First   To create an Advisory Commission on Labor Affairs which shall be charged with analyzing the aspects and features of the process of integration and with making such recommendations to the organs of the Association as it may deem appropriate.

Second   The Advisory Commission shall be composed of representatives of the labor sectors of each country, who may be assisted by advisers. The representatives and advisers shall be accredited by their respective governments. For voting purposes, the delegation of each country shall have a single vote.

Third   The Commission shall meet at least once a year at the call of the Committee, which shall establish the corresponding agenda.

INTER-AMERICAN INSTRUMENTS

INTER-AMERICAN INSTRUMENTS

AGREEMENT ESTABLISHING
THE INTER-AMERICAN DEVELOPMENT BANK
(1959)

(Selected Articles)

The countries on whose behalf this Agreement is signed agree to create the Inter-American Development Bank, which shall operate in accordance with the following provisions:

Article I

PURPOSE AND FUNCTIONS

Section 1 *Purpose*

The purpose of the Bank shall be to contribute to the acceleration of the process of economic development of the member countries, individually and collectively.

Section 2 *Functions*

a) To implement its purpose, the Bank shall have the following functions:

 i) to promote the investment of public and private capital for development purposes;

 ii) to utilize its own capital, funds raised by it in financial markets, and other available resources, for financing the development of the member countries, giving priority to those loans and guarantees that will contribute most effectively to their economic growth;

 iii) to encourage private investment in projects, enterprises, and activities contributing to economic development and to supplement private investment when private capital is not available on reasonable terms and conditions;

 iv) to cooperate with the member countries to orient their development policies toward a better utilization of their re-

341

sources, in a manner consistent with the objectives of making their economies more complementary and of fostering the orderly growth of their foreign trade; and

v) to provide technical assistance for the preparation, financing, and implementation of development plans and projects, including the study of priorities and the formulation of specific project proposals.

b) In carrying out its functions, the Bank shall cooperate as far as possible with national and international institutions and with private sources supplying investment capital.

Article III

OPERATIONS

Section 1 *Use of Resources*

The resources and facilities of the Bank shall be used exclusively to implement the purpose and functions enumerated in Article I of this Agreement.

Section 2 *Ordinary and Special Operations*

a) The operations of the Bank shall be divided into ordinary operations and special operations.
b) The ordinary operations shall be those financed from the Bank's ordinary capital resources, as defined in Article II, Section 5, and shall relate exclusively to loans made, participated in, or guaranteed by the Bank which are repayable only in the respective currency or currencies in which the loans were made. Such operations shall be subject to the terms and conditions that the Bank deems advisable, consistent with the provisions of this Agreement.
c) The special operations shall be those financed from the resources of the Fund in accordance with the provisions of Article IV.

Section 4 *Methods of Making or Guaranteeing Loans*

Subject to the conditions stipulated in this article, the Bank may make or guarantee loans to any member, or any agency or political subdivison thereof, and to any enterprise in the territory of a member, in any of the following ways:

i) by making or participating in direct loans with funds corresponding to the unimpaired paid-in capital and, except as provided in Section 13 of this article, to its reserves and undistributed surplus; or with the unimpaired resources of the Fund;

ii) by making or participating in direct loans with funds raised by the Bank in capital markets, or borrowed or acquired in any other manner for inclusion in the ordinary capital resources of the Bank or the resources of the Fund, and

iii) by guaranteeing in whole or in part loans made, except in special cases, by private investors.

Section 6   *Direct Loan Financing*

In making direct loans or participating in them, the Bank may provide financing in any of the following ways:

a) By furnishing the borrower currencies of members, other than the currency of the member in whose territory the project is to be carried out, that are necessary to meet the foreign exchange costs of the project.

b) By providing financing to meet expenses related to the purposes of the loan in the territories of the member in which the project is to be carried out. Only in special cases, particularly when the project indirectly gives rise to an increase in the demand for foreign exchange in that country, shall the financing granted by the Bank to meet local expenses be provided in gold or in currencies other than that of such member; in such cases, the amount of the financing granted by the Bank for this purpose shall not exceed a reasonable portion of the local expenses incurred by the borrower.

Section 7   *Rules and Conditions for Making or Guaranteeing Loans*

a) The Bank may make or guarantee loans subject to the following rules and conditions:

i) the applicant for the loan shall have submitted a detailed proposal and the staff of the Bank shall have presented a written report recommending the proposal after a study of its merits. In special circumstances, the Board of Executive Directors, by a majority of the total voting power of the member countries, may require that a proposal be submitted to the Board for decision in the absence of such a report;

ii) in considering a request for a loan or a guarantee, the Bank shall take into account the ability of the borrower to obtain the loan from private sources of financing on terms which, in the opinion of the Bank, are reasonable for the borrower, taking into account all pertinent factors;

iii) in making or guaranteeing a loan, the Bank shall pay due regard to prospects that the borrower and its guarantor, if any, will be in a position to meet their obligations under the loan contract;

    iv) in the opinion of the Bank, the rate of interest, other charges and the schedule for repayment of principal are appropriate for the project in question;

    v) in guaranteeing a loan made by other investors, the Bank shall receive suitable compensation for its risk, and

    vi) loans made or guaranteed by the Bank shall be principally for financing specific projects, including those forming part of a national or regional development program. However, the Bank may make or guarantee over-all loans to development institutions or similar agencies of the members in order that the latter may facilitate the financing of specific development projects whose individual financing requirements are not, in in the opinion of the Bank, large enough to warrant the direct supervision of the Bank.

b) The Bank shall not finance any undertaking in the territory of a member if that member objects to such financing.

Section 9   *Use of Loans Made or Guaranteed by the Bank*

a) Except as provided in Article V, Section 1, the Bank shall impose no condition that the proceeds of a loan shall be spent in the territory of any particular country nor that such proceeds shall not be spent in the territories of any particular member or members.

b) The Bank shall take the necessary measures to ensure that the proceeds of any loan made, guaranteed, or participated in by the Bank are used only for the purposes for which the loan was granted, with due attention to considerations of economy and efficiency.

Section 10   *Payment Provisions for Direct Loans*

Direct loan contracts made by the Bank in conformity with Section 4 i) or ii) of this article shall establish:

a) All the terms and conditions of each loan, including among others, provision for payment of principal, interest and other charges, maturities, and dates of payment; and

b) The currency or currencies in which payments shall be made to the Bank.

Section 11   *Guarantees*

a) In guaranteeing a loan the Bank shall charge a guarantee fee, at a rate determined by the Bank, payable periodically on the amount of the loan outstanding.

b) Guarantee contracts concluded by the Bank shall provide that the Bank may terminate its liability with respect to interest if, upon default by the borrower and by the guarantor, if any, the Bank offers to purchase, at par and interest accrued to a date designated in the offer, the bonds or other obligations guaranteed.

c) In issuing guarantees, the Bank shall have power to determine any other terms and conditions.

Article IV

FUND FOR SPECIAL OPERATIONS

Section 1 *Establishment, Purpose, and Functions*

A Fund for Special Operations is established for the making of loans on terms and conditions appropriate for dealing with special circumstances arising in specific countries or with respect to specific projects.

The Fund, whose administration shall be entrusted to the Bank, shall have the purpose and functions set forth in Article I of this Agreement.

Section 2 *Applicable Provisions*

The Fund shall be governed by the provisions of the present article and all other provisions of this Agreement, excepting those inconsistent with the provisions of the present article and those expressly applying only to the ordinary operations of the Bank.

Section 4 *Operations*

a) The operations of the Fund shall be those financed from its own resources, as defined in Section 3 h) of the present article.

b) Loans made with resources of the Fund may be partially or wholly repayable in the currency of the member in whose territory the project being financed will be carried out. The part of the loan not repayable in the currency of the member shall be paid in the currency or currencies in which the loan was made.

Section 5 *Limitation on Liability*

In the operations of the Fund, the financial liability of the Bank shall be limited to the resources and reserves of the Fund, and the liability of members shall be limited to the unpaid portion of their respective quotas that has become due and payable.

Section 9 *Voting*

a) In making decisions concerning operations of the Fund, each member country of the Bank shall have the voting power in the Board of Governors accorded to it pursuant to Article VIII,

Section 4 a) and b), and each Director shall have the voting power in the Board of Executive Directors accorded to him pursuant to Article VIII, Section 4 a) and c).

b) All decisions of the Bank concerning the operations of the Fund shall be adopted by a two-thirds majority of the total voting power of the member countries, unless otherwise provided in this article.

Article V

CURRENCIES

Section 1   *Use of Currencies*

a) The currency of any member held by the Bank, either in its ordinary capital resources or in the resources of the Fund, however acquired, may be used by the Bank and by any recipient from the Bank, without restriction by the member, to make payments for goods and services produced in the territory of such member.

b) Members may not maintain or impose restrictions of any kind upon the use by the Bank or by any recipient from the Bank, for payments in any country, of the following:

   i) gold and dollars received by the Bank in payment of the 50 per cent portion of each member's subscription to shares of the Bank's capital and of the 50 per cent portion of each member's quota for contribution to the Fund, pursuant to the provisions of Article II and Article IV, respectively;

   ii) currencies of members purchased with the gold and dollar funds referred to in i) of this paragraph;

   iii) currencies obtained by borrowings, pursuant to the provisions of Article VII, Section 1 i), for inclusion in the ordinary capital resources of the Bank;

   iv) gold and dollars received by the Bank in payment on account of principal, interest, and other charges, of loans made from the gold and dollar funds referred to in i) of this paragraph; currencies received in payment of principal, interest, and other charges, of loans made from currencies referred to in ii) and iii) of this paragraph; and currencies received in payment of commissions and fees on all guarantees made by the Bank; and

   v) currencies, other than the member's own currency, received from the Bank pursuant to Article VII, Section 4 c) and Article IV, Section 10, in distribution of net profits.

c) A member's currency held by the Bank, either in its ordinary capital resources or in the resources of the Fund, not covered by paragraph b) of this section, also may be used by the Bank or any recipient from the Bank for payments in any country without restriction of any kind, unless the member notifies the Bank of its desire that such currency or a portion thereof be restricted to the uses specified in paragraph a) of this section.

d) Members may not place any restrictions on the holding and use by the Bank, for making amortization payments or anticipating payment of, or repurchasing part or all of, the Bank's own obligations, of currencies received by the Bank in repayment of direct loans made from borrowed funds included in the ordinary capital resources of the Bank.

e) Gold or currency held by the Bank in its ordinary capital resources or in the resources of the Fund shall not be used by the Bank to purchase other currencies unless authorized by a two-thirds majority of the total voting power of the member countries.

Section 2 *Valuation of Currencies*

Whenever it shall become necessary under this Agreement to value any currency in terms of another currency, or in terms of gold, such valuation shall be determined by the Bank after consultation with the International Monetary Fund.

Section 3 *Maintenance of Value of the Currency Holdings of the Bank*

a) Whenever the par value in the International Monetary Fund of a member's currency is reduced or the foreign exchange value of a member's currency has, in the opinion of the Bank, depreciated to a significant extent, the member shall pay to the Bank within a reasonable time an additional amount of its own currency sufficient to maintain the value of all the currency of the member held by the Bank in its ordinary capital resources, or in the resources of the Fund, excepting currency derived from borrowings by the Bank. The standard of value for this purpose shall be the United States dollar of the weight and fineness in effect on January 1, 1959.

b) Whenever the par value in the International Monetary Fund of a member's currency is increased or the foreign exchange of such member's currency has, in the opinion of the Bank, appreciated to a significant extent, the Bank shall return to such member within a reasonable time an amount of that member's currency equal to the increase in the value of the amount of such currency which is held by the Bank in its ordinary capital resources or in the resources of the Fund, excepting currency derived from borrowings by the Bank. The standard of value for this purpose shall be the same as that established in the preceding paragraph.

c) The provisions of this section may be waived by the Bank when a uniform proportionate change in the par value of the currencies of all the Bank's members is made by the International Monetary Fund.

Section 4 *Methods of Conserving Currencies*

The Bank shall accept from any member promissory notes or similar securities issued by the government of the member, or by the depository designated by each member, in lieu of any part of the currency of the member representing the 50 per cent portion of its subscription to the Bank's authorized capital and the 50 per cent portion of its subscription to the resources of the Fund, which, pursuant to the provisions of Article II and Article IV, respectively, are payable by each member in its national currency, provided such currency is not required by the Bank for the conduct of its operations. Such promissory notes or securities shall be non-negotiable, non-interest-bearing, and payable to the Bank at their par value on demand.

Article VI

TECHNICAL ASSISTANCE

Section 1 *Provision of Technical Advice and Assistance*

The Bank may, at the request of any member or members, or of private firms that may obtain loans from it, provide technical advice and assistance in its field of activity, particularly on:

i) the preparation, financing, and execution of development plans and projects, including the consideration of priorities, and the formulation of loan proposals on specific national or regional development projects; and

ii) the development and advanced training, through seminars and other forms of instruction, of personnel specializing in the formulation and implementation of development plans and projects.

Article VII

MISCELLANEOUS POWERS AND DISTRIBUTION OF PROFITS

Section 1 *Miscellaneous Powers of the Bank*

In addition to the powers specified elsewhere in this Agreement, the Bank shall have the power to:

i) borrow funds and in that connection to furnish such collateral or other security therefor as the Bank shall determine, provided that, before making a sale of its obligations in the markets of a country, the Bank shall have obtained the approval of that country and of the member in whose currency the obligations are denominated. In addition, in the case of borrowings of funds to be included in the Bank's ordinary capital resources, the Bank shall obtain agreement of such countries that the proceeds may be exchanged for the currency of any other country without restriction;

ii) buy and sell securities it has issued or guaranteed or in which it has invested, provided that the Bank shall obtain the approval of the country in whose territories the securities are to be bought or sold;

iii) with the approval of a two-thirds majority of the total voting power of the member countries, invest funds not needed in its operations in such obligations as it may determine;

iv) guarantee securities in its portfolio for the purpose of facilitating their sale; and

v) exercise such other powers as shall be necessary or desirable in furtherance of its purpose and functions, consistent with the provisions of this Agreement.

Article VIII

ORGANIZATION AND MANAGEMENT

Section 1 *Structure of the Bank*

The Bank shall have a Board of Governors, a Board of Executive Directors, a President, an Executive Vice President, a Vice President in charge of the Fund, and such other officers and staff as may be considered necessary.

Section 2 *Board of Governors*

a) All the powers of the Bank shall be vested in the Board of Governors. Each member shall appoint one governor and one alternate, who shall serve for five years, subject to termination of appointment at any time, or to reappointment, at the pleasure of the appointing member. No alternate may vote except in the absence of his principal. The Board shall select one of the governors as Chairman, who shall hold office until the next regular meeting of the Board.

b) The Board of Governors may delegate to the Board of Executive Directors all its powers except power to:

   i) admit new members and determine the conditions of their admission;

  ii) increase or decrease the authorized capital stock of the Bank and contributions to the Fund;

 iii) elect the President of the Bank and determine his remuneration;

  iv) suspend a member, pursuant to Article IX, Section 2;

   v) determine the remuneration of the executive directors and their alternates;

  vi) hear and decide any appeals from interpretations of this Agreement given by the Board of Executive Directors;

 vii) authorize the conclusion of general agreements for cooperation with other international organizations;

viii) approve, after reviewing the auditors' report, the general balance sheet and the statement of profit and loss of the institution;

  ix) determine the reserves and the distribution of the net profits of the Bank and of the Fund;

   x) select outside auditors to certify to the general balance sheet and the statement of profit and loss of the institution;

  xi) amend this Agreement; and

 xii) decide to terminate the operations of the Bank and to distribute its assets.

c) The Board of Governors shall retain full power to exercise authority over any matter delegated to the Board of Executive Directors under paragraph b) above.

d) The Board of Governors shall, as a general rule, hold a meeting annually. Other meetings may be held when the Board of Governors so provides or when called by the Board of Executive Directors. Meetings of the Board of Governors also shall be called by the Board of Executive Directors whenever requested by five members of the Bank or by members having one fourth of the total voting power of the member countries.

e) A quorum for any meeting of the Board of Governors shall be an absolute majority of the total number of governors, representing not less than two thirds of the total voting power of the member countries.

f) The Board of Governors may establish a procedure whereby the Board of Executive Directors, when it deems such action appropriate, may submit a specific question to a vote of the governors without calling a meeting of the Board of Governors.

g) The Board of Governors, and the Board of Executive Directors to the extent authorized, may adopt such rules and regulations as may be necessary or appropriate to conduct the business of the Bank.

h) Governors and alternates shall serve as such without compensation from the Bank, but the Bank may pay them reasonable expenses incurred in attending meetings of the Board of Governors.

Section 3   *Board of Executive Directors*

a) The Board of Executive Directors shall be responsible for the conduct of the operations of the Bank, and for this purpose may exercise all the powers delegated to it by the Board of Governors.

b) There shall be seven executive directors, who shall not be governors, and of whom:

   i) one shall be appointed by the member having the largest number of shares in the Bank;

   ii) six shall be elected by the governors of the remaining members pursuant to the provisions of Annex C of this Agreement.

Executive directors shall be appointed or elected for terms of three years and may be reappointed or reelected for successive terms. They shall be persons of recognized competence and wide experience in economic and financial matters.

c) Each executive director shall appoint an alternate who shall have full power to act for him when he is not present. Directors and alternates shall be citizens of the member countries. None of the elected directors and their alternates may be of the same citizenship. Alternates may participate in meetings but may vote only when they are acting in place of their principals.

d) Directors shall continue in office until their successors are appointed or elected. If the office of an elected director becomes vacant more than 180 days before the end of his term, a successor shall be elected for the remainder of the term by the governors who elected the former director. An absolute majority of the votes cast shall be required for election. While the office remains vacant, the alternate shall have all the powers of the former director except the power to appoint an alternate.

e) The Board of Executive Directors shall function in continuous session at the principal office of the Bank and shall meet as often as the business of the Bank may require.

f) A quorum for any meeting of the Board of Executive Directors shall be an absolute majority of the total number of directors representing not less than two thirds of the total voting power of the member countries.

g) A member of the Bank may send a representative to attend any meeting of the Board of Executive Directors when a matter especially affecting that member is under consideration. Such right of representation shall be regulated by the Board of Governors.

h) The Board of Executive Directors may appoint such committees as it deems advisable. Membership of such committees need not be limited to governors, directors, or alternates.

i) The Board of Executive Directors shall determine the basic organization of the Bank, including the number and general responsibilities of the chief administrative and professional positions of the staff, and shall approve the budget of the Bank.

j) Upon the admission to the Bank of new members, having votes totaling not less than 22,000, the Board of Governors may, by a two-thirds majority of the total number of governors representing not less than three-fourths of the total voting power of the member countries, increase by one the number of Executive Directors to be elected.[1]

Section 4 *Voting*

a) Each member country shall have 135 votes plus one vote for each share of capital stock of the Bank held by that country.

b) In voting in the Board of Governors, each governor shall be entitled to cast the votes of the member country which he represents. Except as otherwise specifically provided in this Agreement, all matters before the Board of Governors shall be decided by a majority of the total voting power of the member countries.

c) In voting in the Board of Executive Directors:

  i) the appointed director shall be entitled to cast the number of votes of the member country which appointed him;

---

[1] This subsection was added by action of the Board of Governors on January 28, 1964.

ii) each elected director shall be entitled to cast the number of votes that counted toward his election, which votes shall be cast as a unit; and

iii) except as otherwise specifically provided in this Agreement, all matters before the Board of Executive Directors shall be decided by a majority of the total voting power of the member countries.

Section 5 *President, Executive Vice President, and Staff*

a) The Board of Governors, by an absolute majority of the total number of governors representing not less than a majority of the total voting power of the member countries, shall elect a President of the Bank who, while holding office, shall not be a governor or an executive director or alternate for either.

Under the direction of the Board of Executive Directors, the President of the Bank shall conduct the ordinary business of the Bank and shall be chief of its staff. He also shall be the presiding officer at meetings of the Board of Executive Directors, but shall have no vote, except that it shall be his duty to cast a deciding vote when necessary to break a tie.

The President of the Bank shall be the legal representative of the Bank. The term of office of the President of the Bank shall be five years, and he may be reelected to successive terms. He shall cease to hold office when the Board of Governors so decides by a majority of the total voting power of the member countries.

b) The Executive Vice President shall be appointed by the Board of Executive Directors on the recommendation of the President of the Bank. Under the direction of the Board of Executive Directors and the President of the Bank, the Executive Vice President shall exercise such authority and perform such functions in the administration of the Bank as may be determined by the Board of Executive Directors. In the absence or incapacity of the President of the Bank, the Executive Vice President shall exercise the authority and perform the functions of the President.

The Executive Vice President shall participate in meetings of the Board of Executive Directors but shall have no vote at such meetings, except that he shall cast the deciding vote, as provided in paragraph a) of this section, when he is acting in place of the President of the Bank.

c) In addition to the Vice President referred to in Article IV, Section 8 b), the Board of Executive Directors may, on recommendation of the President of the Bank, appoint other Vice Presidents who shall exercise such authority and perform such functions as the Board of Executive Directors may determine.

d) The President, officers, and staff of the Bank, in the discharge of their offices, owe their duty entirely to the Bank and shall recognize no other authority. Each member of the Bank shall respect the international character of this duty.

e) The paramount consideration in the employment of the staff and in the determination of the conditions of service shall be the necessity of securing the highest standards of efficiency, competence, and integrity. Due regard shall be paid to the importance of recruiting the staff on as wide a geographical basis as possible.

f) The Bank, its officers and employees shall not interfere in the political affairs of any member, nor shall they be influenced in their decisions by the political character of the member or members concerned. Only economic considerations shall be relevant to their decisions, and these considerations shall be weighed impartially in order to achieve the purpose and functions stated in Article I.

Article XI

STATUS, IMMUNITIES AND PRIVILEGES

Section 1 *Scope of Article*

To enable the Bank to fulfill its purpose and the functions with which it is entrusted, the status, immunities, and privileges set forth in this article shall be accorded to the Bank in the territories of each member.

Section 2 *Legal Status*

The Bank shall possess juridical personality and, in particular, full capacity:

a) to contract;

b) to acquire and dispose of immovable and movable property; and

c) to institute legal proceedings.

Section 3 *Judicial Proceedings*

Actions may be brought against the Bank only in a court of competent jurisdiction in the territories of a member in which the Bank has an office, has appointed an agent for the purpose of accepting service or notice of process, or has issued or guaranteed securities.

No action shall be brought against the Bank by members or persons acting for or deriving claims from members. However, member countries shall have recourse to such special procedures to settle controversies between the Bank and its members as may be prescribed in this

Agreement, in the by-laws and regulations of the Bank or in contracts entered into with the Bank.

Property and assets of the Bank shall, wheresoever located and by whomsoever held, be immune from all forms of seizure, attachment or execution before the delivery of final judgment against the Bank.

Section 4 *Immunity of Assets*

Property and assets of the Bank, wheresoever located and by whomsoever held, shall be considered public international property and shall be immune from search, requisition, confiscation, expropriation or any other form of taking or foreclosure by executive or legislative action.

Section 5 *Inviolability of Archives*

The archives of the Bank shall be inviolable.

Section 6 *Freedom of Assets from Restrictions*

To the extent necessary to carry out the purpose and functions of the Bank and to conduct its operations in accordance with this Agreement, all property and other assets of the Bank shall be free from restrictions, regulations, controls and moratoria of any nature, except as may otherwise be provided in this Agreement.

Section 7 *Privilege for Communications*

The official communications of the Bank shall be accorded by each member the same treatment that it accords to the official communications of other members.

Section 8 *Personal Immunities and Privileges*

All governors, executive directors, alternates, officers and employees of the Bank shall have the following privileges and immunities:

a) Immunity from legal process with respect to acts performed by them in their official capacity, except when the Bank waives this immunity.

b) When not local nationals, the same immunities from immigration restrictions, alien registration requirements and national service obligations and the same facilities as regards exchange provisions as are accorded by members to the representatives, officials, and employees of comparable rank of other members.

c) The same privileges in respect of traveling facilities as are accorded by members to representatives, officials, and employees of comparable rank of other members.

Section 9 *Immunities from Taxation*

a) The Bank, its property, other assets, income, and the operations and transactions it carries out pursuant to this Agreement, shall be immune from all taxation and from all customs duties. The Bank shall also be immune from any obligation relating to the payment, withholding or collection of any tax or duty.

b) No tax shall be levied on or in respect of salaries and emoluments paid by the Bank to executive directors, alternates, officials or employees of the Bank who are not local citizens or other local nationals.

c) No tax of any kind shall be levied on any obligation or security issued by the Bank, including any dividend or interest thereon, by whomsoever held:

   i) which discriminates against such obligation or security solely because it is issued by the Bank; or

   ii) if the sole jurisdictional basis for such taxation is the place or currency in which it is issued, made payable or paid, or the location of any office or place of business maintained by the Bank.

d) No tax of any kind shall be levied on any obligation or security guaranteed by the Bank, including any dividend or interest thereon, by whomsoever held:

   i) which discriminates against such obligation or security solely because it is guaranteed by the Bank; or

   ii) if the sole jurisdictional basis for such taxation is the location of any office or place of business maintained by the Bank.

Section 10 *Implementation*

Each member, in accordance with its juridical system, shall take such action as is necessary to make effective in its own territories the principles set forth in this article, and shall inform the Bank of the action which it has taken on the matter.

Article XII

AMENDMENTS

a) This Agreement may be amended only by decision of the Board of Governors by a two-thirds majority of the total number of governors representing not less than three fourths of the total voting power of the member countries.

b) Notwithstanding the provisions of the preceding paragraph, the unanimous agreement of the Board of Governors shall be required for the approval of any amendment modifying:

i) the right to withdraw from the Bank as provided in Article IX, Section 1;

ii) the right to purchase capital stock of the Bank and to contribute to the Fund as provided in Article II, Section 3 b) and in Article IV, Section 3 g), respectively; and

iii) the limitation on liability as provided in Article II, Section 3 d) and Article IV, Section 5.

c) Any proposal to amend this Agreement, whether emanating from a member or the Board of Executive Directors, shall be communicated to the Chairman of the Board of Governors, who shall bring the proposal before the Board of Governors. When an amendment has been adopted, the Bank shall so certify in an official communication addressed to all members. Amendments shall enter into force for all members three months after the date of the official communication unless the Board of Governors shall specify a different period.

Article XIII

INTERPRETATION AND ARBITRATION

Section 1 *Interpretation*

a) Any question of interpretation of the provisions of this Agreement arising between any member and the Bank or between any members of the Bank shall be submitted to the Board of Executive Directors for decision.

Members especially affected by the question under consideration shall be entitled to direct representation before the Board of Executive Directors as provided in Article VIII, Section 3 g).

b) In any case where the Board of Executive Directors has given a decision under a) above, any member may require that the question be submitted to the Board of Governors, whose decision shall be final. Pending the decision of the Board of Governors, the Bank may, so far as it deems it necessary, act on the basis of the decision of the Board of Executive Directors.

Section 2 *Arbitration*

If a disagreement should arise between the Bank and a country which has ceased to be a member, or between the Bank and any member after adoption of a decision to terminate the operation of the Bank, such disagreement shall be submitted to arbitration by a tribunal of three arbitrators. One of the arbitrators shall be appointed by the Bank, another by the country concerned, and the third, unless the parties otherwise agree, by the Secretary General of the Organization of American States. If all efforts to reach a unanimous agreement fail, decisions shall be made by a majority vote of the three arbitrators. The third arbitrator shall be empowered to settle all questions of procedure in any case where the parties are in disagreement with respect thereto.

Article XIV
GENERAL PROVISIONS

Section 1 *Principal Office*

The principal office of the Bank shall be located in Washington, District of Columbia, United States of America.

Section 2 *Relations with other Organizations*

The Bank may enter into arrangements with other organizations with respect to the exchange of information or for other purposes consistent with this Agreement.

Section 3 *Channel of Communication*

Each member shall designate an official entity for purposes of communication with the Bank on matters connected with this Agreement.

Section 4 *Depositories*

Each member shall designate its central bank as a depository in which the Bank may keep its holdings of such member's currency and other assets of the Bank. If a member has no central bank, it shall, in agreement with the Bank, designate another institution for such purpose.

INTER-AMERICAN DEVELOPMENT BANK
REGULATIONS FOR THE FINANCING OF EXPORTS OF CAPITAL GOODS
Chapter I
PURPOSES

Article 1 It is the purpose of these Regulations to establish the basic rules to put into effect a program for the medium-term financing of intra-regional exports of capital goods among the Latin American member countries of the Bank (hereinafter called "the Program"), with a view to promoting the integration and economic development of the region by expanding and diversifying its commerce.

Chapter II

PARTICIPATING COUNTRIES

Article 2 There may participate in the Program, in their capacity of these Regulations, whose attributes and objectives are, in the Bank's as exporters, those Latin American member countries of the Bank which have designated a national agency as provided for in Chapter V opinion, appropriately related to the purpose of the Program.

Chapter III

ELIGIBLE GOODS

Exports Eligible for Financing

Article 3 The Program shall be limited exclusively to the financing of intra-regional exports of capital goods which, for the purpose of these Regulations, shall be understood to be those goods, which, either by their nature or their use, are generally considered in international trade practice to be capital goods and which are normally subject to medium-term financing. These goods shall be set forth in the list specified in Article 6.

The financing may include, in conformance with customary international trade practices and within the percentages set by the Bank, exports of spare parts for goods specified in the list, provided such exportation forms part of a transaction financed under this Program.

Origin of Goods

Article 4 The Program shall be limited to the financing of exports of capital goods originating in the Latin American member countries of the Bank. Goods shall be considered to have originated in such a country when they are produced or manufactured therein from raw materials or parts coming from that country, or any other Latin American member country of the Bank. Goods incorporating imported components not originating in Latin American member countries also shall be considered to have originated in a member country when they meet the following requirements:

a) That there has been effected in the exporting country the last process which substantially altered the character of the goods provided that the CIF value of the imported component not originating in Latin American member countries of the Bank is less than 50% of the total FOB price of the item. The Bank shall follow the policy of diminishing this percentage for specific categories of goods when in its judgment there exists in the intra-regional commerce a reasonable supply of such goods with a smaller component imported from outside the region.

b) That the imported components originate in countries where the Bank's ordinary capital resources may be expended with the understanding, however, that imported components not exceeding in the aggregate more than 10% of the FOB price of the item may originate in other countries.

Exports Not Eligible for Financing

Article 5   The Program shall not finance: a) exports of goods, which, in the judgment of the Bank, will not promote the economic development of the importing country; b) exports of used goods; c) reexportations; d) export transactions which depart from normal commercial practice.

List of Goods

Article 6   The Bank shall distribute to the national agencies a list of the goods whose exportation may be financed under the Program. The list may be revised when deemed appropriate particularly for the purpose of including new capital goods that the Latin American member countries may be in a position to export.

Chapter IV

OPERATING PRINCIPLES

Types of Operations

Article 7   In the execution of the Program, the Bank may conduct loan operations through the following procedures: a) granting global loans to the national agencies to which Chapter V refers; b) concluding line-of-credit agreements with those agencies, either for acquiring credit documents which they may issue or for discounting credit documents which such agencies may have acquired; c) effecting such other operations as the Bank may determine.

Periods of Financing

Article 8   The Program shall finance export credit transactions considered to be at medium term, that is between 180 days and, in general, 5 years. In establishing the periods, there shall be taken into consideration the conditions and practices customarily available in international financing for the respective goods.

The Bank shall establish maximum payment periods taking into account the type of goods, their unit values, and the total amounts of the respective transactions. Such periods may extend beyond 5 years in order to allow the member countries to adjust to the variations which may exist in international competition. The periods shall normally be determined from the date of shipment of the goods.

Percentage of Financing

Article 9 The Bank may finance up to 70% of the invoice value of the export.

Conditions of Financing

Article 10 To qualify an exportation for financing under the Program, it shall be requisite that: a) the importer, at the time of delivery of the shipping documents or prior thereto, shall have made a cash payment of not less than 20% of the invoice value of the export or a lesser percentage which in special cases the Bank deems acceptable to adjust to international competition; b) the exporter has assumed and continues to assume the financial responsibility for at least 15% of the amount owed by the importer; c) the periods of amortization and interest charges applied to the portion not financed by the Bank shall be consistent with the practices of international competition in export financing; d) the importer's obligation shall be payable in United States dollars; e) reliable evidence shall be furnished to the Bank that the goods in question have been shipped with the necessary documentation and protected by the insurance customary in commercial practice; f) in the case of exportations which are to be effected through partial deliveries, the special requirements which the Bank may establish shall have been fulfilled, and g) all other provisions which the Bank may establish in connection with the Program have been fulfilled.

Global Loans

Article 11 The global loans granted by the Bank to the national agencies under the Program shall conform to the following provisions: a) the Bank may charge a commitment fee on undisbursed balances of the loan; b) the period of the loan shall be in keeping with the objectives of the Program; c) the respective contract shall contain all the provisions necessary to ensure that the national agency concerned shall utilize the funds in accordance with the purposes of the Program, the provisions of these Regulations, and the principles and practices of international trade.

Credit Documents

Article 12 The credit documents which the Bank may acquire or discount under these Regulations shall: a) be payable in United States dollars; b) have been prepared in the form and in compliance with requirements stipulated by the Bank; c) provide for payment of interest in semiannual installments; d) have been issued or unconditionally guaranteed by the national agency or such other institution of the exporting country as approved by the Bank; e) be accompanied by such documents and other proof as the Bank may deem appropriate. (As amended April 1, 1964.)

Interest Rate and Guarantee

Article 13   In the operations financed under the Program, the Bank shall charge a rate of interest which may in no case be less than the rate which it applies in its other operations from the ordinary capital resources and the Bank may require the guarantee of the government of the exporting country or of a financing institution of that country acceptable to the Bank.

Chapter V

NATIONAL AGENCIES

Designation

Article 14   The Program shall be carried out through National Agencies appointed by the member countries for that purpose, which agencies, in the opinion of the Bank, shall have legal and financial capacity for the execution of the Program.

Powers of the National Agencies

Article 15   The National Agencies shall be empowered to perform those of the following functions which the Bank determines are necessary to conduct the transactions under these Regulations: a) enter into agreements and loan contracts with the Bank for the purpose of executing the Program; b) discount credit documents deriving from exports included under the Program; c) issue credit documents in favor of the Bank resulting from the financing of exports eligible under the Program; d) rediscount with the Bank, with its full and unconditional guarantee or that of such other institution satisfactory to the Bank, credit documents which it has acquired through the financing of exports eligible under the Program; e) verify that the exports financed under the Program are in keeping with its purposes, the provisions of these Regulations, and the instructions issued by the Bank; f) issue or authenticate certificates as to the origin and the dates of shipment of the goods, as well as certify the fulfillment of the legal and other formalities pertaining to the exportation, and g) to perform all other functions which are their responsibility to fulfill in the implementation of the Program.

Chapter VI

RESOURCES

Resources of the Program

Article 16   The Program will be financed with the ordinary capital resources of the Bank. There shall also be utilized for the Program such resources as the Bank may obtain in the capital market without giving its guarantee, through the sale of credit documents or participations in such documents or in the global loan contracts resulting from operations financed under the Program.

Chapter VII

APPLICATION OF THESE REGULATIONS

Criteria for Application of the Regulations

Article 17   The provisions of these Regulations are to be applied with due consideration in each case of the transaction as a whole, the norms of international competition in the field of export financing, the regional content of the goods, the need for placing the Latin American exporter who lacks other adequate sources of financing on an equal footing relative to international competition, and the extent to which the economic and social development of the member countries will be furthered.

Discretionary Power of the Bank

Article 18   None of the provisions of these Regulations shall limit or restrict the Bank's power to accept or reject any of the operations envisaged in the Program and to determine the legality or propriety of the export transactions.

Coordination of Financing Practices

Article 19   In order to attain the greatest possible coordination and uniformity in export financing practices, the Bank shall maintain liaison with the extra-regional organizations concerned with the subject as well as stimulate and facilitate contacts among the national agencies themselves.

Additional Instructions

Article 20   The Bank shall issue such additional instructions as may be necessary to ensure the quickest and most effective execution of the Program.

Chapter VIII

TRANSITORY PROVISION

The Bank shall begin the execution of this Program not later than January 1, 1964; it may, however, finance exports initiated not more than 90 days prior to the date on which the Program shall have been initiated, provided they are consonant with the terms and purposes of these Regulations.

INTER-AMERICAN DEVELOPMENT BANK RESOLUTIONS ON THE PREINVESTMENT FUND FOR LATIN AMERICAN INTEGRATION

Resolution AG-7/66

(Approved by the Board of Governors in the Fourth Plenary Session, April 28, 1966)

PREINVESTMENT FUND FOR LATIN AMERICAN INTEGRATION

WHEREAS:

A letter of August 10, 1965, from the Inter-American Committee on the Alliance for Progress (CIAP) to the Presidents of the American Republics stated that the President of CIAP had been asked "to explore the possibilities of support by governments of the Hemisphere and the external financing agencies for a revolving fund which would finance project preparation and feasibility studies related to regional integration, the fund to be replenished from the loans flowing from these studies."

This suggestion accords with the Charter of Punta del Este, which in Title III establishes that, "In the application of resources under the Alliance for Progress, special attention should be given not only to investments for multinational projects that will contribute to strengthening the integration process in all its aspects, but also to the necessary financing of industrial production, and to the growing expansion of trade in industrial products within Latin America," and that "the cooperation of the Inter-American Development Bank should be sought in channeling extraregional contributions which may be granted for these purposes."

In response to the letter of the President of CIAP, the President of the United States, in a speech of August 17, 1965, on the Fourth Anniversary of the Charter of Punta del Este, stated that, "the United States will, as CIAP suggests, contribute from its Alliance resources to the creation of a new fund for preparing multinational projects."

In his message on foreign aid submitted to the United States Congress on February 1, 1966, President Johnson reiterated these concepts when he said that the United States would support the proposal of the Inter-American Committee on the Alliance for Progress and the Inter-American Development Bank to establish a new fund for feasibility studies of multinational projects.

In a resolution adopted in Montevideo on November 6, 1965, the

Foreign Ministers of the Latin American Free Trade Association (LAFTA) member countries agreed "to recommend that the Inter-American Development Bank establish, as soon as possible, a fund on which LAFTA may draw to finance preinvestment studies proposed for the Association on programs and projects of interest to regional integration, particularly in the fields of infrastructure, basic industry development, the prospecting and exploitation of the natural resources of major importance to industrial development, and the development of geoeconomic regions affecting two or more countries."

The Second Special Inter-American Conference meeting at Rio de Janeiro on November 17–30, 1965, approved the Socio-Economic Act of Rio de Janeiro, in which Chapter V provides that "with the objective of strengthening and accelerating integration in all its aspects, special priority must be given to the preparation and execution of multinational projects, and to the financing thereof, and the already existing economic integration agencies should coordinate their activities with a view to the earliest possible establishment of the Latin American Common Market. Likewise, the economic and financial institutions of the region should continue to give their fullest support to the organizations for regional integration."

At the Ninth Meeting of the Committee for Economic Cooperation on the Central American Isthmus, its Chairman offered the broadest support of the Central American countries to the negotiations for the establishment of a regional preinvestment fund.

At its VI Meeting held at Asuncion in April 1965, the Board of Governors of the Bank adopted a resolution which, after emphasizing and providing its broadest possible support for the Bank's efforts to expedite and promote the process of Latin American integration, recommended "that the Board of Executive Directors request the Management to formulate programs of technical and financial assistance, and to study, in coordination with other agencies participating in the process of Latin American integration, all aspects of that process relating to the purposes for which the Bank was established."

At the Meeting mentioned in the above paragraph, the Board of Governors gave full support to the creation of the Institute for Latin American Integration as a dependency of the Bank.

The Board of Governors

RESOLVES:

1. That the Board of Executive Directors is requested to take, prior to July 31, 1966, the necessary steps to establish a Pre-investment Fund for Latin American Integration destined to finance studies and the preparation of projects which may help to accelerate the process of Latin American integration.

2. That for the establishment of the Fund referred to in the preceding paragraph and for its use in conformity with the basic rules and mechanisms provided in the Agreement Establishing the Bank, it is recommended that the Board of Executive Directors earmark a suitable sum from the Fund for Special Operations, such sum not to affect in any case the other activities financed by said Fund.

3. That the regional preinvestment studies which may be financed on a nonreimbursable or contingent recovery basis with Bank resources allocated through the Bank's Technical Assistance Budget, may be included in the annual work program of the Preinvestment Fund referred to in the present resolution.

4. That the Bank may also receive contributions for the purposes of the Preinvestment Fund from member and nonmember countries and from other national and international institutions and agencies.

5. Except to the extent that other possibilities are established in documents providing contributions to the Fund, its resources shall be utilized to grant loans to national or regional institutions, for the financing of studies, chiefly in the following fields:

a. Multinational infrastructure works, such as highway systems, air transportation, marine and river transportation, communications, and the promotion of the related services on a regional scale.
b. The integrated development of geoeconomic zones embracing areas in more than one country, as in the joint development of international river basins, including energy sources, river navigation, irrigation, land settlement and forest resources.
c. Basic industries on a regional scale operating in a market combining the consumer requirements of several countries.
d. Other activities oriented toward integration, such as studies and programs for the joint exploitation of natural resources, the establishment of multinational agencies and enterprises, research and the exchange of scientific and technical knowledge, the study of the legal and institutional infrastructure of integration, the training of technical personnel and, in general, the mobilization of human resources.

6. That, whenever possible, the Bank, in granting loans resulting from studies financed with the Fund, whether granted out of its own resources or from funds entrusted to it for administration, shall endeavor as far as possible to include in such loans the entire cost of those studies, including the cost of related studies performed previously as nonreimbursable technical assistance.

7. That the Bank shall prepare annual work programs for regional preinvestment matters, taking into account the projects and studies that

the Latin American Free Trade Association (LAFTA) and the Secretariat for Central American Economic Integration (SIECA) may have under consideration. These programs shall be presented by the Bank to the Inter-American Committee on the Alliance for Progress (CIAP) for consultation, in order that they be evaluated with the participation of representatives of LAFTA and SIECA.

8. That the existence of the Fund shall not prejudice the right of the Bank to make either national or multinational preinvestment loans in keeping with the provisions of its constituent Agreement, utilizing only its own resources or acting in collaboration with other multilateral or governmental sources of financing.

Resolution DE-92/66

(Approved by the Board of Executive Directors, July 21, 1966)

PREINVESTMENT FUND FOR LATIN AMERICAN INTEGRATION

The Board of Executive Directors

WHEREAS:

The Seventh Annual Meeting of the Board of Governors of the Inter-American Development Bank requested the Board of Executive Directors to take, prior to July 31, 1966, the necessary steps to establish a Preinvestment Fund for Latin American Integration destined to finance studies and the preparation of projects which might help to accelerate the process of Latin American integration and, for that purpose, to earmark a suitable sum from the Fund for Special Operations which shall not in any case affect the other activities financed by the latter;

RESOLVES THAT:

1. The Preinvestment Fund for Latin American Integration (hereinafter called "the Fund") is established, in accordance with the provisions of the Agreement Establishing the Bank, Resolution AG-7/66 of the Board of Governors and the stipulations contained in the present resolution.

2. The Fund shall have available for its operations such resources as the Board of Executive Directors may allocate and such others as the Bank may have at its disposal by virtue of special agreements. In addition, the Bank may also receive contributions for the purposes of the Fund from member and nonmember countries and from other national and international institutions and agencies.

3. The resources of the Fund shall be utilized to finance the execution of preinvestment studies which may help to accelerate the process of Latin American integration, chiefly in the following fields:

a. Multinational infrastructure works, such as highway systems, air transportation, marine and river transportation, communications, and the promotion of the related services on a regional scale.

b. The integrated development of geoeconomic zones embracing areas in more than one country, as in the joint development of international river basins, including energy sources, river navigation, irrigation, land settlement and forest resources.

c. Basic industries on a regional scale operating in a market combining the consumer requirements of several countries.

d. Other activities oriented toward integration, such as studies and programs for the joint exploitation of natural resources, the establishment of multinational agencies and enterprises, research and the exchange of scientific and technical knowledge, the study of the legal and institutional infrastructure of integration, the training of technical personnel and, in general, the mobilization of human resources.

4. Depending on the nature of resources available to the Fund, the Bank may extend loans, grant reimbursable and nonreimbursable technical assistance and carry out studies at its own expense.

5. Operations which the Bank may finance with the resources of the Fund may be carried out with governments, governmental agencies, development corporations, multinational entities in charge of integration activities, and organizations of the private sector.

6. In authorizing nonreimbursable technical assistance or conducting studies at its own expense the Bank shall take the necessary steps to recover the respective cost wherever possible.

7. The existence of the Fund shall not prejudice the right of the Bank to make either national or multinational preinvestment loans in keeping with the provisions of its constituent Agreement, utilizing only its own resources or acting in collaboration with other multilateral or governmental sources of financing.

8. The Bank shall prepare annual work programs for regional preinvestment matters, taking into account the projects and studies that the Latin American Free Trade Association (LAFTA) and the Secretariat for Central American Economic Integration (SIECA) may have under consideration. These programs shall be presented by the Bank to the Inter-American Committee on the Alliance for Progress

(CIAP) for consultation, in order that they be evaluated with the participation of representatives of LAFTA and SIECA.

9. The President of the Bank is authorized to adopt all such measures as may be necessary to achieve the objectives of this resolution.

Resolution DE-93/66

(Approved by the Board of Executive Directors, July 21, 1966)

UTILIZATION OF RESOURCES FOR THE PREINVESTMENT FUND FOR LATIN AMERICAN INTEGRATION

The Board of Executive Directors

RESOLVES THAT:

1. The utilization of up to the equivalent of US$15,000,000, from the resources of the Fund for Special Operations is authorized to grant loans for the specific purposes stipulated for the Preinvestment Fund for Latin American Integration established by Resolution DE-92/66.

2. The authorized resources shall be allocated as the applications for credits to execute the respective preinvestment studies are approved.[1]

CHARTER OF PUNTA DEL ESTE

(Signed at Punta del Este, Uruguay, August 17, 1961)

Title III

ECONOMIC INTEGRATION OF LATIN AMERICA

The American republics consider that the broadening of present national markets in Latin America is essential to accelerate the process of economic development in the Hemisphere. It is also an appropriate

---

[1] Moreover, pursuant to an amendment to Section 1.05 of the Social Progress Trust Fund Agreement, it was agreed that the Inter-American Bank, in its capacity as Administrator of that Trust Fund, may use its resources to grant technical assistance in accordance with the terms of the Preinvestment Fund, up to such amounts as shall be determined jointly from time to time for this purpose by the Bank and the United States Government. On the same date it was agreed to allocate an initial amount of up to US$1,000,000 and up to the equivalent of 500,000 dollars in the local currencies of the Bank's Latin American member countries. These resources and those annually assigned by the Bank in its Technical Assistance Budget from its own resources may be used to finance studies performed at its own expense, joint programs with other entities, and the technical assistance granted from the Fund on a nonreimbursable or contingent recovery basis.

means for obtaining greater productivity through specialized and complementary industrial production which will, in turn, facilitate the attainment of greater social benefits for the inhabitants of the various regions of Latin America. The broadening of markets will also make possible the better use of resources under the Alliance for Progress. Consequently, the American republics recognize that:

1. The Montevideo Treaty (because of its flexibility and because it is open to the adherence of all of the Latin American nations) and the Central American Treaty on Economic Integration are appropriate instruments for the attainment of these objectives, as was recognized in Resolution No. 11 (III) of the Ninth Session of the Economic Commission for Latin America.

2. The integration process can be intensified and accelerated not only by the specialization resulting from the broadening of markets through the liberalization of trade but also through the use of such instruments as the agreements for complementary production within economic sectors provided for in the Montevideo Treaty.

3. In order to insure the balanced and complementary economic expansion of all of the countries involved, the integration process should take into account, on a flexible basis, the condition of countries at a relatively less advanced stage of economic development, permitting them to be granted special, fair, and equitable treatment.

4. In order to facilitate economic integration in Latin America, it is advisable to establish effective relationships between the Latin American Free Trade Association and the group of countries adhering to the Central American Economic Integration Treaty, as well as between either of these groups and other Latin American countries. These arrangements should be established within the limits determined by these instruments.

5. The Latin American countries should coordinate their actions to meet the unfavorable treatment accorded to their foreign trade in world markets, particularly that resulting from certain restrictive and discriminatory policies of extracontinental countries and economic groups.

6. In the application of resources under the Alliance for Progress, special attention should be given not only to investments for multinational projects that will contribute to strengthening the integration process in all its aspects, but also to the necessary financing of industrial production, and to the growing expansion of trade in industrial products within Latin America.

7. In order to facilitate the participation of countries at a rela-

tively low stage of economic development in multinational Latin American economic cooperation programs, and in order to promote the balanced and harmonious development of the Latin American integration process, special attention should be given to the needs of these countries in the administration of financial resources provided under the Alliance for Progress, particularly in connection with infrastructure programs and the promotion of new lines of production.

8. The economic integration process implies a need for additional investment in various fields of economic activity and funds provided under the Alliance for Progress should cover these needs as well as those required for the financing of national development programs.

9. When groups of Latin American countries have their own institutions for financing economic integration, the financing referred to in the preceding paragraph should preferably be channeled through these institutions. With respect to regional financing designed to further the purposes of existing regional integration instruments, the cooperation of the Inter-American Development Bank should be sought in channeling extra-regional contributions which may be granted for these purposes.

10. One of the possible means for making effective a policy for the financing of Latin American integration would be to approach the International Monetary Fund and other financial sources with a view to providing a means for solving temporary balance-of-payments problems that may occur in countries participating in economic integration arrangements.

11. The promotion and coordination of transportation and communications systems is an effective way to accelerate the integration process. In order to counteract abusive practices in relation to freight rates and tariffs, it is advisable to encourage the establishment of multinational transport and communication enterprises in the Latin American countries, or to find other appropriate solutions.

12. In working toward economic integration and complementary economies, efforts should be made to achieve an appropriate coordination of national plans, or to engage in joint planning for various economies through the existing regional integration organizations. Efforts should also be made to promote an investment policy directed to the progressive elimination of unequal growth rates in the different geographic areas, particularly in the case of countries which are relatively less developed.

13. It is necessary to promote the development of national Latin American enterprises, in order that they may compete on an equal footing with foreign enterprises.

14. The active participation of the private sector is essential to economic integration and development, and except in those countries in which free enterprise does not exist, development planning by the pertinent national public agencies, far from hindering such participation, can facilitate and guide it, thus opening new perspectives for the benefit of the community.

15. As the countries of the Hemisphere still under colonial domination achieve their independence, they should be invited to participate in Latin American economic integration programs.

SELECTED RESOLUTIONS APPROVED BY THE FIRST, SECOND, THIRD, AND FIFTH ANNUAL MEETINGS OF THE INTER-AMERICAN ECONOMIC AND SOCIAL COUNCIL

Resolution B-1/M62

REPORT ON THE STUDY OF POINTS A AND B OF TOPIC II: "PROBLEMS OF ECONOMIC INTEGRATION"

The First Annual Meeting of the Inter-American Economic and Social Council at the Ministerial Level (IA-ECOSOC) studied point A, "The Latin American Common Market," and point B, "The Economic Integration of Central America," of Topic II, "Problems of Economic Integration." Taking the presentation made by the Delegate of Argentina as a basis, and selecting from it the points it considered pertinent, the meeting agreed to subdivide the study of these questions into three groups, as follows:

I. Questions that are common to the two integration processes under way in Latin America; II. Questions related to the Latin American Free Trade Association (LAFTA), and III. Questions related to the Central American Economic Integration Program.

The meeting agreed, for the purpose of this report to present the results of discussions in the report given below:

I. QUESTIONS THAT ARE COMMON TO THE TWO INTEGRATION PROCESSES UNDER WAY IN LATIN AMERICA

a. *Annual review of the progress made in the economic integration of Latin America*

The meeting, taking as a basis the fact that the Charter of Punta del Este states that one of the goals of the Alliance for Progress is "to strengthen existing agreements on economic integration, with a view to the ultimate fulfillment of aspirations for a Latin American common market that will expand and diversify trade among the Latin American countries and thus contribute to the economic growth of the region," felt that the annual review of the economic and social progress of the Latin American countries that is made by the Inter-American Economic and Social Council at the Ministerial Level should include consideration of the development of the process of integration in the Latin American Free Trade Association and in the Central American Integration Program, recognizing that, although both have specific objectives and jurisdictions of their own, they constitute an essential part of the economic development of the region and, therefore, contribute to the attainment of the goals of the Alliance for Progress program.

b. *Desirability of the presentation of reports on their activities to the Inter-American Economic and Social Council by the two integration movements*

The meeting was of the opinion that, for most effective annual review of the development of the two integration movements, it would be most desirable that they be invited to present reports on their activities to the Inter-American Economic and Social Council, so that the Annual Meeting at the Ministerial Level may have the most exact information on the subject, without prejudice to the studies and documents that the Executive Secretariat of the Inter-American Economic and Social Council may consider it appropriate to present on its own initiative.

c. *Relations between Latin American Free Trade Association and the Central American Economic Integration Program*

In view of the recommendation in point 4 of Title III of the Charter of Punta del Este, concerning the establishment of effective relationships between the two economic integration movements, as well as between either of them and other Latin American countries, the meeting took cognizance of the fact that the two integration organizations have already established relations for the exchange of information. In expressing its satisfaction with this step, the meeting again urges the two groups to strengthen their ties, with a view to more rapid integration of Latin America. In this connection it is recommended that the Executive Secretariats of the Inter-American Economic and Social Council, Economic Commission for Latin America (ECLA), Latin American Free Trade Association (LAFTA), and the General Treaty for Central American Economic Integration extend technical advisory service to those countries that request it.

d. *Financial cooperation for the promotion of intrazonal trade in industrial products*

The meeting recognized the urgent importance of financing systems to quicken the process of integration among the countries of the area and emphasized its satisfaction with the studies that the Inter-American Development Bank (IDB) is carrying out on the establishment of appropriate machinery for the financing of export of capital goods and intermediate goods moving between Latin American countries, as well as investments for financing development plans.

The meeting stressed the need for intensifying representations to the International Monetary Fund and other financing agencies to have them provide the means for solving the temporary balance-of-payments problems caused by the carrying out of integration programs.

e. The meeting also noted with satisfaction the offer from the IDB to initiate a technical assistance program for studying measures and promoting projects that are designed to encourage and speed up the Latin American economic integration process. The IDB stated that it was willing to establish the necessary contacts and collaboration with the Latin American Free Trade Association and the agencies of the General Treaty for Central American Economic Integration and to join their efforts with those of other regional or extra-regional organizations pursuing the same goals.

II. SPECIFIC ASPECTS OF LATIN AMERICAN FREE TRADE ASSOCIATION IN RELATION TO THE CHARTER OF PUNTA DEL ESTE

a. *Desirability of accelerating the program of liberation of trade and coordinating the national policies of the signatory countries.*

In studying the achievements of the Latin American Free Trade Association, the meeting recognized that the program of reduction or elimination of duties has been carried out satisfactorily up to now, but that it would be desirable from the point of view of the interested countries for this aspect of the provisions of the Treaty of Montevideo to be carried out more rapidly, which would contribute to the attainment of the goals of the Alliance for Progress program.

The meeting recognized that, to this end, it would be desirable for the Latin American Free Trade Association member countries to accelerate, as much as possible, the coordination of their respective national policies in fields other than that of duties on intra-Area trade, in order to facilitate progress toward closer economic integration.

b. *Economic integration as national policy*

In the course of discussion of the activities of the Latin American Free Trade Association, the meeting considered that it would be a great help to the process of integration for that Association and likewise for the Central American Program, if the idea of economic integration received more decisive support from the government sector and were taken as an essential goal of national policy, encouraging the most active participation of the private national sectors, especially management and labor groups, in this task.

c. *Commercial policy measures designed to facilitate attainment of the goals of the Free Trade Zone*

The meeting recognized that the programs of liberation of trade already under way in Latin America include not only the removal of duties but also the elimination of the other obstacles to trade.

d. *Program of investigation and promotion of industrial and commercial opportunities in Latin America*

The meeting feels that, as proposed by the Delegation of Uruguay, it is of great importance to achieve a more rapid and balanced development of Latin American economic integration, a systematic program of personnel training should be carried out for the exploration and promotion of industrial, commercial and financing opportunities that can be derived by the different countries, especially those countries and areas of relatively less economic development, as a consequence of the liberation of commercial interchange. This program would also include investigation concerning concrete industrialization and commercialization projects and should initiate the compiling of existing information, which should be exchanged, in addition to data that may be obtained in the course of this program, between integration agencies and the member countries of the Organization of American States.

The meeting noted that the Government of Uruguay has made a formal offer to have the headquarters of the program in Montevideo.

This program, which was conceived to aid the processes of integration, should benefit all the member countries of the Organization.

Along this line the program is considered to be an instrument capable of helping all these countries to discover their potential and effective possibilities for industrialization and commercialization, especially those that may be derived from their adherence to existing instruments of economic integration.

There was also a consensus that the program should rely on the technical and financial collaboration of the OAS, ECLA, and the IDB, as well as on other agencies participating in the programs for technical and financial assistance connected with the Alliance for Progress.

Therefore, the First Annual Meeting of the Inter-American Economic and Social Council at the Ministerial Level suggests that $100,000 be set aside from the budget for the Program of Technical Cooperation of the OAS, for the fiscal year 1963, which would be earmarked to cover part of the expenditures required for financing the program and its work, in collaboration with other agencies, with the understanding that development of the project will commence next year.

III. THE CENTRAL AMERICAN ECONOMIC INTEGRATION PROGRAM AND THE CHARTER OF PUNTA DEL ESTE

Special characteristics of this program

The meeting recognized the progress made by the Central American countries in their Economic Integration Program and felt that that international cooperation measures of a specific nature are needed for it. Along this line, it is understood that these measures should deal basically with financial cooperation for projects concerning infrastructure, agricultural development, and industries of regional interest, and that it would be desirable for the financing agencies connected with the Alliance for Progress program to give greater support to the financial agency of the Central American program.

The meeting also recommended that the technical assistance machinery of the inter-American system should continue to cooperate with the agencies of the Central American Economic Integration Program.

Resolution B-2/M62

ECONOMIC DEVELOPMENT OF BORDER REGIONS WITHIN THE OBJECTIVES OF THE ALLIANCE FOR PROGRESS

WHEREAS:

One of the main objectives of the Alliance for Progress, as established in the Charter of Punta del Este, is the economic integration of Latin America;

Measures should be adopted that will lead to such integration, and the starting point therefor is a balanced regulation of existing regional conditions where there are traditional common interests among two or more adjacent countries; and

Joint planning and execution of specific economic development projects by such countries within their border zones and joint internal or external financing therefore are advisable, since they further this economic integration process,

The First Annual Meeting of the Inter-American Economic and Social Council at the Ministerial Level

RESOLVES:

1. To recommend that the countries interested in joint economic development of border zones promote the formation of mixed committees to study programs leading to the development of those zones, and that they strive for the appropriate coordination of planning organizations, for the purpose of preparing specific development programs for the said zones, with a view to obtaining internal or external financing.

2. To request the Executive Secretariat of the Inter-American Economic and Social Council, on the basis of data presented by the governments, to report to the Council's next meeting on activities in Latin America directed at the objectives set forth in the previous paragraph.

Resolution B-3/M62

INTENSIFICATION AT THE NATIONAL AND REGIONAL LEVELS OF STANDARDIZATION ACTIVITIES

WHEREAS:

A program for standardization of products on a regional scale is important and facilitates commercial exchange and furthers the work of economic integration, by eliminating the disparities in product characteristics;

An inter-American agency exists whose purpose it is to promote and present to national standards associations proposed standards of a regional scope for their approval; and

There should be a close relationship between the goals of the Pan American Standards Committee and the purpose of the program of trade liberalization which is the aim of the instruments of economic integration of Latin America,

The First Annual Meeting of the Inter-American Economic and Social Council at the Ministerial Level

RESOLVES:

1. To recommend the intensification at the national and regional levels of standardization activities and the granting of greater support and recognition to the work of the national and regional standards associations and the Pan American Standards Committee.

2. To recommend to the Pan American Standards Committee that when deciding upon a permanent location for its Secretariat it consider the close relationship between the activities of economic integration and standardization on a regional scale.

Resolution B-4/M62

TRANSPORTATION

The First Annual Meeting of the Inter-American Economic and Social Council at the Ministerial Level

RESOLVES:

1. To declare that the formulation and execution of a policy on transportation is of basic importance in order to strengthen and accelerate the processes of economic integration.

2. To take note of the reference document on this subject, which is the report of the meeting of experts on waterborne transportation ("Informe sobre la Reunión de Expertos en Transporte Marítimo y Fluvial") that met in Montevideo last July, convoked by the Permanent Executive Committee of the Latin American Free Trade Association; and of the account given by the representative of that Association of the work done at its Second Conference, following the general lines of that report.

3. To express its satisfaction with the concern shown by the Latin American Free Trade Association and the General Treaty for Central American Economic Integration with regard to this subject, consistent with what is stated in the Charter of Punta del Este.

4. To express its determination to cooperate, to the extent of its competence and resources, with the Latin American Free Trade Association and the Central American integration instruments in formulating and carrying out their transportation policies and in coordinating them with the policies of those other countries that do not as yet belong to one system or the other.

Resolution 1-M/63

CREATION OF THE INTER-AMERICAN COMMITTEE ON THE ALLIANCE FOR PROGRESS (CIAP)

WHEREAS:

The First Annual Meeting of the Inter-American Economic and Social Council adopted Resolution A-8, calling for a study of the inter-

American system in order to ascertain whether its present structure meets the requirements of the Alliance for Progress program;

Resolution A-8 begins by recognizing "that the inter-American system as presently constituted, was in the main established prior to the Alliance for Progress, and, in consequence, may not possess a type of structure permitting of achievement of the objectives of the Charter of Punta del Este in the dynamic and efficient way called for";

That resolution charged two outstanding Latin Americans with studying the structure and activities of those organizations and agencies of the inter-American system that have responsibilities in regard to the Alliance, and empowered them to make, if necessary, recommendations regarding those structural and procedural changes that are required in the system and in its various organs in order that the Alliance for Progress may take on the efficiency and the dynamic qualities called for by the Charter of Punta del Este;

The Council of the Organization, after approving Resolution A-8, entrusted the former presidents of Brazil and Colombia, Juscelino Kubitschek and Alberto Lleras, with the preparation of a report and conclusions, to be brought to the attention of the governments of the member states and submitted to the Inter-American Economic and Social Council for consideration, if need be, at a special meeting;

Former presidents Kubitschek and Lleras accepted and carried out the mandate of the Inter-American Economic and Social Council, and rendered their conclusions in separate reports presented to the Council of the Organization, for transmittal to the governments at the Special Meeting held on June 15, 1963;

The reports of former presidents Kubitschek and Lleras, which have been presented to the Second Annual Meetings of the Inter-American Economic and Social Council for consideration, are in agreement regarding the need to create a permanent, multilateral body representing the Alliance for Progress, and for this purpose proposed the creation of an inter-American development committee;

The recommendations of the former presidents, which have been examined by the Inter-American Economic and Social Council, suggest ways of organizing the proposed new body so that the Alliance for Progress may have multilateral representations and possess functional mechanisms and sufficient authority to permit it to discharge its responsibilities with the dynamic qualities and efficiency required; and

Consideration has been given to the views expressed in this regard in the Memorandum of the General Secretariat of the Organization of American States (Doc. OEA/Ser.H/X.4, CIES/344), the Report of the Panel of Experts (Doc. OEA/Ser.H/X.4, CIES/370), and the Observations of the Board of Executive Directors of the Inter-American Development Bank,

The Second Annual Meeting of the Inter-American Economic and Social Council at the Ministerial Level,

RESOLVES:

To create an Inter-American Committee on the Alliance for Progress (CIAP), in accordance with the following provisions:

I. NATURE AND PURPOSE

1. The Inter-American Committee on the Alliance for Progress (CIAP) shall be a special, permanent committee of the Inter-American Economic and Social Council for the purpose of representing multilaterally the Alliance for Progress and, in the same way, coordinating and promoting its implementation in accordance with the Charter of Punta del Este, and of carrying out the mandate of this resolution and those it receives from the Council of the Organization of American States or the Inter-American Economic and Social Council.

II. DUTIES AND FUNCTIONS

2. The Inter-American Committee on the Alliance for Progress shall carry out its duties and functions in keeping with the general orientation and lines of policy established by the Inter-American Economic and Social Council in its meetings at the ministerial level.

3. To fulfill the purpose set forth in the preceding chapter, the Inter-American Committee on the Alliance for Progress shall have the following duties and functions:

   a. To study the problems that may arise in connection with the Alliance for Progress and to resolve them or suggest solutions to the competent authority in each case, in accordance with the standards and policies established therefor.

   b. To promote continuing improvements in the process of giving the Alliance a more multilateral character.

   c. To make an annual estimate of the financing actually needed for Latin American development and of the total funds that may be available from the various domestic and external sources.

   d. To make a continuing review of national and regional plans, steps taken, and efforts made within the framework of the Alliance, and to make specific recommendations to the members of the Alliance and to the regional organizations in the Hemisphere concerning those plans, steps and efforts. In discharging this duty, consideration shall be given to the evaluation reports of the ad hoc committees set up under the Charter of Punta del Este or those deriving from steps taken pursuant to paragraph 9 of this resolution.

e. On the basis of the estimates referred to in paragraph 3.c and the review and the recommendations referred to in paragraph 3.d:

  i. To prepare and present proposals on the amount and sort of domestic resources each country would have to utilize to achieve the objectives of the Alliance, and

  ii. To prepare and present annual proposals for determining the distribution among the several countries of public funds under the Alliance for Progress, referred to in Chapter V.7 of Title II of the Charter of Punta del Este, which contribute to the external financing of general plans and specific programs for the development of the Latin American countries, giving special consideration to the progress which, in line with its basic characteristics, each country makes toward reaching the objectives of the Charter of Punta del Este, and being especially mindful of Title I.1 of the Charter.

f. To cooperate with each country and with the Inter-American Development Bank or other financial agents which the country may designate, in their negotiations with governments and with any other source of financing for the purpose of obtaining the external assistance required to finance their development programs and plans.

g. To coordinate those efforts within the Alliance which require multilateral action, such as economic integration, foreign trade policies of the area, and, in general, those activities which are related to the economic and social development of Latin America and which are not specifically assigned to any other body.

h. To obtain information on the progress made in multilateral investment programs for integration purposes and, upon request by the countries concerned, to help in obtaining financing for such investments, in accordance with established criteria and procedures.

i. To coordinate the work of the special committees of the Inter-American Economic and Social Council and to decide upon the necessity for their meetings, which shall be convoked by the Chairman of the Inter-American Committee on the Alliance for Progress.

j. To review the budget of the Pan American Union for the Alliance for Progress, the budget of the Program of Technical Cooperation, and that of any other specific multilateral fund, as prepared by the

General Secretariat for approval by the Inter-American and Social Council.

k. To review the program and budget prepared by the Secretary General with respect to the regular operations of the Secretriat within the purview of the Inter-American Economic and Social Council—including the items for permanent professional and administrative personnel; for the operation of the Inter-American Economic and Social Council, the Inter-American Committee on the Alliance for Progress, and the Panel of Experts and for overhead directly related to these operations—for approval by the Inter-American Economic and Social Council, in accordance with Article 19.f of its Statutes.

l. To establish its Regulations and the rules of procedure it considers advisable for the performance of its functions.

4. The member states agree that, when providing financial and technical assistance through their own agencies and when instructing their representatives in the various international organizations that provide such assistance, they shall give special consideration to the recommendations of the Inter-American Committee on the Alliance for Progress, in accordance with paragraph 3.e (ii), regarding the distribution of external public funds under the Alliance for Progress.

III. MEMBERSHIP AND OPERATION

5. The Inter-American Committee on the Alliance for Progress shall be composed of a chairman and seven representatives of the member states of the Organization of American States. Each representative shall be entitled to one vote.

The chairman shall be elected for a three-year period and shall be eligible for re-election for one term only.

The representatives of the countries, proposed thereby, shall be appointed by the Inter-American Economic and Social Council for a two-year period, on the basis of the same distribution agreed upon for electing the Executive Directors of the Inter-American Development Bank (IDB) at the election immediately prior to each period. Such distribution shall not apply to the five countries of Central America, which, as a group, shall propose one representative.

At the time of the first appointment, three of the six members who represent the Latin American countries shall be selected by lot to serve for one year.

A member of the Inter-American Committee on the Alliance for Progress may be re-elected only in the event that the countries which proposed their appointment indicate to the Inter-American Economic and Social Council that this be done.

When in the exercise of its functions the Inter-American Committee on the Alliance for Progress is to consider matters specifically concerning a given country, it shall invite that country to appoint an ad hoc representative.

6. The Secretary General of the Organization of American States (OAS), the President of the Inter-American Development Bank (IDB), the Coordinator of the Panel of Experts, and the Principal Director of the Economic Commission for Latin America (ECLA) shall serve as permanent advisors to the Inter-American Committee on the Alliance for Progress and in that capacity may attend its meetings.

7. The Panel of Experts shall be the technical arm of the Inter-American Committee on the Alliance for Progress in carrying out its functions of evaluating development plans and programs, in the spirit of the provisions of Title II, Chapter V.3 of the Charter of Punta del Este, and, in general, it may be consulted by the Inter-American Committee on the Alliance for Progress in relation to other matters relating to its functions. The Inter-American Development Bank shall be the technical arm of the Committee in matters concerning the financing of Latin American development.

The Inter-American Committee on the Alliance for Progress may request the technical advice of the Latin American Free Trade Association (LAFTA) and the Permanent Secretariat of the General Treaty on Central American Economic Integration (SIECA) on matters of economic integration.

8. In conformity with existing provisions, the Inter-American Committee on the Alliance for Progress may invite representatives of governmental and non-governmental agencies, who are recognized international authorities and who may have a particular interest in matters to be taken up at given meetings, to attend these meetings as observers. The Organization for Economic Cooperation and Development (OECD) and the European Economic Community (EEC) shall be among the entities to be so invited.

9. Those countries which have only sectoral programs and those which have national development plans but do not request the formation of an ad hoc committee may come to an agreement with the Inter-American Committee on the Alliance for Progress as to the best way of evaluating their programs or plans in consonance with the aims of the Charter of Punta del Este.

10. In order to ensure more frequent information on the progress of

the activities of the Inter-American Committee on the Alliance for Progress, the Chairman of the Inter-American Economic and Social Council, pursuant to Article 20 of its Statutes, shall convoke special meetings of the Inter-American Economic and Social Council at the ministerial level, when such shall be considered necessary.

11. The Inter-American Committee on the Alliance for Progress shall submit to the Inter-American Economic and Social Council for consideration an annual report on the fulfillment of its mandate and the draft resolutions that it may agree upon.

IV. CHAIRMAN

12. The Inter-American Economic and Social Council at the Ministerial Level shall elect an outstanding personality of the nationality of one of its members to be chairman of the Inter-American Committee on the Alliance for Progress. In addition to the functions and powers normal to the position, and to those which may be entrusted to him by the Inter-American Economic and Social Council and, on occasion by the Council of the Organization of American States, the Chairman shall be the permanent representative of the Inter-American Committee on the Alliance for Progress in actions required for rapid and effective execution of its decisions.

In the discharge of his duties, the Chairman shall be responsible only to the Inter-American Committee on the Alliance for Progress and the Inter-American Economic and Social Council.

The Chairman shall take office at a special ceremony in the presence of the Council of the Organization of American States.

V. SECRETARIAT AND HEADQUARTERS

13. The Executive Secretary of the Inter-American Economic and Social Council shall be the Secretary of the Inter-American Committee on the Alliance for Progress. Secretariat services shall be provided by the General Secretariat. Whenever the Chairman of the Inter-American Committee on the Alliance for Progress considers it indispensable to enlist the services of additional personnel in order to carry out the functions of the Committee more efficiently, he may request the Secretary General of the Organization of American States to take the necessary steps to appoint suitable persons.

14. The Inter-American Committee on the Alliance for Progress shall have its headquarters in Washington, D.C., United States of America, but it may hold meetings in any other city in the member states of the Organization of American States.

Resolution 10-M/63

REGIONAL INTEGRATION

WHEREAS:

Economic integration is an indispensable tool in promoting economic and social development in Latin America; and

Although the statements made by the observers for the Permanent Secretariat of the General Treaty for Central American Economic Integration and the Latin American Free Trade Association reveal that significant progress has been achieved in the field of Latin American economic integration during the past year, nevertheless measures must be taken to speed up said integration,

The Second Annual Meeting of the Inter-American Economic and Social Council at the Ministerial Level

RECOMMENDS:

That the governments of the Latin American countries which are members of the Organization intensify their search for means which will permit an acceleration of the integration process, which, among other aims, seeks to lessen the differences in level of economic development of the countries of the region.

Resolution 10-M/64

ECONOMIC INTEGRATION OF LATIN AMERICA

WHEREAS:

Regional economic integration is a fundamental factor in accelerating the economic and social development of the Latin American countries;

The Montevideo Treaty, whereby the Latin American Free Trade Association was established, and the General Treaty for Central American Economic Integration constitute the basic existing instruments for the attainment of the ultimate objective: the economic integration of Latin America;

Though significant progress has been achieved and worthwhile efforts have been made by the parties to the General Treaty for Central American Economic Integration, it is necessary to intensify the endeavors of Latin American countries to attain the objectives of economic integration and development; and,

For attainment of these objectives it is important to seek adequate coordination of the economic policies of the Latin American countries and of such overall and sectorial goals as may be established for development plans,

The Third Annual Meeting of the Inter-American Economic and Social Council at the Ministerial Level

RESOLVES:

1. To recommend that, with regard to problems affecting the Latin American Free Trade Association, the member states lend it their fullest political support, in order that the objectives of the Montevideo Treaty may be attained and, consequently, the process of economic integration of the associated states may be accelerated, with a view to achieving harmonious development of their economies. In this regard, the Inter-American Economic and Social Council believes that the member countries should adopt decisions at the highest political level, establish definite objectives, and define the fundamental characteristics of national and regional operative mechanisms which permit the attainment of the goals of integration.

2. To recommend to the executive bodies of the Alliance for Progress—the Inter-American Committee on the Alliance for Progress and the Inter-American Development Bank—that they make available maximum technical and financial support to facilitate and expedite the Latin American integration process, in accordance with the principles of the Charter of Punta del Este.

3. To recommend that, within the framework of the Alliance for Progress, special attention be devoted to the operation of multinational and national projects aimed at the regional market—with respect to investment in both infrastructure and production—and that particular consideration be given to the situation of countries showing a relatively lesser degree of development.

4. To recognize the importance of increased participation by developed countries, whether or not they are members of the inter-American system, in support of specific initiatives that may favor the Latin American integration process.

5. To recommend that national planning agencies in Latin America maintain a close relationship with one another.

6. To recommend to the Inter-American Committee on the Alliance for Progress that, with the collaboration of the Economic Commission for Latin America, the Inter-American Institute for Economic and Social Planning, and regional organizations, it draft as soon as possible a ten-year industrialization plan to serve as a frame of reference for the first stage of Latin American economic integration.

II. ACTION PLAN OF VIÑA DEL MAR

(Approved at the Fifth Annual Meeting of the IA-ECOSOC,
Viña del Mar, Chile, June 15–26, 1967)

D. INTEGRATION

The measures for carrying out the decisions contained in the Declaration of the Presidents of America on financial and technical cooperation, in order to accelerate integration, have to do with mobilizing resources to meet the needs arising from section 5 of Chapter I and sections 4 and 5 of Chapter II of the Declaration. The machinery and principles recommended for proceeding with the implementation of these measures are as follows:

37. CIAP will convene a meeting of government representatives of the member countries of LAFTA and CACM, representatives of Latin American countries that do not belong to either of these integration systems, and a United States representative—in the capacity of observer—to study the financial implications of the process of regional economic integration.

The government representatives will suggest courses of action and formulate specific recommendations on the following points:

a. Financial implications; evaluation of needs and supplementary sources of external funds; criteria for application; and methods of administering resources and determining priorities in accordance with the provisions of section 5 of Chapter I and sections 4 and 5 of Chapter II of the Declaration of the Presidents of America;
b. Establishment of a fund or other financial mechanism to meet the requirements of integration;
c. Establishment of formulas for Latin American economic and financial cooperation, with a view to the mobilization of larger amounts of national resources to be used in financing regional integration; and
d. Special financing needs that will arise for Latin American business in the course of integration, so as to ensure its adequate capacity to participate intensively in the investment opportunities opened up by the process.

Representatives of the CABEI, CEMLA, ECLA, IBRD, the IDB, the IMF, LAFTA, OECD, and SIECA will be invited to attend as advisors.

The first stage of the meeting will be held in Rio de Janeiro next September and will determine a schedule of activities that will enable the meeting to conclude its work and present a report to the governments prior to the Sixth Annual Meetings of the IA-ECOSOC.

It is considered desirable that, until this work is completed, the Inter-

American Development Bank and other Alliance for Progress agencies, in programming the allocation of funds for integration, try to heed the orientation and priorities decided upon for their systems by the directing bodies of the Latin American Free Trade Association and the Central American Common Market, together with those of the governments of countries not attached to either of them. These organizations should especially take account of financial needs arising from balance-of-payments problems, industrial readaptation, reorientation of manpower, and financing of exports, resulting from the accelerated process of tariff reduction.

38. With respect to the mobilization of funds to meet the needs of the Central American Common Market, it is recommended:

a. That a working group be formed representing the CIAP, IDB, SIECA, and the Central American Economic Integration Bank to attend to the needs of Central America for financing and technical assistance, and to determine the funds that will be provided, in accordance with paragraph 5.e of Chapter I of the Declaration of the Presidents of America; and

b. That the Alliance for Progress financing agencies decide promptly on the request made by the Central American Economic Integration Bank for an expansion in the resources of the Central American Fund for Economic Integration.

39. With respect to granting funds to undertake the preparatory studies and work involved in converting LAFTA into a common market, in accordance with Chapter I.5.f of the Declaration of the Presidents of America, CIAP, the IDB, and the Executive Secretariat of LAFTA will determine the funds that will be furnished to LAFTA to carry out the various programs designed to fulfill the objectives indicated.

40. To provide a solution for problems arising during the period of transition of LAFTA and CACM to a Latin American Common Market, it is decided that financial and technical resources should be mobilized to help solve the problems of balance of payments, industrial adaptation, and reorientation of manpower that may arise during this period of transition, including those that may arise in the operation of subregional agreements that may be entered into as integral steps in the transition to a Latin American Common Market.

41. In order to promote harmonious, balanced development, which implies bearing in mind the different degrees of development of the participating countries, both those with inadequate markets and those relatively less developed economically, and taking into account the special situation of the latter, it is resolved:

a. To request CIAP and the IDB, in order to give full effect to the provisions of the Declaration of the Presidents in regard to financial cooperation, they clearly define the specific modes of the financial aid envisaged on a priority basis for the countries less developed economically, as regards the study and implementation both of national and multinational infrastructure projects of special interest to them, and of projects connected with the establishment in them of industries for the regional market. Also, in accordance with section 2 of Chapter I of the Declaration of the Presidents of America, these organizations shall bear in mind the decision to promote immediate action to facilitate free access of products of the LAFTA member countries of relatively less economic development to the market of the other LAFTA countries; and

b. To recommend that, to this end, CIAP and the IDB take into account, among other things, the conclusions reached at the meeting of the relatively less economically developed countries to be convened by ECLA in the near future for the purpose of considering specific proposals for measures in favor of those countries within the context of Latin American economic integration.

42. With regard to the mobilization of resources for multinational projects and industries, it is resolved:

a. To recommend to the member countries of the Inter-American System that, pursuant to the decision of the Presidents, they adopt the necessary measures to ensure that the resources of the IDB Preinvestment Fund may be increased immediately and that a substantial part of such resources may be used to finance on a nonreimbursable or contingent recovery basis the conduct of studies aimed at meeting the need for the promotion of multinational projects to stimulate Latin American economic integration; and

b. To suggest to the IDB that as soon as possible it begin consultations with its member states for the prompt fulfillment of the provisions of the Declaration of the Presidents of America in this respect.

43. In addition, since the process of Latin American integration should tend towards a steady growth of employment opportunities, it is resolved:

a. That the international financial institutions, in dealing with multinational projects, should take into particular account the creation and maintenance of sources of employment and the improvement of the workers' living standards, with priority consideration of the employment situation in the countries less economically developed or having insufficient market; and

b. That the international financial institutions, in studying multinational infrastructure projects, should make them consonant with the priorities established in the national plans, taking into account a joint evaluation of all investment opportunities and the respective debt capacities.

44. With respect to the establishment of multinational airlines and programs in the field of maritime transport, to which reference is made in section 2 of Chapter II of the Declaration of the Presidents, it is resolved:

a. To recommend to the governments of the Inter-American System that they further the studies on the possibility of granting treatment to multinational regional air transport companies in each country that will be no less favorable than that applied to the airlines of each country of the hemisphere. At least one of the states involved in the multinational enterprise will be a member of the ICAO;

b. To recommend to these governments that they should study, jointly, the measures that would help the development of the multinational companies referred to;

c. To continue the studies initiated by the OAS/ECLA Transport Program on the level and structure of maritime freight rates, adapting them to the principles, regulations, and objectives contained in the LAFTA Declaration on Water Transport Policy (Resolution 120-V) and in the Convention on Water Transport; taking into account the situation and special interest of the CACM countries and of the other countries of Latin America;[1]

d. To support the maritime transport programs of the Latin American countries, in accordance with the resolution mentioned, as an effective contribution to the development of their economies, and to obtain, insofar as possible, cooperation in such programs by all developed countries.

45. Furthermore, in order to facilitate the establishment of the Latin American Common Market, it is desirable that all OAS member states have complete information on it; it is therefore resolved:

a. To request the General Secretariat of the OAS to secure from the Secretariat of LAFTA and the CACM information as to any new developments on the convergence of the two systems and to disseminate this information to countries not yet associated with these systems; and

b. To request the executive organs of LAFTA and the CACM to invite Latin American countries not yet members of LAFTA or

---

[1] Approved with the reservation of the United States.

the CACM to send representatives to any joint meetings or consultations held by the member states of LAFTA and of the CACM, pursuant to the provisions laid down in Chapter I, section 4.g, of the Declaration of the Presidents of America, prior to the formation of the bodies referred to therein.

46. To emphasize the importance of intense and effective participation by the private sector in the integration process, in order to assist the attainment of the goals outlined on the subject by the Declaration of the Presidents of America.

ECONOMIC AND SOCIAL ACT OF RIO DE JANEIRO

(Resolution II of the Second Special Inter-American Conference, Rio de Janeiro, Brazil, 1965)

Chapter V—*Economic Integration*

27. The American states recognize that the economic integration of the developing countries of the hemisphere should be one of the basic objectives of the inter-American system and, for that reason, will orient their efforts and take the measures that are necessary to accelerate the process of integration.

28. With the object of strengthening and accelerating integration in all its aspects, special priority must be given to the preparation and execution of multinational projects, and to the financing thereof, and the already existing economic integration agencies should coordinate their activities with a view to the earliest possible establishment of the Latin American common market. Likewise, the economic and financial institutions of the region should continue to give their fullest support to the organizations for regional integration.

29. Within the framework of mutual assistance, the participation of the comparatively less developed countries in Latin American programs of multinational economic cooperation should be encouraged, and the smooth balanced development of Latin American integration promoted, with special importance attached to the needs of those countries and particularly to their infrastructure programs and programs for the promotion of new lines of production.

30. National development plans should take into account the market expansion resulting from regional integration, in accordance with their own goals and objectives, in order to achieve adequate levels of employment, stimulate investment, increase technological capacity, and improve the conditions of cost, competition, and productivity.

PROTOCOL OF AMENDMENT TO THE CHARTER OF THE ORGANIZATION OF AMERICAN STATES "PROTOCOL OF BUENOS AIRES"

(Signed at Buenos Aires, Argentina, February 27, 1967)
(Selected Articles)

Article 39

The Member States, in order to accelerate their economic development, regional integration, and the expansion and improvement of the conditions of their commerce, shall promote improvement and coordination of transportation and communication in the developing countries and among the Member States.

Article 40

The Member States recognize that integration of the developing countries of the Hemisphere is one of the objectives of the inter-American system and, therefore, shall orient their efforts and take the necessary measures to accelerate the integration process, with a view to establishing a Latin American common market in the shortest possible time.

Article 41

In order to strengthen and accelerate integration in all its aspects, the Member States agree to give adequate priority to the preparation and carrying out of multinational projects and to their financing, as well as to encourage economic and financial institutions of the inter-American system to continue giving their broadest support to regional integration institutions and programs.

Article 42

The Member States agree that technical and financial cooperation that seeks to promote regional economic integration should be based on the principle of harmonious, balanced, and efficient development, with particular attention to the relatively less-developed countries, so that it may be a decisive factor that will enable them to promote, with their own efforts, the improved development of their infrastructure programs, new lines of production, and export diversification.

Article 44

The Member States recognize that, in order to facilitate the process of Latin American regional integration, it is necessary to harmonize the social legislation of the developing countries, especially in the labor and social security fields, so that the rights of the workers shall be equally protected, and they agree to make the greatest efforts possible to achieve this goal.

Article 50

The Member States, with due respect for the individuality of each of them, agree to promote cultural exchange as an effective means of consolidating inter-American understanding; and they recognize that regional integration programs should be strengthened by close ties in the fields of education, science, and culture.

Article 101

To accomplish its purpose the Inter-American Council for Education, Science, and Culture shall:
  m) Recommend appropriate procedures for intensifying integration of the developing countries of the Hemisphere by means of efforts and programs in the fields of education, science, and culture;

Article 105

The purpose of the Inter-American Juridical Committee is to serve the Organization as an advisory body on juridical matters; to promote the progressive development and the codification of international law; and to study juridical problems related to the integration of the developing countries of the Hemisphere and, insofar as may appear desirable, the possibility of attaining uniformity in their legislation.

IDEAS ON SOCIAL AND ECONOMIC MATTERS FOR THE MEETING OF CHIEFS OF STATE[1]

F. OTHER MEASURES TO ASSURE THE CONTINUITY OF THE POLICY OF INTEGRATION

The group of decisions set forth in the preceding sections outlines an immediate action plan designed to strengthen and accelerate the two processes of integration presently under way, as well as to establish

---

[1] Prepared in January 1967 by the group of Special Advisers to the Committee on Preparation for the Eleventh Meeting of Consultation of Ministers of Foreign Affairs. The Eleventh Meeting was charged with preparing the Agenda for a meeting of Chiefs of State to be held during 1967. The Special Advisers were: José A. Mora, Secretary General of the Organization of America States; Felipe Herrera, President of the Inter-American Development Bank; Carlos Sanz de Santamaría, Chairman of the Inter-American Committee on the Alliance for Progress; Raúl Prebisch, Executive Secretary of the United Nations Conference on Trade and Development; José Antonio Mayobre, Executive Secretary of the Economic Commission for Latin America; Alberto Solá, Executive Secretary of the Latin American Free Trade Association; Albino Román y Vega, Secretary General of the Organization of Central American States; Carlos Manuel Castillo, Executive Secretary of the Permanent Secretariat of the General Treaty on Central American Economic Integration, and Gustavo Guerrero, President of the Central American Bank for Economic Integration.

closer ties between those processes themselves and between them and the Latin American countries that have not yet adhered to either of them.

To give permanence and continuity to the integrationist policy on the national level, each Latin American country should create or designate an authority of a rank equivalent at least to a division of a government department, headed by an Under-secretary, charged with assuming responsibility for the corresponding national actions.

For the same purpose, on the regional level, the presidents of the Latin American countries would name a Coordinating Committee, whose task would be to study and evaluate the processes of integration and make suggestions with regard to the formation of the Latin American Common Market. The basic guidelines for attaining this objective would be the following:

1. That it is desired to adopt the policies and establish the systems necessary to establish progressively a common market that will cover all the countries of Latin America, within a period that should not exceed 10 years beginning in 1973;

2. That by its very nature this common market presupposes free movement of persons, goods and services, and capital within the region;

3. That there is an aspiration to adopt a common external tariff and to harmonize other instruments regulating foreign trade;

4. That efforts be made to achieve a coordinated investment policy designed to physically integrate the regional market, to assure the effective and dynamic participation of the countries that are relatively less developed or have insufficient markets, and to correct the imbalances now shown by the economic development of the various countries of the region;

5. That harmonization of monetary, exchange, fiscal, and social policies be sought among the countries that will form part of the common market;

6. That there is an aspiration to harmonize the various national legal systems in the fields directly related to the process of integration; and

7. That the Common Market should have an adequate institutional framework, which would include the standards and the agencies necessary for its effective functioning.

The presidents could invite executive officials of the functioning integration agencies and of the regional agencies connected with the process to make up a Coordination Committee. This committee would report annually to the presidents of the Latin American countries on the progress made and the problems encountered in the process of integration and would propose the measures it deemed appropriate for each stage of the process.

DECLARATION
OF THE
PRESIDENTS OF AMERICA

Signed at the Meeting of American Chiefs of State
Punta del Este, Uruguay, April 14, 1967

THE PRESIDENTS OF THE AMERICAN STATES AND THE PRIME MINISTER OF TRINIDAD AND TOBAGO MEETING IN PUNTA DEL ESTE, URUGUAY,

RESOLVED to give more dynamic and concrete expression to the ideals of Latin American unity and of solidarity among the peoples of America, which inspired the founders of their countries;

DETERMINED to make this goal a reality within their own generation, in keeping with the economic, social and cultural aspirations of their peoples;

INSPIRED by the principles underlying the inter-American system, especially those contained in the Charter of Punta del Este, the Economic and Social Act of Rio de Janeiro, and the Protocol of Buenos Aires amending the Charter of the Organization of American States;

CONSCIOUS that the attainment of national and regional development objectives in Latin America is based essentially on self-help;

CONVINCED, however, that the achievement of those objectives requires determined collaboration by all their countries, complementary support through mutual aid, and expansion of external cooperation;

PLEDGED to give vigorous impetus to the Alliance for Progress and to emphasize its multilateral character, with a view to encouraging balanced development of the region at a pace substantially faster than attained thus far;

UNITED in the intent to strengthen democratic institutions, to raise the living standards of their peoples and to assure their increased participation in the development process, creating for these purposes suitable conditions in the political, economic and social as well as labor fields;

RESOLVED to maintain a harmony of fraternal relations in the Americas, in which racial equality must be effective;

PROCLAIM

The solidarity of the countries they represent and their decision to achieve to the fullest measure the free, just, and democratic social order demanded by the peoples of the Hemisphere.

I

Latin America will create a common market.

THE PRESIDENTS OF THE LATIN AMERICAN REPUBLICS resolve to create progressively, beginning in 1970, the Latin American Common Market, which shall be substantially in operation in a period of no more than fifteen years. The Latin American Common Market will be based on the complete development and progressive convergence of the Latin American Free Trade Association and of the Central American Common Market, taking into account the interests of the Latin American countries not yet affiliated with these systems. This great task will reinforce historic bonds, will promote industrial development and the strengthening of Latin American industrial enterprises, as well as more efficient production and new opportunities for employment, and will permit the region to play its deservedly significant role in world affairs. The ties of friendship among the peoples of the Continent will thus be strengthened.

THE PRESIDENT OF THE UNITED STATES OF AMERICA, for his part, declares his firm support for this promising Latin American initiative.

THE UNDERSIGNED PRESIDENTS AFFIRM THAT:

We will lay the physical foundations for Latin American economic integration through multinational projects.

Economic integration demands a major sustained effort to build a land transportation network and to improve transportation systems of all kinds so as to open the way for the movement of both people and goods throughout the Continent; to establish an adequate and efficient telecommunications system; to install interconnected power systems; and to develop jointly international river basins, frontier regions, and economic areas which include the territory of two or more countries.

We will join in efforts to increase substantially Latin American foreign-trade earnings.

To increase substantially Latin American foreign-trade earnings, individual and joint efforts shall be directed toward facilitating nondiscriminatory access of Latin American products in world markets, toward increasing Latin American earnings from traditional exports, toward avoiding frequent fluctuations in income from such commodities, and, finally, toward adopting measures that will stimulate exports of Latin American manufactured products.

We will modernize the living conditions of our rural populations, raise agricultural productivity in general, and increase food production for the benefit of both Latin America and the rest of the world.

The living conditions of the rural workers and farmers of Latin America will be transformed, to guarantee their full participation in economic and social progress. For that purpose, integrated programs of modernization, land settlement, and agrarian reform will be carried out as the countries so require. Similarly, productivity will be improved and agricultural production diversified. Furthermore, recognizing that the Continent's capacity for food production entails a dual responsibility, a special effort will be made to produce sufficient food for the growing needs of their own peoples and to contribute toward feeding the peoples of other regions.

We will vigorously promote education for development.

To give a decisive impetus to education for development, literacy campaigns will be intensified, education at all levels will be greatly expanded, and its quality improved so that the rich human potential of their peoples may make their maximum contribution to the economic, social, and cultural development of Latin America. Educational systems will be modernized taking full advantage of educational innovations, and exchanges of teachers and students will be increased.

We will harness science and technology for the service of our peoples.

Latin America will share in the benefits of current scientific and technological progress so as to reduce the widening gap between it and the highly industrialized nations in the areas of production techniques and of living conditions. National scientific and technological programs will be developed and strengthened and a regional program will be started; multinational institutes for advanced training and research will be established; existing institutes of this kind in Latin America will at the same time be strengthened and contributions will be made to the exchange and advancement of technological knowledge.

We will expand programs for improving the health of the American peoples.

The fundamental role of health in the economic and social development of Latin America demands that the prevention and control of communicable diseases be intensified and that measures be taken to eradicate those which can be completely eliminated by existing techniques. Also programs to supply drinking water and other services essential to urban and rural environmental sanitation will be speeded up.

Latin America will eliminate unnecessary military expenditures.

THE PRESIDENTS OF THE LATIN AMERICAN REPUB-

LICS, conscious of the importance of armed forces to the maintenance of security, recognize at the same time that the demands of economic development and social progress make it necessary to devote to those purposes the maximum resources available in Latin America.

Therefore, they express their intention to limit military expenditures in proportion to the actual demands of national security in accordance with each country's constitutional provisions, avoiding those expenditures that are not indispensable for the performance of the specific duties of the armed forces and, where pertinent, of international commitments that obligate their respective governments. With regard to the Treaty on the Banning of Nuclear Arms in Latin America, they express the hope that it may enter into force as soon as possible, once the requirements established by the Treaty are fulfilled.

IN FACING THE PROBLEMS CONSIDERED IN THIS MEETING, which constitute a challenge to the will of the American governments* and peoples, the Presidents proclaim their faith in the basic purpose of the inter-American system: to promote in the Americas free and democratic societies, existing under the rule of law, whose dynamic economies, reinforced by growing technological capabilities, will allow them to serve with ever-increasing effectiveness the peoples of the Continent, to whom they announce the following program.

* When the term "Latin America" is used in this text, it is to be understood that it includes all the member states of the Organization of American States, except the United States of America. The term "Presidents" includes the Prime Minister of Trinidad and Tobago. The term "Continent" comprises both the continental and insular areas.

II

ACTION PROGRAM

Chapter I

LATIN AMERICAN ECONOMIC INTEGRATION AND INDUSTRIAL DEVELOPMENT

1. *Principles, objectives, and goals*

Economic integration is a collective instrument for accelerating Latin American development and should constitute one of the policy goals of each of the countries of the region. The greatest possible efforts should be made to bring it about, as a necessary complement to national development plans.

At the same time, the different levels of development and economic and market conditions of the various Latin American countries must be borne in mind, in order that the integration process may promote their harmonious and balanced growth. In this respect, the countries of relatively less economic development, and, to the extent required, those of insufficient market, will have preferential treatment in matters of trade and of technical and financial cooperation.

Integration must be fully at the service of Latin America. This requires the strengthening of Latin American enterprise through vigorous financial and technical support that will permit it to develop and supply the regional market efficiently. Foreign private enterprise will be able to fill an important function in assuring achievement of the objectives of integration within the pertinent policies of each of the countries of Latin America.

Adequate financing is required to facilitate the economic restructuring and adjustments called for by the urgent need to accelerate integration.

It is necessary to adopt all measures that will lead to the completion of Latin American integration, above all those that will bring about, in the shortest time possible, monetary stability and the elimination of all restrictions, including administrative, financial, and exchange restrictions, that obstruct the trade of the products of the area.

To these ends, the Latin American Presidents agree to take action on the following points:

a. Beginning in 1970, to establish progressively the Latin American Common Market, which should be substantially in operation within a period of no more than fifteen years.

b. The Latin American Common Market will be based on the improvement of the two existing integration systems: the Latin American Free Trade Association (LAFTA) and the Central American Common Market (CACM). The two systems will initiate simultaneously a process of convergence by stages of cooperation, closer ties, and integration, taking into account the interest of the Latin American countries not yet associated with these systems, in order to provide their access to one of them.

c. To encourage the incorporation of other countries of the Latin American region into the existing integration systems.

2. *Measures with regard to the Latin American Free Trade Association (LAFTA)*

The Presidents of the member states of LAFTA instruct their respective Ministers of Foreign Affairs, who will participate in the next meeting of the Council of Ministers of LAFTA, to be held in 1967, to adopt the measures necessary to implement the following decisions:

a. To accelerate the process of converting LAFTA into a common market. To this end, starting in 1970, and to be completed in a period of not more than fifteen years, LAFTA will put into effect a system of programmed elimination of duties and all other nontariff restrictions, and also a system of tariff harmonization,

in order to establish progressively a common external tariff at
levels that will promote efficiency and productivity, as well as
the expansion of trade.

b. To coordinate progressively economic policies and instruments
and to harmonize national laws to the extent required for integration. These measures will be adopted simultaneously with the
improvement of the integration process.

c. To promote the conclusion of sectoral agreements for industrial
complementation, endeavoring to obtain the participation of the
countries of relatively less economic development.

d. To promote the conclusion of temporary subregional agreements,
with provision for reducing tariffs within the subregions and harmonizing treatments toward third nations more rapidly than in
the general agreements, in keeping with the objectives of regional integration. Subregional tariff reductions will not be extended to countries that are not parties to the subregional
agreement, nor will they create special obligations for them.

Participation of the countries of relatively less economic development in all stages of the integration process and in the formation of the
Latin American Common Market will be based on the provisions of
the Treaty of Montevideo and its complementary resolutions, and these
countries will be given the greatest possible advantages, so that balanced development of the region may be achieved.

To this same end, they have decided to promote immediate action to
facilitate free access of products of the LAFTA member countries of
relatively less economic development to the market of the other
LAFTA countries, and to promote the installation and financing in the
former countries of industries intended for the enlarged market.

The countries of relatively less economic development will have the
right to participate and to obtain preferential conditions in the subregional agreements in which they have an interest.

The situation of countries characterized as being of insufficient market shall be taken into account in temporary preferential treatments
established, to the extent necessary to achieve a harmonious development in the integration process.

It is understood that all the provisions set forth in this section fall
within or are based upon the Treaty of Montevideo.

3. *Measures with regard to the Central American economic integration
program*

The Presidents of the member states of the Central American Common Market commit themselves:

a. To carry out an action program that will include the following
measures, among others:

(1) Improvement of the customs union and establishment of a Central American monetary union;
(2) Completion of the regional network of infrastructure;
(3) Promotion of a common foreign-trade policy;
(4) Improvement of the common market in agricultural products and implementation of a joint, coordinated industrial policy;
(5) Acceleration of the process of free movement of manpower and capital within the area;
(6) Harmonization of the basic legislation required for economic integration.

b. To apply, in the implementation of the foregoing measures, and when pertinent, the temporary preferential treatment already established or that may be established, in accordance with the principle of balanced development among countries.

c. To foster closer ties between Panama and the Central American Common Market, as well as rapid expansion of trade and investment relations with neighboring countries of the Central American and Caribbean region, taking advantage, to this end, of their geographic proximity and of the possibilities for economic complementation; also, to seek conclusion of subregional agreements and agreements of industrial complementation between Central America and other Latin American countries.

4. *Measures common to Latin American countries*

The Latin American Presidents commit themselves:

a. Not to establish new restrictions on trade among Latin American countries, except in special cases, such as those arising from equalization of tariffs and other instruments of trade policy, as well as from the need to assure the initiation or expansion of certain productive activities in countries of relatively less economic development.

b. To establish, by a tariff cut or other equivalent measures, a margin of preference within the region for all products originating in Latin American countries, taking into account the different degrees of development of the countries.

c. To have the measures in the two preceding paragraphs applied immediately among the member countries of LAFTA, in harmony with the other measures referring to this organization contained in the present chapter and, insofar as possible, to extend them to nonmember countries in a manner compatible with existing international commitments, inviting the latter countries to extend similar preferences to the members of LAFTA, with the same qualification.

d. To ensure that application of the foregoing measures shall not hinder internal readjustments designed to rationalize the instruments of trade policy made necessary in order to carry out national development plans and to achieve the goals of integration.

e. To promote acceleration of the studies already initiated regarding preferences that LAFTA countries might grant to imports from the Latin American countries that are not members of the Association.

f. To have studies made of the possibility of concluding agreements of industrial complementation in which all Latin American countries may participate, as well as temporary subregional economic integration agreements between the CACM and member countries of LAFTA.

g. To have a committee established composed of the executive organs of LAFTA and the CACM to coordinate implementation of the foregoing points. To this end, the committee will encourage meetings at the ministerial level, in order to ensure that Latin American integration will proceed as rapidly as possible, and, in due course, initiate negotiation of a general treaty or the protocols required to create the Latin American Common Market. Latin American countries that are not members shall be invited to send representatives to these meetings and to those of the committee of the executive organs of LAFTA and the CACM.

h. To give special attention to industrial development within integration, and particularly to the strengthening of Latin American industrial firms. In this regard, we reiterate that development must be balanced between investments for economic ends and investments for social ends.

5. *Measures common to member countries of the Organization of American States (OAS)*

The Presidents of the member states of the OAS agree:

a. To mobilize financial and technical resources within and without the hemisphere to contribute to the solution of problems in connection with the balance of payments, industrial readjustments, and retraining of the labor force that may arise from a rapid reduction of trade barriers during the period of transition toward the common market, as well as to increase the sums available for export credits in intra-Latin American trade. The Inter-American Development Bank and the organs of both existing integration systems should participate in the mobilization of such resources.

b. To mobilize public and private resources within and without the hemisphere to encourage industrial development as part of the integration process and of national development plans.

c. To mobilize financial and technical resources to undertake specific feasibility studies on multinational projects for Latin American industrial firms, as well as to aid in carrying out these projects.

d. To accelerate the studies being conducted by various inter-American agencies to promote strengthening of capital markets and the possible establishment of a Latin American stock market.

e. To make available to Central America, within the Alliance for Progress, adequate technical and financial resources, including those required for strengthening and expanding the existing Central American Economic Integration Fund, for the purpose of accelerating the Central American economic integration program.

f. To make available, within the Alliance for Progress and pursuant to the provisions of the Charter of Punta del Este, the technical and financial resources needed to accelerate the preparatory studies and work involved in converting LAFTA into a common market.

Chapter II

MULTINATIONAL ACTION FOR INFRASTRUCTURE PROJECTS

The economic integration of Latin America demands a vigorous and sustained effort to complete and modernize the physical infrastructure of the region. It is necessary to build a land transport network and improve all types of transport systems to facilitate the movement of persons and goods throughout the hemisphere; to establish an adequate and efficient telecommunications system and interconnected power systems; and jointly to develop international watersheds, frontier regions and economic areas that include the territory of two or more countries. In Latin America there are in existence projects in all these fields, at different stages of preparation or implementation, but in many cases the completion of prior studies, financial resources, or merely the coordination of efforts and the decision to bring them to fruition are lacking.

The Presidents of the member states of the OAS agree to engage in determined action to undertake or accelerate the construction of the infrastructure required for the development and integration of Latin America and to make better use thereof. In so doing, it is essential that the groups of interested countries or multinational institutions determine criteria for assigning priorities, in view of the amount of human and material resources needed for the task.

As one basis for the criteria, which will be determined with precision upon consideration of the specific cases submitted for study, they stress the fundamental need to give preferential attention to those projects that benefit the countries of the region that are at a relatively lower level of economic development.

Priority should also be given to the mobilization of financial and technical resources for the preparation and implementation of infrastructure projects that will facilitate the participation of landlocked countries in regional and international trade.

In consequence, they adopt the following decisions for immediate implementation:

1. To complete the studies and conclude the agreements necessary to accelerate the construction of an inter-American telecommunications network.

2. To expedite the agreements necessary to complete the Pan American Highway, to accelerate the construction of the Bolivarian Highway (Carretera Marginal de la Selva) and its junction with the Trans-Chaco Highway and to support the studies and agreements designed to bring into being the new highway systems that will join groups of countries of continental and insular Latin America, as well as the basic works required to develop water and airborne transport of a multinational nature and the corresponding systems of operation. As a complement to these agreements, negotiations should be undertaken for the purpose of eliminating or reducing to a minimum the restrictions on international traffic and of promoting technical and administrative cooperation among land, water, and air transport enterprises and the establishment of multinational transport services.

3. To sponsor studies for preparing joint projects in connection with watersheds, such as the studies commenced on the development of the River Plate basin and that relating to the Gulf of Fonseca.

4. To allocate sufficient resources to the Preinvestment Fund for Latin American Integration of the IDB for conducting studies that will make it possible to identify and prepare multinational projects in all fields that may be of importance in promoting regional integration. In order that the aforesaid Fund may carry out an effective promotion effort, it is necessary that an adequate part of the resources allocated may be used without reimbursement, or with reimbursement conditioned on the execution of the corresponding projects.

5. To mobilize, within and outside the hemisphere, resources in addition to those that will continue to be placed at the disposal of the countries to support national economic development programs, such resources to be devoted especially to the implementation of multinational infrastructure projects that can represent important advances in the

Latin American economic integration process. In this regard, the IDB should have additional resources in order to participate actively in the attainment of this objective.

Chapter III

MEASURES TO IMPROVE INTERNATIONAL TRADE CONDITIONS IN LATIN AMERICA

The economic development of Latin America is seriously affected by the adverse conditions in which its international trade is carried out. Market structures, financial conditions, and actions that prejudice exports and other income from outside Latin America are impeding its growth and retarding the integration process. All this causes particular concern in view of the serious and growing imbalance between the standard of living in Latin American countries and that of the industrialized nations and, at the same time, calls for definite decisions and adequate instruments to implement the decisions.

Individual and joint efforts of the member states of the OAS are essential to increase the incomes of Latin American countries derived from, and to avoid frequent fluctuations in, traditional exports, as well as to promote new exports. Such efforts are also essential to reduce any adverse effects on the external earnings of Latin American countries that may be caused by measures which may be taken by industrialized countries for balance of payments reasons.

The Charter of Punta del Este, the Economic and Social Act of Rio de Janeiro and the new provisions of the Charter of the OAS reflect a hemispheric agreement with regard to these problems, which needs to be effectively implemented; therefore, the Presidents of the member states of the OAS agree:

1. To act in coordination in multilateral negotiations to achieve, without the more highly developed countries' expecting reciprocity, the greatest possible reduction or the elimination of tariffs and other restrictions that impede the access of Latin American products to world markets. The Government of the United States intends to make efforts for the purpose of liberalizing the conditions affecting exports of basic products of special interest to Latin American countries, in accordance with the provisions of Article 37. a) of the Protocol of Buenos Aires.

2. To consider together possible systems of general nonreciprocal preferential treatment for exports of manufactures and semimanufactures of the developing countries, with a view to improving the condition of the Latin American export trade.

3. To undertake a joint effort in all international institutions and organizations to eliminate discriminatory preferences against Latin American exports.

4. To strengthen the system of intergovernmental consultations and carry them out sufficiently in advance, so as to render them effective and ensure that programs for placing and selling surpluses and reserves that affect the exports of the developing countries take into account the interests of the Latin American countries.

5. To ensure compliance with international commitments to refrain from introducing or increasing tariff and nontariff barriers that affect exports of the developing countries, taking into account the interests of Latin America.

6. To combine efforts to strengthen and perfect existing international agreements, particularly the International Coffee Agreement, to obtain favorable conditions for trade in basic products of interest to Latin America and to explore all possibilities for the development of new agreements.

7. To support the financing and prompt initiation of the activities of the Coffee Diversification Fund, and consider in due course the creation of other funds to make it possible to control the production of basic products of interest to Latin America in which there is a chronic imbalance between supply and demand.

8. To adopt measures to make Latin American export products more competitive in world markets.

9. To put in operation as soon as possible an inter-American agency for export promotion that will help to identify and develop new export lines and to strengthen the placing of Latin American products in international markets, and to improve national and regional agencies designed for the same purpose.

10. To initiate such individual or joint action on the part of the member states of the OAS as may be required to ensure effective and timely execution of the foregoing agreements, as well as those that may be required to continue the execution of the agreements contained in the Charter of Punta del Este, in particular those relating to foreign trade.

With regard to joint action, the Inter-American Committee on the Alliance for Progress (CIAP) and other agencies in the region shall submit to the Inter-American Economic and Social Council (IA-ECOSOC), for consideration at its next meeting, the means, instruments, and action program for initiating execution thereof.

At its annual meetings, IA-ECOSOC shall examine the progress of the programs under way with the object of considering such action as may ensure compliance with the agreements concluded, inasmuch as a substantial improvement in the international conditions in which Latin American foreign trade is carried on is a basic prerequisite to the acceleration of economic development.

Chapter IV

MODERNIZATION OF RURAL LIFE AND INCREASE OF AGRICULTURAL PRODUCTIVITY, PRINCIPALLY OF FOOD

In order to promote a rise in the standard of living of farmers and an improvement in the condition of the Latin American rural people and their full participation in economic and social life, it is necessary to give greater dynamism to agriculture in Latin America, through comprehensive programs of modernization, land settlement, and agrarian reform when required by the countries.

To achieve these objectives and to carry out these programs, contained in the Charter of Punta del Este, it is necessary to intensify internal efforts and to provide additional external resources.

Such programs will be oriented toward increasing food production in the Latin American countries in sufficient volume and quality to provide adequately for their population and to meet world needs for food to an ever-increasing extent, as well as toward improving agricultural productivity and toward a diversification of crops, which will assure the best possible competitive conditions for such production.

All these development efforts in agriculture must be related to the overall development of the national economies in order to harmonize the supply of agricultural products and the labor that could be freed as a result of the increase in farm productivity with the increase in demand for such products and with the need for labor in the economy as a whole.

This modernization of agricultural activities will furthermore create conditions for a development more in balance with the effort toward industrialization.

To achieve these goals, the Latin American Presidents undertake:

1. To improve the formulation and execution of agricultural policies and to ensure the carrying out of plans, programs, and projects for pre-investment, agricultural development, agrarian reform, and land settlement, adequately coordinated with national economic development plans, in order to intensify internal efforts and to facilitate obtaining and utilizing external financing.

2. To improve credit systems, including those earmarked for the resettlement of rural workers who are beneficiaries of agrarian reform, and for increased productivity, and to create facilities for the production, marketing, storage, transportation, and distribution of agricultural products.

3. To provide adequate incentives, including price incentives, to promote agricultural production under economic conditions.

4. To foster and to finance the acquisition and intensive use of those

agricultural inputs which contribute to the improvement of productivity, as well as the establishment and expansion of Latin American industries producing agricultural inputs, particularly fertilizers, pesticides, and agricultural machinery.

5. To ensure the adequacy of tax systems that affect the agricultural sector, so that they may contribute to the increase of productivity, more production, and better land distribution.

6. To expand substantially programs of specialized education and research and of agricultural extension, in order to improve the training of the rural worker and the education of technical and professional personnel, and, also, to intensify animal and plant sanitation campaigns.

7. To provide incentives and to make available financial resources for the industrialization of agricultural production, especially through the development of small and medium industry and the promotion of exports of processed agricultural products.

8. To facilitate the establishment of multinational or international programs that will make it possible for Latin America to supply a larger proportion of world food needs.

9. To foster national programs of community development and of self-help for small-scale farmers, and to promote the creation and strengthening of agricultural cooperatives.

By recognizing the importance of the stated objectives, goals and means, the Presidents of the member states of the OAS undertake, within the spirit of the Alliance for Progress, to combine intensified internal efforts with additional external support especially earmarked for such measures.

They call upon CIAP, when analyzing the agricultural sector as included in national development plans, to bear in mind the objectives and measures indicated herein, giving due attention to agrarian reform programs in those countries that consider these programs an important basis for their agricultural progress and economic and social development.

Chapter V

EDUCATIONAL, TECHNOLOGICAL, AND SCIENTIFIC DEVELOPMENT AND INTENSIFICATION OF HEALTH PROGRAMS

A. *Education and Culture*

Education is a sector of high priority in the overall development policy of Latin American nations.

The Presidents of the member states of the OAS recognize that, during the past decade, there has been development of educational services in Latin America unparalleled in any other period of the history of their countries.

Nevertheless, it must be admitted that:

a. It is necessary to increase the effectiveness of national efforts in the field of education;
b. Educational systems should be more adequately adjusted to the demands of economic, social, and cultural development;
c. International cooperation in educational matters should be considerably intensified, in accordance with the new standards of the Charter of the OAS.

To these ends, they agree to improve educational administrative and planning systems; to raise the quality of education so as to stimulate the creativity of each pupil; to accelerate expansion of educational systems at all levels; and to assign priority to the following activities related to economic, social, and cultural development:

1. Orientation and, when necessary, reorganization of educational systems, in accordance with the needs and possibilities of each country, in order to achieve:

a. The expansion and progressive improvement of preschool education and extension of the period of general education;
b. An increase in the capacity of secondary schools and the improvement of their curricula;
c. An increase in opportunities following general education, including opportunities for learning a trade or a specialty or for continuing general education;
d. The gradual elimination of barriers between vocational and general education;
e. The expansion and diversification of university courses, so that they will include the new professions essential to economic and social development;
f. The establishment or expansion of graduate courses through professional schools;
g. The establishment of refresher courses in all branches and types of education, so that graduates may keep their knowledge up to date in this era of rapid scientific and technological progress;
h. The strengthening and expansion of adult education programs;
i. The promotion of special education for exceptional students.

2. Promotion of basic and advanced training for teachers and administrative personnel; development of educational research and experimentation, and adequate expansion of school building programs.

3. Broadening of the use of educational television and other modern teaching techniques.

4. Improvement of rural elementary schools to achieve a level of quality equal to that of urban elementary schools, with a view to assuring equal educational opportunities to the rural population.

5. Reorganization of vocational education, when necessary, taking into account the structure of the labor force and the foreseeable manpower needs of each country's development plan.

6. An increase in private financing of education.

7. Encouragement of local and regional communities to take an effective part in the construction of school buildings and in civic support to educational development.

8. A substantial increase in national scholarship and student loan and aid programs.

9. Establishment or expansion of extension services and services for preserving the cultural heritage and encouraging intellectual and artistic activity.

10. Strengthening of education for international understanding and Latin American integration.

Multinational efforts

1. Increasing international resources for the purposes set forth in this chapter.

2. Instructing the appropriate agencies of the OAS to:

a. Provide technical assistance to the countries that so request:
   i) In educational research, experimentation, and innovation;
   ii) For training of specialized personnel;
   iii) In educational television. It is recommended that study be made of the advisability of establishing a multinational training center in this field;
b. Organize meetings of experts to recommend measures to bring national curricula into harmony with Latin American integration goals;
c. Organize regional volunteer teacher programs;
d. Extend inter-American cooperation to the preservation and use of archeological, historic, and artistic monuments.

3. Expansion of OAS programs for fellowships, student loans, and teacher exchange.

National educational and cultural development efforts will be evaluated in coordination by CIAP and the Inter-American Council for Education, Science, and Culture (now the Inter-American Cultural Council).

B. *Science and technology*

Advances in scientific and technological knowledge are changing the economic and social structure of many nations. Science and technology offer infinite possibilities for providing the people with the well-being that they seek. But in Latin American countries the potentialities that this wealth of the modern world offers have by no means been realized to the degree and extent necessary.

Science and technology offer genuine instruments for Latin American progress and must be given an unprecedented impetus at this time. This effort calls for inter-American cooperation, in view of the magnitude of the investments required and the level attained in such knowledge. In the same way, their organization and implementation in each country cannot be effected without a properly planned scientific and technological policy within the general framework of development.

For the above reasons the Presidents of the member states of the OAS agree upon the following measures:

Internal efforts

Establishment, in accordance with the needs and possibilities of each country, of national policies in the field of science and technology, with the necessary machinery and funds, the main elements of which shall be:

1. Promotion of professional training for scientists and technicians and an increase in their numbers.

2. Establishment of conditions favoring full utilization of the scientific and technological potential for solving the economic and social problems of Latin America, and to prevent the exodus of persons qualified in these fields.

3. Encouragement of increased private financial contributions for scientific and technological research and teaching.

Multinational efforts

1. Establishment of a Regional Scientific and Technological Development Program designed to advance science and technology to a degree that they will contribute substantially to accelerating the economic development and well-being of their peoples and make it feasible to engage in pure and applied scientific research of the highest possible quality. This Program shall complement Latin American national programs in the area of science and technology and shall take special account of the characteristics of each of the countries.

2. The Program shall be oriented toward the adoption of measures to promote scientific and technological research, teaching, and information; basic and advanced training of scientific personnel; and ex-

change of information. It shall promote intensively the transfer to, and adaptation by, the Latin American countries of knowledge and technologies originating in other regions.

3. The Program shall be conducted through national agencies responsible for scientific and technological policy, through institutions—national or international, public or private—either now existing or to be established in the future.

4. As part of the Program, they propose that multinational technological and scientific training and research institutions at the postgraduate level be established, and that institutions of this nature already existing in Latin America be strengthened. A group, composed of high-ranking, qualified persons, experienced in science, technology, and university education, shall be established to make recommendations to the Inter-American Council for Education, Science, and Culture (now the Inter-American Cultural Council) on the nature of such multinational institutions, including such matters as their organization, the characteristics of their multinational administration, financing, location, coordination of their activities among themselves and with those of pertinent national institutions, and on the other aspects of their operation. The aforementioned group, selected and convoked by the Inter-American Council for Education, Science, and Culture (now the Inter-American Cultural Council) or, failing this, by CIAP, shall meet within 120 days after the close of this meeting.

5. In order to encourage the training of scientific and technological personnel at the higher academic levels, they resolve that an Inter-American Fund for Scientific and Technological Training shall be established as part of the Program, so that scientists and research workers from Latin American countries may pursue advanced scientific and technological studies, with the obligation to engage in a period of scientific work in Latin America.

6. The Program shall be promoted by the Inter-American Council for Education, Science, and Culture (now the Inter-American Cultural Council), in cooperation with CIAP. They shall coordinate their activities with similar activities of the United Nations and other interested organizations.

7. The Program may be financed by contributions of the member states of the inter-American system, inter-American or international institutions, technologically advanced countries, universities, foundations, and private individuals.

C. *Health*

Improvement of health conditions is fundamental to the economic and social development of Latin America.

Available scientific knowledge makes it possible to obtain specific results, which, in accordance with the needs of each country and the provisions of the Charter of Punta del Este, should be utilized to attain the following objectives:

a. Control of communicable diseases and eradication of those for which methods for total elimination exist. Pertinent programs shall receive international coordination when necessary.
b. Acceleration of programs for providing drinking-water supplies, sewerage, and other services essential to environmental sanitation in rural and urban areas, giving preference to lower-income groups. On the basis of studies carried out and with the cooperation of international financing agencies, national revolving fund systems shall be used to assure the continuity of such programs.
c. Greater and more rapid progress in improving nutrition of the neediest groups of the population, taking advantage of all possibilities offered by national effort and international cooperation.
d. Promotion of intensive mother and child welfare programs and of educational programs on overall family guidance methods.
e. Priority for basic and advanced training of professional, technical, administrative, and auxiliary personnel, and support of operational and administrative research in the field of health.
f. Incorporation, as early as the preinvestment phase, of national and regional health programs into general development plans.

The Presidents of the member states of the OAS, therefore, decide:

1. To expand, within the framework of general planning, the preparation and implementation of national plans that will strengthen infrastructure in the field of health.

2. To mobilize internal and external resources to meet the needs for financing these plans. In this connection, to call upon CIAP, when analyzing the health sector in national development programs, to take into account the objectives and needs indicated.

3. To call upon the Pan American Health Organization to cooperate with the governments in the preparation of specific programs relating to these objectives.

Chapter VI

ELIMINATION OF UNNECESSARY MILITARY EXPENDITURES

The Latin American Presidents, conscious of the importance of the armed forces in maintaining security, at the same time recognize that the demands of economic development and social progress make it necessary to apply the maximum resources available in Latin America to these ends.

Consequently, they express their intention to limit military expenditures in proportion to the actual demands of national security, in accordance with each country's constitutional provisions, avoiding those expenditures that are not indispensable for the performance of the specific duties of the armed forces and, where pertinent, of international commitments that obligate their respective governments.

With regard to the Treaty on the Banning of Nuclear Arms in Latin America they express the hope that it may enter into force as soon as possible, once the requirements established by the Treaty are fulfilled.

DONE at Punta del Este, Uruguay, in the English, French, Portuguese, and Spanish languages, this Pan American Day, the fourteenth of April of the year one thousand nine hundred sixty-seven, the seventy-seventh anniversary of the founding of the inter-American system.

Juan Carlos Onganía
President of Argentina

Arturo Costa e Silva
President of Brazil

Carlos Lleras Restrepo
President of Colombia

Eduardo Frei Montalva
President of Chile

José Joaquín Trejos Fernández
President of Costa Rica

Fidel Sánchez
President Elect of El Salvador

Lyndon B. Johnson
President of the United States of America

Julio César Méndez Montenegro
President of Guatemala

Arthur Bonhomme
Representative of the President of Haiti

Oswaldo López A.
President of Honduras

Gustavo Díaz Ordaz
President of Mexico

Lorenzo Guerrero
President of Nicaragua

Marco A. Robles
President of Panama

Alfredo Stroessner
President of Paraguay

Fernando Balaúnde Terry
President of Peru

Joaquín Balaguer
President of the Dominican Republic

Eric Williams
Prime Minister of Trinidad and Tobago

Raúl Leoni
President of Venezuela

APPENDIX

BIBLIOGRAPHY ON ECONOMIC INTEGRATION

IN LATIN AMERICA[1]

By

HELEN L. CLAGETT

Books and Pamphlets

Agreement establishing the Central American Bank for Economic Integration. [n.p.] 1961. 11 leaves (pamphlet).

Aguiar—*See* Pinto de Aguiar.

Aguilar Silles, Oscar. El Tratado de Montevideo y la integración de América Latina. Mexico, 1963. 229 p. [Thesis, Univ. of Mexico].

Ajia Keizai Kenkyujo, *Tokyo*. [Title first in Japanese]. Bibliography on the economic integration in Latin America. Tokyo, Institute of Asian Economic Affairs, 1964. 56 p.

Argentine Republic. Consejo Federal de Inversiones. Zona latinoamericana de libre comercio; reseña jurídica; trabajo elaborado por Alberto Ricardo González Arzac, asesor del Consejo. Buenos Aires, 1963. 110 p.

————. Dirección Nacional de Estadística y Censos. Intercambio comercial argentino con los países de la A.L.A.L.C. Buenos Aires, 1962. 16 p.

Arias, G. Mercado común. Estudio de la C.E.P.A.L. Panama, 1962.

Asociación Latinoamericana de Libre Comercio. Acta de negociaciones. Montevideo, 1962. (Various pagings).

————. Lista consolidada de concesiones. Montevideo, 1965. 2 vols.

————. Argentina: lista nacional y listas especiales para Ecuador y Paraguay. Montevideo, 1963. 1 vol. unpaged.

————. Chile: lista nacional y listas especiales para Ecuador y Paraguay. Montevideo, 1963. 1 vol. unpaged.

————. Colombia: lista nacional y listas especiales para Ecuador y Paraguay. Montevideo, 1963. 1 vol. unpaged.

————. Ecuador: lista nacional y lista especial para Paraguay. Montevideo, 1963. 1 vol. unpaged.

————. Estados Unidos de Brasil: lista nacional y listas especiales para Ecuador y Paraguay. Montevideo, 1963. 1 vol. unpaged.

————. Paraguay: lista nacional y lista especial para Ecuador. Montevideo, 1963. 1 vol. unpaged.

————. Peru: lista nacional y listas especiales para Ecuador y Paraguay. Montevideo, 1963. 1 vol. unpaged.

————. Uruguay: lista nacional y lista especiales para Ecuador y Paraguay. Montevideo, 1963. 1 vol. unpaged.

---

[1] Items are divided into "Books and pamphlets," "Articles in Periodicals" and "Legislation." Selected items are included on related matters such as Alliance for Progress, economic development, etc., where there is any substantial discussion on CACM or LAFTA.

————. Comité Provisional. La Asociación Latinoamericana de Libre Comercio. Buenos Aires, 1961. 75 p.

————. Reunión de la Comisión Especial de la ALALC. Montevideo, Uruguay, 7 a 18 de septiembre de 1964. México, Banco de Comercio Exterior, 1964, 41 págs.

Aspectos legales de la Asociación Latinoamericana de Libre Comercio. Seminario organizado por Federación Interamericana de Abogados, Facultad de Derecho y Ciencias Sociales del Uruguay [y] Colegio de Abogados del Uruguay, realizado en Montevideo del 20 al 29 de noviembre de 1963. Montevideo, 1966. 482 p.

Avances y obstáculos en la ALALC vistos por los representantes de sus países miembros. México, Publicaciones Especializadas, 1963. 149 p. [Individual essays on progress of LAFTA contributed by the nine countries].

Baerresen, Donald W. Latin American trade patterns by . . ., Martin Carnoy and Joseph Grunwald. Washington, Brookings Institution, 1965. 329 p. [Part 3 on common markets. Bibliography 325–329.]

Balassa, Bela A. El desarrollo económico y la integración. Mexico, Centro de Estudios Monetarios Latinoamericanos, 1965. 151 p.

————. Economic development and integration. Mexico, Centro de Estudios Monetarios Latinoamericanos, 1965. 157 p.

————. Integración económica y desarrollo de América Latina. Mexico, Centro de Estudios Monetarios Latinoamericanos, 1964.

————. La teoría de la integración económica. Mexico, Uteha, 1964. 350 p.

Baltra Cortés, Alberto. Crecimiento económico de América Latina; problemas fundamentales. Santiago de Chile, Edit. del Pacífico, 1959. 260 p.; 4. ed. 1964. 288 p.

————. El futuro económico de Chile y de América Latina por . . ., Felipe Herrera y René Silva. Santiago de Chile, Edit. Universitaria, 1957. 129 p.

Banco de México, Departmento de Investigaciones Industriales. Información del mercado común y bibliografía preliminar sobre actividades económicas de los países latinoamericanos. Mexico, 1960. 86 p. (Servicio Bibliografíco y Archivo Técnico).

————. La planeación económica regional. Una política nacional de desarrollo regional; por Lloyd Rodwin. Introducción a la planeación regional, por Sergio de la Peña. Mexico, Banco de México, 1960. 140 pp.

Banco Interamericano de Desarrollo—See Inter-American Development Bank.

Banco Nacional de Comercio Exterior, S.A., Mexico. La integración económica latinoamericana. Mexico, 1963. 957 p. [Selection of articles published in Comercio Exterior, 1957–1963].

Basulto Verduzco, Daniel. El problema del origen de las mercancías en la Asociación Latinomericana de Libre Comercio. Mexico, 1964. 161 p. (Thesis).

Black, Eugene Robert. Tales of two continents: Africa and South America. Athens, Univ. of Georgia, 1961. 36 p. (Ferdinand Phinizy lectures).

Brown, Robert T. Transport and the economic integration of South America. Washington, Brookings Institution, Transport Research Program, 1965. 288 p.

Business International Corporation, New York. LAFTA: Key to Latin America's 200 million consumers. New York, 1966. 67 p.

————. Latin America's merging market; the challenge of economic integration. New York, 1964. 55 p.

————. Winning the Colombian market operating in and from a gateway to LAFTA. New York, 1964. 41 p.

Calderón Martínez, Antonio. De la ALALC al mercado común lationamericano; análisis de algunos problemas para la formación de la tarifa externa común. Mexico, 1964. 161 p. (Thesis).

Castillo, Carlos M. Growth and integration in Central America. New York, Praeger, 1966. 188 p.

Centro de Estudios Monetarios Latinoamericanos. Cooperación financiera en América Latina (Documentos preparados para la última (VII) Reunión Operativa del CEMLA cuyo tema general fué "Contribución de los sistemas financieros a la integración económica de América Latina," y que se celebró en México del 3 al 14 de septiembre de 1962, Mexico, 1963. 293 p.

Clark, John W. Economic regionalism and the Americas. New York, Hauser Press, 1966. 64 p.

Cole, John P. Latin America; an economic and social geography. London, Butterworths, 1965. 468 p. [Chapter 10 on Central America, and Chapter 20 on Foreign Trade and Economic Union].

Committee for Economic Development. Cooperation for progress in Latin America. New York, 1961. 56 p.

———. Economic development of Central America; a statement on national policy by the Research and Policy Committee of the Committee for Economic Development. New York, 1964. 123 p. (English and Spanish texts).

Conference on Latin America. London, 1964. Latin America; prospect and challenge, official report. London, Hispanic and Luso-Brazilian Councils, 1964. 79 p.

Conference on Tensions Development in the Western Hemisphere. Salvador, Brazil, 1962. Latin America: Evolution or Explosion? Edited by Mildred Adams. New York, Dodd, Mead, 1963. 277 p.

Conferencia de Organismos de Fomento de la Producción de la Estabilización de Precios del Istmo Centroamericano. 1st, Guatemala, 1958. Memoria. Guatemala, 1958. 1 vol (various pagings.)

Cruz de Schlesinger, Lucía and Marta S. Fernández. Proyecciones de demanda para Colombia de trece productos industriales, 1965–67. Proyecto sobre interacción económica regional de industrias dentro del area de la A.L.A.L.C. Bogotá, 1965.

Dell, Sidney Samuel. A Latin American common market? London, Issued under auspices of the Royal Institute of International Affairs by Oxford Univ. Press, 1966. 336 p.

———. Problemas de un mercado común latinoamericano. Mexico, Centro de Estudios Monetarios Latinoamericanos, 1959. 219 p.

———. Trade blocs and common markets. New York, A. A. Knopf, 1963. 384 p. (See chapters on LAFTA and CACM).

Dyer, John M. United States—Latin American trade and financial relations. Coral Gables, Fla., Univ. of Miami Press, 1961. 188 p.

Economic Conference of the Organization of American States. Buenos Aires, 1957. Summary of the basic documents presented to the Economic Conference. Washington, Pan American Union, 1957. 57 p.

———. Liberalización del comercio inter-latinoamericano. Buenos Aires, Doc. No. 3, Pan American Union. Washington, 1957.

Ehrman, Libert. Opportunities for investment in Chile: a program for encouragement of private industry. New York, Published for Surveys & Research Corp. by Praeger, 1966. 169 p. (Contract with Agency for International Development).

Escobar Cerda, Luis. Organización para el desarrollo económico. Santiago de Chile, Edit. Universitaria, 1961. 187 p.

Fernández-Shaw, Félix Guillermo. La integración de Centro América. Madrid, Ediciones Cultura Hispánica, 1965. 1086 p. (Appendix of documents, and bibliography).

Ferrer, Aldo. The Argentine economy. Berkeley, University of California Press, 1967. 239 p. (Translated by Marjory M. Urquidi).

Ferrero, Rómulo A. El mercado común latinoamericano. Lima, Cámara de Comercio de Lima, 1959. 23 p.

First National City Bank of New York. Central American community—a report on economic conditions and progress towards integration. New York, 1961. 11 p.

Flores Rodríguez, Roberto. La integración industrial latinoamericana y la política industrial de México. Mexico, 1964. 183 p. (Thesis).

Foreign private investment in the Latin American Free Trade Area; report of the consultant group jointly appointed by the Economic Commission for Latin America and the Organization of American States. New York, United Nations Department of Economic and Social Affairs, 1961. 30 p.

García Reynoso, Plácido. Integración económica latinoamericana. Primera etapa 1960–1964. Mexico, 1965.

General Agreement on Tariffs and Trade (GATT). Central American free trade area. Entry into force of instruments for El Salvador, Guatemala and Nicaragua. (Doc. L/1058. Oct. 12, 1959).

———. Central American free trade area. First annual report by the government of Nicaragua, including Central American agreement on the equalization of import duties and charges. (Doc. L/1303/Add. 1, Oct. 12, 1960).

———. Central American free trade area. Participation of Nicaragua (Docs. L/1302/Add. 2, Nov. 12, 1960; L/1302/Sept. 30, 1960; L/891, Oct. 23, 1958; L/1639, Nov. 22, 1961).

Gerassi, John. The great fear; the reconquest of Latin America by Latin Americans. New York, Macmillan, 1963. 457 p.

Gnazzo, Edison. Integración económica de América Latina, por . . . y Roberto González Casal. Montevideo, 1960. 66 p. (Facultad de Ciencias Económicas y de Administración. Universidad. Instituto de la Hacienda Pública).

González Laris Casillas, Jorge Eduardo. La integración económica latinoamericana. Mexico, 1960. 180 p. (Thesis).

Gordon, Lincoln. A new deal for Latin America: the Alliance for Progress. Cambridge, Mass., Harvard Univ. Press, 1963. 146 p. (Also Portuguese text).

Gordon, Wendell C. The political economy of Latin America. New York, Columbia University Press, 1965. 401 p. [Chapter 21 on "Common Markets"].

Gutiérrez Olivos, Sergio. Subdesarrollo, integración, y alianza. Buenos Aires, Emecé editores, 1963. 189 p.

Haas, Ernst B. The politics of economics in Latin American regionalism; the Latin American Free Trade Association after four years of operation, by . . . and Philippe C. Schmitter. Denver, University of Denver, 1965. 78 p.

Hacia la integración acelerada de América Latina: Proposiciones a los presidentes latinoamericanos presentados por José Antonio Mayobre [et al]. Con un estudio técnico de CEPAL. México, Fondo de Cultura Económica, 1965. 195 p.

A handbook of facts for persons considering investments. San José, Costa Rica, Imprenta Nacional, 1963.

Hartmann, Hans Joachim. América Latina y la Comunidad Económica Europea; nuevas bases de cooperación, por . . . y Jurgen Westphalen. [versión castellana: Ramón Jovani]. Hamburg, Ubersee-Verlag, 1965. 96 p.

Herrarte, Alberto. Panamá en la integración centroamericana. Guatemala, Edit. del Ministerio de Educación Pública, José de Pineda Ibarra, 1961. 83 p.

Herrera Lane, Felipe. Address prepared for delivery at the Conference of the contracting parties of the Latin American Free Trade Association, second period of sessions, in Mexico, D.F., on Aug. 28, 1962. Washington, D.C. Inter-American Development Bank, 1962. 14 p.

———. América Latina: integración económica y reintegración política. Washington, BID, 1962. 29 p.; Publ. also in Bahia, Brazil, 1963. 29 p.

————. América Latina integrada. Buenos Aires, Losada, S.A., 1964. 249 p.

Hirshman, Alberto O. (editor). Latin American issues: essays and comments. New York, Twentieth Century Fund, 1961. 201 p. (Includes essays by Raymond Mikesell, "The Movement toward regional trading groups in Latin America," and by Victor Urquidi "The common market as a tool of economic development.") (Spanish translation also).

Honduras. Consejo Nacional de Economía. Plan nacional de desarrollo económico y social de Honduras, 1965–69. Tegucigalpa, Secretaría del Consejo Nacional de Economía, 1965. 4 vols.

Illanes Benítez, Fernando. El sistema económico interamericano: problemas y posibilidades. Santiago de Chile, Edit. Andrés Bello, 1963. 82 p.

Instituto Interamericano de Estudios Jurídicos Internacionales. Instrumentos relativos a la integración económica en América Latina. Washington, D.C., 1964. 345 p. [Bibliography pages 325–345].

Instituto Torcuato di Tella. Centro de Investigaciones Económicas. Argentina en la A.L.A.L.C.; estadísticas comerciales, 1959–1963. Buenos Aires, 1963. 47 p. (On Project 15: "Costos industriales comparados con los países de la ALALC").

Inter-American Conference. 11th Quito, 1961. América y sus problemas económicos sociales; conferencias. Quito, Edit. La Unión Católica, 1961.

Inter-American Development Bank. Economic integration; financial aspects. Caracas, April, 1963. [Also in Spanish, Caracas, 1963].

————. Factores para la integración latinoamericana. México, Fondo de Cultura Económica, 1966. 247 p.

————. Programa de integración económica de Centroamérica. March 17, 1961 11 p. and appendix (Document DEI/61–9).

Inter-American Economic and Social Council. Alianza para el progreso; documentos oficiales emanados de la reunión extraordinaria del Consejo Interamericano Económico y Social al nivel ministerial, Punta del Este, Uruguay, 5 a 17 de agosto de 1961. Montevideo, 1961. 65 p.

————. 1st Annual Meeting, Mexico, October, 1962. Consultation on economic and social development planning. Report of Meeting of February–March 1962 at Santiago, Chile, Washington, D.C., Pan American Union, 1962. 135 p.

Inter-American Institute of International Legal Studies. SEE ALSO: Instituto Interamericano de Estudios Jurídicos Internacionales. (See complete list of the Institute's publications on pp. 451-452.

————. Seminar on legal and institutional aspects of Central American integration. Report of the General Secretariat. Washington, 1964. (Also Spanish text). [Center for Advanced International Studies, University of Miami, August 17–21, 1964].

International Bank for Reconstruction and Development. World Bank activities in Latin America; a report for the Economic Conference of the Organization of American States, Buenos Aires, 1957. Washington, 1957. 62 p.

————. The World Bank and IDA in the Americas: a summary of activities. Washington, 1962. 103 p.

International Economic Association. El desarrollo económico y América Latina; trabajos y comentarios presentados en la Conferencia de la Asociación Económica Internacional celebrada en Rio de Janeiro en agosto de 1957. Mexico, Fondo de Cultura Económica, 1960. 553 p.

————. Economic development for Latin America; proceedings of a conference held by the International Economic Association. Edited by Howard S. Ellis. New York, St. Martin's Press, 1961. 478 p.

Johnson, Warren Eames. The Montevideo Treaty for a Latin American Free Trade Area (In International Trade, Investment and Organization, edited by Wayne R. LeFave and Peter Hay. Chicago, Univ. of Chicago Press, 1967).

Jordán Sandoval, Santiago. Alternativa de Bolivia para ingresar a la zona de libre comercio. La Paz, Min. de Educación y Bellas Artes, 1962. 101 p. (Oficialía Mayor de Cultura Nacional).

Jornadas "Chile y la Zona Libre de Comercio." Chile y la ALALC; un análisis en profundidad. Santiago de Chile, Edit. del Pacífico, 1963. 143 p.

Latin American Free Trade Association. *Comité Intersecretarial Mexicana de la ALALC.* Documentos informativos del Comité Provisional de Montevideo en relación con la Zona Latinoamericana de Libre Comercio. Mexico, Banco de Mexico, S.A., 1961.

Lauterbach, Albert T. Enterprise in Latin America; business attitudes in a developing economy. Ithaca, N.Y., Cornell University Press, 1966. 207 p.

Lawson, R. C. International regional organizations. New York, 1962. (On pages 345–360, material on LAFTA and CACM).

Lima, A. A. Interaccão económica, social é política da América Latina. Rio de Janeiro, Libr. Agir Editora, 1958. 86 p.

Lockley, Lawrence Campbell, A guide to market data in Central America. Tegucigalpa, 1964. 161 p. [Central American Bank for Economic Integration].

Lower, Milton D. Some aspects of Latin American trade policies; three essays by M. D. Lower, Raymond E. Hannigan and Rudolf K. Jansen. Austin, Bureau of Business Research, University of Texas, 1964. 83 p.

Loyola Montemayor, Elias. Los productos agrícolas en la Asociación Latinoamericana de Libre Comercio. México, 1964. 264 p. (Theses).

MacLeish, William H. Experiment in union: Latin America broadens its market. New York, Vision, Inc., 1961. 24 p.

Mallory, Lester Dewitt. Social implications of the Act of Bogotá. Washington, Department of State, 1961. 15 p.

Massad, Carlos. La zona de libre comercio en América; algunos problemas por resolver; por Carlos Massad y John Strasma. Santiago de Chile, Inst. de Economía, Univ. de Chile, 1961. 39 p.

Mayobre, José Antonio. The economic realities of Latin America, by the Venezuelan Minister of Finance at the Commission of the 21, in Bogotá. Caracas, Impr. Nacional, 1960. 14 p. (Spanish edition, 16 p.).

McLean Cortina, Carlos. América Latina y un mercado común; ensayo de fundamentación de una organización económica de los países de América. Bogotá, 1962. 89 p. (Thesis).

McVicker, Roy H. Central America: some observations on its common market, binational centers and housing programs. Washington, U.S. Govt. Printing Office, 1966. 33 p. [89th Cong., 2d Sess. Subcommittee on Inter-American Affairs].

Mexico City. Cámara Nacional de Comercio. El Tratado de Montevideo y la Asociación Latinoamericana de Libre Comerico. Ciclo de conferencias. Mexico, 1960. 144 p.

Mexico. Dirección General de Estudios Hacendarios. La Asociación Latinoamericana de Libre Comercio. Mexico, Sec. de Hacienda y Crédito Público, 1960–61. 3 vols.

Mikesell, Raymond F. Liberalization of inter-Latin American trade (Topic III, item B of the Agenda). Washington, Pan American Union, 1957. 94 p. (Economic Conference of the Organization of American States, Buenos Aires, 1957).

———. (*See also* contribution in Hirschman's Latin American Issues).

Morgan Guaranty Trust Company of New York. The Central American common market. New York. International Banking Division, Morgan Guaranty Trust, 1964. 35 p.

Musich, Arnaldo T. La política económica argentina y su proyección internacional. Buenos Aires, Editorial Concordia, 1962. 103 p.

Myrdal, Gunnar. Solidaridad o desintegración. 2. ed. Mexico, Fondo de Cultura Económica, 1963.

National Planning Association. United States-Latin American relations; United States and Latin American policies affecting their economic relations. A study prepared at the request of the Subcommittee on American Republics Affairs of the Committee on Foreign Relations, U.S. Senate, No. 5. Washington, Government Printing Office, 1960. 140 p. (86th Cong., 2d sess. Committee print).

Nye, Joseph S. Central American regional integration. New York, Carnegie Endowment for International Peace, 1967. 66 p. [International Conciliation, No. 572].

Organization of American States. General Secretariat. Latin American economic integration. Official records of OAS-OEA/Ser. H/X, 1-ES-Re-Doc. 3, 1961.

———. Secretary General. Development of regional markets in Latin America; background information. Washington, Pan American Union, 1958. 17 p. (Also Spanish).

Ortiz Urzúa, Gastón. La Asociación Latinoamericana de Libre Comercio y el Tratado de Montevideo. Santiago, Editorial Jurídica de Chile, 1964. 296 p. (Thesis).

Ossío Sanjinés, Luis. Integración económica, defensa de la soberanía de los estados latinoamericanos y motor de su industrialización. Potosí, Bolivia, 1960. 90 p. (Thesis).

[Los] Países de la ALALC vistos desde México. Mexico, Publicaciones Especializadas, 1962. 143 p.

Peaslee, Amos. International governmental organizations. 2. ed. The Hague, 1961 [Vol. 2, pp. 1573–1588].

Peirano Facio, Jorge. Política comercial y desarrollo económico. Montevideo, 1964. 59 p. (Consejo Interamericano de Comercio y Producción, Sección Uruguaya).

Pellegrini, Vicente. Argentina y el Mercado Común Europeo. Buenos Aires, Edit. Sudamericana, 1963. 91 p.

Perlaza Contreras, Santander. Pactos internacionales de comercio. Bogotá, 1965. 67 p. (Thesis).

Perloff, Harvey S. and Romulo Almeida. La integración económica regional. Washington, Pan American Union, Sept. 15, 1963. (CIES/OEA).

Pincus, Joseph. The Central American Common Market. Washington, Department of State, Agency for International Development. Regional Offices for Central America and Panama Affairs, 1962. 231 p.

———. The five Central American economic integration agreements. Washington, U.S. International Cooperation Administration, Public Administration Division, Technical Resources Branch, 1960. 15 p.

Pincus, Joseph. The industrial development laws of Central America. Washington, U.S. Dept. of State, Agency for International Development, Communications Resources Division, 1961. 90 p.

Pinto de Aguiar, Manōel. América Latina, comercio internacional e mercado regional. Salvador, Brasil, Univ. de Bahía, 1958. 83 p.

Pinto Santa Cruz, Aníbal. Chile, una economía difícil. Mexico, Fondo de Cultura Económica, 1964. 184 p.

Ponce Carapia, Antonio. El comercio exterior de México y la Asociación Latinoamericana de Libre Comercio. Mexico, 1964. 118 p. (Thesis).

Postweiler, Rudolph August. Problems concerning the supply and demand for direct United States investment in Latin America for the years 1957–1965. Ann Arbor, Michigan, University Microfilms, 1959. 275 p. (Univ. of Wisconsin thesis).

426 ECONOMIC INTEGRATION IN LATIN AMERICA

Powelson, John P. Latin America; today's economic and social revolution. New York, McGraw-Hill, 1964. 303 p. (Chapter 8 on Economic Integration).

Prat Echaurren, Carlos. Una América grande y generosa; beneficios de la integración, perjuicios de las nacionalizaciones. Santiago de Chile, Edit. del Pacífico, 1963. 189 p.

Prieto Aceves, Carlos. Integración económica y comunidad internacional. Mexico, 1960. 130 p. (Thesis).

Proyecciones del Tratado de Montevideo. Mexico, Editorial Loa, 1962. 103 p.

Puiggrós, Rodolfo. Integración de América Latina; factores ideológicos y políticos. Buenos Aires, J. Alvarez, 1965. 80 p.

Ray, Philip Alexander. South wind red; our hemisphere crisis. Chicago, Reguey, 1962. 242 p.

Rizzuto, Francisco Antonio. Necesidad e idea del mercado común latinoamericano; disertación en la Bolsa de Comercio de Córdoba el 12 de mayo de 1961. Buenos Aires, Veritas Edit., 1961. 29 p.

El Salvador. Ministro de Economía. Program for the economic integration of Central America. San Salvador, 1959. 29 p.

──────. El programa de integración económica de Centroamérica. San Salvador, 1958. 82 p. (Two appendices with treaty and other texts).

San Salvador. Universidad Nacional. Facultad de Ciencias Económicas. Desarrollo económico latinoamericano. San Salvador, Edit. Universitaria, 1962. 99 p.

Schmitter, Philippe C. Mexico and Latin American economic integration, by . . . and Ernest B. Haas. Berkeley, Institute of International Studies, University of California, 1964. 43 p.

Selser, Gregorio. Alianza para el progreso, la mal nacida. Buenos Aires, Ediciones Iguazú, 1964. 133 p. (Colección Documentos, 5).

Seminario de Integración Económica Centroamericana. *1st, San Salvador,* 1957. Integración económica de Centroamérica. San Salvador, Organización de Estados Centroamericanos, Secretaría General, 1959. Vol. 1.

──────. *Seminario de Integración Económica Centroamericana. (SIECA). Secretaría Permanente del Tratado General.* Arancel de aduanas centroamericano. Guatemala, 1964.

Seminario sobre Aplicación y Administración de los Tratados del Mercado Común Centroamericano. San José, Costa Rica, 1961. Informe, San José, 1961. 83 p. (Escuela Superior de Administración Pública, América Central).

Sol, Jorge. (*See* Seminario de Integración Económica, *supra.*)

Solá, Alberto. Asociación Latinoamericana de Libre Comercio. Charla . . . en la Bolsa de Comercio de Caracas el día 25 de abril de 1963. Caracas, Bolsa de Comerico, 1963. 39 p.

Soltero Peralta, Rafael. El Mercado Común, el mundo de hoy y él de mañana. San Juan, P.R., 1962. 86 p.

Stanford Research Institute. International Development Center. Common markets and free trade areas; problems and issues for the United States. Menlo Park, California, 1960. 37 p.

Stark, Harry. Social and economic frontiers in Latin America. Dubuque, Iowa, W. C. Brown Co., 1961. 421 p.

Strasma, John. Reform finance and a Latin American common market; some harmonization problems in tax policy. Madison, Wis., 1965. 38 p.

Streeter, Paul. Economic integration: aspects and problems, 2 ed. Leyden, Sythoff, 1964. 176 p.

Thomas Gallardo, Frank J. Successful entrepreneurship in Central America. San José, Costa Rica, Latin American Business Publications, Ltd., 1964. 184 p.

Tres industrias mexicanas ante la ALALC; siderurgía, manufacturas eléctricas, automotriz. Mexico, Publicaciones Especializadas, 1962. 120 p.

Triffin, Robert. Possibility of effecting multilateral compensation settlements between Latin American and European countries through the European Payments Agreement. Santiago, Chile, March 4, 1956—(United Nations Doc. E/CN.12/299).

United Nations. Central American Economic Cooperation Committee. La integración económica de Centroamérica, 1956. (E/CN.12/422; E/CN.12/CCE/33) revised 2 U.N. Nov. 1956. 98 p.[1]

———. Committee on Economic Integration in the Central American Isthmus. Report of the Committee . . . February 25, 1957 to June 10, 1958. New York; Mexico, May 1959. 72 p. (E/CN.12/CCE/151).

——— ———. Report of the Committee . . . 1958–1959. (E/CN.12/533). New York, 1959. 169 p.

——— ———. Report of the Committee . . . 1959–1960. Mexico, 1960 (E/CN.12/522; also E/CN.12/CCE/224).

——— ———. Report of the 2nd extraordinary meeting (Spanish text) 1960. 13 p. (E/CN.12/542).

United Nations. Economic Commission for Africa. The significance of recent common market developments in Latin America. Addis Ababa, 1960. 90 p. (E/CN.14/64).

——— ———. Economic Commission for Latin America. Central American economic integration and development. New York, United Nations, 1961. (E/CN.12/586).

——— ———. El comercio internacional y el desarrollo de América Latina. Mexico, Fondo de Cultura Económica, 1964. 396 p.

——— ———. Consultations on trade policy; report of the third series of meetings between Colombia, Ecuador and Venezuela. Quito, Dec. 7–10, 1960. Santiago de Chile, 1961. (E/CN.12/555).

——— ———. A contribution to economic integration policy in Latin America. New York, 1965. 185 p. (E/CN.12/728).

——— ———. Economic development, planning and international cooperation. Santiago, Chile, 1961. 65 p.; Caracas, 1961. 76 p.

——— ———. Estudio sobre la posible incorporación de Panamá al mercado común centroamericano (texto preliminar). Documento elaborado por la Secretaría de la CEPAL a solicitud del Gobierno de Panamá. Panama, Departamento de Relaciones Públicas del Ministerio de Hacienda y Tesoro, 1962. 101 p. (Cover-title: Mercado común).

——— ———. Government policies affecting private foreign investment in Latin American regional market. New York, March 28, 1959. 25 p. (E/CN.-12/C. 1/12).

——— ———. Informe del director principal a cargo de la Secretaría Ejecutiva sobre el estado actual del programa de integración y reciprocidad económica centroamericana. New York, 1953. (Various pagings).

——— ———. Inter-Latin American trade; current problems. International cooperation in a Latin American development policy. Study of Inter-Latin American trade and its prospects; Southern zone of Latin America. New York, 1957. 105 p. (E/CN.12/423).

——— ———. The Latin American common market, prepared by the Secretariat of the Economic Commission for Latin America. New York, 1959. 146 p. (E/CN.12/531).

---

[1] Spanish and English texts available for majority of U.N. entries, although not always indicated.

—— ——. The Latin American economy in 1965. New York, 1966. 49 p. (U. N. Doc. E/CN.12/754).

—— ——. The Latin American movement towards multilateral economic integration. Santiago, Chile, March, 1961. (E/CN.12/567).

—— ——. Multilateral economic cooperation in Latin America. New York, 1962. (E/CN.12/621). [Also Spanish text].

—— ——. Papers on financial problems prepared by the Secretariat for the use of the Latin American Free Trade Association. Santiago, Chile, March, 1961. New York. (E/CN.12/569).

—— ——. Política comercial y libre comercio en Centroamérica. July 20, 1955. (E/CN.12/368).

—— ——. Possibilities of integrated industrial development in Central America. New York, United Nations, 1964. 54 p. (E/CN.12/683/rev.1).

—— ——. Problemas y perspectivas del desarrollo industrial latinoameri-cano. Buenos Aires, Solar-Hachette, 1964. 168 p. (U.N. Doc. E/CN.12/664).

—— ——. Recent developments and trends in Latin American trade with the European Economic Community. New York, 1963. 88 p. (E/CN.12/631).

—— ——. Repercusiones fiscales de la equiparación de impuestos a la im-portación y del libre comercio en Centroamérica. New York, 1959. (E/CN. 12/CCE.110, March 20, 1959).

—— ——. Report submitted by the Executive Secretary concerning the programme for economic integration and reciprocity in Central America. New York, 1953. (Various pagings).

—— ——. Report of the Central American Economic Cooperation Commit-tee, Sept. 3, 1959 to December 13, 1960. (E/CN.12/552; also 1961 UN Publ. No. 60 II G.7); Report as of Dec. 13, 1960 to Jan. 29, 1963. (U.N. Doc. E/CN.12/CCE 303 Rev.) 1964.

—— ——. Report of the third special session of Central American economic cooperation committee, San José, Costa Rica, July 23–31, 1962. New York, 1963. 83 p. (E/CN.12/657).

—— ——. Report of the trade committee on the first meeting of the work-ing group on customs matters. Santiago, Chile, March, 1961. (E/CN.12/568).

—— ——. Towards a dynamic development policy for Latin America. New York, April 14, 1963. 155 p. (E/CN.12/680).

—— ——. Committee of the Whole. 7th Session, Santiago, Chile, March 28, 1960. Progress report submitted by the Secretariat concerning the common market programme. New York, 1960. 47 p. (E./CN.12/AC.45/e).

—— ——. Food and Agriculture Organization. The role of agricultural prod-ucts in a regional market, April 7, 1959. (E/CN.12/499).

—— ——. The role of agriculture in the Latin American common market, and free trade area arrangements. Santiago, Chile, January, 1961. (E/CN. 12/551).

—— ——. Trade Committee. Consultations on trade policy. Summary record of meetings held at the ECLA headquarters, Santiago, Chile, August 26, 1958.

—— ——. Sugestiones sobre el mercado regional latinoamericano. Santiago de Chile, January, 1958.

—— ——. Some problems of the Latin American regional market. Santiago, Chile, January 25, 1958. (E/CN.12/C.1/WG.2/2).

U.S. Agency for International Development. The alliance for progress; an Ameri-can partnership. Washington, 1965. 30 p.

——. Regional Office for Central America and Panama Affairs. A collection of some of the most important economic integration treaties of Central America. Unofficial translations compiled by ROCAP. Guatemala, 1964. 1 vol. (Various pagings). Rev. ed. 1966. 186 p.

U.S. *Congress Joint Economic Committee.* Economic developments in South America. Hearings before the Subcommittee on Inter-American Relationships of the Joint Economic Committee, Congress of the United States (87th Cong. 2d sess.) pursuant to Sec. 5 (a) of the Public Law 304 (79th Cong.) May 10–11, 1962. Washington, Government Printing Office, 1962. 151 p. (*Also* Report of Subcommittee, 1962, 12 p.).

———. Economic policies and programs in Middle America. A report of the Subcommittee on Inter-American Relationships, by Representative Martha W. Griffiths. Washington, Government Printing Office, 1962. 31 p. (88th Cong., 1st sess.).

———. Economic policies and programs in South America by the Subcommittee on Inter-American Relationships of the Joint Economic Committee, Congress of the United States (87th Cong. 2d sess.). Washington, Government Printing Office, 1962. 123 p.

———. Latin American development and Western Hemisphere Trade. Hearings . . . Sept. 8, 9 and 10, 1965. Washington, Government Printing Office, 1965. 293 p. (Includes reprinted studies and addresses on LAFTA and CACM in appendix).

U.S. *Congress. Senate. Committee on Foreign Relations.* United States-Latin American relations. Compilation of studies prepared under the direction of the Subcommittee on American Republics Affairs, of the Committee on Foreign Relations. Washington, Government Printing Office, 1960. 827 p. (Study No. 5, pp. 399–539 on United States and Latin American policies affecting their economic relations).

U.S. *Depart. of Commerce. Bureau of International Commerce.* Trade and investment in Central America. Washington, Government Printing Office, 1965. 88 p. (Suppl. to "International Commerce").

U.S. *Department of State. Bureau of Public Affairs.* The Alliance for Progress. (Office of Media Services). Washington, Government Printing Office, 1964. 6 p. (Address by Thomas C. Mann).

U.S. *Library of Congress. Legislative Reference Service.* Free trade, tariff legislation and common markets for the Western Hemisphere; a collection of excerpts and selected references. Prepared by the Economics Division, Legislative Reference Service . . . Washington, Government Printing Office, 1962. 70 p. (U.S. Cong. 87th Cong. 2d sess., House Doc. 598).

U.S. *Tariff Commission.* The Latin American Free Trade Association. Washington, 1962. 21 p. (*Its* T. C. Publication 60).

Urquidi, Victor L. Free trade and economic integration in Latin America; the evolution of a common market policy. Translated from the Spanish by Marjory M. Urquidi. Berkeley, University of California Press, 1962. 190 p.

———. El mercado común y el desarrollo económico nacional. Mexico, Banco Nacional de México, 1959. 26 p.

———. Trayectoria del mercado común latinoamericano. Mexico. Centro de Estudios Monetarios Latinoamericanos, 1960, 178 p. (Appendix contains: Cronología del mercado común. Bibliografía selecta, *and* Tratado de Montevideo).

———. Viabilidad económica de América Latina. Mexico, Fondo de Cultura Económica, 1962. 205 p.

———. (*See also* Hirshman's Latin American Issues).

Venezuela. *Dirección de Comercio Exterior y Consulados.* Mercado común centroamericano. Caracas, 1965. 71 leaves. (*Its* Estudios sobre comercio exterior, 16).

Ventura, Ovidio S. Hacia la integración de Latinoamérica, una salida para los problemas de su desarrollo. Buenos Aires, Edic. Sigla, 1959. 62 p.

Viera Altamirano, Napoleón. Gran Bretaña, el estado tutelar y el Mercado Común otra vez frente a la esfinge. San Salvador, El Diario de Hoy, 1962. 102 p.

————. Instituciones y revoluciones. San Salvador, El Diario de Hoy, 1963. 154 p. (Chapters on "El mercado común latinoamericano y nuestra industrialización" and "La integración económica de Centro América y su mercado común").

Villeda Morales, Ramón (President of Honduras). Discurso al inaugurar la reunión de Ministros de Relaciones Exteriores y de Economía del Istmo Centroamericano. Tegucigalpa, Tip. Nacional, 1961. 17 p.

Weisbord, Albert. Latin America: actuality. New York, Citadel Press, 1964. 256 p. (Occasional references to common markets only).

Wilkinson, Joe R. Latin America and the European Economic Community: an appraisal. Denver, University of Denver, 1965. 65 p.

Wionczek, Miguel S. Integración de la América Latina; experiencias y perspectivas, por Bela Balassa, et al. Mexico, Fondo de Cultura Económica, 1964. 381 p. [Appendix, pp. 331–374, containing documents and bibliography).

————. Latin American economic integration; experiences and prospects. New York, Praeger, 1966. 310 p. (Translation of "Integración de la América Latina").

————. Latin American Free Trade Association. New York, Carnegie Endowment for International Peace, 1965. 80 p.

Wish, John R. Economic development in Latin America; an annotated bibliography. New York, Praeger, 1965. 144 p.

Withers, William. The economic crisis in Latin America. New York, Free Press of Glencoe, 1964. 307 p.

World Peace Through the Rule of Law. Working paper for the First World Conference, Athens, Greece, June 30–July 6, 1963. (American Bar Association's Committee on World Peace Through Law). (Pages 174–184).

Zook, Paul D. Foreign trade and human capital. Dallas, Southern Methodist Univ. Press, 1962. 102 p. (Contains 7 studies).

Periodical Articles, Notes, etc.

"Adam Smith away from home; idea of a Latin American common market". *Economist*, London, 188:448 (Aug. 8, 1958).

"Adiós to Latin tariff barriers". *Business Week*, New York, June 9, 1962, p. 78.

Alemann, Roberto. "Unity south of the Rio Grande". *Statist*, London, 175:101 (Jan. 12, 1962).

Alexander, Robert J. "Development, then trade: the goals of Latin America's common market". *Challenge*, New York, 8:50 (June, 1960).

————. "Trade policies in Latin America". *Current History*, Philadelphia, 43:77–81 (August, 1962).

Allen, Robert Loring. "Integration in less developed areas". *Kyklos, International Review for Social Sciences*, Switzerland, 14:315 (1961).

Almeida, Rómulo. "The rôle of regional organizations in Latin America". *Temas Del B I D* (Banco Interamericano de Desarrollo), Washington. Ed. especial, 1965.

"[Una] América sin fronteras". *Visión, Revista Internacional*, New York. (July, 1961) pp. 64–77.

Andrade M., Carlos. "México en la Zona de Libre Comercio Latinoamericano". *Combate*, San José, Costa Rica, (May–June, 1961) pp. 58–64.

"Argentina to grant Paraguay special concessions in LAFTA". *Foreign Commerce Weekly*, U.S. Dept. of Commerce, 66:21 (1961).

Arnold, Elting. "The rôle of the Inter-American Development Bank with respect to economic integration in Latin America". *Bulletin of Section of International and Comparative Law,* American Bar Association, Chicago. 8:12 (Dec. 1963).

Asociación Latinoamericana de Libre Comercio. "Resoluciones de la II Conferencia de las Partes Contratantes". *El Mercado de Valores,* Semanario de Nacional Financiera, S.A. Mexico, 24:19–33 (Jan. 1964).

"Audiencias del Senado acerca de la participación de México en la Zona Latinoamericana de Libre Comercio". *Comercio Exterior,* Mexico, 10:534 (1960).

Ayensa, Alfonso *and* Juan Bloc. "Comercio de México con los países de América Latina". *Comercio Exterior,* Mexico. 8:398–402 (1960).

Baer, Werner. "The economics of Prebisch and ECLA". *Economic Development and Cultural Change,* Chicago (Univ. of Chicago) 10:169–182 (1962).

Bailey, Norman A. "Common market to rise in Central America". *Magazine of Wall Street,* New York, 112:79 (April 6, 1963).

———. "What prospects for success in Latin American common markets today?" *Magazine of Wall Street,* New York, 107:181–183 (Nov. 5, 1960).

Baranson, Jack. "Industrialización y regionalismo en Centroamérica". *Combate,* San José, Costa Rica, 24:52 (Sept.–Oct. 1962).

———. "Industrialization and regionalism in Central America". *Inter-American Economic Affairs,* Washington, 16:87 (Autumn, 1962).

Barnouin, Jack. "El mercado común y Latinoamérica". *Combate,* San José, Costa Rica, 16:31–38 (May/June, 1961).

"Bases para la formación del mercado regional lationamericano". *Comercio Exterior,* Mexico, 8:66 (1958).

Beaulac, Willard L. "Cooperation in international economic affairs." *U.S. Dept of State Bulletin,* Oct. 21, 1957, p. 647.

Bello, Daniel: "Mercado común latinoamericano. Recomendaciones sobre estructura y normas". *Revista de la Facultad de Ciencias Económicas y de Administración,* Montevideo, Sept., 1959, pp. 1195–1217.

———. Miguel S. Wionczek *and* Victor L. Urquidi. "Tres conferencias sobre mercado común latinoamericano". *Comercio Exterior,* Mexico, 9:641–52 (1959).

Bertrand, Raymond. "Precio, concurrencia y armonización en el mercado común". *Revista del Banco de la Rep. Oriental del Uruguay,* 11:45–53 (Jan. 1958).

Beteta, Ramón. "Una opinión mexicana para América Latina". *Mercado Común América-Latina,* Montevideo, 3:22 (April–May, 1961).

"Blueprint for boom?" *Newsweek,* Dayton, Ohio, 60:62 (Sept. 10, 1962).

Blumenthal, William. "Trade problems and the Alliance for Progress; address". *U.S. Dept. of State Bulletin,* Washington, 47:777–82 (Nov. 19, 1962).

Bolton, George (Sir). "Problems of economic development in Latin America". *International Affairs,* London, 39:184–97 (April, 1963).

Branco, R. "Brazilian finances and their implication for economic integration". *Inter-American Economic Affairs,* Washington, D.C. 19:87–97 (Autumn, 1965).

Brewster, J. Alan. "The Central American program for integrated industrial development". *Public and International Affairs,* Princeton, N. J., 4:12 (Spring, 1966).

Bueno, Gerardo M. "El financiamiento de las exportaciones y la Zona Latinoamericana de Libre Comercio". *Comercio Exterior,* Mexico, 10:672 (1960).

———. "La zona de libre comercio y el problema de pagos". *Comercio Exterior,* Mexico, 10:77–81 (1960).

"Buglecall for Latin unity". *Economist,* London, 215:506 (May 1, 1965).

Burck, Gilbert, "Latin America: bureaucracy or the market?" *Fortune,* Chicago, 65:85 (Feb. 1962).

"Business picks up in Nicaragua, boosted by high export earnings. Central American treaty ratified". *Foreign Commerce Weekly*, U.S. Dept. of Commerce, 66:7 (1961).

Calderón M., Antonio. "Hacia el mercado común en América Latina". *Comercio Exterior*, Mexico, 9:17 (1959).

———. "Problemas de comercio entre los países latinoamericanos". *Comercio Exterior*, Mexico, 7:17 (1957).

Campos Salas, Octaviano. "El Banco Centroamericano de Integración Económica". *Revista de Economía*, Mexico, 24: 239 (July, 1961).

———. "Comercio inter-latinoamericano e integración regional". *Comercio Exterior*, Mexico, 9:595 (1959).

———. "La Zona de Libre Comercio de América Latina". *Comercio Exterior*, Mexico, 10:140 (1960).

———. "La Zona de Libre Comercio de América Latina". *Nuevos Aspectos de la Política Económica*, Mexico, Universidad, 1960, pp. 131–139.

Cárdenas, José C. "El mercado común lationamericano y sus proyecciones en el desarrollo regional y nacional". *Boletin del Banco Central del Ecuador*, Quito, 32:15–35 (Jan.–Feb. 1959). Also: *Boletin Trimestral de Informaciones Económicas*, March, 1959, pp. 32–73.

Carrillo Flores, Antonio. "Cooperación economica interamericana". *Foro Internacional*, Mexico, 1:1–13 (July–Sept. 1960).

Castellanos, Diego L. "Algunos aspectos del mercado común y la Asociación Latinoamericana de Libre Comercio en relación con la economía venezolana". *Comercio Exterior*, Mexico, Vol. 12, 1962, p. 239.

Castillo, Luciano *and* Julio Olavarría A. "Influencia de la Zona Latinoamericana de Libre Comercio en el derecho comercial de los países que la integran". *Revista de Derecho Mercantil*, Madrid, 36:399 (Oct.–Dec., 1963).

"Central America closes ranks". *Business Week*, N.Y., March 16, 1963, pp. 47–8.

"Central America. Regional integration". *Quarterly Review of the Bank of London and South America, Ltd.*, 4:36–46 (Jan. 1964).

"Central America set for growth". *Engineering News Record*, N.Y., 170:57 (Mar. 21, 1963).

"Central American common market moves closer to fully integrated status". *Business International*, N.Y., Feb. 23, 1962, p. 3.

"Central American common market two-week experts conference ended". *Business International*, N.Y., Feb. 9, 1962, p. 8.

"The Central American community". *Latin American Business Highlights*, Chase-Manhattan Bank, N.Y., 9:1–5 (No. 4, 1959).

"Central American countries create common market". *Foreign Commerce Weekly*, U.S. Dept. of Commerce, Washington, 66:7 (1961).

"Central American economic integration moves apace; uniform duties set". *Foreign Commerce Weekly*, U.S. Dept. of Commerce, 66:31 (No. 17, 1961).

"Central American economic protocols signed". *Foreign Commerce Weekly*, U.S. Dept. of Commerce, 64:8 (No. 2, 1960).

"Central American integration in economics, education and culture". *United Nations Review*, New York, 3:62 (Sept. 1956).

"Central American plans for economic integration". *United Nations Review*, New York, 3:10 (Sept. 1956).

"Central Americans draw closer". *Business Week*, N.Y., March 2, 1957, p. 100.

"Central Americans take lead in race for world's first total common market". *Business International*, N.Y., Jan. 5, 1962, p. 6.

Centro de Estudios Monetarios Latinoamericanos. "Contribución de los sistemas financieros a la integración económica latinoamericana. Relatorias de la VII Reunión Operativa de la C.E.M.L.A." *Técnicas Financieras(CEMLA)*, Mexico, 2:3–121 (Sept.–Oct. 1962).

Chamaro, Pedro Ramón. "El Tratado: un medio de negociación permanente". *Mercado Común, América-Latina,* Montevideo, 6:9 (Feb. 1960).

Cintra, Nivaldo Ulmoa. "O mercado regional latinoamericano". *Digesto Económico,* São Paulo, Brasil. 15:115 (Jan.–Feb. 1959).

Cochrane, J. D. "Central American economic integration". *Américas,* Washington, 18:1–5 (May, 1966).

———. "Central American economic integration: the 'integrated industries' scheme". *Inter-American Economic Affairs,* Washington, 19:63 (Autumn, 1965).

———. "U.S. attitudes toward Central American integration". *Inter-American Economic Affairs,* Washington, 18:73 (Autumn, 1964).

"Colombia grants LAFTA concessions—effective April 1, 1962". *Foreign Commerce Weekly,* U.S. Dept. of Commerce, 67:627 (No. 15, 1962).

"Comentarios de la prensa latinoamericana sobre el Tratado de Montevideo". *Comercio Exterior,* Mexico, 10:195 (1960).

"Comité Ejecutivo Permanente de la Asociación Latinoamericana de Libre Comercio, 1962. El problema del transporte en la ALALC y sus vinculaciones con el desarrollo económico general de la Zona". *La Marina Mercante Argentina,* Buenos Aires, 1962, pp. 176 et seq.

"Common market for Latin America". *United Nations Review,* N.Y., 5:46 (Oct. 1958).

"Common market for Latin America". *U.S. News and World Report,* 58:93 (May 3, 1965).

"Common market: Argentine-Brazilian doubts". *Review of the River Plate,* Buenos Aires, April 30, 1965, p. 132.

"Common markets south of the border". *Dun's Review and Modern Industry,* N.Y., 81:51 (March, 1963).

"Concesiones acordadas en la primera serie de negociaciones de las partes contratantes del Tratado de Montevideo". *Comercio Exterior,* Mexico, 11:Supp. (Dec. 1961).

"Conferencia económica interamericana de la Organización de Estados Americanos. Declaración económica de Buenos Aires". *Boletin de la Dirección General Impositiva,* Buenos Aires, 7:255 (Oct. 1957).

Cornejo, B. "Common market for Latin America?" *The Rotarian,* Evanston, Ill., 96:28 (March, 1960).

Correa Avila, Carlos M. "El mercado común europeo, la Zona de Libre Comercio Latinoamericano, y el intercambio con América Latina; la Asociación Europea de Libre Comercio". *Revista de la Cámara Argentina de Comercio,* Buenos Aires, 337:49–63 (2. trim. 1960).

"Curious common marketing". *Time,* Chicago, 81:82 (Jan. 25, 1963).

Daza, A. M. "Comentarios sobre la integración económica iberoamericana". *Moneda y Crédito,* Madrid, 62:49–57 (Sept. 1957).

"Declaration of the Presidents of America (signed at Punta del Este, Uruguay April 14, 1967)". *The Dept. of State Bulletin,* Washington, 56:712 (May 8, 1967).

Delegación de la Barra Mexicana ante el Seminario sobre aspectos legales de la ALALC. "México y la Asociación Latinoamericana de Libre Comercio". *El Foro,* Mexico, 43:31 (Oct.–Dec. 1963).

Dell, Sidney S. "Métodos alternativos para establecer un mercado común". *Mercado Común América-Latina,* Montevideo, 8:7–12 (Aug. 1960).

———. "Las perspectivas del Tratado de Montevideo". *Panorama Económico,* Santiago de Chile, May, 1960, pp. 117–119.

———. "El Tratado de Montevideo". *Boletin Quincenal, Centro de Estudios Monetarios Latinoamericanos,* Mexico, April, 1960, suppl., pp. 89–92.

Delmas, G. "Togetherness in Central America; urge toward reunion". *Reporter,* 34:34–37 (April 7, 1966).

Díaz Poblete, Marco Antonio. "Integración latinoamericana". *Revista de Derecho Público*, Chile, 5:42 (July/Dec. 1966).

Dillon, Douglas. "Inter-American cooperation in the economic field". *U.S. Dept. of State Bulletin*, Washington, Jan. 12, 1959, p. 48.

"Disappointments and achievements—LAFTA's six month balance sheet". *Business International*, N.Y., June 15, 1962, p. 6.

Doeker, Richard S. "The Montevideo Treaty and the European Economic Community; a comparative legal analysis". *Australian Outbook*, Melbourne, 15:153–168 (1961).

Dosik, Richard S. "The Montevideo Treaty and new trade". *Inter-American Economic Affairs*, Washington, 14:117 (Winter, 1960).

Duvall, Donald K. "The integration industries regime of the Central American common market". *The International Lawyer* (American Bar Association, Section of International and Comparative Law) 1:667 (July, 1967).

———. *and* Harry A. Inman. "Latin American economic integration developments". *Bulletin—Section of International and Comparative Law*, American Bar Association (Various issues 1964 through 1967).

Echeverría, Vicente. "La integración regional en América Latina". *Panorama Económico*, Santiago de Chile, Nov.–Dec. 1959.

"Economic integration in Latin America: in the long run LAFTA may contribute substantially to the solution of Latin America's economic problems". *International Economic Review*, Chicago, March, 1963, pp. 1–7.

"Economic integration in Latin America: the Central American program of economic integration and the Latin American Free Trade Association; a report by the Committee on Foreign Law, Association of the Bar of the City of New York". *The Record*, Asso. of the Bar of City of N.Y., 17 (No. 6, 68 p.) (June, 1962).

"Economistas latinoamericanos tratan del mercado común y del desarrollo regional. Extractos de una Mesa Redonda". *Comercio Exterior*, Mexico, 10:539–544 (1960).

Ely, Roland T. "Economic integration in Latin America". *The Financial Analyst's Journal*, N.Y., 8:9–19; 55–60 (July, 1962).

"The emerging common markets in Latin America". *Monthly Review, Federal Reserve Bank of New York*, 42:154–160 (Sept. 1960).

Emiro Valencia, Luis. "Mercado común democrático". *Cuadernos Americanos*, Mexico, 18:100–119 (Nov.–Dec. 1959).

"En camino de la integración. La Asociación Latinoamericana de Libre Comercio". *Comercio Exterior*, Mexico, Sept./Oct., 1962 (suppl.) and Dec. 1962 (suppl.).

Escobedo, Manuel G. "Regional economic American organization". *Bulletin of the Section of International and Comparative Law*, American Bar Association, 8:17 (Dec. 1963).

Estéves, Vernon R. "Desarrollo del mercado común latinoamericano". *El Trimestre Económico*, Mexico, 26:398–409 (July–Sept. 1959).

Farag, Attiat A. "Economic integration in Latin America". *Economía Internazionale*, Geneva, 16:714–724 (Nov. 1963).

———. "The Latin American Free Trade Area". *Inter-American Economic Affairs*, Washington, 17:73–84 (Summer, 1963).

Feder, Ernst. "Some reflections on Latin America's 'Common market'." *American Journal of Economics and Sociology*, N.Y., 20:433 (July, 1961).

Fernández Shaw, Felix G. "La integración económica iberoamericana". *Revista de Estudios Políticos*, Madrid, 121:169 (Jan.–Feb. 1962).

Ferraris, J. "Mercado común latinoamericano como exigencia del desarrollo económico". *Boletín de la Biblioteca del Congreso de la Nación*, Buenos Aires, 81:13 (May–Oct. 1960).

Ferrero, Rómulo. "El mercado común latinoamericano". *Informaciones Comerciales*, Lima, 10:13–24 (Sept. 1959).
———. "O mercado comum latino-americano". *Revista Brasileira de Economía*, Rio de Janeiro, 15:21–31 (June, 1961).
Flammang, Robert A. "The common market movement". *Iowa Business Digest*, Salt Lake 32:17 (June, 1961). Issue on Latin America.
Frondizi, Arturo. "Integración nacional e integración latinoamericana". *Economía*, Santiago de Chile. 18:1–25, (2. trim. 1958).
Fueyo Laneri, Fernando. "Legislación social y ALALC". *Revista de Derecho y Ciencias Sociales*, Chile, 32:115 (July–Sept. 1964).
García, Norberto. "El mercado común, la industrialización y el desarrollo económico de América Latina". *Revista de Economía y Estadística*, Córdoba, Arg., 11:11–26, (Jan.–Dec. 1960).
García Amador, Francisco V. "Latin American integration—its legal and institutional aspects". *Américas*, Washington, D.C., 17:50–53 (April, 1965).
García Reynoso, Plácido. "Comentarios sobre el Tratado de Montevideo". *Comercio Exterior*, Mexico, 10:128–130 (1960).
——— (*and* José Gómez Gordoa). "Conferencias sobre el Tratado de Montevideo". *Comercio Exterior*, Mexico, 10:253 (1960).
———. "Dos conferencias sobre el mercado común latinoamericano". *El Trimestre Económico*, Mexico, 26:541–560 (Jan.–Mar. 1960).
———. "La integración industrial de Latinoamérica". *Industria*, Mexico, 11:23 (Oct. 1959).
———. "El mercado común latinoamericano". *Ciencias políticas y sociales*, Mexico, Jan.–March, 1960, pp. 15–38.
———. "Mercado común latinoamericano". *Comercio Exterior*, Mexico, 9:373 (1959). [Same title: *Revista Bancaria*, (Asociación de Banqueros de México) 7:284, (July–Aug. 1959).]
———. "Papel del empresario en un area de libre comercio". *Comercio Exterior*, Mexico, 11:140 (1961). Also in: *Mercado Común, América Latina*, Montevideo, 3:7 (April–May, 1961).
———. "Problemas de integración industrial latinoamericana". *Comercio Exterior*, Mexico, 9:591 (1959).
Garrido Torres, José. "O Brasil e o Mercado Comum Latino-Americano". *Journal of Inter-American Studies*, Gainesville, Fla., 3:195 (April, 1961).
———. "El imperativo urgente de la cooperación económica interamericana". *Foro Internacional*, Mexico, April–June, 1961, pp. 571–586.
———. "The Latin American Free Trade Zone". *Journal of Inter-American Studies*, Gainesville, Fla., 2:421 (Oct. 1960).
———. "Porqué un mercado regional latinoamericano?" *Revista Brasileira de Política Internacional*, Rio de Janeiro, 1:74–121 (June, 1958).
Gelsi Bidart, Adolfo. "Agropecuaria y Asociación Latinoamericana de Libre Comercio (A.L.A.L.C.)". *La Justicia Uruguaya*, Montevideo, 49:97 (1964).
Gianazza, Pedro Antonio. "Integración económica centroamericana". *La Aduana Uruguaya*, Montevideo, 41:7057–62 (Oct. 1954).
Gibert, Y. "América Latina, Europa e la tendenze di integrazione economica". *Mondo Aperto*, Rome, 15:377–391 (Dec. 1961).
Gigax, William R. "The Central American common market". *Inter-American Economic Affairs*, Washington, 16:59–77 (Autumn, 1962).
Goldman, Marvin G. "Arbitration in inter-American trade relations: Regional market aspects". *Inter-American Law Review* 7:67 (Jan./June, 1965). (Also printed in Spanish).
Gómez, Rodrigo *and* Rafael Urrutia Millán. "Dos conferencias sobre el Tratado de Montevideo". *Comercio Exterior*, Mexico, 10:189–194 (1960).

González Aninat, Hernán. "Algunas ideas en torno a la integración de América Latina". *Revista de Derecho y Ciencias Sociales,* Chile, 34:82 (Jan./Mar. 1966).

Gordon, F. "Condiciones fundamentales sobre un mercado común". *Mercado Común, América Latina,* Montevideo, 2:12 (Aug. 1960).

Gordon, Lincoln. "Economic regionalism reconsidered". *World Politics,* Princeton, N.J., 13: No. 2 (Jan. 1961).

————. "Private enterprise, economic integration and the Alliance for Progress; address". *U.S. Dept. of State Bulletin,* Washington, 55:18–23 (July 4, 1966).

Griffin, Keith B. "The potential benefits of Latin American integration". *Inter-American Economic Affairs,* 17:3–20 (Spring, 1964).

Guier, Enrique. "La justicia en el Mercado Común Centroamericano". *Revista de Ciencias Jurídicas,* Costa Rica, No. 6:7 (Nov. 1965).

Haas, E. B. *and* P. C. Schmitter. "Economics and differential patterns of political integration: projections about unity in Latin America". *International Organization* (Boston), 18:705–37 (Autumn, 1964).

"Hacia la solución de los problemas del comercio exterior de América Latina, y la realización de su integración económica; Período de sesiones del Comité Plenario de la CEPAL". *Noticias de la CEPAL,* Santiago de Chile, No. 11:1–12 (Feb. 1964).

Hall, L. "J.F.K. co-stars in a new common market: Latinos have a hit". *Life,* Chicago, 154:26–35 (March 29, 1963).

Harmon, F. "Toward more trade". *Américas,* Washington, D.C. 16:31–35 (April 11, 1964).

Hazera, Jorge. "What happened at Buenos Aires: a report on the OAS Economic Conference; with Economic Declaration of Buenos Aires". *Américas,* Washington, D.C., 9:14 (Nov. 1957).

Herman, Emilio. "El mercado común latinoamericano". *Informaciones Comerciales,* Lima, 10:22 (Jan. 1959).

Herrera Lane, Felipe. "El financiamiento de la integración latinoamericana". *Revista de Derecho y Ciencias Sociales,* Chile, 30:83 (Jan.–March, 1963).

————. "Integración económica y reintegración política". *Combate,* San José, Costa Rica, 24:9–17 (Sept.–Oct. 1962).

————. "Opportunities and obstacles in Latin America". *Vital Speeches,* Pelham, N.Y., 29:242–245 (Feb. 1, 1963).

Hess, Raúl. "La integración económica centroamericana: ¿Espectro o esperanza?" *Combate,* San José, Costa Rica, 16:23–30 (May–June, 1961).

Huelin, David. "Economic integration in Latin America: progress and problems". *International Affairs,* London, 40:430–439 (July, 1964).

————. "A free trade area in South America". *World Today,* London, 16:79–88, (Feb. 1960).

————. "Latin American Free Trade Association". *F.B.I. Review,* London, Nov. 1960, p. 51.

Hughes, L. A. "Zona de Libre Comercio". *Mercado Común, América Latina,* Montevideo, 3:15 (April–May, 1961).

"Instituto para la integración de América Latina". *Temas del BID* (Banco Interamericano de Desarrollo) Washington, 2:57 (No. 3, Feb. 1965).

"Integration in Latin America; the need for coordinated policies". *Quarterly Review of the Bank of London and South America, Ltd.,* London, 4:1–15 (Jan. 1964).

"Inter-American Development Bank: Proposals for creation of the Latin American Common Market". *International Legal Materials* (American Society of International Law, Washington), 4:651 (July, 1965).

James, D. "Five countries with one idea". *Readers' Digest,* N.Y., 74:225 (Feb. 1959).

Johnson, Lyndon B. "U.S. support for Central American common market reaffirmed". *U.S. Dept. of State Bulletin*, Washington, 54:1004–5 (June 27, 1966).

"Joint venture opportunities, lucrative LAFTA markets beckon U.S. manufacturers operating in Ecuador". *Foreign Commerce Weekly*, U.S. Dept of Commerce, 67:5–14 (No. 5, 1960).

Keller, Frank L. "Central American common market; economic integration amidst political diversity". *Annals of Association of American Geographers*, Washington, D.C., 52:343 (Sept. 1962).

———. "ODECA: common market experiment in an under-developed area". *Journal of Inter-American Affairs*, 5:267–275 (April, 1963).

King Vanoni, Luis. "La Zona Latinoamericana de Libre Comercio en la economía ecuatoriana". *Planificación*, Quito, (Junta Nacional de Planificación y Coordinación Económica) 1:97–108 (Sept.–Dec. 1962).

Kybal, Milic. "Integración de los mercados de capital en América Latina". *Temas del BID* (Banco Interamericano de Desarrollo), Washington, 2:19 (No. 3, Feb. 1965).

Labastida, Horacio. "La integración económica centroamericana y la política social". *Ciencias Políticas y Sociales*, México, 11:215 (April, 1965).

"LAFTA considers ocean cargo, ports, customs procedure". *International Commerce*, U.S. Dept. of Commerce, 68:29 (Oct. 15, 1962).

"LAFTA members prepare for tariff negotiations". *Foreign Commerce Weekly*, U.S. Dept. of Commerce, 66:9 and 39(1961).

"LAFTA. Resolution 100(IV): Basic directives for economic policy". *International Legal Materials* (American Society of International Law), Washington, 4:761 (July, 1965).

"LAFTA. Summary of activities". *International Organization*, Boston, 16:650 and 18:650. (Summer, 1962 and Summer, 1964).

"LAFTA tariff negotiations concluded, concessions cover over 2450 items". *Foreign Commerce Weekly*, U.S. Dept. of Commerce, 67:170 (No. 5, 1962).

Lagunilla Iñarritu, Alfredo. "Cuatro temas sobre el mercado común latinoamericano". *Comercio Exterior*, Mexico, 9:726 (1959).

———. "Integración y reciprocidad económica en América Latina". *Revista de la Secretaría de Estado de Economía y Comercio*, Ciudad Trujillo, Rep. Dominicana, 31:36 (Nov.–Dec. 1953).

Lamboglia, Santiago. "Mercados comunes latinoamericanos". *La Aduana Uruguaya*, Montevideo, 27:33 (Feb.–March, 1961). Also in: *Mercado Común, América-Latina*, Montevideo, 2:3 (Dec. 1960).

Lang, J. T. "The Montevideo Treaty for a Latin American Free Trade Area". *Univ. of Illinois Law Forum* 1965: 617 (Winter, 1965).

Laris Casillas, J. E. "El mercado común latinoamericano". *Revista de Economía*, Mexico, 24:6–34; 39–66 (Jan.–Feb. 1961).

"Latin America and financial integration". *Comercio Exterior*, Mexico, 11:3 (Oct. 1965).

"Latin American common market". *Time*, Chicago, 79:32 (Jan. 12, 1962).

"The Latin American Free Trade Association". *Latin American Business Highlights*, (Chase-Manhattan Bank), New York, 11:25–31 (No. 2, 1961).

"Latin American Free Trade Association confounds skeptics with hefty tariff cuts". *Business International*, N.Y., Jan. 12, 1962, p. 5.

"Latin American Free Trade Association. Implementation of resolutions outlined". *Foreign Commerce Weekly*, U.S. Dept of Commerce, 67:25 (No. 1, 1965).

"Latin American Free Trade Association—problems and prospects". *Foreign Information Service* (First National City Bank of New York), Sept. 1961, pp. 1–8.

"Latin American Free Trade Association: Report of activities to G.A.T.T." *International Legal Materials*, Washington, D.C., 4:682 (July, 1965).

"Latin American Free Trade Association. Summary of activities". *International Organization*, Boston, 16:650 (Summer, 1962).

"Latin American Free Trade Association tariff negotiations in progress". *Foreign Commerce Weekly*, U.S. Dept. of Commerce, 66:5–7; 27 (No. 21, 1961).

"Latin American regional market proposed by ECLA group". *Foreign Commerce Weekly*, U.S. Dept. of Commerce, 59:18 (March 10, 1958).

Linfield, Seymour L. "Latin American free trade and American industry". *Commercial and Financial Chronicle*, N.Y., 191:10 (April 28, 1960). Reprinted in: *Congressional Record*, April 29, 1960: A3671–A3673).

——. "El libre comercio latinoamericano y la industria norteamericana" (Spanish text). *Comercio Exterior*, Mexico 10:315 (1960).

Lops, C. "Le prospettive dell'Associazione Latino-Americana del Libero Scambio". *Idea*, Rome, 17:156–161 (March, 1961).

Lukes, F. "Basic legal research and sources on the Latin American economic integration". *Law Library Journal*, Chicago, 58:270 (Aug. 1965).

Manoliu, Florín. "La Zona de Libre Comercio y sus problemas de pago". *Revista de Ciencias Económicas*, Buenos Aires, 48:3–32 (Jan.–Mar. 1960).

Mansfield, Mike. "Common market for Latin America". *New Leader*, N.Y., 43:8 (Jan. 25, 1960).

Mansholt, S. L. "Convenios regionales para mercados agrícolas". *Comercio Exterior*, Mexico, 11:599 (1961).

Manterola, Miguel. "Los problemas del comercio exterior de Mexico". *Comercio Exterior*, Mexico, 7:580 (1957).

Marini, José Felipe. "Mercado común latinoamericano". *Revista Argentina Jurídica LA LEY* (daily suppl.) 113:1, Feb. 12, 1964.

Martínez Sotomayor, Carlos. "Integración económica latinoamericana". *Revista de Derecho y Ciencias Sociales*, Chile, 30:21 (Jan.–Mar. 1963).

Martínez Villa, Juan. "El futuro del Tratado de Montevideo". *Comercio Exterior*, Mexico, 11:341 (1961).

Massad, Carlos and John Strasma. "Coordinación de la política económica dentro de la Zona Latinoamericana de Libre Comercio". *Comercio Exterior*, Mexico, 11:205, (1961).

Medina Mora, Alejandro. "Problemas actuales de intercambio entre México y los países de la Zona Latinoamericana de Libre Comercio". *Revista Bancaria*, Asociación de Banqueros de Mexico, 8:305 (July–Aug. 1960).

Melchor Llerena, Orlando. "Latin American Free Trade Area (LAFTA); significance and purposes". *Review of the River Plate*, Buenos Aires, 132:333 (Nov. 30, 1962).

"Members of Central American free trade area and Latin American free trade association. Annual summary of exchange and foreign trade regulations, as of January 1, 1962". *Foreign Information Service, of First National City Bank of New York*.

Mendez, Jorge. "La zona latinoamericana de libre comercio: una grave responsabilidad colombiana". *Nueva Economía*, Bogotá, 1:1 (Feb. 1961).

Méndez Delfino, Eustaquio. "La integración económica y el mercado común de Latinoamérica". *Anales de la Academia de Ciencias Económicas*, Buenos Aires, ser. 3, 3:39–64 (1959).

"Mexican economy in slump; regional planning studied". *Foreign Commerce Weekly*, U.S. Dept. of Commerce, 67:646 (1962).

"Mexico too? Common markets". *Américas*, Washington, D.C., 9:2 (June, 1958).

Mignone, Emilio Fermín. "Naturaleza jurídica de los órganos de la Asociación

Latinoamericana de Libre Comercio". *Jurisprudencia Argentina,* Buenos Aires, Sec. Doctrina, p. 3 (May–June, 1960).

Mikesell, Raymond Frech. "Latin American economic development: some basic issues". *Journal of International Affairs,* N.Y., 14:126–139 (No. 2, 1960).

"The Montevideo Treaty". *Fortnightly Review,* Bank of London and South America, Ltd., 25:357–380 (No. 611, 1960).

Monti, Angel. "Notas sobre la política económica del Mercado Común". *Desarrollo Económico,* La Plata, 1:109–130 (Oct.–Dec. 1958).

Mora, José A. "Latin American Free Trade Zone: a summary of address". *Américas,* Washington, D.C., 14:43 (Oct. 1962).

Morales, Cecilio. "Trade liberalization and economic integration". *Social Science,* Philadelphia, 35:231 (Oct. 1960).

Morizon, Ives. "Algunas consideraciones sobre el area de libre comercio". *Comercio Exterior,* Mexico, 12:530 (1962).

Mur de Lara, M. E. "El mercado común latinoamericano". *Revista de la Facultad de Ciencias Económicas,* Lima, 59:258 (July–Dec. 1959).

Mussio, Juan Carlos. "La Asociación Latinoamericana de Libre Comercio". *Combate,* San José, Costa Rica, 16:39–47 (May–June, 1961).

Nattier, Frank E. "Latin American Free Trade Association (LAFTA)". *Business Lawyer,* (American Bar Association), Chicago, 21:515 (Jan. 1966).

"New kind of revolution in Central America". *U.S. News and World Report,* 60:62–66 (May 30, 1966).

"New octopus: Mexico's trade with CACM". *Newsweek,* 67:38 (Jan. 10, 1966).

"Nómina consolidada de productos en relación con los que los gobiernos de Argentina, Brazil, Chile, Paraguay, Perú y Uruguay solicitan del Gobierno Mexicano reducción o eliminación de gravámenes y demás restricciones vigentes a su importación". *Comercio Exterior,* Mexico, 11 (Suppl. Aug. 1961).

Norberg, Charles R. "Central American economic integration". *Studies in Law and Economic Development* (Geo. Washington Univ. Law School, Wash., D.C.) 1:1 (April, 1966).

"ODECA. Integración económica centroamericana. Compilación de tratados". *Boletin Informativo de ODECA,* San Salvador, Aug. 15, 1961 (special issue), 251 p.

Olavarría Avula, Julio. "La legislación comercial y la integración latinoamericana". *Revista de la Univ. Externado de Colombia.* 6:285 (Dec. 1965).

Oreamuno, J. Rafael. "The bases of inter-American economic cooperation". *Social Science,* Kansas City, Mo., 28:216 (Oct. 1953).

"Patterns of regional trade groupings adopted by Latin American governments". *Foreign Commerce Weekly,* U.S. Dept of Commerce, 64:8 (No. 11, 1960).

Pegurier, Atututo. "O mercado comum latino-americano". *Economía Brasileira,* Rio de Janeiro, 4:nos. 3–4 (1958).

"A penetrating look at the growing regional markets of Latin America: CAFTA and LAFTA are playing a vital role in the economic growth of the continent's developing nations". *Export Trade,* N.Y., 86:8–11 (Oct. 1, 1962).

Pinto Santa Cruz, Anibal. "Antecedentes y razón de ser de la integración económica regional". *Panorama Económico,* Santiago de Chile, Feb.–March, 1960.

Plaza, Galo. "For a regional market in Latin America". *Foreign Affairs,* N.Y., 37:607–616 (July, 1959).

Poirier, Anthony J. "Latin American Free Trade Association now in operation". *Foreign Commerce Weekly,* U.S. Dept. of Commerce, 66:42 (1961).

Pons, J. B. "Strutture e prospettive del Trattato di Montevideo". *Mondo Aperto,* Rome, 15:355–364 (No. 6, Dec. 1961).

"La posición de Argentina respecto a una Zona de Libre Comercio en el sur de Latinoamérica". *Comercio Exterior,* Mexico, 9:537–541 (1959).

Prebisch, Raúl. "Economic aspects of the Alliance". (*The Alliance for Progress, Problems and Perspectives.* Baltimore, Johns Hopkins Press, 1962, pp. 24–65).

———. "Joint responsibilities for Latin American progress". *Foreign Affairs,* N.Y., July, 1961.

———. "El mercado común latinoamericano". *Comercio Exterior,* Mexico, 9:258 (1959).

———. "El mercado común latinoamericano". *Comercio Exterior,* Mexico, 9:509 (1959).

———. "Los obstáculos estructurales y la necesaria revisión de la política de desarrollo y de cooperación internacional". *Comercio Exterior,* Mexico, 11:276 (1961).

———. "Los pagos multilaterales en una política de mercado común latino-americano". *Boletin Quincenal,* Centro de Estudios Monetarios Latinoamericanos, Mexico, *Suppl.* to issue Dec. 1958, pp. 274–283.

———. Same title in: *Revista del Banco de la República Oriental del Uruguay,* Montevideo, 17:No. 68 (Jan. 1960).

———. "Pagos y la Zona de Libre Comercio en América Latina". *Comercio Exterior,* Mexico, 10:9–13 (1960).

———. "Reflexiones sobre la integración económica latinoamericana". *Comercio Exterior,* Mexico, 11:650 (1961); Same in: *Revista de Economía y Estadística,* Córdoba, Arg., 6:No. 1 (Jan.–March, 1962).

"Preparing for a Latin American common market". *United Nations Review,* N.Y., 6:No. 1 (July, 1959).

"Presidents' meeting at San José: statements, addresses and remarks". with Declaration of Central America (March 18–21, 1963). *U.S. Dept. of State Bulletin,* Washington, 48:511–520 (April 8, 1963).

"Primeros pasos hacia la formación del mercado común latinoamericano". *Comercio Exterior,* Mexico, 8:243 (1958).

"Los problemas del comercio latinoamericano en la reunión de la CEPAL en La Paz". *Comercio Exterior,* Mexico, 7:275 (1957).

"Progress report: LAFTA." *Latin American Business Highlights,* Chase Manhattan Bank, N.Y., 13:3–7 (2. quarter, 1963).

"Proposed changes in structure of L.A.F.T.A. Final act and resolutions of meeting of foreign ministers of Latin American Free Trade Association countries; Montevideo, Uruguay, November 3–6, 1965". *International Legal Materials,* (American Society of International Law) Washington, D.C., 5:125 (Jan. 1966).

"Proposals for the creation of the Latin American Market". *International Legal Materials,* Washington, D.C., 4:651 (July, 1965).

"Proyecto de acuerdo de zona de libre comercio en la parte meridional de América Latina". *Comercio Exterior,* Mexico, 9:307 (1959).

"Proyecto de Tratado de Zona de Libre Comercio". *Comercio Exterior,* Mexico, 9:567 (1959).

"Public relations takes a continental look at the problems affecting implementation and development of Latin America's two great projects: the Alliance for Progress and the free trade zone". *Comments on Argentine Trade,* American Chamber of Commerce in Argentina, 42:issues for Jan. 16, and 17, and others in Feb. 1963.

Rafferty, William A. *and* Robert L. Pritchard. "Mexican-Central American market needs close aggressive attention". *Foreign Commerce Weekly,* U.S. Department of Commerce, June 27, 1960.

"Recomendaciones acerca de la estructura y normas del mercado común latino-americano". *Comercio Exterior*, Mexico, 9:124 (1959).

"Regímenes de comercio exterior en los países de la Zona Latinoamericana de Libre Comercio". *Comercio Exterior*, Mexico, 11, Suppl., July, 1961.

"A regional market for Latin America. The proposal for a regional market for Latin Amercia was one of the few items on the agenda of the Inter-American Economic Conference in August, 1957, that was both constructive and attracted a considerable measure of support". *Review of the River Plate*, Buenos Aires, Feb. 20, 1958. p. 17.

"Regional market to the South". *Américas*, Washington, D. C., 97:614 (Sept. 21, 1957).

"Resoluciones de la CEPAL sobre el mercado común latinoamericano". *Comercio Exterior*, 9:316 (1959).

Ribas, José Miguel. "Latin America's European market". *Americas*, Washington, D.C., 14:1–7 (Oct. 1962).

Rice, R. P. "Common market for five Central American nations makes rapid progress". *International Commerce*, U.S. Dept. of Commerce, 69:4 (March 18, 1963).

Rivero, Nicolás. "Central American common market". *Américas*, Washington, D.C., 15:3 (Jan. 1963).

Roche, E. "La France, le marché commun et l'Amérique Latine". *Revue Politique et Parlementaire*, Paris, 63:25–47 (April, 1961).

Sammons, Robert L. "Proposals for the common market in Latin America". *Public Policy*, Yearbook of Harvard's Graduate School of Public Administration, 10:268–296 (1960).

San Miguel, Manuel. "Factores dinámicos de la Zona Latinoamericana de Libre Comercio". *Revista de Ciencias Económicas*, Buenos Aires, 48:259–276 (July–Sept. 1960).

Sánchez Fontans, José. "El mercado común y su influencia en el derecho privado". *Revista de Derecho Español y Americano*, Madrid, 6:505 (Jan.–March, 1961).

Sanz Manrique, Fernando. "Colombia en la Asociación Latino-americana de Libre Comercio". *Comercio Exterior*, Mexico, 11:402 (1961).

Sedwitz, Walter J. "A common market for Latin America?" *Current History*, Philadelphia, 43:1 (July, 1962).

Shreiberg, Sheldon L. "The United States private investor and the Central American Common Market". *Studies in Law and Economic Development* (Geo. Wash. Univ. Law School, Wash., D.C.) 2:170 (Sept. 1966).

Shonfield, A. "Latin American integration; a new phase". *The World Today*, London, 21:460–69 (Nov. 1965).

Shoup, Carl S. "Tax problems of a common market in Latin America". *Tax Policy*, Princeton, N.J., 29:3 (Nov. 1962).

Solá, Alberto. "Consideración de algunos problemas financieros en la Asociación Latinoamericana de Libre Comercio". *Industria*, San Salvador, 4:38–43 (Feb. 1964).

Solórzano V., Victor M. "La reunión de la CEPAL en La Paz". *Comercio Exterior*, Mexico, 7:357 (1957).

"South America's seven". *The Commonweal*, N.Y., 71:38 (Oct. 9, 1959).

"Special Punta del Este issue". *Américas*, Washington, D.C. 13:1–42 (Oct. 1961).

Staley, C. E. "Central American economic integration". *Southern Economic Journal*, New Mexico, 29:88–95 (Oct. 1962).

Stanley, A. O. "Common markets south of the border". *Dun's Review and Modern Industry*, N.Y., 81:51 (March, 1963).

——. "International markets". *Dun's Review and Modern Industry*, N.Y., 80:113 (Oct. 1962).

————. "Latin American common market". *Dun's Review and Modern Industry*, N.Y., 75:58 (Aug. 1961).

Stokes, C. J. "El mercado común latinoamericano: una defensa clásica". *Revista de Economía y Estadística*, Córdoba, Arg., 4:55–73 (1960).

Sumberg, Theodore A. "Free-trade zone in Latin America". *Inter-American Economic Affairs*, Washington, D.C., 14:51–64 (Summer, 1960).

Tapia Valdés, Jorge. "Competencia y órganos de una autoridad supranacional". *Revista de Derecho Privado*, Chile, 1:9 (July/Sept. 1966).

"Taxes, land and trade: Alliance for Progress briefs". *Américas*, Washington, D.C. 14:17 (Jan. 1962).

Tinbergen, Jan. "La industria pesada y el mercado común latinoamericano". *Comercio Exterior*, Mexico, 10:418 (1960).

"To get bolder or give up". *Time*, New York, 84:103 (Oct. 30, 1964).

Torres, Abelardo. "El Estado Federal de Centroamérica y su política económica". *Economía Salvadoreña*, San Salvador, 5:59–66 (July–Dec. 1958).

Torres, G. "Cooperação econômica interamericana". *Digesto Económico*. São Paulo, Brasil, 17:75–84 (May–June, 1961).

Torres Campana, Manuel. "Dos conferencias sobre el mercado común latino-americano". *El Trimestre Económico*, Mexico, 26: 541–560 (1959).

Torres Gaitán, Ricardo. "El Mercado Común Latinoamericano". *Cuadernos Americanos*, Mexico, 17:29–41 (1958).

————. "La política de comercio exterior". *Comercio Exterior*, Mexico, 12:211 (1962).

Torres Manzo, Carlos. "Comentarios alrededor de dos preguntas sobre comercio internacional". *Investigación Económica*, Mexico, 21:475–95 (No. 83, 1961).

"Toward Middle American unity". *Américas*, Washington, D. C., 10:19 (Oct. 1958).

"Towards a Latin American common market". *Review of the River Plate*, Buenos Aires, (April 18, 1958).

Trombetta, M. "L'integrazione economica latino americana ed i suoi riflessi in campo internazionale". *Mondo Aperto*, Rome, 15:364–376 (Dec. 1961).

"Two new protocols further define economic cohesion: Central American ministers take steps on integration of industries". *International Commerce*, 69:7 (March 18, 1963).

"Unions on paper; schemes of economic cooperation". *Economist*, London, 194:328, (Feb. 1960).

Urquidi, Victor L. "Apreciación preliminar del Proyecto de Montevideo". *Comercio Exterior*, Mexico, 9:562 (1959).

————. "Centroamérica avanza hacia la integración económica". *Comercio Exterior*, Mexico, 7:105 (1957).

————. "En torno a la Zona Latinoamericana de Libre Comercio". *Comercio Exterior*, Mexico, 11:474 (1961).

————. "The idea of the Latin American common market". *Economic and Statistics Review of Puerto Rico*, San Juan, 2:1 (1. sem. 1961).

————. "México ante los mercados comunes". *Comercio Exterior*, Mexico, 12:421 (1962).

————. "Montevideo Treaty: a comment on Mr. Sumberg's views". *Inter-American Economic Affairs*, Washington, D.C. 14:19–27 (Fall, 1960).

————. "¿Progresará el mercado común latinoamericano?" *Comercio Exterior*, Mexico, 9:307 (1959).

Valencia, Luis Emiro. "Mercado común democrático". *Combate*, San José, Costa Rica, 10:7–17 (May–June, 1960).

Vallejo, Joaquin. "Comentarios sobre el proyecto de mercado regional inter-latinoamericano". *Ciencias Económicas*, Medellin, Colombia, 5:no. 12 (May, 1958).

Vernon, Raymond. "México ante los mercados comunes (otro punto de vista)". *Comercio Exterior*, Mexico, 12:527 (1962).
Viera Altamirano, Napoleón. "El mercado común latinoamericano y nuestra industrialización". *Cuadernos Americanos*, Mexico, 19:67–89 (March–April, 1960).
Villagrán Kramer, Francisco. "Los partidos políticos y las organizaciones obreras ante la integración económica centroamericana". *Ciencias Políticas y Sociales*, Mexico. 11:189 (April/Sept. 1965).
Wallich, H. C. "New common market". *Newsweek*, N.Y., 65:80 (March 8, 1965).
"What's ahead for United States-Latin American trade?" *International Trade Review*, N.Y., 36:21–42 (April, 1962).
"Why Central America moves to a faster beat". *Business Week*, 114 (Sept. 11, 1965).
Wilhelm, Marion B. "The Latin American common market: how it stands, where it's going; trends towards industrial integration among the nine member nations of LAFTA". *Mexican-American Review*, American Chamber of Commerce in Mexico, 30:10 (Nov. 1962).
Wilson, C. M. "Trade or suffocate". *National Review*, N.Y., 13:99–101 (Aug. 14, 1962).
Wionczek, Miguel S. "La actitud de los Estados Unidos frente al problema de la integración económica de América Latina". *Comercio Exterior*, Mexico, 12:18 (1962).
———. Same title in: *Revista de Economía y Estadística*, Córdoba, Arg. 5:7–25 (1961).
———. "El financiamiento de la integración económica de América Latina". *El Trimestre Económico*, Mexico, 27:15–33 (Jan.–March, 1960).
———. "Latin American Free Trade Association: with text of Montevideo Treaty". *International Conciliation*, 551:3–80 (Jan. 1965).
———. "The Montevideo Treaty and Latin American integration". *Moneta é Credito*, Banca Nazionale del Lavoro, Rome, 14:197–240 (June, 1961).
Yañez Perez, Luis. "El instituto latinoamericano de administración de negocios y el mercado común latinoamericano". *Comercio Exterior*, Mexico, 10:380 (1960).

Legislation

I. LATIN AMERICAN FREE TRADE ASSOCIATION

Argentina

Law 15,378 of Oct. 6, 1960, ratifies the Treaty establishing a free trade area and creating the Latin American Free Trade Association (LAFTA), signed in Montevideo, Feb. 18, 1960 [*Boletin Oficial*, Oct. 18, 1960].
Decree 12,108 of Dec. 28, 1961, provides tariffs to be applied to imports from Brazil, Chile, Mexico, Paraguay, Peru, and Uruguay, on items in the national lists, pursuant to the Montevideo Treaty. [*Boletin Oficial*, April 5, 1962].
Decree 14,241 of Dec. 31, 1962, approves substitute National List for that of 1961 (*supra*), to include also imports from Ecuador and Colombia, now adherents to Montevideo Treaty. [*Boletin Oficial*, Feb. 6, 1963].
Decree 970 of Feb. 13, 1964, approves lengthy (200 pages of charts in book-sized pages) National List, with corresponding duties and fees to be applied to imports from members of ALALC. [*Boletin Oficial*, March 28, 1964].
Decree 3288 of May 8, 1964, limits exportation of live cattle only to member nations of ALALC. [*Boletin Oficial*, May 12, 1964].
Resolution 265 of July 31, 1964, creates an advisory committee on Latin American Free Trade Associations matters, with representation from the most

important industrial and commercial organizations and unions. [*Boletin Oficial,* August 11, 1964].

Decree 1329 of Feb. 19, 1965, adopts rules and procedures to regulate the exchange of goods with member countries in LAFTA [*Boletin Oficial,* March 4, 1965].

Resolution 106 of April 2, 1965, provides that the *Dirección Nacional de Industrias* shall take charge of implementing Decree 1329 (*supra*) on trade with LAFTA members. [*Boletin Oficial,* April 26, 1965].

Brazil

Legislative Decree 1 of Feb. 3, 1961, approves text of the Montevideo Treaty, establishing a Free Trade Zone. [*Diario Oficial,* Feb. 4, 1961].

Decree 50,656 of May 24, 1961, promulgates the Montevideo Treaty, to become law of the land. [*Diario Oficial,* May 25, 1961].

Decree 387 of Dec. 20, 1961, provides for the execution of agreements resulting from negotiations in the free trade zone created under the Montevideo Treaty of 1960, and adds a list of products and concessions for Members of LAFTA. [*Diario Oficial,* Dec. 27, 1961].

Circular 116 of Dec. 27, 1961, of the Director of Customs, relating to the Latin American Free Trade Zone. [*Diario Oficial,* Feb. 4, 1962].

Decree 1451 of Oct. 11, 1962, provides for the execution of industrial agreements as complementary to the Montevideo Treaty, and pursuant to the protocols thereto, signed on July 20, 1962. [*Diario Oficial,* Oct. 17, 1962].

Decree 1972–A of Dec. 31, 1962, provides for the execution or implementation of the agreements reached at the second annual negotiations of LAFTA. The Brazilian national list for 1963 is included, as applicable to imports from member nations. [*Diario Oficial,* Jan. 30, 1963 (suppl. 1.)].

Decree 52,087 of May 31, 1963, creates the *Comissão Nacional para os Assuntos da Associação Latino-Americana de Livre Comercio* (C.L.C.) within the Ministry of Foreign Relations, to deal with matters concerning participation in LAFTA [*Diario Oficial,* June 3, 1963].

Decree 52,111 of June 17, 1963, gives permanent character to the delegation representing Brazil in LAFTA. Repeals earlier legislation in this regard. [*Diario Oficial,* June 18, 1963].

Decree 55,780 of Feb. 19, 1965, provides for implementation of the annual negotiations agreed upon by LAFTA members at the Bogotá meeting in December, 1964. Includes national list of products for importation from member countries. [*Diario Oficial,* March 3, 1965].

Decree 58,033 of March 22, 1966, provides for execution of objectives of the 5th annual series of negotiations for Free Trade Zone established by Montevideo Treaty. [*Diario Oficial,* April 6, 1966].

Chile

Decree 269 of May 2, 1961, promulgates the Montevideo Treaty of 1960, creating the Latin American Free Trade Association. [*Diario Oficial,* May 24, 1961].

Law 14,840 of Jan. 26, 1962, authorizes the President of the Nation to impose, increase, decrease or repeal any taxes or duties, or grant loans, and to take any necessary measures to implement Article 28(b) of Chapter VII of the Montevideo Treaty on LAFTA. [*Diario Oficial,* Feb. 6, 1962].

Decree-with-force-of-Law 450 of Dec. 6, 1963, creates a National Advisory Commission, with representatives of government and industry, to assist the President in implementation of the Montevideo Treaty. [*Diario Oficial,* Dec. 30, 1963].

Decree-with-force-of-Law 451 of Dec. 6, 1963, organizes the Secretariat-General or Executive Secretariat for LAFTA matters, listing duties, personnel, etc. [*Diario Oficial*, Feb. 20, 1964].

Colombia

Law 88 of May 2, 1961, promulgates the Treaty of Montevideo, signed in 1960, creating the Latin American Free Trade Association. [*Diario Oficial*, Oct. 9, 1961].

Decree 207 of Feb. 1, 1963, orders the observance of certification of origin on merchandise exported to member countries of LAFTA, pursuant to the resolutions adopted at the II. Conference held in Mexico, in December, 1962. [*Diario Oficial*, Feb. 20, 1963].

Decree 437 of March 6, 1963, authorizes the holding of an International Exposition Fair in Bogotá in August or September, 1963, to exhibit merchandise imported and exported to and from signatory countries of the Montevideo Treaty. [*Diario Oficial*, March 21, 1963].

Decree 768 of April 7, 1964, provides for LAFTA fairs every two years commencing in 1964. [*Diario Oficial*, April 17, 1964].

Decree 146 of Feb. 2, 1965, revises tariff reductions for member countries of LAFTA based on resolutions adopted at Bogotá meeting in 1964. [*Diario Oficial*, Feb. 12, 1965(?)].

Decree 160 of Jan. 27, 1966, concerns special tariff concessions for LAFTA members. Amended by Decree 533 of March 7, 1966.

Ecuador

Decree 1825 of Oct. 20, 1961, approves adherence by Ecuador to the Treaty of Montevideo, creating a free trade zone and establishing the Latin American Free Trade Association. [*Registro Oficial*, Nov. 16, 1961].

Resolution of Nov. 16, 1961, approves the Treaty of Montevideo, pursuant to authorization to adhere thereto (*supra*). [*Registro Oficial*, Dec. 1, 1961].

Decree 14 of Jan. 3, 1963, approves the National List of products for Ecuador, with accompanying reduced duty fees in favor of LAFTA members, to become effective Jan. 1, 1963. [*Registro Oficial*, Jan. 3, 1963].

Decree 201 of Feb. 4, 1964, incorporates changes in import duties pursuant to the III Conference of the contracting parties of LAFTA; National List is incorporated. [*Registro Oficial*, March 2, 1964].

Decree 199 of Feb. 4, 1964, creates the *Grupo de Trabajo* or task force to identify the industries which may be established in Ecuador, and to draft projects for submission to the Permanent Commission (Executive), of LAFTA, pursuant to the III Conference of the contracting parties. [*Registro Oficial*, April 1, 1964].

Mexico

Decree of Nov. 7, 1960, approves the Treaty of Montevideo, of Feb. 18, 1960, which created the Latin American Free Trade Association and established a free trade area. [*Diario Oficial*, Dec. 29, 1960].

Numerous administrative orders of the Ministry of Industry deal with items of import and export to and from LAFTA countries, import licenses, etc.

Decree of May 27, 1967, promulgates the Agreement on Water Transportation for the Latin American Free Trade Association. [*Diario Oficial*, July 8, 1967].

Paraguay

Law 668 of Sept. 6, 1960, approves and ratifies the Treaty of Montevideo, which created the Latin American Free Trade Association. [*Gaceta Oficial*, Sept. 6, 1960].

Decree 19,857 of Dec. 30, 1961, provides for the enforcement of application of import duties pursuant to the National List, agreed upon at the first Conference of LAFTA [*Registro Oficial*, 6.bimestre p. 339, 1961].

Decree 21,290 of March 30, 1962, provides for special treatment for imports from LAFTA members, in this case to Colombian products. [*Registro Oficial*, 2.bimestre, p. 468, 1962].

Decree 22,699 of June 8, 1962, creates the *Consejo Nacional de Comercio Exterior* as an advisory organ to the Government for promotion and orientation of international and foreign trade. This eliminates the former government agency of *Consejo Nacional de Zona de Libre Comercio*, which was created by Decree 10,665 of June 3, 1960. [*Registro Oficial*, 3.bimestre, p. 284, 1962].

Decree 7,140 of Sept. 14, 1964, puts into effect the National List of Paraguay as of Jan. 1st. Repeals Decree 2,916 of Feb. 17, 1964, on same subject. [*Gaceta Oficial*, Sept. 15, 1964].

Peru

Legislative Decree 13,463 of Nov. 19, 1960, approves the Montevideo Treaty signed Feb. 18, 1960, which set up a free trade area or zone, and created the Latin American Free Trade Association. [*El Peruano*, Nov. 23, 1960].

Decree 12 of March 31, 1962, extends to Colombia the same treatment on imports commencing April 1, 1962, as is given to other members of LAFTA. [*El Peruano*, April 18, 1962].

Decree of Jan. 10, 1964 orders customs houses to apply new tariff concessions to imports from member countries of LAFTA, pursuant to agreements reached at the recent sessions of LAFTA conference. [*El Peruano*, Jan. 11, 1964].

Decree 2-H of Jan. 6, 1965, provides changes in import duties to be applied to imports from LAFTA countries, pursuant to agreements reached at the 1964 Bogotá Conference of the Association. [*El Peruano*, Jan. 11, 1965].

Law 15,905 of Jan. 7, 1966, authorizes the *Banco Central de Reserva* to undertake necessary operations and functions to implement LAFTA's agreement on multilateral compensation of balances and reciprocal credits. [*El Peruano*, Jan. 10, 1966].

Uruguay

Law of April 28, 1961, approves the Treaty of Montevideo, signed Feb. 18, 1960, creating the Latin American Free Trade Association (LAFTA). [*Diario Oficial*, May 24, 1961].

Decree of June 18, 1963, specifies duties and restrictions on importation of products subject to negotiation under the Montevideo Treaty, incorporated either in national lists or special lists. [*Diario Oficial*, July 2, 1963].

Decree of July 16, 1963, creates a division within the organization of the Ministry of Foreign Relations to deal with LAFTA matters, to be called "*Sección A.L.A.L.C.*" [*Diario Oficial*, Aug. 2, 1963].

Decree of Jan. 9, 1964, creates an advisory body known as *Comisión Nacional Asesora de Transporte*, to coordinate and develop intra-zonal transportation of goods related to LAFTA [*Diario Oficial*, Jan. 29, 1964].

Decree of Jan. 16, 1964, provides for importation of specified merchandise included on the Uruguayan national list, imported from member countries of A.L.A.L.C., setting the duties and concessions in each case. [*Diario Oficial*, Feb. 14, 1964].

Decree 386 of June 20, 1967, creates a Department of Latin American Integration Affairs within the scope of the Ministry of Foreign Relations, as authorized in Article 6 of the new 1967 Constitution. [*Diario Oficial*, June 27, 1967].

Provisions implementing Decree 14 of 1964, dealing with importation of merchandise specified in the National List for Uruguay. [*Diario Oficial,* October 1, 1964].

Venezuela

Law of June 11, 1966, approves the Montevideo Treaty of 1960, establishing a free Trade zone and creating the Latin American Free Trade Association. [*Gaceta Oficial,* August 11, 1966, extr. issue].

Decree 102 of August 11, 1964, creates a commission to be known as the National Commission on the Latin American Free Trade Association, and establishes its functions. [*Gaceta Oficial,* August 11, 1964].

II. CENTRAL AMERICAN COMMON MARKET

Costa Rica

Law 1730 of Jan. 30, 1954, approves the Treaty on Free Trade and Economic Integration between Costa Rica and El Salvador, signed on Oct. 5, 1953. [*La Gaceta,* Feb. 6, 1954].

Law 2149 of July 19, 1957, approves the enforcement of the Treaty on Free Trade and Economic Integration between Costa Rica and Guatemala. [*La Gaceta,* July 27, 1957].

Decree 10 of Oct. 10, 1959, amends Law 2149 (*supra*) by issuing additional lists of merchandise to be subject to the Treaty of 1957. [*La Gaceta,* Oct. 24, 1959].

Law 2992 of June 8, 1962, approves the Treaty of Preferential Exchange and Free Trade between Costa Rica and Nicaragua. [*La Gaceta,* June 12, 1962].

Law 3315 of July 29, 1964, approves the Protocol to the Central American Agreement on Equalization of Import Duties, signed in San Salvador, on Jan. 29, 1963. [*La Gaceta,* August 25, 1964].

Law 3320 of July 30, 1964, approves the Protocol to the Agreement on a System of Central American Integrated Industries, signed in San Salvador, on January 29, 1963. [*La Gaceta,* Aug. 25, 1964].

Law 3421 of Oct. 6, 1964, approves the Protocol to the General Treaty on Central American Economic Integration, adopting a Central American Uniform Customs Code, signed in Guatemala on Dec. 13, 1963. [*La Gaceta,* Nov. 10, 1964 (suppl.)].

Legislative Decree 3319 of July 3, 1964, authorizes the President to adopt, as he believes necessary, the uniform rates on imports which were included in the "B" List of the Central American Agreement on Equalization of Import Duties.

Law 3488 of Jan. 29, 1965, ratifies the Protocol to the Central American Agreement on Equalization of Import Duties, signed in Guatemala Aug. 1, 1964.

Decree 3820 of Aug. 4, 1966 puts into force the import duties agreed upon in the Protocol to the Central American Agreement on Equalization of Import Duties, signed in 1964, and ratified by Costa Rica on Jan. 29, 1965 (*supra*) [*La Gaceta,* Aug. 10, 1966].

Decree 15 of May 7, 1966, puts into force the Regulation to the Uniform Central American Customs Code (RECAUCA). [*La Gaceta,* May 19, 1966, suppl.]

Decree 20 of June 8, 1966, suspended the enforcement of the above regulation for another 180 days computed from June 16, 1966. [*La Gaceta,* June 16, 1966].

Guatemala

Legislative Decree 1262 of Dec. 22, 1958, ratifies the Treaty on Free Trade and Economic Union of Central America. [*El Guatemalteco,* March 11, 1959].

Law 1273 of March 16, 1959, approves the Central American Treaty on Industrial Integration, signed in Honduras, on June 10, 1958. [*El Guatemalteco*, April 9, 1959].

Law 1348 of April 7, 1960, ratifies the Treaty on Economic Union, signed by Guatemala, El Salvador and Honduras on Feb. 6, 1960. [*El Guatemalteco*, May 4, 1960].

Law 1383 of Sept. 20, 1960, approves the additional Protocol to the Treaty of Economic Association, signed on June 9, 1960. Ratified on Sept. 20, 1960. [*El Guatemalteco*, Oct. 8, 1960].

Law 1350 of May 16, 1960, approves the Treaty on Central American Equalization of Import Duties, and the Protocol on Central American Tariff Preferences, ratified by Guatemalan President on May 16, 1960. [*El Guatemalteco*, Oct. 15, 1960].

Legislative Decree 1435 of April 20, 1961, approves the General Treaty on Central American Economic Integration. [*El Guatemalteco*, June 5, 1961].

Legislative Decree 1437 of April 20, 1961, approves the protocol to the Central American Agreement on Equalization of Import Duties. [*El Guatemalteco*, June 1, 1961].

Decree-law 3 of April 4, 1963, eliminates the special Ministry on Central American Economic Integration, transferring its duties and powers to the Ministry of Economy. [*El Guatemalteco*, April 20, 1963].

Resolution of April 30, 1963, creates within the Ministry of Economy a special department on Central American Integration. [*El Guatemalteco*, June 12, 1963].

Decree 1560 of April 3, 1963, approves the Protocol to the General Treaty on Central American Economic Integration, signed in Tegucigalpa, on Nov. 16, 1962. [*El Guatemalteco*, Oct. 25, 1963]. Instrument of ratification, [Oct. 25–26, 1963].

Decree 1582 of March 27, 1963, approves Protocol to the Central American Agreement on Equalization of Import Duties, signed in San José July 31, 1962. Instruments of ratification of agreement included. [*El Guatemalteco*, Jan. 21 and 24, Feb. 10–26, 1964].

Decree-law 169 of Jan. 28, 1964, approves Protocol to the General Treaty of Central American Economic Integration, signed in Guatemala on Dec. 13, 1963. Instrument of ratification of protocol included. [*El Guatemalteco*, Jan. 31 and April 10, 1964].

Honduras

Decree 89 of Feb. 2, 1960, approves Resolution 104, on agreement to integrate Central American industry. [*La Gaceta*, March 4, 1960].

Law 199 of March 23, 1960, approves the Protocol of the Treaty on Free Trade and Economic Integration of Central America, signed in 1957. [*La Gaceta*, May 21, 1960].

Decree 64 of April, 1962, approves the Central American Agreement on Equalization of Import Duties. [*La Gaceta*, March 28–31, 1962].

Decree 47 of March 9, 1962, approves with reservations the Treaty on Economic Integration of Central America, signed Dec. 13, 1960. [*La Gaceta*, April 5–6, 1962].

Decree 65 of April, 1962, approves the Protocol of Dec. 13, 1960, to the Central American Agreement on Equalization of Import Duties. [*La Gaceta*, June 1–4, 1962].

Decree 49 of March 15, 1963, approves the new Charter of the Organization of Central American States (ODECA), replacing that of 1951. [*La Gaceta*, April 16, 1963].

Decree 123 of June 14, 1963, approves the Agreement on the Central American Bank of Economic Integration, signed Jan. 7, 1963. [*La Gaceta*, July 4, 1963].

Decree 92 of June 4, 1963, approves the Protocol of Jan. 29, 1963, to the Central American Agreement on Equalization of Import Duties. [*La Gaceta*, July 9, 1963].

Decree 91 of June 4, 1963, approves the Protocol of Jan. 29, 1963, to the Agreement on Administration of Central American Integrated Industries. [*La Gaceta*, July 11, 1963].

Decree 130 of May, 1963, approves the Protocol of July 31, 1962, to the Central American Agreement on Equalization of Import Duties. [*La Gaceta*, July 15–26, 1963].

Decree 15 of April 4, 1966, approves Resolution 4 of March 22, 1966, approving the second Protocol to the Agreement on the System of Central American Integrated Industries, signed in San Salvador, Nov. 5, 1965. [*La Gaceta*, May 18, 1966].

Nicaragua

Decree 1 of Jan. 13, 1959, ratifies the Convention on Central American Integrated Industries, signed June 10, 1958. [*La Gaceta*, Jan. 20, 1959].

Decree 4 of Jan. 13, 1959, ratifies the Treaty on Free Trade and Economic Integration of Central America, signed June 10, 1958. [*La Gaceta*, Jan. 21 and 29, 1959]. [Ratification in *La Gaceta*, Feb. 26, 1959].

Resolution 4 of May 23, 1960 approves the Central American Agreement on Equalization of Import Duties and Protocol on Central American import preferences. [*La Gaceta*, May 31, 1960].

Ratification of charter of *Banco Centroamericano de Integración Económica.* [*La Gaceta*, May 26, 1961].

Ratification of Protocol to the Central American Agreement on Economic Integration. [*La Gaceta*, June 2, 1961].

Ratification of the Protocol to the Central American Agreement on Equalization of Import Duties. [*La Gaceta*, June 8, 1961].

Acuerdo 6 of Aug. 30, 1961, approved Treaty on Preferential Exchange and Free Trade signed in Panama on Aug. 2, 1961, between Nicaragua, Panama and Costa Rica. Ratified by Decree 8 of Dec. 21, 1961, and instrument deposited and dated June 13, 1962. [*La Gaceta*, July 19, 1962]. Exchange of ratifications August 1, 1962. [*La Gaceta*, Oct. 22, 1962].

Resolution 1 of Jan. 16, 1964, approves the Protocol signed in Guatemala on Dec. 13, 1963, to the General Treaty of Central American Economic Integration. [*La Gaceta*, Jan. 24, 1964].

Resolution 3 of April 4, 1964, approves the Protocols signed in San Salvador in 1963, to the Agreement on the System of Central American Integrated Industries, and to the Central American Agreement on Equalization of Import Duties. [*La Gaceta*, April 14, 1964].

Decree 5 of May 13, 1964, ratifies the Protocol signed in Guatemala Dec. 13, 1963, to the General Treaty on Central American Economic Integration (uniform customs code). [*La Gaceta*, June 4, 1964]. List of products in [*La Gaceta*, June 15, 1964]

Decree 6 of Oct. 10, 1964, ratifies the Protocol signed Jan. 1963 on the Agreement on Central American Integrated Industries and the Protocol to the Central American Agreement on Equalization of Import Duties. [*La Gaceta*, Feb. 20, 1965]. [See also *La Gaceta*, March 15, 1965].

Panama

Law 33 of Jan. 31, 1962, approves the Treaty on Preferential Exchange and Free Trade entered into with Nicaragua and Costa Rica, signed in Panama on Aug. 2, 1961. [*Gaceta Oficial*, Feb. 16, 1962].

Decree-law 25 of June 18, 1964, creates a Foreign Commerce Advisory Department and a Department of International Trade within the Ministry of Foreign Relations, and establishes their functions. [*Gaceta Oficial,* June 22, 1964].

Law 54 of Feb. 2, 1967, approves the text of the Protocol on the Entry of Panama to the Central American Commission on Geography and Cartography, a subsidiary of ODECA. [*Gaceta Oficial,* March 29, 1967].

El Salvador

Legislative Decree 2778 of Jan. 19, 1959, ratifies the Central American Treaty on Free Trade and Economic Integration. [*Diario Oficial,* April 7, 1959].

Ratification of above Treaty [*Diario Oficial,* May 7, 1959].

Legislative Decree 3012 of Feb. 17, 1960, ratifies the agreement on economic union, signed by El Salvador, Honduras and Guatemala. [*Diario Oficial,* March 23, 1960].

Law 3085 of July 12, 1960, ratifies the Protocols to the Central American Treaty on Free Trade and Economic Integration, concerning development and assistance funds, and the administrative offices of the Association. [*Diario Oficial,* July 18, 1960].

Resolution 13 and Resolution 72 approve the protocol on equalization of customs or import duties and the charter of the *Banco Centroamericano de Integración Económica.* [*Diario Oficial,* March 10, 1961].

Decree 348 of July 15, 1963, ratifies the Agreement signed in Panama on Dec. 12, 1962, on the Charter of the Organization of Central American States (ODECA) replacing that of 1951. [*Diario Oficial,* July 25, 1963].

Resolution 280 of June 13, 1963, and Decree 400 of Sept. 26, 1963, approve and ratify the Protocol of Adherence of Costa Rica to the Agreement on Equalization of Import Duties. [*Diario Oficial,* Oct. 4, 1963].

Decree 464 of Dec. 5, 1963, approves Protocol to the Central American Agreement on Equalization of Import Duties, signed in San Salvador, Jan. 29, 1963. [*Diario Oficial,* Dec. 13, 1963].

Decree 488 of Jan. 20, 1964, approves Central American Agreement on Tax Incentives to Industrial Development, signed in Costa Rica, July 31, 1962. [*Diario Oficial,* Jan. 30, 1964].

Decree 489 of Jan. 20, 1964, ratifies the Protocol to the General Treaty on Central American Economic Integration, signed in Honduras Nov. 16, 1962. [*Diario Oficial,* Jan. 31, 1964].

Ratification instrument on Central American Agreement on Tax Incentives to Industrial Development, dated Feb. 11, 1964. [*Diario Oficial,* Feb. 26, 1964].

Ratification instrument on Protocol to General Treaty on Central American Economic Integration, dated Feb. 11, 1964. [*Diario Oficial,* Feb. 26, 1964].

Protocol to Agreement on the System of Central American Integration Industries, signed in San Salvador Jan. 29, 1963, and approved by Resolution 283 of June 13, 1963, ratified by Decree 70 of Sept. 16, 1964. [*Diario Oficial,* October 1, 1964].

Protocol to Central American Agreement on the Equalization of Import Duties, signed in San José, on July 31, 1962, approved by Resolution 282 of June 13, 1964, and ratified by Decree 69 of Sept. 16, 1964. [*Diario Oficial,* October 1, 1964].

Decree 187 of Dec. 23, 1964, creates the Under-Secretariat on Economic Integration and International Trade, under the Ministry of Economy. [*Diario Oficial,* December 24, 1964].

OTHER PUBLICATIONS OF THE INSTITUTE

Roundtable of Western Hemisphere International Law Scholars, San José, Costa Rica, March 31-April 5, 1963. Final Report. (In cooperation with the Carnegie Endowment for International Peace), 125 p. (out of print) (Also in Spanish, out of print)

Material de Referencia sobre la Enseñanza del Derecho Internacional y Materias Afines en Latinoamérica y Canadá (Publicación provisional) (1964) 157 p. (out of print)

Organizaciones Internacionales No Americanas, Instrumentos Constitucionales (1964). v-567 p.

Instrumentos Relativos a la Integración Económica de America Latina. 2ª edición. (in press.)

Inaugural Meeting, Bogotá, March 18-23, 1964, Report of the General Secretariat (1964). (Also in Spanish)

Special Meeting on Legal and Institutional Aspects of Foreign Private Investment, Rio de Janeiro, March 25-28, 1964, Report of the General Secretariat (1964). (Also in Spanish)

Seminar on Legal and Institutional Aspects of Central American Integration, Center for Advanced International Studies, University of Miami, 17-21 August 1964, Report of the General Secretariat (1964). (Also in Spanish)

Outline for a Basic Course on Public International Law, Report of the Special Committee (1964), 97 p. (Also in Spanish) (out of print)

Quién es Quién en Latinoamérica en Derecho Internacional y Materias Afines (Publicación provisional) (1965) 172 p. (out of print)

Instrumentos Relativos a la Integración Europea, Tratado que Establece la Comunidad Económica Europea y otros Instrumentos (1965), vii-333 p. (out of print)

Instrumentos Relativos a la Integración Europea, Tratado que Establece la Comunidad Europea del Carbón y del Acero y otros Instrumentos (1965), vii-196 p. (out of print)

Instrumentos Relativos a la Integración Europea, Tratado que Establece la Comunidad Europea de Energía Atómica y otros Instrumentos (1965), vii-178 p. (out of print)

Seminar on Legal and Institutional Aspects of the Latin American Free Trade Association, LAFTA Secretariat, Montevideo, October 18-22, 1965, Report of the General Secretariat (1966). (Also in Spanish) (out of print)

Meeting on Teaching and Research Regarding Legal and Institutional Problems of Latin American Integration, Institute for the Integration of Latin America, Buenos Aires, November 25-29, 1965, Report of the General Secretariat (1966). (Also in Spanish)

Second Special Meeting on Legal and Institutional Aspects of Foreign Private Investment, Rio de Janeiro, November 1-5, 1965, Report of the General Secretariat (1966). (Also in Spanish)

The Inter-American System, Its Development and Strengthening (1966), xxxvi-530 p. (Also in Spanish)

Problemas Jurídicos e Institucionales de la Integración Europea. Relaciones entre el Derecho Comunitario y el Derecho Nacional (1967), vi-316 p.

Roundtable on the Integration of Latin America and the Question of Constitucional. Universidad Nacional de Colombia, Bogotá, 6-8 ary 6-8, 1967. Report of the General Secretariat (1967). (Also in Spanish)

Mesa Redonda sobre la Integración de América Latina y la Cuestión Constitucional. Universidad Nacional de Colombia. Bogotá, 6-8 febrero 1967, Informe de la Secretaría General. ANEXO: ACTAS Y DOCUMENTOS (1967), 370 p. (Spanish only)

Problemática Jurídica e Institucional de la Integración de América Latina, Ensayo de Sistematización (Publicación provisional, 1967). 831 p. (out of print)

Primer Seminario de Profesores de Derecho Internacional. Fundación Universidad de Bogotá "Jorge Tadeo Lozano", Instituto de Estudios Diplomáticos e Internacionales, Bogotá, 7-8 julio 1967. Actas de las Sesiones. (1967)